WITHDRAWN

business solutions

Tricks of the Microsoft® Office Gurus

Paul McFedries

W9-BKI-149

Contents

800 E. 96th Street
Indianapolis, Indiana 46240

Tricks of the Microsoft Office Gurus

Copyright © 2005 by Sams Publishing

All rights reserved. No part of this book shall be reproduced, stored in a retrieval system, or transmitted by any means, electronic, mechanical, photocopying, recording, or otherwise, without written permission from the publisher. No patent liability is assumed with respect to the use of the information contained herein. Although every precaution has been taken in the preparation of this book, the publisher and author assume no responsibility for errors or omissions. Nor is any liability assumed for damages resulting from the use of the information contained herein.

International Standard Book Number: 0-7897-3369-2

Library of Congress Catalog Card Number: 2005920841

Printed in the United States of America

First Printing: May 2005

08   07   06   05   4   3   2

Trademarks

All terms mentioned in this book that are known to be trademarks or service marks have been appropriately capitalized. Sams Publishing cannot attest to the accuracy of this information. Use of a term in this book should not be regarded as affecting the validity of any trademark or service mark.

Warning and Disclaimer

Every effort has been made to make this book as complete and as accurate as possible, but no warranty or fitness is implied. The information provided is on an "as is" basis. The author and the publisher shall have neither liability nor responsibility to any person or entity with respect to any loss or damages arising from the information contained in this book.

Bulk Sales

Sams Publishing offers excellent discounts on this book when ordered in quantity for bulk purchases or special sales. For more information, please contact

U.S. Corporate and Government Sales
1-800-382-3419
corpsales@pearsontechgroup.com

For sales outside the United States, please contact

International Sales
international@pearsoned.com

Associate Publisher
Michael Stephens

Acquisitions Editor
Loretta Yates

Development Editor
Sean Dixon

Managing Editor
Charlotte Clapp

Project Editor
Mandie Frank

Copy Editor
Barbara Hacha

Indexer
Bill Meyers

Proofreader
Tricia Liebig

Technical Editor
Greg Perry

Publishing Coordinator
Cindy Teeters

Designer
Anne Jones

Table of Contents

II OFFICE 2003 SHARING AND COLLABORATION TRICKS

III OFFICE 2003 CUSTOMIZATION TRICKS

About the Author

Paul McFedries is the president of Logophilia Limited, a technical writing company. Now primarily a writer, Paul has worked as a programmer, a consultant, a spreadsheet developer, and a website developer. He has written more than 40 books that have sold nearly three million copies worldwide. These books include *Formulas and Functions with Microsoft Excel 2003* (Sams Publishing, 2004), *Microsoft Access 2003 Forms, Reports, and Queries* (Sams Publishing, 2004), *The Absolute Beginner's Guide to VBA* (Que Publishing, 2004), and *The Complete Idiot's Guide to Windows XP 2/E* (Alpha, 2005).

Dedication

To Karen and Gypsy, with love.

Acknowledgments

Substitute damn every time you're inclined to write very; your editor will delete it and the writing will be just as it should be.

—Mark Twain

I didn't follow Mark Twain's advice in this book (the word *very* appears throughout), but if my writing still appears "just as it should be," then it's because of the keen minds and sharp linguistic eyes of the editors at Sams. Near the front of the book you'll find a long list of the hard-working professionals whose fingers made it into this particular paper pie. However, there are a few folks that I worked with directly, so I'd like to single them out for extra credit. A big, heaping helping of thanks goes out to Acquisitions Editor Loretta Yates, Development Editor Sean Dixon, Project Editor Mandie Frank, Copy Editor Barbara Hacha, and Tech Editor Greg Perry.

We Want to Hear from You!

As the reader of this book, *you* are our most important critic and commentator. We value your opinion and want to know what we're doing right, what we could do better, what areas you'd like to see us publish in, and any other words of wisdom you're willing to pass our way.

As an associate publisher for Sams Publishing, I welcome your comments. You can email or write me directly to let me know what you did or didn't like about this book—as well as what we can do to make our books better.

Please note that I cannot help you with technical problems related to the topic of this book. We do have a User Services group, however, where I will forward specific technical questions related to the book.

When you write, please be sure to include this book's title and author as well as your name, email address, and phone number. I will carefully review your comments and share them with the author and editors who worked on the book.

Email: feedback@sampublishing.com

Mail: Michael Stephens
         Associate Publisher
         Sams Publishing
         800 East 96th Street
         Indianapolis, IN 46240 USA

For more information about this book or another Sams Publishing title, visit our website at www.sampublishing.com. Type the ISBN (excluding hyphens) or the title of a book in the Search field to find the page you're looking for.

Introduction

It has been estimated that although Microsoft Office 2003 contains more than 10,000 features, the average user is familiar with only about 150 of them. That means that most people have left a whopping 98.5 percent of Office territory unexplored. In practical terms, it also means that most people aren't taking advantage of the power of the Office suite. It means that most people are working inefficiently by trying to make the techniques they know serve a wide range of situations, and it means that most people are working ineffectively because they aren't aware of techniques that could solve their problems and add sophistication to their documents.

You'll no doubt be happy to hear that the goal of this book is *not* to give you a tour of the 98.5 percent (or whatever) of Office features that you may be unfamiliar with. I don't know anyone who wants to learn *all* of Office. Instead, my purpose here is to share with you the tips and shortcuts and little-known techniques—in short, the *tricks*—that I've amassed in my more than 15 years of wrestling with the Office programs. You'll also no doubt be happy to hear that this book shuns what I call "stunt tricks": those arcane and useless tips that have no purpose in the real world and serve only to show off the knowledge and smarts of the writers. A pox on their houses! This book is grounded firmly in the real world of business and other practical concerns, and the tricks I offer are designed to help you work better, faster, safer, and smarter.

What's in This Book

This book isn't meant to be read from cover to cover, although you're certainly free to do just that if the mood strikes you. Instead, most of the chapters are set up as self-contained units that you can dip into at will to extract whatever nuggets of information you need. The book is divided into four main parts. To give you the big picture before diving in, here's a summary of what you'll find in each part:

- Part 1, "Office 2003 Application Tricks"—The five chapters in Part 1 offer up a collection of tricks for each of the five main Office 2003 programs: Word (Chapter 1), Excel (Chapter 2), PowerPoint (Chapter 3), Access (Chapter 4), and Outlook (Chapter 5).

- Part 2, "Office 2003 Sharing and Collaboration Tricks"—The four chapters in Part 2 focus on two of the Office suite's most powerful features: sharing data and collaborating with other users. You learn how to share data between programs (Chapter 6), collaborate on documents (Chapter 7), use Office documents on the Web (Chapter 8), and collaborate using a Tablet PC (Chapter 9).

- Part 3, "Office 2003 Customization Tricks"—This part presents four chapters that help you take Office to the next level. You learn how to customize the Office programs to work faster and more efficiently (Chapter 10), the basics of the VBA programming language (Chapter 11), a fistful of useful VBA macros (Chapter 12), and how to automate Access without programming (Chapter 13).

- Part 4, "Office 2003 Security Tricks"—Security is high on everyone's mind these days, so the book closes with two chapters that explore Office security issues and solutions. You learn security tricks for Office as a whole in Chapter 14, and for Outlook email in particular in Chapter 15.

This Book's Special Features

Tricks of the Microsoft Office Gurus is designed to give you the information you need without making you wade through ponderous explanations and interminable technical background. To make your life easier, this book includes various features and conventions that help you get the most out of the book and Excel itself.

- Steps—Throughout the book, each Office task is summarized in step-by-step procedures.
- Things you type—Whenever I suggest that you type something, what you type appears in a **bold** font.
- Commands—I use the following style for Excel menu commands: File, Open. This means that you pull down the File menu and select the Open command.
- Code-continuation characters (➥)—When a line of code is too long to fit on a single line of this book, it's broken at a convenient place, and the code-continuation character appears at the beginning of the next line.

This book also uses the following boxes to draw your attention to important (or merely interesting) information.

Headings Let You See What a Sidebar Is About at a Glance

The Note box presents asides that give you more information about the topic under discussion. These tidbits provide extra insights that give you a better understanding of the task at hand.

➔ These cross-reference elements point you to related material elsewhere in the book.

Office 2003 Application Tricks

Building Dynamic Documents in Word

Most Word documents are relatively static affairs, with only your additions, edits, formats, and deletions providing anything resembling dynamism. That's fine because most memos, letters, articles, and proposals exist as is and don't require dynamic elements.

Not that Word is without dynamic features, even if all you're doing is typing all day. For example, Word's AutoCorrect feature fixes spelling blunders on-the-fly, and AutoText enables you to enter long chunks of text by typing just a few characters. Smart tags appear after certain operations, giving you context-sensitive options for modifying your most recent operation.

But beyond this day-to-day dynamism, Word offers a slew of powerful features that enable you to make a document jump through all kinds of hoops. With fields, for example, you can insert text based on document properties or the contents of bookmarks, run macros, get input from the user, and even create reasonably powerful formulas for such things as summing the contents of a table. With data entry forms, you can create sophisticated interfaces that get data from the user with ease and accuracy.

In this chapter you'll learn about these and other dynamic features that you can add to your Word arsenal.

AutoCorrect Tricks

The economists tell us that productivity has increased dramatically over the past 10 years or so. They have many explanations for this rise (they are economists, after all), but as far as I know, no one has studied what I believe is the *real* reason productivity is up: the AutoCorrect feature that has been part of Word for most of those 10 years.

This likely sounds preposterous to you, and of course, it is. But not by much. We're all now so used to AutoCorrect that we forget (and certainly don't notice) that several times each day we still spell "the" as "teh," "other" as "otehr," and "different" as "differnet"; in each case, AutoCorrect is there to catch and repair the blunders. Without any fanfare, AutoCorrect quietly adds the proper accents to "cliché" and "café," fixes finger fumbles such as "I;ll" and "showinf," and sorts out nonsense such as "andt he" and "sot hat." If you type a lot, this probably happens dozens of times a day, perhaps even hundreds if your eye-finger coordination isn't what it used to be. Imagine how much time it would take out of your busy day to have to go back and fix all those typos? One shudders to think about it.

So AutoCorrect is certainly a useful productivity booster, whether the economists realize it yet or not. But it can be made even better, as the next few sections show.

Reversing AutoCorrect

If AutoCorrect changes a word and you prefer to keep your original spelling, you can reverse the correction immediately by pressing Ctrl+Z or selecting Edit, Undo AutoCorrect. However, this works only if the correction was the last action performed in the document. If you did anything else after the correction—typed or deleted text, applied formatting, and so on—the Undo command won't work.

Luckily, you can still reverse the correction by placing the mouse pointer over the word until you see an underline appear. Move the mouse over the underline to reveal the AutoCorrect Smart Tag. Click the Smart Tag and then click Change Back to "*text*," where text is the uncorrected version of the text, as shown in Figure 1.1.

This Chapter's Examples
You'll find the Word files used as examples in this chapter on my website at www.mcfedries.com/OfficeGurus.

Figure 1.1
Click the AutoCorrect Smart Tag to reverse the correction.

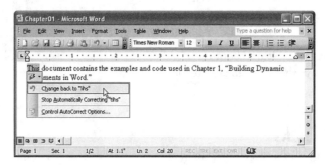

Note, too, that you can also tell Word to stop making this correction permanently by clicking Stop Automatically Correcting "*text*", where *text* is the original text.

Avoiding an AutoCorrect

If you want to use an "incorrect" version of a word or phrase that AutoCorrect normally jumps all over, you can use a simple trick. Type the incorrect text and then type the AutoCorrect trigger (space, punctuation mark, Tab, or Enter) that you'd normally add after the incorrect text. After AutoCorrect does its thing, press Ctrl+Z to undo the correction, and then continue on your merry way.

Moving AutoCorrect Entries to Another Computer

If you've spent seemingly endless hours adding your own AutoCorrect entries (and perhaps also deleting some of the default entries), it can be daunting to contemplate replicating your customized list on another computer. Fortunately, you don't have to go to all that much trouble because Word 2003 comes with an AutoCorrect Utility that automates this process. The idea is that you first back up your existing AutoCorrect entries to a file, and then you apply that file to the other computer.

To use the AutoCorrect Utility, open the `Support.dot` template found in the following folder:

```
C:\Program Files\Microsoft Office\Office11\Macros
```

Installing `Support.dot`

If you don't see the `Support.dot` template, you need to install it. Run the Office 2003 setup, click Add or Remove Features, and then click Next. Activate the Choose Advanced Customization of Applications check box, and then click Next. Expand the Microsoft Office Word branch and then the Wizards and Templates branch. Click More Templates and Macros and then click Run All from My Computer. Click Update to install the feature, which includes the `Support.dot` template.

Click the AutoCorrect Backup macro button to launch the AutoCorrect Utility, shown in Figure 1.2. Click Backup to gather the AutoCorrect entries. When the Save As dialog box appears, choose a location for the backup file and then click Save. (Note that the default AutoCorrect Backup file is about 600KB, so you should be able to fit yours on a floppy, if necessary.)

Now move to the other computer, open `Support.dot`, and click the AutoCorrect Backup button. Click Restore and then click Yes when the macro asks if you want to continue. In the Open dialog box, select the AutoCorrect Backup file and then click Open.

Saving Your Settings

If you have other Office 2003 settings that you want to migrate to another computer, consider using the Save My Settings Wizard, which can gather *all* your Office settings. To run this wizard, select Start, All Programs, Microsoft Office, Microsoft Office Tools, Microsoft Office 2003 Save My Settings Wizard.

Figure 1.2
In the Support.dot template, click the AutoCorrect Backup macro button to launch the AutoCorrect Utility.

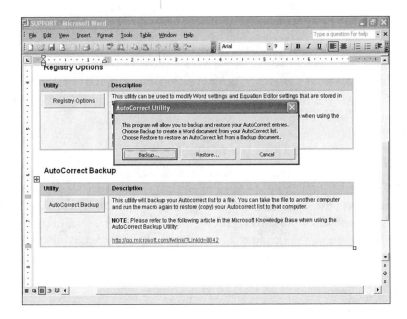

Entering Boilerplate Text Automatically

Do you have a phrase, a sentence, or even multiple paragraphs that you use regularly? Typing these bits of boilerplate text can be tedious and it's certainly time-wasting. To stop throwing away those precious seconds and minutes, you can convince Word to store the boilerplate and then recall it with a few keystrokes. You can do this using either AutoCorrect or AutoText.

Using AutoCorrect to Enter Boilerplate Text

Here's how to store and use boilerplate text with Word's AutoCorrect feature:

1. Select the boilerplate text.
2. Select Tools, AutoCorrect Options to display the AutoCorrect dialog box.
3. Select the AutoCorrect tab. Your boilerplate text appears in the With text box.
4. If the boilerplate includes formatting and you want to include that formatting each time you insert the boilerplate, activate the Formatted Text option; otherwise, leave the Plain Text option activated.

Formatted Versus Plain Text Corrections

The AutoCorrect feature is available in all the major Office applications. However, the formatted AutoCorrect replacements are available only in Word. This can lead to problems if you have a formatted entry defined in Word and a plain text entry from another program that uses the same original text. For example, you might have a formatted entry for *addr* in Word, and a plain text entry for *addr* that was defined in Access. If you insert the *addr* entry in Word, you always get the formatted correction. To avoid this confusion, never use the same original text for two different entries.

---

5. In the Replace text box, type a short abbreviation or code. For example, if the boilerplate consists of your contact information, you might type **addr**, as shown in Figure 1.3.

6. Click Add.

7. Click OK.

Figure 1.3
Use the AutoCorrect tab to enter an abbreviation that "corrects" to display boilerplate text you use often.

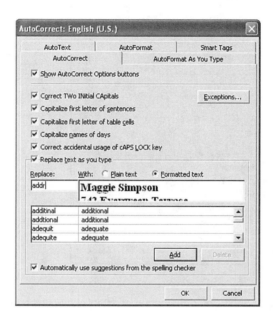

To use the boilerplate, type the abbreviation you entered in step 5 and then type a space or punctuation mark, or press Tab or Enter.

Using AutoText to Enter Boilerplate Text

Instead of using AutoCorrect for boilerplate, you can use Word's AutoText feature. The difference is that with an AutoText entry you need to type the first few characters of the boilerplate text. Word then displays an AutoComplete balloon showing you the rest of the text, and you press Enter to complete the text. Some people prefer this route because it doesn't require remembering various abbreviations, as does the AutoCorrect technique.

Here's how to store and use boilerplate text with Word's AutoText feature:

1. Select the boilerplate text.

Including Boilerplate Formatting

Another compelling feature of AutoText is its capability to preserve the formatting of the boilerplate text. To ensure that this happens, when you select the boilerplate text, you must include the paragraph mark at the end of the text.

---

2. Select Tools, AutoCorrect Options to display the AutoCorrect dialog box.

3. Select the AutoText tab. Your boilerplate text appears in the Enter AutoText Entries Here text box, as shown in Figure 1.4.

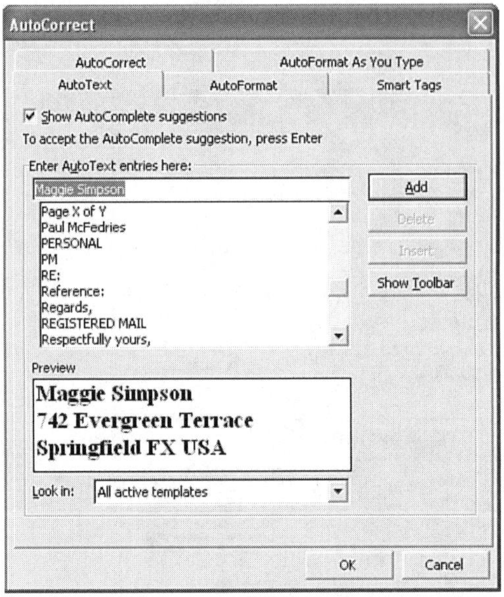

Figure 1.4
Use the AutoText tab to define an entry that enables you to insert boilerplate text by typing just the first few characters and pressing Enter.

4. Make sure that the Show AutoComplete Suggestions check box is activated.

5. Click Add.

6. Click OK.

To use the boilerplate, type the first few letters of the text and then press Enter.

You can also access AutoText entries via the AutoText toolbar. Right-click any toolbar and then click AutoText to display the toolbar, as shown in Figure 1.5. Click All Entries, click an AutoText category, and then click the entry you want to insert.

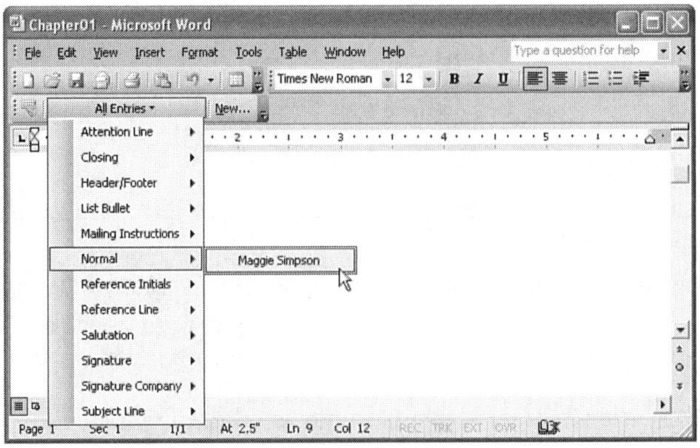

Figure 1.5
For easy access to AutoText entries, display the AutoText toolbar.

Note, too, that you can add an AutoText entry by selecting the text, clicking the AutoText toolbar's New button, and entering the text in the Create AutoText dialog box.

Printing AutoText Entries

To get a hard-copy listing of all Word's AutoText entries, select File, Print to display the Print dialog box. In the Print What list, select AutoText Entries.

Creating a Customizable AutoCorrect Entry

Most boilerplate text is static and can be inserted into documents without modification. However, you may occasionally use boilerplate text that requires customization. For example, you might need to replace a date within the boilerplate with the current date. You could insert the boilerplate and then edit the date by hand, but our goal in this chapter is to create dynamic documents. To that end, you can handle this kind of customization chore by replacing the boilerplate text that requires customization with a field that performs the customization automatically. For example, by replacing the date with a { DATE } field, AutoCorrect automatically uses the current date each time you insert the boilerplate text.

Field Info

To learn how to insert and work with Word's fields, see the section "Using Fields to Insert Dynamic Data" later in this chapter.

For an even higher level of customization, you can get Word to prompt you (or a user) to insert the required data. You do this by replacing the boilerplate text that requires customizing with the { FILLIN *Prompt* } field, where *Prompt* is a message that prompts the user. When AutoCorrect inserts the boilerplate, it displays a dialog box to prompt for the required data.

Using AutoCorrect to Insert Your Signature

One of AutoCorrect's most powerful—but, inexplicably, one of its least used—features is its capability to insert graphics. You can associate any image with a bit of text, and AutoCorrect will replace that text with the image. There are many uses for this, but perhaps the handiest is inserting a scanned version of your signature. This is a great way to "sign" any document that you're going to fax or distribute without it being printed.

Here are the steps to follow:

1. Sign a piece of paper and insert the paper into your scanner.
2. In Word, select Insert, Picture, From Scanner or Camera.
3. Use the scanning software to crop the signature and then insert it into your document.
4. Select the scanned signature.

5. Select Tools, AutoCorrect Options to display the AutoCorrect dialog box.

6. Select the AutoCorrect tab. Your signature image appears in the With box, as shown in Figure 1.6.

Figure 1.6
When you select your scanned signature and then display the AutoCorrect dialog box, the signature image appears in the With box.

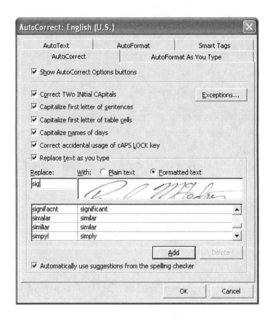

7. Make sure the Formatted Text option is activated.

8. In the Replace text box, type an abbreviation or code for the signature (such as `sig`).

9. Click OK.

Creating Border Lines On-the-Fly

If you want to display a border between two paragraphs, one way to do it (as shown in Figure 1.7) is to drop down the Outside Border tool and then click the Top Border button (assuming the cursor is in the second of the two paragraphs; if it's in the first paragraph, click the Bottom Border tool instead).

If you're a dedicated keyboardist, you can avoid the mouse clicking entirely and insert the same line by pressing hyphen (–) three or more times and then pressing Enter.

Either technique works nicely as long as you want the default border, which is a thin, straight line. If you want a different style—for example, a thicker line or a wavy line—you need to select Format, Borders and Shading and then choose your options in the Borders and Shading dialog box.

Border   **Outside Border tool**

Figure 1.7
Use the Outside Border tool to add a border between paragraphs.

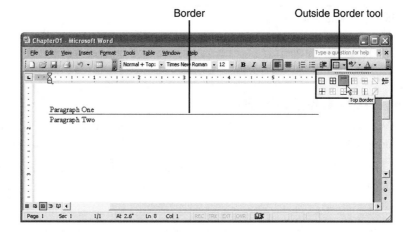

Or do you? Interestingly, the ———+Enter keyboard shortcut has five cousins that produce different line styles:

Character	Key Combo	Resulting Line Style
_ (underscore)	___+Enter	Thick
= (equal sign)	===+Enter	Double
# (pound)	###+Enter	Triple (two thin, one thick)
~ (tilde)	~~~+Enter	Wavy
* (asterisk)	***+Enter	Dotted

Figure 1.8 shows the resulting lines.

Figure 1.8
Examples of borders you can create on-the-fly using your keyboard.

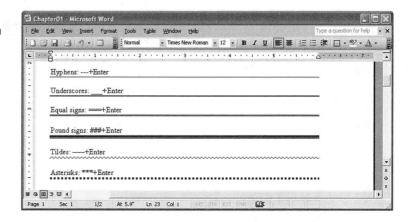

Turning Off AutoFormat Borders

These automatic borders are one of Word's AutoFormat features. If you prefer not to use them, select Tools, AutoCorrect Options, click the AutoFormat as You Type tab, and deactivate the Border Lines check box.

Creating Table Cells On-the-Fly

Word offers some powerful tools for building document tables. But if all you need is one or more cells in a single row, you can create a table with just a few keystrokes.

The secret here is that Word interprets the following keys as the instruction to make a single table cell:

```
+--+
```

That is, if you type a plus sign (+), two hyphens (--), another plus sign (+), and then press Enter, Word converts your typing into a table cell. For multiple cells in the same row, just extend the idea. For example, pressing Enter after entering the following text creates a one-row table with four cells:

```
+--+--+--+--+
```

For wider cells, type more hyphens, as in this example:

```
+--+----+--------+----------------+
```

For multiple-row tables, enter the plus signs and hyphens on consecutive lines, as in this example that creates a table with three rows and four columns:

```
+--+--+--+--+
+--+--+--+--+
+--+--+--+--+
```

Figure 1.9 shows several tables created using this method.

Figure 1.9
Examples of tables that you can create on-the-fly using your keyboard.

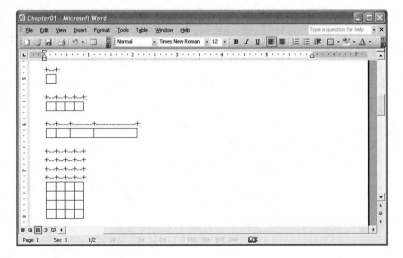

Turning Off AutoFormat Tables

This on-the-fly table building is another of Word's AutoFormat features. To turn it off, select Tools, AutoCorrect Options, click the AutoFormat as You Type tab, and deactivate the Tables check box.

Creating Custom Bulleted Lists On-the-Fly

When you need a bulleted list, the usual route is to select Format, Bullets and Numbering, and use the Bullets and Numbering dialog box to set up the list. However, AutoCorrect also enables you to create bulleted lists on-the-fly. The easiest way to go about this is to first type any of the following characters (to type an em dash, press Ctrl+Alt+-, the minus sign on your numeric keypad):

```
*
o
—  (em dash)
-
--
>
->
=>
```

Then press Tab or the spacebar, enter the first bullet text, and press Enter. (If you use the lowercase *o* as the starting character, you must press Tab to create the bulleted list.) Word converts the paragraph into a bulleted list and starts a second bullet. Figure 1.10 shows the various bullet styles created by each character in the left column.

Using Symbols as Bullets

This trick also works with characters from a symbol typeface such as Symbol, Webdings, Wingdings, or ZapfDingbats. Select Insert, Symbol to choose the symbol you want to use as the bullet.

This also works if you want to use a picture as the bullet. Select Insert, Picture, From File, and use the Insert Picture dialog box to select the image you want to use. Note that the following folder contains a number of images suitable for bullets:

```
C:\Program Files\Microsoft Office\Media\Office11\Bullets
```

Click Insert to add the picture to the document. Press Tab or the spacebar, type the bullet text, and then press Enter to convert the text into a list with the picture as the bullet.

Use Small Images as Bullets

To use an image as a bullet, the image must be no taller than about 15 pixels. To ensure that you don't choose a larger image, in the Insert Picture dialog box, pull down the Views menu and select Details. In the Details view, the Dimensions column tells you the width and height of each image.

Figure 1.10
Examples of bullets you can create on-the-fly using your keyboard.

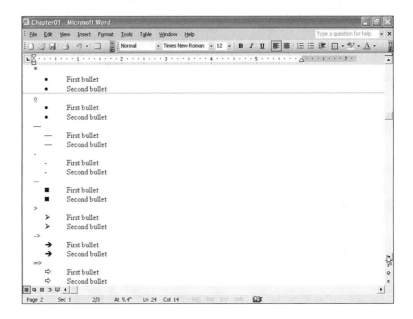

Turning Off Automatic Bulleted Lists
To turn off these on-the-fly bulleted lists, select Tools, AutoCorrect Options, click the AutoFormat as You Type tab, and deactivate the Automatic Bulleted Lists check box.

Using Custom Document Properties

Word maintains a collection of properties for each document, and these properties represent *metadata*—data about the document itself. The default properties include the document's title, subject, author, and statistics such as the number of characters, words, paragraphs, and pages. Word generates the values of many of these properties automatically. For example, Word calculates all the statistics based on the document content, and the default values for the Author and Company properties are the values you entered when you installed Word. The other properties you fill in by hand by selecting the File, Properties command and clicking the Summary tab.

Change Your Name and Company
Office stores the default Author and Company values in the Registry. To change the Author value, select Tools, Options, click the User Information tab, and then change the Name value. The default Company name is trickier to change. First, open the Registry Editor and navigate to the following branch (see Appendix A "Working with the Windows Registry"):

```
HKEY_LOCAL_MACHINE\Software\Microsoft\Windows\CurrentVersion\Installer\
➥UserData\S-1-5-18\Products\9040111900063D11C
```

Edit the `RegCompany` setting with the new company name you want to use. Now navigate to the following branch:

`HKEY_CURRENT_USER\Software\Microsoft\Office\11.0\Common\UserInfo`

Rename the `Company` setting (to `OldCompany`, for example). The next time you start Word, any new documents you create will use the new company name as the Company property.

Creating a Custom Document Property

You can also create your own custom properties, and you can set these up to be filled in either automatically or manually. For example, if you are passing a document among a number of people, you may want to keep track of who last read the document. To do that, you could create a "Last Read By" property and have each user fill in his or her initials. Here are just a few other custom property ideas:

- The name of the person who edited or proofread the document.
- The date the document was completed.
- The department the document belongs to.
- The project that the document is part of.
- The current status of the document.
- A telephone number to call for more information about the document.

Before creating your custom property, you need to decide whether you want the value of the property to be generated automatically by content within the document itself. In Word, custom property values are generated by the current values of bookmarks. Therefore, you must first create a bookmark:

1. Select the text that you want to use as the bookmark.
2. Select Insert, Bookmark to display the Bookmark dialog box.
3. Type a name for the bookmark in the Bookmark Name text box.
4. Click Add.

View Your Bookmarks

Using a bookmark as a dynamic property value placeholder works only if the other users (or you, in a few weeks, when you've forgotten you've done all this) update the bookmark text in the appropriate spot. You can help ensure that this happens by turning on Word's bookmark indicators, which are gray brackets that surround the text. To turn on these indicators, select Tools, Options, click the View tab, and activate the Bookmarks check box.

With that done, you can create the custom property by following these steps:

1. Select File, Properties to display the document's Properties dialog box.
2. Click the Custom tab.

3. Type a name for the property in the Name text box (or select one of the existing names provided by Word in the list).

4. Use the Type list to choose a data type for the property: Text, Date, Number, or Yes or No.

5. If you want the property value generated automatically by a bookmark, activate the Link to Content check box.

6. Specify the value of the property as follows:

    - If you activated Link to Content, use the Value list to choose the name of the bookmark you want to associate with the property.

    - Otherwise, enter the property value in the Value text box.

7. Click Add. Word adds the property to the Properties list. Figure 1.11 shows an example.

8. Click OK.

Figure 1.11
A custom document property named BookTitle is added to the document and linked to the TitleOfBook book-mark.

Prompting for User Input
If you're relying on users to enter the data necessary to update a custom property, you can get Word to prompt the user to enter the data by using a FILLIN field. See "Prompting the User for Input," later in this chapter.

Searching via Document Properties

One of the main advantages of using custom properties is that they enable you to organize documents based on those properties. Specifically, you can use the Search task pane to search for documents that not only include a custom property but also have that property set to a particular value. Follow these steps:

1. Select File, File Search to display the Basic File Search task pane.
2. Click Advanced File Search to switch to the Advanced File Search task pane.
3. Use the Property list to choose the property you want to include in the search. If your custom property doesn't appear in the list, type the property name into the text box.
4. In the Condition list, choose an operator. (For example, to find those documents in which the property exactly matches a certain value, choose the is (exactly) operator.
5. Use the Value text box to enter the property value you want to search for.
6. Click Add to add the criteria to the search expression. Figure 1.12 shows an Advanced File Search pane ready to search on the BookTitle custom document property.

Figure 1.12
Use the Advanced File Search pane to search for files based on document properties.

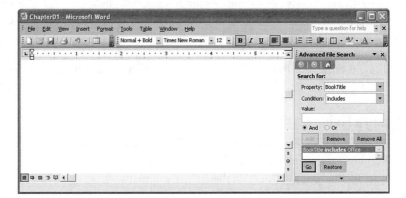

7. Repeat steps 3–6 to add other criteria. (Be sure to click And or Or before adding the criteria to the expression.)
8. Fill out the rest of the search options, as needed.
9. Click Go. Word searches for documents that match your criteria.

Using Fields to Insert Dynamic Data

The real secret to creating truly dynamic documents in Word is a little-known and even less understood feature called the *field*. A field is a miniprogram that generates or calculates a result and then displays that result in your document or stores it in a bookmark. Each field consists of code that resides inside a placeholder that you can put anywhere inside your document. Word has dozens of these codes, and they all generate data based on various kinds of information, such as the following:

■ Information that lies elsewhere in the document—For example, a document property or the value stored in a bookmark.

- Information from the environment—For example, the current date or time, or input supplied by the user.

- Information that results from a calculation—For example, the sum of a table column or the average of a set of numeric values stored in bookmarks.

The dynamism of the field comes from the fact that any of this information can change over time. When it does, the result displayed by the field also changes when the field is updated.

Even if you've never used fields directly (or haven't even heard of them), you've probably worked with fields at least indirectly. For example, if you select Insert, Date and Time, you're actually inserting a field that displays the current date or time (or both, depending on the format you select in the Date and Time dialog box). Similarly, if you've ever inserted page numbers, a table of contents, or a cross-reference, you've inserted a field in each case.

These examples serve as a reminder for an important field caveat: Fields can be amazingly powerful, but remember that Word often provides easier and more direct methods for accomplishing a field-related task. In general, if a field or field equivalent is also available via a menu command, a toolbar button, or some other part of the Word interface, you should always use the interface method. It saves times and reduces the chances that you'll make a mistake.

Inserting a Field

Besides using Word's built-in features (such as the Insert menu's Date and Time or Page Numbers commands) to insert fields, you can also add fields to your document using two other methods: using the Field dialog box and manually, as discussed in the next few sections.

Using the Field Dialog Box

The Field dialog box is the quickest and safest way to insert a field, because it acts as a front end for the 70-odd Word fields and their myriad properties and switches. (A *switch* is extra code added to the field that determines the look or behavior of the field.) Here are the general steps to follow to insert a field:

1. Position the cursor where you want the field's result to appear.
2. Select Insert, Field to display the Field dialog box.
3. If you know the category assigned to the field, use the Category list to select it. Otherwise, select (All) in the Category list.
4. Use the Field Names list to click the field you want to insert. Depending on the field you selected, the Field dialog box displays one or more controls in the Field Properties and Field Options areas. In Figure 1.13, for example, the Date field shows controls in both areas.

Figure 1.13
To avoid errors, use the Field dialog box to insert a field along with any properties or switches.

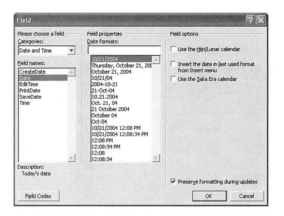

5. Use the Field Properties controls to customize the field output.
6. Use the Field Options controls to customize how the field operates.
7. Click OK. Word inserts the field and displays its current value.

Understanding Field Code Syntax

Before you learn how to insert a field manually, you need to know the syntax used by field codes. The Field dialog box can help. First, here's the general syntax:

```
{ FIELD instructions }
```

The braces serve to enclose the field code. The *FIELD* part is the name of the field. This is usually seen with all uppercase letters, but field names aren't case sensitive. (In this book, I use the all-uppercase format in the code examples. However, when I discuss fields in the main text, I'll use the initial caps or inner caps format: Date, EditTime, and so on.) The *instructions* part consists of the elements that control the behavior of the field and the look of its result. They correspond to the controls displayed in the Field Properties and Field Options areas of the Fields dialog box. There are often several items in the field instructions, and these items can include document elements (such as the name of a bookmark) and switches. Most instructions are not case sensitive, but a few are, as you'll see a bit later (for example, see Table 1.1).

The Ref field, for instance, displays the value of a bookmark. Among the many switches you can add to this field, the * lower switch formats the displayed text as lowercase, and the \h switch sets the field as a hyperlink (that is, Ctrl+clicking the field takes you to the bookmark). Here's the field code that displays the value of a bookmark named FileName in lowercase as a hyperlink to the bookmark:

```
{ REF FileName \* lower \h }
```

To help you learn not only the field names but also the instructions that go along with each field, open the Field dialog box, select the field, and then click the Field Codes button. The dialog box changes to show the field code and the general syntax for the field, as shown in Figure 1.14.

Figure 1.14
Click Field Codes to see this version of the Field dialog box.

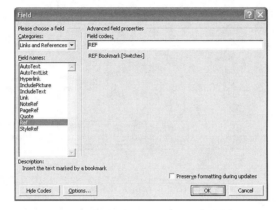

To add further instructions to the code, click Options to display the Field Options dialog box, the layout of which depends on the field. Figure 1.15 shows the Field Options dialog box for the REF field.

Figure 1.15
Click Options to display the Field Options dialog box for the selected field.

For most fields, the Field Options dialog box has two tabs: General Switches and Field-Specific Switches. As the name implies, the items in the Field-Specific Switches tab are specific to the field you're working with. The General Switches are used in multiple fields, and they fall into three categories: format, numeric picture, and date-time picture.

The format switches all begin with the characters * (followed by a space) and they handle character formatting, case conversion, and number conversion, as detailed in Table 1.1.

1

Table 1.1   General Format (*) Switches

Switch	Description
Character Formatting	
* charformat	Applies the formatting of the field code's first (nonblank) character to the entire result.
* mergeformat	Applies the formatting of the original result to any new result that occurs when the field is updated.
Case Conversion	
* caps	Converts the first character of each word in the result to uppercase.
* firstcap	Converts the first character of the first word in the result to uppercase.
* lower	Converts all the characters in the result to lowercase.
* upper	Converts all the characters in the result to uppercase.
Number Conversion	
* alphabetic	Converts the result to lowercase, alphabetic characters. The numbers 1 to 26 are converted to a through z, 27 becomes aa, 28 becomes bb, and so on. Zero displays a blank, and negative numbers generate an error.
* Alphabetic	Converts the result to uppercase, alphabetic characters. The numbers 1 to 26 are converted to A through Z, 27 becomes AA, 28 becomes BB, and so on. Zero displays a blank, and negative numbers generate an error.
* arabic	Converts the result to an Arabic number. (*Arabic numbers* are what the rest of us call *cardinal numbers*; that is, they're just the numbers 0 through 9.) For example, the result 3rd is converted to 3. Decimal results are rounded to the nearest whole number.
* cardtext	Converts the result to a cardinal number written as text. For example, the result 32 is converted to thirty-two. Decimal results are rounded to the nearest whole number.
* dollartext	Converts the whole number part of the result to cardinal text, replaces the decimal place with and, and displays the decimal part (rounded to two places) as a numerator over 100. For example, the result 10.95 is converted to ten and 95/100.
* hex	Converts the result to hexadecimal numbers. For example, the result 30 is converted to 1E.
* ordinal	Converts the result to an ordinal number. For example, the result 21 is converted to 21st.

continues

Table 1.1   Continued

Switch	Description
Number Conversion	
* ordtext	Converts the result to ordinal number written as text. For example, the result 21 is converted to twenty-first.
* roman	Converts the result to lowercase Roman numerals. For example, the result 14 is converted to xiv.
* Roman	Converts the result to uppercase Roman numerals. For example, the result 14 is converted to XIV.

A numeric picture switch begins with the characters \# (followed by a space). You use it to specify how you want Word to display a numeric result. You build a numeric picture switch using the symbols described in Table 1.2.

Enter Picture Switches First

If you're inserting or editing the field by hand, make sure you enter the numeric picture or date-time picture switches *before* the format switches. If you insert the format switch first, Word displays an error as the field result.

Table 1.2   Symbols Used in Numeric Picture (\ #) Switches

Symbol	Description
#	Holds a place for a digit, but displays nothing if no digit exists in the position. For example, if the result is 5 and the switch is \# ##, Word displays 5.
0	Holds a place for a digit. Displays zero if no digit is present in the position. For example, if the result is 5 and the switch is \# 00, Word displays 05.
. (period)	Displays the decimal point. For example, if the result is 24 and the switch is #0.00, Word displays 24.00.
, (comma)	Displays a comma as the thousands separator in results greater than or equal to 1,000 and less than or equal to –1,000.
$ or %	Displays the character.

Displaying Other Characters

Except for the standard numeric picture symbols—# 0 . and ,—you can insert any character within the numeric picture and Word will display that character. For example, the following numeric picture switch appends the degree symbol to the result:

\# #0.0°

If you want to include a word or phrase within the results, you must enclose the entire numeric picture in quotation marks. For example, the following switch adds the phrase ° Celsius to the result:

```
\# "#0.0° Celsius"
```

Inserting Special Symbols

Symbols such as the degree sign (°) aren't available directly via your keyboard, of course. You can use Word's Insert, Symbol command to insert them, or, if you know the symbol's ANSI code, you can use your keyboard's numeric keypad (make sure the NumLock key is activated). For example, to enter the degree sign, press Alt+0176 on the numeric keypad. Here are some common ANSI characters you can use:

Key Combination	ANSI Character
Alt+0163	£
Alt+0162	¢
Alt+0165	¥
Alt+0169	©
Alt+0174	®
Alt+0176	°

If you want to use a different numeric picture for a result depending on whether it's positive, negative, or zero, use the following syntax:

```
\# positive;negative;zero
```

The three parts, separated by semicolons, determine how various numbers are presented. The first part defines how a positive number is displayed; the second part defines how a negative number is displayed; and the third part defines how zero is displayed. For example, the following switch specifies different pictures for positive, negative, and zero results (note the parentheses specified for the negative result):

```
\# $0;($0);0
```

If you leave out the *zero* picture, a zero result uses the *positive* picture:

```
\# $0;($0)
```

A date-time picture switch begins with the characters \@ (followed by a space). You use it to specify how you want Word to display a date or time result. You build a date-time picture switch using the symbols described in Table 1.3.

1

Table 1.3   Symbols Used in Date-Time Picture (\@) Switches

Symbol	Description
Date Formats	
d	Displays the day part of the result without a leading zero (1 to 31).
dd	Displays the day part of the result with a leading zero (01 to 31).
ddd	Displays the day part of the result as a three-letter day abbreviation (Mon, for example).
dddd	Displays the day part of the result as the full day name (Monday, for example).
m	Displays the month part of the result without a leading zero (1 to 12).
mm	Displays the month part of the result with a leading zero (01 to 12).
mmm	Displays the month part of the result as a three-letter month abbreviation (Aug, for example).
mmmm	Displays the month part of the result with the full month name (August, for example).
yy	Displays the year part of the result as a two-digit year (00 to 99).
yyyy	Displays the year part of the result as the full year (1900 to 2078).
Time Formats	
h	Displays the hour part of the result without a leading zero (0 to 24).
hh	Displays the hour part of the result with a leading zero (00 to 24).
m	Displays the minute part of the result without a leading zero (0 to 59).
mm	Displays the minute part of the result with a leading zero (00 to 59).
s	Displays the seconds part of the result without a leading zero (0 to 59).
ss	Displays the seconds part of the result with a leading zero (00 to 59).
AM/PM or am/pm	Displays the time using a 12-hour clock and either AM or PM or am or pm.
/ or :	Separates parts of dates or times.

Displaying Other Characters

If you need to include spaces in your date-time picture, enclose the picture in quotation marks, as shown here:

```
\@ "m/d/yyyy h:mm AM/PM"
```

As with numeric pictures, you can insert any character within the date-time picture and Word will display that character. If you want to include a word or phrase within the results, you must enclose the entire numeric picture in quotation marks. For example, the following switch adds the phrase Eastern Time to the result:

```
\@ "h:mm Eastern Time"
```

Inserting a Field Manually

If you know the code for the field you want to insert and that code is relatively simple, it's often fastest to insert the field by hand. To do that, move the cursor to where you want to insert the field and then press Ctrl+F9. As you can see in Figure 1.16, Word inserts a new, empty field that includes only the braces. Type the code between the braces, as shown in Figure 1.17. When you're done, press F9 to update the field and display its result.

Figure 1.16
Press Ctrl+F9 to start a new field.

Figure 1.17
Type the field code between the braces.

Viewing and Navigating Fields

After you insert a field, Word displays the field results. If you want to do further work with any of a document's field, you need to be able to view and navigate the fields, as described in the next two sections.

Toggling Field Codes

If you want to view a field's underlying code, you need to toggle the field from showing its results to showing its code. You can use either of two methods:

- To toggle between results and code for a single field, either click inside the field and then press Shift+F9, or right-click the field and then select Toggle Field Codes.
- To toggle between results and code for all the document's fields, press Alt+F9.

Showing Field Codes All the Time
If you always prefer to see the field codes when you first open a document, you can force Word to display them. Select Tools, Options to display the Options dialog box, select the View tab, and then activate the Field Codes check box.

Navigating a Document's Fields

Before you can work with a field, you need to navigate to it within the document. This isn't a problem if you're dealing with only a couple of fields and you know exactly where they are. You just click inside the field and Word marks the occasion by shading the full field result. If you need to select the entire field (to move it or delete it, for example), either use your mouse to click and drag over the entire field, or move to the right of the field and press Backspace.

Controlling Field Shading

Normally, Word shows the field shading only when you click inside or select a field. If you have trouble finding your fields, you might prefer to see the field shading even when fields aren't selected. Conversely, if other people will be working with your document, you might prefer that no shading appears, making it less likely that others will edit the fields. To control the shading, select Tools, Options to display the Options dialog box, and then select the View tab. In the Field Shading list, select Never, Always, or When Selected (the default).

However, fields have a nasty habit of blending in with the surrounding text; it's easy to lose fields and have trouble finding them. Toggling all the document's fields to code can help, but many people find it easier to navigate from field to field. Word gives you two techniques to work with:

- Press F11 to move forward to the next field in the document.
- Press Shift+F11 to move backward to the previous field in the document.

As you navigate, Word selects each field. Unfortunately, these techniques don't wrap. That is, after you've navigated to the last field in a document, pressing F11 doesn't take you to the first field in the document; similarly, pressing Shift+F11 in the first field doesn't take you to the last field.

Updating a Field

Fields are dynamic, which means that the data underlying the field can change. For example, if you insert a field to show the current date, the underlying data changes each day. However, Word does not automatically update the field result. To update fields on-the-fly, use any of the following techniques:

- Navigate to a field and press F9. Alternatively, right-click the field and then click Update Field.
- To update multiple fields, select the text that includes all the fields and then press F9.

Updating All Fields with a Macro

When you're working with fields, it's common to need to update all of a document's fields at once. One way to do this is to select the entire document and press F9. This works, but it's a hassle because not only must you perform the extra step of selecting the entire document, but that extra step also means that you lose your current cursor position.

To avoid this problem, create a VBA macro that updates all the document's fields. Press Alt+F11 to open the VBA Editor, add a module to the Normal project, and then enter the sub-procedure shown in Listing 1.1 (see Figure 1.18).

Listing 1.1   A Macro to Update All the Fields in the Active Document

```
Sub UpdateAllFields()
    ActiveDocument.Fields.Update
End Sub
```

Figure 1.18
Add the
UpdateAllFields
procedure to the Normal
project to make it avail-
able for all your docu-
ments.

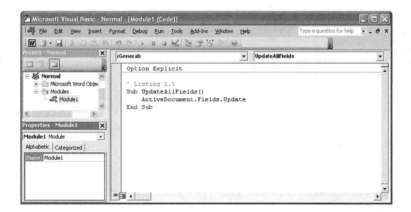

Assign this macro to a toolbar button or keyboard shortcut. (I use Ctrl+Alt+Shift+F9.)

Cross-Reference
See Chapter 11, "Maximizing Office with VBA Macros," to learn how to work with the VBA Editor and create macros. To learn how to customize Word's toolbars, see Chapter 10, "Customizing Office to Suit Your Style," particularly the "Creating Custom Toolbars" section. For custom Word keyboard shortcuts, see Chapter 10's "Creating Custom Keyboard Shortcuts in Word" section.

Updating Fields When Opening a Document

It's often useful to update all of a document's fields when the document is opened. Word doesn't do that by default, but you can create a macro that does.

Launch the VBA Editor and open the project that corresponds to your document. In the project's Microsoft Word Objects branch, double-click the ThisDocument object. In the code window that appears, select Document in the object list and select Open in the event list. Add the following statement to the Document_Open() stub that appears:

```
ThisDocument.Fields.Update
```

Figure 1.19 shows the completed code.

Object list   Event list

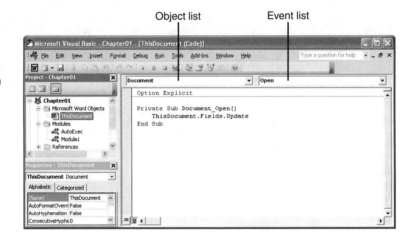

Figure 1.19
Add this code to your document's Open event to update all fields each time the document is opened.

Change Your Macro Security

For a macro to work with the document's Open event, macro security must be set to Medium or Low (in Chapter 14, see the section titled "Setting the Macro Security Level"). Alternatively, apply a digital signature to the project, as described in Chapter 14's "Self-Certifying Your VBA Projects" section.

Updating Fields by Field Type

Rather than updating all the fields in a document, you might prefer to update only fields of a particular type. For example, the EditTime field displays the total time, in minutes, that the document has had the system focus (and, presumably, has been edited) since the document was created. This is the same as the Total editing time value displayed in the Statistics tab of the document's Properties dialog box (select File, Properties). If you want to track the total editing time, it's often convenient to add the EditTime field to the document rather than opening the dialog box. But if you have other fields in the document that you'd rather not update at the same time, it would be useful to be able to update only the EditTime field.

You can do this quite simply using a VBA macro. In VBA, Word's field types are implemented as constants with the following form:

```
wdFieldFieldType
```

Here, *FieldType* is the type of field, such as `EditTime`. So the constant for the `EditTime` field is `wdFieldEditTime`.

To put this to use, Listing 1.2 provides some code that updates only the `EditTime` field.

Listing 1.2 Updating the `EditTime` Field

```
Sub UpdateEditTime()
    Dim f As Field
    For Each f In ThisDocument.Fields
        If f.Type = wdFieldEditTime Then
            f.Update
            Exit For
        End If
    Next 'f
End Sub
```

This procedure runs through all the fields in the document and looks for one where the `Type` property is `wdFieldEditTime`. When the property is found, the `Update` method refreshes the field and then exits the `For` loop.

Updating Multiple Fields of the Same Type

If your document has more than one field of a particular type and you want to update all such fields, delete the `Exit For` statement in the code. This forces Word to loop through all the fields in the document, so each instance of the field type you want to update is found by the loop.

Updating Fields by Name

If you have a specific field you want to update, looping through all the fields to find the field's type is often inefficient. If you know the field's position within the document, you can specify the position as the index number of the `Fields` collection in a VBA macro. For example, the following statement updates the first field in the active document:

```
ActiveDocument.Fields(1).Update
```

However, that's a bit of a blunt instrument because the index numbers of the fields change as fields are added and deleted.

A better solution is to reference fields by name. You can't do this directly, but you can assign a bookmark to a field and then use the bookmark's name. For example, suppose you select the `EditTime` field and insert a bookmark named `TotalEditTime`. Then the following statement will update the field:

```
ActiveDocument.Bookmarks("TotalEditTime").Range.Fields.Update
```

Preventing Updates by Locking a Field

At times, you might not want a field updated. For example, you may have edited the field result, so updating the field will overwrite your changes. Similarly, if you're updating all the fields in a document, you might want to skip those fields that prompt for information. Use the following techniques to lock and unlock the current field:

- Press Ctrl+F11 to lock the field.
- Press Ctrl+Shift+F11 to unlock the field.

Converting a Field Result to Text

You might decide that the current field result should remain permanent. For example, you might have novice users working with the document, and you don't want them getting confused by or editing the field codes. Instead of locking all the fields, a better solution is to convert the current field results to plain text. You do that by selecting one or more fields and then pressing Ctrl+Shift+F9.

Keyboard Shortcuts for Fields

Table 1.4 provides a reference to the various keyboard shortcuts that you can use to work with fields. The table also gives the Word command equivalent for each action, in case you want to create custom toolbar buttons for those field techniques you use most often.

Table 1.4   Keyboard Shortcuts for Working with Fields

Key Combo	Command Equivalent	Action
F9	UpdateFields	Updates the selected field or fields.
Ctrl+F9	InsertField	Begins a new field.
Shift+F9	ToggleFieldDisplay	Displays the code for the selected field.
Alt+F9	ViewFieldCodes	Displays the codes for all the document's fields.
Alt+Shift+F9	DoFieldClick	Activates a GOTOBUTTON or MACROBUTTON field.
F11	NextField	Goes to the next field.
Shift+F11	PrevField	Goes to the previous field.
Ctrl+F11	LockFields	Locks the selected fields to prevent them from being updated.
Ctrl+Shift+F11	UnlockFields	Unlocks the selected field.
Ctrl+Shift+F9	UnlinkFields	Converts the selected field's result to text.

Putting Fields to Good Use

Word 2003 has a huge repertoire of fields—more than 70 in all. A full accounting of all the fields would require a chapter several times the length of this one. In any case, no such accounting is necessary because Word's online Help provides an excellent field reference.

Instead, the next few sections highlight a few of the most useful fields and take you through some examples that show the fields in their best and most practical light.

Viewing Total Editing Time Updated in Real-Time

Earlier I mentioned the EditTime field, which reflects the total amount of time, in minutes, that the document has been edited (or at least has held the system focus). The total amount of time that a document has been edited is useful for freelancers, lawyers, consultants, and other professionals who bill for their time. Knowing how long you have spent working on a document enables you to provide a more accurate accounting of your time.

If you have a time budget that you're trying to stick to, you may find yourself constantly checking the document's properties to view the Total editing time value. Rather than wasting time performing that chore, add the EditTime field to your document. Here's some code that displays the total editing time with the word minutes added for clarity:

```
Total Editing Time: {EDITTIME \# "0 minutes" \* mergeformat }
```

Now all you have to do is update the field to check the total editing time.

If even that sounds like a hassle, you can add a relatively simple macro to the document that will update the EditTime field in real-time. Open the VBA Editor and insert a module in the document's project. Add the code in Listing 1.3 to the module.

Listing 1.3 Updating the EditTime Field in Real-time

```
Sub UpdateEditTime()
    Dim f As Field
    For Each f In ThisDocument.Fields
        If f.Type = wdFieldEditTime Then
            f.Update
            Exit For
        End If
    Next 'f
    Application.OnTime Now + TimeValue("00:01:00"), _
        "Chapter01.Module1.UpdateEditTime"
End Sub
```

This procedure runs through all the fields in a document looking for one where the Type property is wdFieldEditTime, which corresponds to the EditTime field. When the property is found, the Update method refreshes the field. The key to the real-time updating is the Application.OnTime statement, which sets up the UpdateEditTime procedure to run again in one minute.

Displaying the Editing Time in the Status Bar

To constantly monitor the EditTime field as it's updated in real-time, you can place the field at the top or bottom of the document and then split the window (select Window, Split) so that the field remains visible in one pane. If that's not convenient for some reason, you can display the latest EditTime result in the status bar. In Listing 1.3, insert the following statement after the f.Update method:

```
    Application.StatusBar = f.Result
```

The Field object's Result property returns the current result of the specified field.

Tracking the Number of Words

If you're a professional writer or editor, you may be more concerned with the number of words in your documents. This value is available in the document's Properties dialog box, in the Statistics tab. However, you can also track this value outside of the dialog box by using a field. Insert the NumWords field and use the macro techniques in this section to update the field in real-time.

Running a Macro

If you have a macro that you want to make available for yourself or other users, you can assign it a shortcut key or a toolbar button. But what if you want an in-text reference to a macro? That is, what if you want some text or an image that the user can double-click to launch the macro? You can do this using a MacroButton field:

```
{ MACROBUTTON MacroName DisplayText }
```

Here, *MacroName* is the name of the macro you want to run, including the project name and module name; *DisplayText* is the text the user double-clicks to launch the macro. (You can also launch the macro by clicking the field and then pressing Alt+Shift+F9.)

For example, the following code creates a MacroButton field that displays Update Editing Time and runs the Chapter01.Module1.UpdateEditTime macro:

```
{ MACROBUTTON Chapter01.Module1.UpdateEditTime Update Editing Time }
```

Figure 1.20 shows the field in a document with surrounding text. In this case, I've underlined the field text and changed the text color (it's blue) to ensure that the reader knows what text to double-click.

EditTime field

Figure 1.20
In this example, double-clicking the MacroButton field runs the UpdateEditTime macro to update the EditTime field.

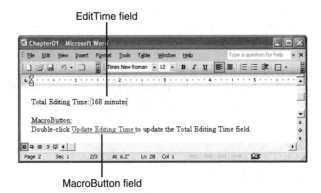

MacroButton field

Another way to do this is to display a small image instead of text. You do this by inserting an InsertPicture field as the MacroButton field's *DisplayText* property:

```
{ INSERTPICTURE FileName }
```

Replace *FileName* with the full path and filename of the image you want to use. If the path contains spaces, replace each backslash (\) with double backslashes (\\). Here's an example:

```
{ MACROBUTTON Chapter01.Module1.UpdateEditTime { INSERTPICTURE
➡C:\\Documents and Settings\\Paul\\My Documents\\My Pictures\\clock.jpg } }
```

Figure 1.21 shows the result.

Figure 1.21
Use the
`InsertPicture`
field within a
`MacroButton` field to
have the user double-
click an image to run the
macro.

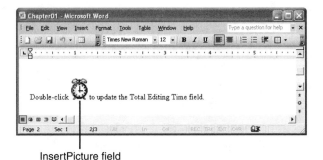

InsertPicture field

Creating "Click-and-Type" Text Placeholders

Another use for the `MacroButton` field is to create "click-and-type" text placeholders. Figure 1.22 shows some examples of what I mean. I created this document using Word's Professional Fax template. As you can see, there are placeholders such as [Click here and type name]. The idea is that you click the placeholder and then type the required text.

Figure 1.22
Word's Professional Fax
template includes "click-
and-type" text place-
holders.

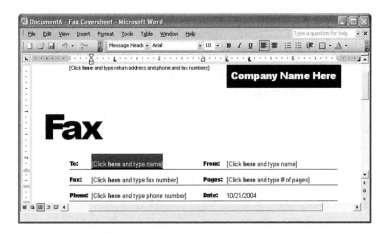

Interestingly, look what happens when you click one of these placeholders and then press Shift+F9, as shown in Figure 1.23.

Figure 1.23
The placeholders are really just MacroButton fields that reference a nonexistent macro.

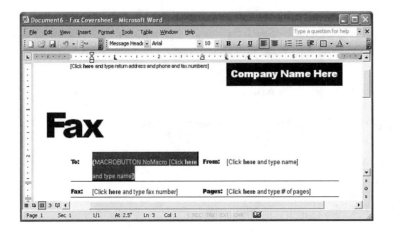

As you can see, the placeholder is actually a MacroButton field:

```
{ MACROBUTTON NoMacro [Click here and type name] }
```

The NoMacro option refers to a nonexistent macro. When you click within the field and begin to type, the field is replaced by the text.

Watch the Fake Macro Name

Make sure the fake macro name you use for the placeholder MacroButton field is not the same as any built-in or custom macro that you've created. This ensures that the user won't accidentally run the macro.

Creating a Shortcut Menu of AutoText Entries

Word's AutoText feature comes with a handy AutoComplete option. When you type the first few letters of the AutoText entry, a banner appears with the complete entry, and you press Enter to insert the full entry. (To ensure that this option is turned on, select Tools, AutoCorrect Options, display the AutoText tab, and make sure the Show AutoCorrect Suggestions check box is activated.) This is useful, but it requires knowing the available AutoText entries. The other problem is that you might prefer to choose from among a selection of AutoText entries. You can do this via the menu bar by selecting Insert, AutoText, selecting a style such as Salutation, and then selecting the entry you want. However, Word gives you a much easier way to do this, and it also solves the problem of knowing the first characters of the AutoText entries.

The solution is the AutoTextList field, which, when right-clicked, displays a menu of AutoText entries from a particular style:

```
{ AUTOTEXTLIST LiteralText [\s Style] [\t Tooltip] }
```

Using Quotation Marks

If the *LiteralText*, *Style*, or *Tooltip* values contain spaces, be sure to surround them with quotation marks.

LiteralText is the text that is displayed as a prompt inside the document. The optional *Style Name* is an AutoText style such as Salutation or Closing. If you omit this option, Word displays all the AutoText entries. The *Tooltip text* option specifies the text that appears in a banner when the user hovers the mouse pointer over the field.

Following is an AutoTextList field example that displays the literal text Choose salutation and displays a list of the AutoText entries in the Salutation category:

```
{ AUTOTEXTLIST "Choose salutation" \s Salutation \t "Right-click to
➥see a list of salutations" }
```

Figure 1.24 shows the list that appears when the user right-clicks the field.

AutoTextList field

Figure 1.24
Use an
AutoTextList field
to give the user a list of
related AutoText entries
when he or she right-
clicks the field.

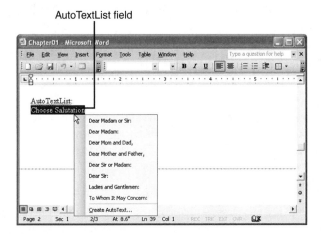

Removing the Create AutoText Command

If you don't want other users to have access to the Create AutoText command that appears at the bottom of the AutoTextList shortcut menu, you can delete it. Select Tools, Customize, and then activate Shortcut Menus in the Toolbars tab. In the Shortcut Menus toolbar that appears, click Text and then click AutoTextList Field. Drag the Create AutoText command from the menu to delete it.

Building a Formula Field

Most fields return predefined results, such as document properties or the current date and time. If you have a custom calculation that you want to appear in your document, you need to build a formula field.

All formula fields have the same general structure: an equal sign (=), followed by one or more *operands*—which can be a literal value, the result of another field, the contents of a bookmark, a table reference, or a function result—separated by one or more *operators*—the symbols that combine the operands in some way, such as the plus sign (+) and the greater-than sign (>). These field formulas come in two varieties: arithmetic and comparison.

Arithmetic formulas are by far the most common type of formula. They combine operands with mathematical operators to perform calculations. I've summarized the mathematical operators used in arithmetic formulas in Table 1.5.

Table 1.5   Word's Formula Field Arithmetic Operators

Operator	Name	Example	Result
+	Addition	{ =10+5 }	15
–	Subtraction	{ =10-5 }	5
*	Multiplication	{ =10*5 }	50
/	Division	{ =10/5 }	2
%	Percentage	{ =10% }	0.1
^	Exponentiation	{ =10^5 }	100000

For example, suppose you want to know the average number of words per page in your document. That is, you need to divide the total number of words (as given by the NumWords field) by the total number of pages (as given by the NumPages field). Here's a formula field that does this:

```
{= { NumWords } / { NumPages } }
```

A *comparison formula* is an expression that compares two or more numeric operands. If the expression is true, the result of the formula is 1. If the statement is false, the formula returns 0. Table 1.6 summarizes the operators you can use in comparison formulas.

Table 1.6   Word's Formula Field Comparison Operators

Operator	Name	Example	Result
=	Equal to	{ =10=5 }	0
>	Greater than	{ =10>5 }	1
<	Less than	{ =10<5 }	0
>=	Greater than or equal to	{ =10>=5 }	1
<=	Less than or equal to	{ =10<=5 }	0
<>	Not equal to	{ =10<>5 }	1

For example, suppose you want to know whether a document's current size on disk (as given by the `FileSize` field) is greater than 50,000 bytes. Here's a comparison formula field that checks this:

```
{= { FileSize } > 50000 }
```

Finally, Word also offers a number of functions that you can plug into your formula fields. Table 1.7 lists the available functions.

Table 1.7   Word's Formula Field Functions

Function	Returns
`ABS(x)`	The absolute value of *x*.
`AND(x,y)`	1 if both *x* and *y* are true; 0 otherwise.
`AVERAGE(x,y,z,…)`	The average of the list of values given by *x*,*y*,*z*,….
`COUNT(x,y,z,…)`	The number of items in the list of values given by *x*,*y*,*z*,…
`DEFINED(x)`	1 if the expression *x* can be calculated; 0 otherwise.
`FALSE`	0.
`INT(x)`	The integer portion of *x*.
`MIN(x,y,z,…)`	The smallest value in the list of values given by *x*,*y*,*z*,….
`MAX(x,y,z,…)`	The largest value in the list of values given by *x*,*y*,*z*,….
`MOD(x,y)`	The remainder after dividing *x* by *y*.
`NOT(x)`	1 is *x* is false; 0 if *x* is true.
`OR(x,y)`	1 if either or both *x* and *y* are true; 0 if both *x* and *y* are false.
`PRODUCT(x,y,z,…)`	The result of multiplying together the items in the list of values given by *x*,*y*,*z*,….
`ROUND(x,y)`	The value of *x* rounded to the number of decimal places specified by *y*.
`SIGN(x)`	1 if *x* is positive; –1 if *x* is negative.
`SUM(x,y,z,…)`	The sum of the items in the list of values given by *x*,*y*,*z*,….
`TRUE`	1.

Suppose you want to know whether your document has more than 1,000 words (as given by the `NumWords` property) or more than 100 lines (as given by the `DocProperty Lines` field). Here's a formula field that checks this using the `OR` function:

```
{ = OR( { NumWords } > 1000, { DOCPROPERTY Lines } > 100) }
```

Calculating Billable Time Charges

You saw earlier that you use the `EditTime` field to return the total editing time for a document. If you bill by the hour based on the amount of time you have worked on a document, you might want to keep track of how much money you've earned so far. If you earn, for instance, $100 per hour, the following formula displays your current billable earnings:

```
{ = { EDITTIME } / 60 * 100 }
```

The `EditTime` result is given in minutes, so you have to divide by 60 to get the number of hours. You then multiply that result by 100 to get the earnings.

To ensure accurate billing, you may want to use the `ROUND` function to round the result to the nearest dollar:

```
{ = ROUND( { EDITTIME } / 60 * 100, 0) \#$0.00 }
```

This formula field also uses a numeric picture to format the result with a dollar sign and two decimal places, as shown in Figure 1.25.

Figure 1.25
A formatted formula field that calculates the billable charge based on the current `EditTime` result.

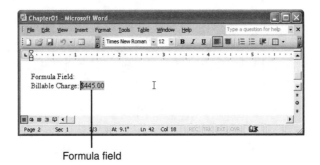

Formula field

Creating Decision-Making Fields

One of the most powerful fields is the `If` field, which compares two expressions and then returns one of two values depending on the result:

```
{ IF Expression1 Operator Expression2 TrueResult FalseResult }
```

`Expression1` and `Expression2` are operands, and `Operator` is one of the comparison operators listed in Table 1.6. If the result of this comparison operation is true, the field displays the `TrueResult` text; if the result of this comparison operation is false, the field displays the `FalseResult` text.

For example, here's a field that checks the `NumWords` field to see whether it's greater than 1,000:

```
{ IF { NumWords } > 1000 "Over word count!" "Word count okay" }
```

If the `NumWords` result is greater than 1,000, the field displays `Over word count!`; if the `NumWords` result is less than or equal to 1,000, the field displays `Word count okay`.

Prompting the User for Input

With many templates, the user is required to fill in certain document properties, such as the title, subject, author, or keywords. Ensuring that these values are entered can be a crucial part of a document management system. One way to do this is to use a Fill-in field, which displays a dialog box that prompts the user for data. The entered data is then displayed as the field result:

```
{ FILLIN Prompt }
```

Prompt is the text that appears as a prompt in the dialog box. Here's an example:

```
{ FILLIN "Please enter the document title:" }
```

If you insert this field in a template, Figure 1.26 shows the dialog box that appears when the user creates a new document based on the template.

Figure 1.26
When you update a Fill-in field, Word displays a dialog box similar to this one.

Although it may occasionally be useful to store user input in the document (see, for example, Chapter 6's "Personalizing Mail Merges with Fill-in Fields"), what if what you really want to do is change the actual document properties? Because each document property has its own field type, you can change many properties by specifying the Fill-in result as the new property value. For example, the following code prompts the user for a document title and then stores the result in the Title property using the Title field:

```
{ TITLE { FILLIN "Please enter a document title:" } }
```

Hiding the Fill-in **Result**

Unfortunately, the result of the Title field appears in the document text. To avoid this, you can hide the result by placing everything inside a Seq field. You normally use this field to create a sequential numbering system, but it comes with a \h switch that hides the field. Here's the hidden form of the Fill-in field:

```
{ SEQ \h { TITLE { FILLIN "Please enter a document title:" } } }
```

Prompting to a Bookmark with Ask

Word also comes with an Ask field type. This works the same as Fill-in, except that the result is stored in a bookmark:

```
{ ASK Bookmark Prompt }
```

Performing Calculations in Tables

Word tables are useful for organizing text into rows and columns and for providing an attractive layout option for lists and other data. But tables get especially powerful and dynamic when you apply formulas to the numeric data contained within a table's rows or columns. For example, if you have a table of sales for various departments, you could display the total sales in a cell at the bottom of the table. Similarly, if your table lists the gross margins from all company divisions, you could display the average gross margin in a cell.

Referencing Table Cells

The trick to using formulas within tables is to reference the table cells correctly. The easiest way to do this is to use the *relative referencing* that's built into Word tables:

Relative Reference	Refers To
ABOVE	All the cells above the formula cell in the same column.
BELOW	All the cells below the formula cell in the same column.
LEFT	All the cells to the left of the formula cell in the same row.
RIGHT	All the cells to the right of the formula cell in the same row.

For example, the following formula field sums all the numeric values in the cells above the formula cell in the same column:

```
{ =SUM(ABOVE) }
```

Figure 1.27 shows an example of this formula field in action in the subtotal cell (D12, showing the result $90.17).

If you need to refer to specific cells in your formula, you should use *absolute referencing*, which is very similar to the cell referencing used by Excel. That is, the table columns are assigned the letters A (for the first column), B (second column), and so on; the table rows are assigned the numbers 1 (for the first row), 2 (second row), and so on. Following are some examples:

Absolute Reference	Refers To
A1	The cell in the first row and first column.
D5	The cell in the fifth row and fourth column.
A1,D5	The cells A1 and D5.
A1:D5	The rectangular range of cells created by A1 in the top-left corner and D5 in the bottom-right corner.
B:B	All the cells in the second column.
3:3	All the cells in the third row.

Formula is =SUM(ABOVE)

Figure 1.27

The subtotal in this invoice document is calculated using a field with the formula =SUM(ABOVE).

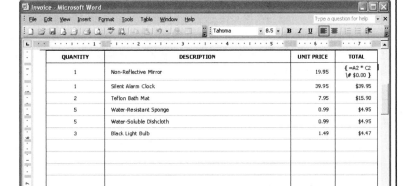

Formula is =Subtotal * .05

In the invoice shown in Figure 1.27, for example, the total for the Non-Reflective Mirror item is derived using the following formula field:

```
{ =A2 * C2 \# $0.00 }
```

An Entire Row/Column Gotcha

If you want to use an absolute reference for an entire column (such as A:A) or an entire row (such as 1:1), make sure you place your formula in a different row or column. For example, consider the following formula field:

```
{ =SUM(A:A) }
```

This sums all the cell values in the first column. However, if you insert the field into a cell in column A, the field result will be included in the sum the next time you update the field. In Excel, this would be flagged as a circular reference. In Word, you just get the wrong answer.

Finally, you can also use bookmarks to create formulas that have "named" operands. For example, if you select a cell and insert a bookmark named GrossMargin, you can refer to that cell using the bookmark name, as in this example:

```
{ =B3 * GrossMargin }
```

In the invoice document shown in Figure 1.27, I assigned a bookmark named Subtotal to the subtotal cell. To calculate the sales tax value, I used the following formula field:

```
{ = Subtotal * .05 }
```

For Sophisticated Formulas, Use Excel

Given the row-and-column format of a table and the use of Excel-like absolute referencing, Word's tables bear some resemblance to an Excel worksheet. However, that resemblance is vague, at best. Given the relatively limited set of functions available with fields, and without any proper spreadsheet tools at your disposal, you should use Word tables for only the simplest of formula tasks. If you need something more powerful, you can always embed an Excel worksheet right into a Word document. See the section in Chapter 6 titled "Inserting an Object from Another Application," to learn how this is done.

This also works for entire tables, although in an annoyingly quirky way. Select your table (via Table, Select, Table) and then insert a bookmark to name it. You can then reference a cell in that table as follows:

```
SUM(TableName Cell)
```

Here, `TableName` is the bookmark name for the table, and `Cell` is an absolute cell reference. For example, the following code refers to cell A1 in a table named Table1:

```
SUM(Table1 A1)
```

You might think I used the preceding SUM function as an example, but that's not the case. To reference a cell in another table in Word, you *must* include the table name and cell reference inside a function! In other words, the following apparently sensible code in fact produces a syntax error in Word:

```
Table1 A1
```

The SUM function is most often used because the sum of a single cell is the value of the cell itself. You can also use AVERAGE, COUNT, MAX, MIN, or PRODUCT, if you want to be different.

For example, to refer to the Total Due cell in the table in Figure 1.27, I first selected the table and assigned a bookmark named `InvoiceDetail`. With that done, the following formula field references the Total Due cell, as shown in Figure 1.28:

```
{ =SUM(InvoiceDetail C15) }
```

Another Reference Gotcha

Why does the formula reference C15 instead of D15? Because the bottom four rows of the table have only three columns. Therefore, the rightmost column is column C for those rows.

Solving a Relative Reference Problem

There's an important limitation to the relative references I mentioned earlier. When it comes upon a relative reference, Word gathers the cells to use in the formula by moving along the column (for ABOVE and BELOW) or the row (for LEFT and RIGHT). Crucially, it stops moving along the row or column when it comes to a cell that's either empty or that contains text. Even if you have more numbers further along the row or column, Word doesn't see them.

Figure 1.28
Assign a bookmark to a table to reference cells in that table from other parts of the document.

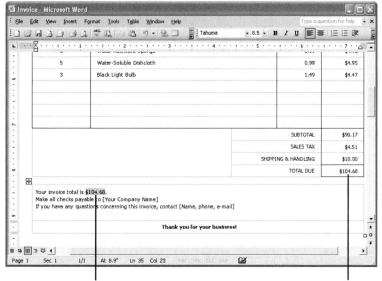

This formula field uses a table name...   ...to reference this cell.

To show you how this works, consider the version of the invoice table shown in Figure 1.29.

...only includes these three cells

Figure 1.29
When you use a relative reference, Word stops when it hits a cell that is blank or that contains text.

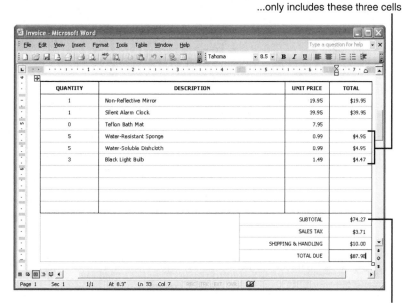

This total...

Notice how the Total cell for the Teflon Bath Mat item (D4) is blank. If you examine the Subtotal, the result is clearly incorrect. That's because the ABOVE relative reference applies only to cells D5 through D11. Because cell D4 is empty, the sum doesn't include the numeric values in cells D2 and D3.

When the Problem Isn't a Problem

This relative reference behavior may seem brain dead, but at times it comes in handy. For example, the formula that calculates the Total Due value in our invoice table is =SUM(ABOVE). This sums the Shipping & Handling, Sales Tax, and Subtotal cells, but then stops because the cell above Subtotal is blank. This is what we want, so in this case, the relative reference "problem" isn't really a problem at all.

One way to work around this problem is to replace the relative reference with an absolute reference:

    { =SUM(D2:D11) }

That works, as you can see in Figure 1.30.

Figure 1.30
One way to work around Word's relative reference problem is to use absolute referencing.

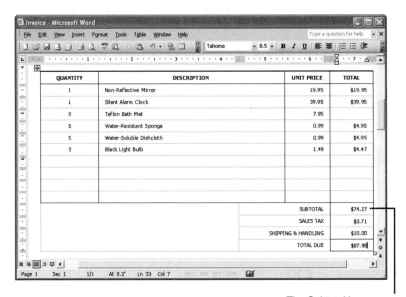

The Subtotal is now correct

The problem with this workaround is that it's not particularly flexible. That is, if you add or delete rows in the table, you must edit the formula by hand.

A better solution is to create two tables by splitting the original table just above the SUM formula. (The easiest way to do this is to place the cursor in the row that will form the top of the second table, and then select the Table, Split Table command.) Now use a bookmark to name the table containing the values you want to sum, and then reference this table in the formula.

Figure 1.31 shows the split invoice table. The top table I've named OrderDetail, and I've changed the Subtotal field to the following:

```
{ =SUM(OrderDetail D:D) }
```

Now, no matter how many rows you add or delete in the OrderDetail table, the formula will always return the correct subtotal.

OrderDetail table

Figure 1.31
To always get an accurate sum, place the SUM formula in a separate table and then reference the table containing the values.

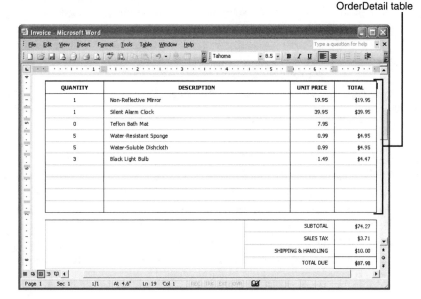

"Hiding" the Table Split
To make this workaround effective, you should hide the paragraph between the two tables. Place the cursor in the paragraph and select Format, Font. Reduce the font size to 1 point, and activate the Hidden effect.

Adding Dummy Text to a Document

When you're working on a document (particularly if you're collaborating with another user), you may need to set up the document's layout and formatting before the text is ready. Most document designers work around this problem by adding dummy text, which enables them to tweak the design without having to wait for the text.

Using the RAND **Function**

Word's RAND function enables you to insert dummy text automatically:

```
=RAND(paragraphs, sentences)
```

Here, the *paragraphs* value specifies the number of paragraphs of dummy text that Word will generate, and *sentences* specifies the number of sentences per paragraph. You can specify up to 200 paragraphs of up to 99 sentences each, or up to 99 paragraphs with up to 200 sentences in each.

For example, to generate five paragraphs with six sentences in each, you'd type the following formula at the spot in the document where you want the dummy text to appear, and then press Enter:

```
=RAND(5,6)
```

In all cases, Word simply repeats the following sentence:

```
The quick brown fox jumps over the lazy dog.
```

This classic sentence is famous for containing all 26 letters of the alphabet.

Using the Repeat Command

There's another road to filler text that you might want to try. As you may know, when you type text in Word without performing any other action (such as deleting characters or applying formatting), Word stores all the text you've typed since the previous nontyping action. This means that you can also force Word to repeat the typing by selecting Edit, Repeat Typing, or by using the faster keyboard shortcuts: F4 or Ctrl+Y. For some quick filler text, type a few words and then press F4 repeatedly until the area you want is filled.

Even better, use that old document designer standby, the semi-Latin text snippet:

> Lorem ipsum dolor sit amet, consectetuer adipiscing elit, sed diam nonummy nibh euismod tincidunt ut laoreet dolore magna aliquam erat volutpat. Ut wisi enim ad minim veniam, quis nostrud exerci tation ullamcorper suscipit lobortis nisl ut aliquip ex ea commodo consequat.

> Duis autem vel eum iriure dolor in hendrerit in vulputate velit esse molestie consequat, vel illum dolore eu feugiat nulla facilisis at vero eros et accumsan et iusto odio dignissim qui blandit praesent luptatum zzril delenit augue duis dolore te feugait nulla facilisi. Nam liber tempor cum soluta nobis eleifend option congue nihil imperdiet doming id quod mazim placerat facer possim assum.

I've pasted this text into the Chapter01.doc example file.

From Here

- For more on the `Fill-in` field, see the section "Personalizing Mail Merges with Fill-in Fields" in Chapter 6.

- For the details on using Word for collaboration, see the section "Collaborating on a Word Document" in Chapter 7.

- To learn how to customize Word's toolbars, see Chapter 10, "Customizing Office to Suit Your Style," particularly the "Creating Custom Toolbars" section.

- For custom Word keyboard shortcuts, see the section "Creating Custom Keyboard Shortcuts in Word" in Chapter 10.

- To learn how to work with the VBA Editor and create macros, see Chapter 11, "Maximizing Office with VBA Macros."

- For more useful Word VBA macros, see the section "Word Macros" in Chapter 12.

- For information on applying a digital signature to a project, see the section "Self-Certifying Your VBA Projects" in Chapter 14.

Analyzing Data with Excel

2

All data has a story to tell. Whether it's sales, expenses, statistics, inventory, or share prices, the data usually hides something interesting or important that you ought to know. However, even Office gurus understand that although it's relatively easy to enter data into an Excel worksheet, it's much harder to hear what that data is telling you. To put it another way, Office gurus know that to glean meaning from static worksheet data, you have to *animate* the data in some way so as to turn the data into *information*.

In Excel, animating data really means *analyzing* it. Using Excel's business-modeling tools, you can analyze worksheet numbers to make them reveal their secrets. This chapter shows you how to do this by examining five of Excel's most useful data-analysis techniques and features: what-if analysis, scenarios, Goal Seek, Solver, and lists.

Performing a What-If Analysis

What-if analysis is perhaps the most basic method for understanding worksheet data. With what-if analysis, you first calculate a formula D, based on the input from variables A, B, and C. You then say, "What if I change variable A? Or B or C? Or all three? What happens to the result?"

For example, Figure 2.1 shows a worksheet that calculates the monthly payment for a loan or mortgage based on three variables: the interest rate, the term, and the initial principal. Cell C8 shows the result of the PMT() function. Now the questions begin: What if the interest rate is 8%? What if the term is 25 years? What if the principal is $125,000? Or $150,000? Answering these questions is a straightforward matter of changing the appropriate variables and watching the effect on the result.

Figure 2.1
The most basic form of what-if analysis involves changing worksheet variables and watching the result.

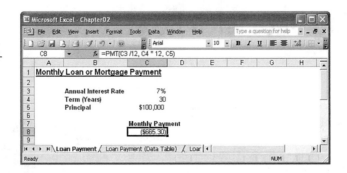

More Info

I adapted some of the material in this chapter from my book *Formulas and Functions for Microsoft Excel 2003* (Que Publishing, 2004). If you need more detail about data analysis in Excel, you can check out the book at your local store or online at www.mcfedries.com/ExcelFormulas/.

This Chapter's Examples

You'll find the workbook that contains this chapter's examples at www.mcfedries.com/OfficeGurus/.

Performing What-If Analysis with a Range Snapshot

The simplest form of what-if analysis involves changing the value of one cell and watching its effect on the values of one or more other cells. However, what if the cells you want to watch reside in another worksheet or workbook? You could arrange the windows accordingly, but Excel has an easier method: the Camera tool. The Camera takes a snapshot of a specified range and enables you to add that snapshot to any worksheet. The snapshot is "live," however, so any changes that occur in the original range will also appear automatically in the snapshot.

To begin, follow these steps to display the Camera tool:

1. Select Tools, Customize to display the Customize dialog box.
2. Select the Commands tab.
3. In the Categories list, select Tools.
4. In the Commands list, click and drag the Camera item and drop it on the menu bar.
5. Click Close.

To use the camera, select the range, click Camera, and then click the spot where you want the snapshot to appear.

Setting Up a One-Input Data Table

Modifying formula variables suffers from a serious drawback: you see only a single result at one time. If you want to study the effect a range of values has on the formula, you need to construct a *data table*. In the loan payment worksheet, for example, suppose that you want to see the payments with the principal varying between $100,000 and $150,000. You could just enter these values into a row or column and then create the appropriate formulas. Setting up a data table, however, is much easier, as the following procedure shows:

1. Add to the worksheet the values you want to input into the formula. You have two choices for the placement of these values:

   - If you want to enter the values in a row, start the row one cell up and one cell to the right of the formula.

   - If you want to enter the values in a column, start the column one cell down and one cell to the left of the cell containing the formula, as shown in Figure 2.2.

Input cell

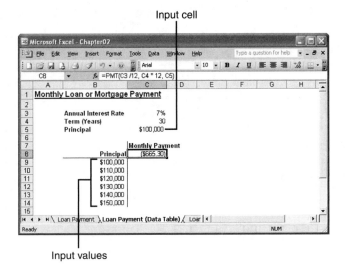

Figure 2.2
To set up the data table, first enter the formula's input values.

Input values

2. Select the range that includes the input values and the formula. (In Figure 2.2, this is B8:C14.)

3. Choose Data, Table. Excel displays the Table dialog box.

4. How you fill in this dialog box depends on how you set up your data table:

   - If you entered the input values in a row, use the Row Input Cell text box to enter the cell address of the input cell.

   - If the input values are in a column, enter the input cell's address in the Column Input Cell text box. In the loan payment example, enter **C5** (the Principal cell) in the Column Input Cell, as shown in Figure 2.3.

Figure 2.3
In the Table dialog box, enter the input cell where you want Excel to substitute the input values.

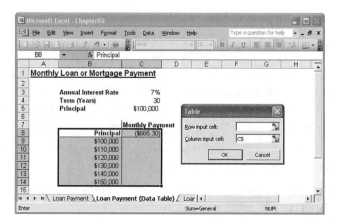

5. Click OK. Excel places each of the input values in the input cell; Excel then displays the results in the data table, as shown in Figure 2.4.

Figure 2.4
Excel substitutes each input value into the input cell and displays the results in the data table.

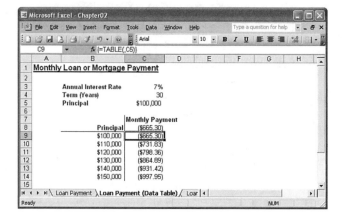

Setting Up a Two-Input Table

You also can set up data tables that take two input variables. For example, this would enable you to see the effect on a loan payment's value when you enter different values for the principal *and* the interest rate, for instance. The following steps show you how to set up a two-input data table:

1. Enter one set of values in a column below the formula and the second set of values to the right of the formula in the same row, as shown in Figure 2.5.

2. Select the range that includes the input values and the formula (B8:G14 in Figure 2.5).

3. Choose Data, Table to display the Table dialog box.

4. In the Row Input Cell text box, enter the cell address of the input cell that corresponds to the row values you entered (C3 in Figure 2.5—the Annual Interest variable).

Figure 2.5
Enter the two sets of values that you want to input into the formula.

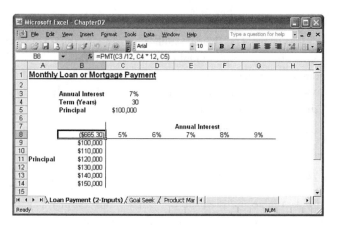

5. In the Column Input Cell text box, enter the cell address of the input cell you want to use for the column values (C5 in Figure 2.5—the Principal variable).

6. Click OK. Excel runs through the various input combinations and then displays the results in the data table, as shown in Figure 2.6.

Figure 2.6
Excel substitutes each input value into the input cell and displays the results in the data table.

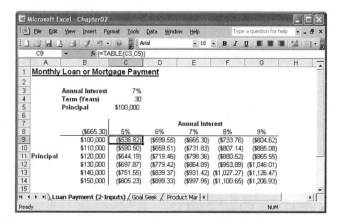

Bypassing Table Recalculation

If you make changes to any of the variables in a table formula, Excel recalculates the entire table. This can be a problem with large tables, which can take a long time to calculate. If you prefer to control the table recalculation, choose Tools, Options. Select the Calculation tab and then activate the Automatic Except Tables check box. This tells Excel not to include data tables when it recalculates a worksheet. To recalculate a table, press F9 (or Shift+F9 to recalculate the current worksheet only).

Editing a Data Table

If you want to make changes to the data table, you can edit the formula (or formulas) as well as the input value. However, the data table results are a different matter. When you run the Data, Table command, Excel enters an array formula in the interior of the data table. This formula is a `TABLE()` function (a special function available only by using the Data, Table command) with the following syntax:

```
{=TABLE(row_input_ref, column_input_ref)}
```

Here, `row_input_ref` and `column_input_ref` are the cell references you entered in the Table dialog box. The braces ({ }) indicate that this is an array, which means that you can't change or delete individual elements of the array. If you want to change the results, you need to select the entire data table and then run the Data, Table command again. If you just want to delete the results, you must first select the entire array and then delete it.

Working with Scenarios

In what-if analysis, a particular set of input values that you plug into a model is called a *scenario*. Because most what-if worksheets can take a wide range of input values, you usually end up with a large number of scenarios to examine. Instead of going through the tedious chore of inserting all these values into the appropriate cells, Excel has a Scenario Manager feature that can handle the process for you.

As you've seen in this chapter, Excel has powerful features that enable you to build sophisticated models that can answer complex questions. The problem, though, isn't in *answering* questions, but in *asking* them. For example, Figure 2.7 shows a worksheet model that analyzes a mortgage. You use this model to decide how much of a down payment to make, how long the term should be, and whether to include an extra principal paydown every month. The Results section compares the monthly payment and total paid for the regular mortgage and for the mortgage with a paydown. It also shows the savings and reduced term that result from the paydown.

Figure 2.7
A mortgage-analysis worksheet.

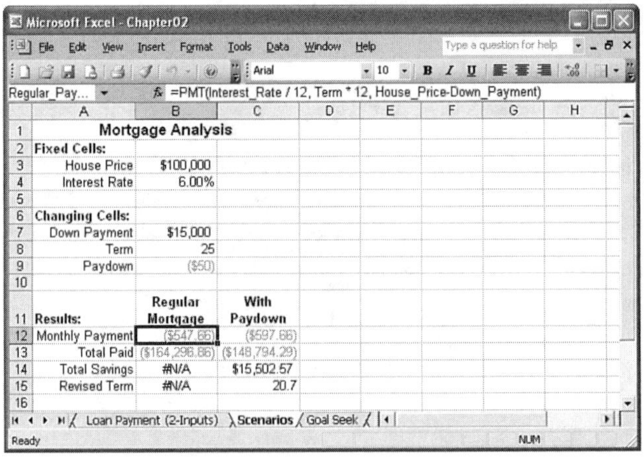

Here are some possible questions to ask this model:

- How much will I save over the term of the mortgage if I use a shorter term and a larger down payment and include a monthly paydown?

- How much more will I end up paying if I extend the term, reduce the down payment, and forego the paydown?

These are examples of *scenarios* that you would plug into the appropriate cells in the model. Excel's Scenario Manager helps by letting you define a scenario separately from the worksheet. You can save specific values for any or all of the model's input cells, give the scenario a name, and then recall the name (and all the input values it contains) from a list.

Setting Up Your Worksheet for Scenarios

Before creating a scenario, you need to decide which cells in your model will be the input cells. These will be the worksheet variables—the cells that, when you change them, change the results of the model. (Not surprisingly, Excel calls these the *changing cells*.) You can have as many as 32 changing cells in a scenario. For best results, follow these guidelines when setting up your worksheet for scenarios:

- The changing cells should be constants. Formulas can be affected by other cells, and that can throw off the entire scenario.

- To make it easier to set up each scenario, and to make your worksheet easier to understand, group the changing cells and label them (see Figure 2.7).

- For even greater clarity, assign a range name to each changing cell.

Adding a Scenario

To work with scenarios, you use Excel's Scenario Manager tool. This feature enables you to add, edit, display, and delete scenarios, as well as create summary scenario reports.

When your worksheet is set up the way you want it, you can add a scenario to the sheet by following these steps:

1. Choose Tools, Scenarios. Excel displays the Scenario Manager dialog box, shown in Figure 2.8.
2. Choose Add. The Edit Scenario dialog box appears. Figure 2.9 shows a completed version of this dialog box.
3. Use the Scenario Name text box to enter a name for the scenario.
4. Use the Changing Cells box to enter references to your worksheet's changing cells. You can type in the references (be sure to separate noncontiguous cells with commas) or select the cells directly on the worksheet.

Figure 2.8
Excel's Scenario Manager enables you to create and work with worksheet scenarios.

Figure 2.9
Use the Add Scenario dialog box to define a scenario.

5. Use the Comment box to enter a description for the scenario. This appears in the Comment section of the Scenario Manager dialog box.

6. Click OK. Excel displays the Scenario Values dialog box, shown in Figure 2.10.

Figure 2.10
Use the Scenario Values dialog box to enter the values you want to use for the scenario's changing cells.

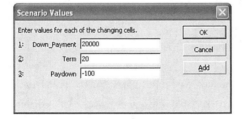

7. Use the text boxes to enter values for the changing cells.

Range Names for the Changing Cells
You'll notice in Figure 2.10 that Excel displays the range name for each changing cell, which makes it easier to enter your numbers correctly. If your changing cells aren't named, Excel displays the cell addresses instead.

---

8. To add more scenarios, click Add to return to the Add Scenario dialog box and repeat steps 3–7. Otherwise, click OK to return to the Scenario Manager dialog box.

9. Click Close to return to the worksheet.

Displaying a Scenario

After you define a scenario, you can enter its values into the changing cells by displaying the scenario from the Scenario Manager dialog box. The following steps give you the details:

1. Choose Tools, Scenarios to display the Scenario Manager.

2. In the Scenarios list, click the scenario you want to display.

3. Click Show. Excel enters the scenario values into the changing cells. Figure 2.11 shows an example.

Figure 2.11
When you click Show, Excel enters the values for the highlighted scenario into the changing cells.

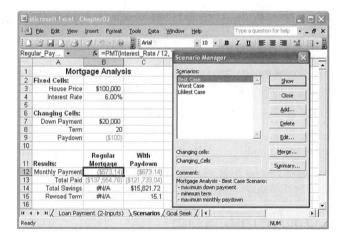

4. Repeat steps 2 and 3 to display other scenarios.

5. Click Close to return to the worksheet.

Using Goal Seek for What-If Analysis

The what-if analysis you've seen so far has concentrated on changing formula variables to see what effect this has on the result. But what if you need to come at the problem from the opposite angle? That is, what if you know what result you're looking for? In that case, what you need to know is the specific set of formula values that will give you the result you seek.

For example, you might know that you need to have $50,000 saved in 15 years for your child's education, or you might know that you have to achieve a 30% gross margin in your next budget. If you need to manipulate only a single variable to achieve these results, you can use Excel's Goal Seek feature. You tell Goal Seek the final value you need and which variable to change, and it finds a solution for you (if one exists). (If you want to manipulate multiple variables, use Solver, instead. See "Solving Complex Problems with Solver," later in this chapter.)

Running Goal Seek

Before you run Goal Seek, you need to set up your worksheet in a particular way. This means doing three things:

- Set up one cell as the *changing cell*. This is the value that Goal Seek will iteratively manipulate to attempt to reach the goal. Enter an initial value (such as 0) into the cell.
- Set up the other input values for the formula and give them proper initial values.
- Create a formula for Goal Seek to use to try to reach the goal.

Let's suppose that you have future monetary goals that you need to reach by a certain date and that you have an initial amount to invest. Given current interest rates, how much extra do you have to deposit into the investment periodically to achieve your goal? For example, suppose that you want to end up with $50,000 in 15 years to finance your child's college education. If you have no initial deposit and you expect to get 7.5% interest over the term of the investment, how much do you need to deposit each month to reach your target? Figure 2.12 shows a worksheet set up to use Goal Seek:

- Cell B4 is the changing cell: the monthly deposit into the fund (with an initial value of 0).
- The other cells (B2 and B3) are used as constants for the FV() function.
- Cell B5 contains the FV() function that calculates the future value of the college fund. When Goal Seek is done, this cell's value should be $50,000.

Figure 2.12
A worksheet set up to use Goal Seek to find out how much to set aside each year to end up with a $50,000 education fund in five years.

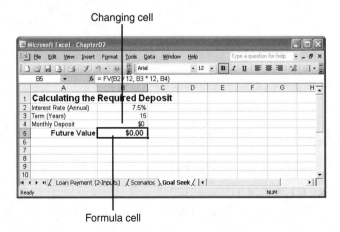

Changing cell

Formula cell

With your worksheet ready to go, follow these steps to use Goal Seek:

1. Choose Tools, Goal Seek. Excel displays the Goal Seek dialog box.

2. Use the Set Cell text box to enter a reference to the cell that contains the formula you want Goal Seek to manipulate. (Cell B5 in Figure 2.12.)

3. Use the To Value text box to enter the final value you want for the goal cell (such as 50000).

4. Use the By Changing Cell text box to enter a reference to the changing cell. (This is cell B4 in Figure 2.12.) Figure 2.13 shows a completed Goal Seek dialog box.

Figure 2.13
The completed Goal Seek dialog box.

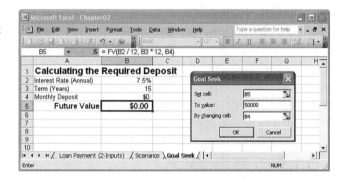

5. Click OK. Excel begins the iteration and displays the Goal Seek Status dialog box. When finished, the dialog box tells you whether Goal Seek found a solution (see Figure 2.14).

Figure 2.14
The Goal Seek Status dialog box shows you the solution (if one was found).

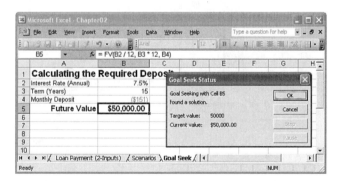

6. If Goal Seek found a solution, you can accept the solution by clicking OK. To ignore the solution, click Cancel.

Goal Seeking with Charts

If you have your data graphed in a 2D bar, column, line, or XY chart, you can run Goal Seek by using the mouse to drag a data marker to a new position. If the data marker represents a formula, Excel uses Goal Seek to work backward and derive the appropriate formula input values.

The following example helps explain this process. Suppose that you want to invest some money every year so that in 10 years, you'll have $150,000. Assuming a constant interest rate, how much do you need to set aside annually to reach your goal? The solution is to adjust the chart data marker at 10 years so that it has the value $150,000. The following procedure shows you the steps to follow:

1. Activate the chart and select the specific data marker you want to adjust. Excel adds selection handles to the marker. For the example, select the data marker corresponding to 10 years on the category axis.

2. Drag the black selection handle to the desired value. As you drag the handle, the current value appears in a pop-up, as shown in Figure 2.15.

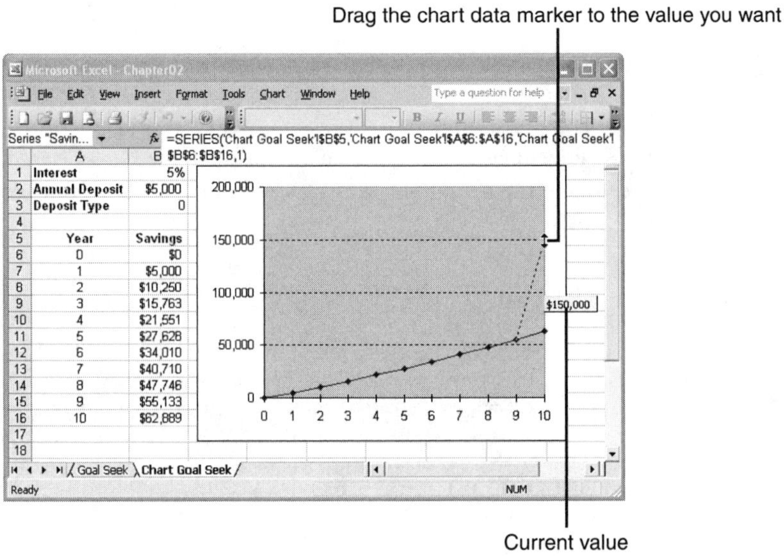

Drag the chart data marker to the value you want

Figure 2.15
Drag the data marker to the desired value.

Current value

3. Release the mouse button. If the marker references a number in a cell, Excel changes the number and redraws the chart. If the marker references a formula, as in the example, Excel displays the Goal Seek dialog box, shown in Figure 2.16. The Set Cell text box shows the cell referenced by the data marker, and the To Value text box shows the new number to which you dragged the marker.

Figure 2.16
If the data marker is derived from a formula, Excel runs Goal Seek.

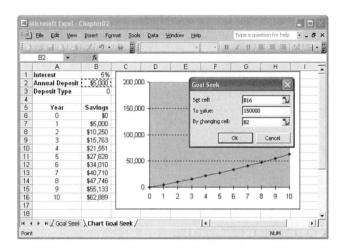

4. Enter the appropriate reference in the By Changing Cell text box. For the example, you enter **B2** to calculate the required annual deposit.

5. Click OK. The Goal Seek Status dialog box appears while Excel derives the solution for the new number.

6. When the iteration is complete, click OK. Excel redraws the chart.

Solving Complex Problems with Solver

Most problems in business aren't as easy as the Goal Seek examples. You'll usually face formulas with at least two and sometimes dozens of variables. Often a problem will have more than one solution, and your challenge will be to find the *optimal* solution (that is, the one that maximizes profit, or minimizes costs, or matches other criteria). For these bigger challenges, you need a more muscular tool. Excel has just the answer: Solver. Solver is a sophisticated optimization program that enables you to find the solutions to complex problems that would otherwise require high-level mathematical analysis.

Solver, like Goal Seek, uses an iterative method to perform its magic. This means that Solver tries a solution, analyzes the results, tries another solution, and so on. However, this cyclic iteration isn't just guesswork on Solver's part. The program looks at how the results change with each new iteration and, through some sophisticated mathematical trickery, it can tell (usually) in what direction it should head for the solution.

However, the fact that Goal Seek and Solver are both iterative doesn't make them equal. In fact, Solver brings a number of advantages to the table:

- Solver enables you to specify multiple adjustable cells. You can use up to 200 adjustable cells in all.

2

- Solver enables you to set up *constraints* on the adjustable cells. For example, you can tell Solver to find a solution that not only maximizes profit, but also satisfies certain conditions, such as achieving a gross margin between 20% and 30%, or keeping expenses less than $100,000. These conditions are *constraints* on the solution.

- Solver seeks not only a desired result (the "goal" in Goal Seek), but also the optimal one. This means that you can find a solution that is the maximum or minimum possible.

- For complex problems, Solver can generate multiple solutions. You then can save these solutions under different scenarios, as described later in this chapter.

Solver is a powerful tool that most Excel users don't need. It would be overkill, for example, to use Solver to compute net profit given fixed revenue and cost figures. Many problems, however, require nothing less than the Solver approach. These problems cover many different fields and situations, but they all have the following characteristics in common:

- They have a single *target cell* that contains a formula you want to maximize, minimize, or set to a specific value. This formula could be a calculation, such as total transportation expenses or net profit.

- The target cell formula contains references to one or more *changing cells* (also called *unknowns* or *decision variables*). Solver adjusts these cells to find the optimal solution for the target cell formula. These changing cells might include items such as units sold, shipping costs, or advertising expenses.

- Optionally, there are one or more *constraint cells* that must satisfy certain criteria. For example, you might require that advertising be less than 10% of total expenses or that the discount to customers be a number between 40% and 60%.

What types of problems exhibit these kinds of characteristics? A surprisingly broad range, as the following list shows:

- The transportation problem—This problem involves minimizing shipping costs from multiple manufacturing plants to multiple warehouses while meeting demand.

- The allocation problem—This problem requires minimizing employee costs while maintaining appropriate staffing requirements.

- The product mix problem—This problem requires generating the maximum profit with a mix of products while still meeting customer requirements. You solve this problem when you sell multiple products with different cost structures, profit margins, and demand curves.

- The blending problem—This problem involves manipulating the materials used for one or more products to minimize production costs, meet consumer demand, and maintain a minimum level of quality.

- Linear algebra—This problem involves solving sets of linear equations.

Loading Solver

Solver is an add-in to Microsoft Excel, so you'll need to load Solver before you can use it. Choose Tools, Add-Ins to display the Add-Ins dialog box. In the Add-Ins Available list, activate the Solver Add-In check box and then click OK. Excel installs the add-in and adds a Solver command to the Tools menu.

Using Solver

Suppose your concern is to find a break-even point for a new product. The break-even point is the number of units that need to be sold to produce a profit of 0. This is a straightforward Goal Seek problem: you change the number of units until your profit formula reaches the value of 0. But what if you need to find the break-even point for *two* products? The goal in this case is to compute the number of units to sell for both products so that the total profit is 0.

The most obvious way to proceed is to use Goal Seek to determine the break-even points for each product separately. Figure 2.17 shows the results.

Figure 2.17
The break-even points for two products (using separate Goal Seek calculations on the Product Profit cells).

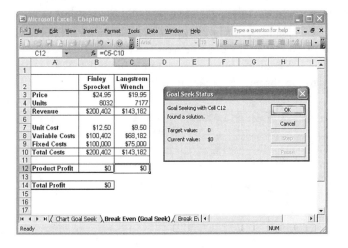

This method works, but the problem is that the two products don't exist in a vacuum. For example, cost savings will be associated with each product because of joint advertising campaigns, combined shipments to customers (larger shipments usually mean better freight rates), and so on. To allow for this, you need to reduce the cost for each product by a factor related to the number of units sold by the other product. In practice, this would be difficult to estimate, but to keep things simple, I'll use the following assumption: The costs for each product are reduced by $1 for every unit sold of the other product. For instance, if the Langstrom wrench sells 10,000 units, the costs for the Finley sprocket are reduced by $10,000. I'll make this adjustment in the Variable Costs formula. For example, the formula that calculates variable costs for the Finley sprocket (cell B8) becomes the following:

```
=B4 * B7 - C4
```

Similarly, the formula that calculates variable costs for the Langstrom wrench (cell C8) becomes the following:

```
=C4 * C7 - B4
```

By making this change, you move out of Goal Seek's territory. The Variable Costs formulas now have two variables: the units sold for the Finley sprocket and the units sold for the Langstrom wrench. I've changed the problem from one of two single-variable formulas, which Goal Seek can easily handle (individually), to a single formula with two variables, which is the terrain of Solver.

To see how Solver handles such a problem, follow these steps:

1. Choose Tools, Solver. Excel displays the Solver Parameters dialog box.

2. In the Set Target Cell text box, enter a reference to the target cell—that is, the cell with the formula you want to optimize. In the example, you enter **B14**.

3. In the Equal To section, select the appropriate option button: Select Max to maximize the target cell, select Min to minimize it, or select Value Of to solve for a particular value (in which case, you also need to enter the value in the text box provided). In the example, you activate Value Of and enter **0** into the text box.

4. Use the By Changing Cells box to enter the cells you want Solver to change while it looks for a solution. In the example, you enter **B4,C4**. Figure 2.18 shows the completed Solver Parameters dialog box for the example (note that Solver changes all cell addresses to the absolute reference format).

Figure 2.18
Use the Solver Parameters dialog box to set up the problem for Solver.

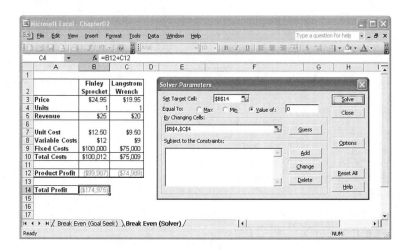

The By Changing Cells Text Box
You can enter a maximum of 200 cells into the By Changing Cells box. Also, the Guess button enters into the By Changing Cells text box all the nonformula cells that are directly or indirectly referenced by the target cell's formula.

5. Click Solve. (I discuss constraints in the next section.) Solver works on the problem and then displays the Solver Results dialog box, which tells you whether it found a solution.

6. If Solver found a solution that you want to use, click the Keep Solver Solution option and then click OK. If you don't want to accept the new numbers, click Restore Original Values and click OK, or just click Cancel.

Figure 2.19 shows the results for the example. As you can see, Solver has produced a total profit of 0 by running one product (the Langstrom wrench) at a slight loss and the other at a slight profit. Although this is certainly a solution, it's not really the one you want. Ideally, for a true break-even analysis, both products should end up with a product profit of 0. The problem is that you didn't tell Solver that was the way you wanted the problem solved. In other words, you didn't set up any constraints.

Figure 2.19
When Solver finishes its calculations, it displays the Solver Results dialog box and enters the solution (if it found one) into the worksheet cells.

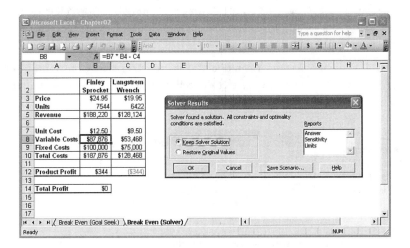

Adding Constraints

The real world puts restrictions and conditions on formulas. A factory might have a maximum capacity of 10,000 units a day, the number of employees in a company has to be a number greater than or equal to zero (negative employees would really reduce staff costs, but nobody has been able to figure out how to do it yet), and your advertising costs might be restricted to 10% of total expenses. All are examples of what Solver calls *constraints*. Adding constraints tells Solver to find a solution so that these conditions are not violated.

To find the best solution for the break-even analysis, you need to tell Solver to optimize both Product Profit formulas to 0. The following steps show you how to do this:

Returning to the Worksheet
If Solver's completion message is still onscreen from the last section, select Cancel to return to the worksheet without saving the solution.

1. Choose Tools, Solver to display the Solver Parameters dialog box. Solver reinstates the options you entered the last time you used Solver.
2. To add a constraint, click Add. Excel displays the Add Constraint dialog box.
3. In the Cell Reference box, enter the cell you want to constrain. For the example, you enter cell **B12** (the Product Profit formula for the Finley sprocket).
4. Use the drop-down list in the middle of the dialog box to select the operator you want to use. The list contains several comparison operators for the constraint—less than or equal to (<=), equal to (=), and greater than or equal to (>=)—as well as two other data type operators—integer (int) and binary (bin). For the example, select the equal to operator (=).

Constraints as Binary or Integer Values

Use the int (integer) operator when you need a constraint, such as total employees, to be an integer value instead of a real number. Use the bin (binary) operator when you have a constraint that must be either TRUE or FALSE (or 1 or 0).

5. If you chose a comparison operator in step 4, use the Constraint box to enter the value by which you want to restrict the cell. For the example, enter 0. Figure 2.20 shows the completed dialog box for the example.

Figure 2.20
Use the Add Constraint dialog box to specify the constraints you want to place on the solution.

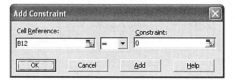

6. If you want to enter more constraints, click Add and repeat steps 3–5. For the example, you also need to constrain cell C12 (the Product Profit formula for the Langstrom wrench) so that it, too, equals 0.
7. When you're done, click OK to return to the Solver Parameters dialog box. Excel displays your constraints in the Subject to the Constraints list box.

Changing or Deleting Constraints

You can add a maximum of 100 constraints. Also, if you need to make a change to a constraint before you begin solving, click the constraint in the Subject to the Constraints list box, click Change, and then make your adjustments in the Change Constraint dialog box that appears. If you want to delete a constraint that you no longer need, click it and then click the Delete button.

8. Click Solve. Solver again tries to find a solution, but this time it uses your constraints as guidelines.

Figure 2.21 shows the results of the break-even analysis after adding the constraints. As you can see, Solver was able to find a solution in which both product margins are 0.

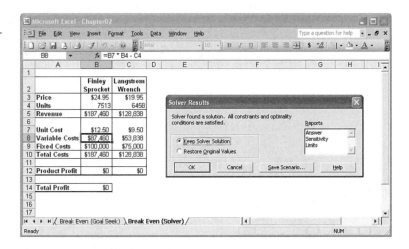

Figure 2.21
The solution to the break-even analysis after adding the constraints.

Analyzing Data with Lists

Excel's forte is spreadsheet work, but its row-and-column layout also makes it a natural flat-file database manager. In Excel, a *list* is a collection of related information with an organizational structure that makes it easy to find or extract data from its contents. Specifically, a list is a worksheet range that has the following properties:

- Field—A single type of information, such as a name, an address, or a phone number. In Excel lists, each column is a field.

- Field value—A single item in a field. In an Excel list, the field values are the individual cells.

- Field name—A unique name you assign to every list field (worksheet column). These names are always found in the first row of the list.

- Record—A collection of associated field values. In Excel lists, each row is a record.

- List range—The worksheet range that includes all the records, fields, and field names of a list.

For example, suppose that you want to set up an accounts-receivable list. A simple system would include information such as account name, account number, invoice number, invoice amount, due date, and date paid, as well as a calculation of the number of days overdue. Figure 2.22 shows how this system would be implemented as an Excel list.

Figure 2.22
Accounts-receivable data in an Excel worksheet.

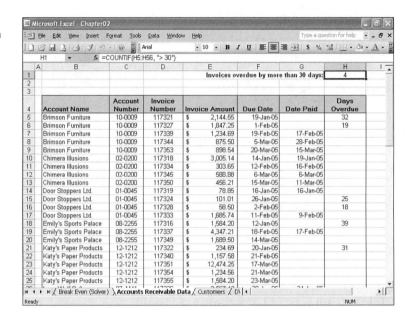

Excel lists don't require elaborate planning, but you should follow a few guidelines for best results. Here are some pointers:

- Always use the top row of the list for the column labels.

- Field names must be unique, and they must be text or text formulas. If you need to use numbers, format them as text.

- Some Excel commands can automatically identify the size and shape of a list. To avoid confusing such commands, try to use only one list per worksheet. If you have multiple related lists, include them in other worksheets in the same workbook.

- If you have nonlist data in the same worksheet, leave at least one blank row or column between the data and the list. This helps Excel to identify the list automatically.

- Excel has a command that enables you to filter your list data to show only records that match certain criteria. (See "Filtering List Data," later in this chapter, for details.) This command works by hiding rows of data. Therefore, if the same worksheet contains nonlist data that you need to see or work with, don't place this data to the left or right of the list.

Converting a Range to a List

Excel has a number of commands that enable you to work efficiently with list data. To take advantage of these commands, you must convert your data from a normal range to a list by following these steps:

1. Click any cell within the range that you want to convert to a list.

2. Choose Data, List, Create List (or press Ctrl+L). Excel displays the Create List dialog box.

3. The Where Is the Data for Your List? box should already show the correct range coordinates. If not, enter the range coordinates or select the range directly on the worksheet.

4. If your range has column headers in the top row (as it should), make sure the My List Has Headers check box is activated.

5. Click OK.

When you convert a range to a list, Excel makes three changes to the range, as shown in Figure 2.23:

- It displays a border around the list.
- It adds drop-down arrows to each field header.
- It displays the List toolbar whenever you select a cell within the list.

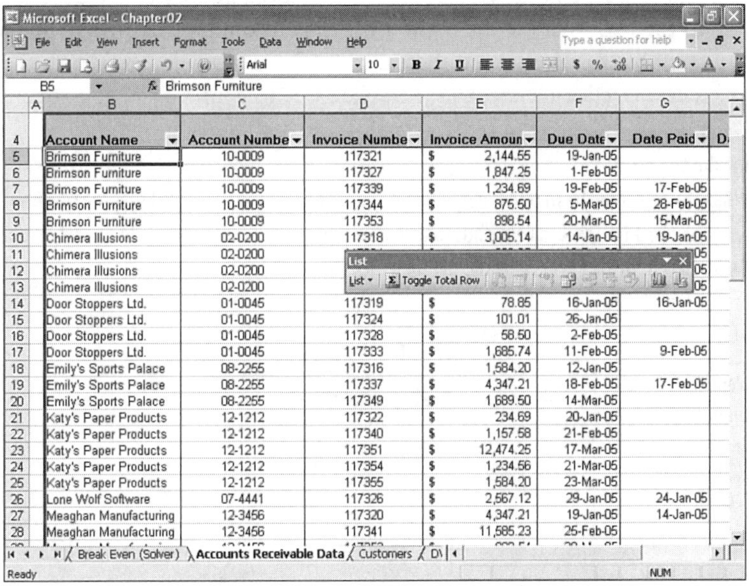

Figure 2.23
The accounts-receivable data converted to a list.

If you ever need to change the list back to a range, select a cell within the list and choose Data, List, Convert to Range.

Basic List Operations

After you've converted the range to a list, you can start working with the data. Following is a quick look at some basic list operations:

- Adding a new record anywhere in the list—Select any cell in a record below which you want to add the new record. In the List toolbar, choose List, Insert, Row. Excel inserts a blank row above the selected cell into which you can enter the new data.

- Adding a new record at the bottom of the list—After you have inserted a row, you'll see an asterisk (*) in the first field below the last record in the list. This is the new record symbol, and it means that you can use this row to add a new record to the list.

Turning Off Excel's Warning Dialog

As soon as you start entering data into the new record, Excel displays a dialog box to tell you that it has inserted a row. You can avoid being pestered by this bit of obvious news by clicking the Do Not Display This Dialog Again check box.

- Deleting a record—Select any cell in the record you want to delete. In the List toolbar, choose List, Delete, Row.

- Working with a record using a data form—Choose Data, Form (or, on the List toolbar, choose List, Form). This displays the list's *data form*, which is a dialog box that enables you to add, edit, delete, and find list records quickly (see Figure 2.24). To add a record to the list, click New and enter the data into the blank fields. To edit a record, use the scrollbar to select it and then edit the fields. To delete a record, use the scrollbar to select it, click Delete, and then click OK to confirm the deletion.

Invalid List Error

When you select the Form command, you may see a dialog box warning you that the `Database or list range is not valid`. This usually means that your workbook has an existing range named *Database*. Select Insert, Name, Define, select the `Database` name, and then click Delete.

Figure 2.24
The data form for the accounts-receivable list.

- Finding a record using criteria—Display the data form, click Criteria, and then enter the criteria you want to use in the corresponding field. For example, if you want to find a record where the Invoice Amount field is greater than $1,000, enter >1000 in the data form's Invoice Amount box. Use the Find Prev and Find Next buttons to scroll through the records that match the criteria.

Sorting a List

One of the advantages of a list is that you can rearrange the records so that they're sorted alphabetically or numerically. This feature enables you to view the data in order by customer name, account number, part number, or any other field. You even can sort on multiple fields, which would enable you, for example, to sort a client list by state and then by name within each state.

The following procedure shows you how to sort a list:

1. Select a cell inside the list.

2. Choose List, Sort on the List toolbar. Excel displays the Sort dialog box, shown in Figure 2.25.

Figure 2.25
Use the Sort dialog box to sort the list on one or more fields.

3. Use the Sort By list to select the field you want to use for the overall order for the sort.

4. (Optional) If you want to sort the data on more than one field, use one or both of the Then By lists to select the field or fields you want to use.

Sorting and Formulas
Be careful when you sort list records that contain formulas. If the formulas use relative addresses that refer to cells outside their own record, the new sort order might change the references and produce erroneous results. If your list formulas must refer to cells outside the list, be sure to use absolute addresses.

---

5. For each sort field, select either Ascending or Descending.

Excel's Sorting Order

How Excel sorts the list depends on the data. Here's the order Excel uses in an ascending sort:

Type (in Order of Priority)	Order
Numbers	Largest negative to largest positive
Text	Space ! " # $ % & ' ( ) * + , - . / 0 through 9 (when formatted as text) : ; < = > ? @ A through Z (Excel ignores case) [\ ] ^ _ ' {,} ~
Logical	FALSE before TRUE
Error	All error values are equal
Blank	Always sorted last (ascending or descending)

6. (Optional) Choose Options to specify one or more of the following sort controls:

First Key Sort Order—Sets a custom sort order (using an AutoFill list) for the field you chose in the Sort By list. For example, to sort by the days of the week, select the Sun, Mon, Tue option.

Case Sensitive—Activate this option to have Excel differentiate between uppercase and lowercase during sorting. In an ascending sort, for example, lowercase letters are sorted before uppercase letters.

Orientation—Excel normally sorts list rows (the Sort Top to Bottom option). To sort list columns, activate Sort Left to Right.

7. Click OK. Excel sorts the range.

Custom AutoFill Lists

You're not stuck with only the few AutoFill lists that Excel recognizes out of the box. You're free to define your own AutoFill lists. To start, choose Tools, Options, click the Custom Lists tab, and then click New List. Type an item from your list into the List Entries box, press Enter, and then repeat for each item. (Make sure that you add the items in the order in which you want them to appear in the series.) Click Add to add the list to the Custom Lists box, and then click OK to return to the worksheet.

Sorting on More Than Three Keys

You're not restricted to sorting on only three fields in an Excel list. By performing consecutive sorts, you can sort on any number of fields. For example, suppose that you want to sort a customer list by the following fields (in order of importance): Region, State, City, ZIP Code, and Name. To use five fields, you must perform two consecutive sorts. The first sort uses the three least important fields: City, ZIP Code, and Name. Of these three, City is the most important, so it's selected in the Sort By field; ZIP Code is selected in the first Then By field, and Name is selected in the second Then By field. When this sort is complete, you must run a second sort using the remaining keys, Region and State. Select Region in the Sort By list and State in the first Then By list.

By running multiple sorts and always using the least important fields first, you can sort on as many fields as you like.

Sorting a List in Natural Order

It's often convenient to see the order in which records were entered into a list, or the *natural order* of the data. Normally, you can restore a list to its natural order by choosing Edit, Undo Sort immediately after a sort.

Unfortunately, after several sort operations, it's no longer possible to restore the natural order. The solution is to create a new field, called, for example, Record, in which you assign consecutive numbers as you enter the data. The first record is 1, the second is 2, and so on. To restore the list to its natural order, you sort on the Record field.

Add the Record Field Up Front

The Record field will work only if you add it either before you start inserting new records in the list or before you've irrevocably sorted the list. Therefore, when planning any list, you might consider always including a Record field just in case you need it.

Follow these steps to add a new field to the list:

1. Select a cell in the field to the right of where you want the new field inserted.
2. In the List toolbar, choose List, Insert, Column. Excel inserts the column.
3. Rename the column header to the field name you want to use.

Figure 2.26 shows the Accounts Receivable list with a Record field added and the record numbers inserted.

Calculating the Next Record Number

If you're not sure how many records are in the list, and if the list isn't sorted in natural order, you might not know which record number to use next. To avoid guessing or searching through the entire Record field, you can generate the record numbers automatically using the MAX() function. Click the formula bar and type (but don't confirm) the following:

```
=MAX(Column:Column)
```

Replace *Column* with the letter of the column that contains the record number (for example, MAX(B:B) for the list in Figure 2.26). Now highlight the formula and press F9. Excel displays the formula result that will be the highest record number used so far. Therefore, your next record number will be one more than the calculated value.

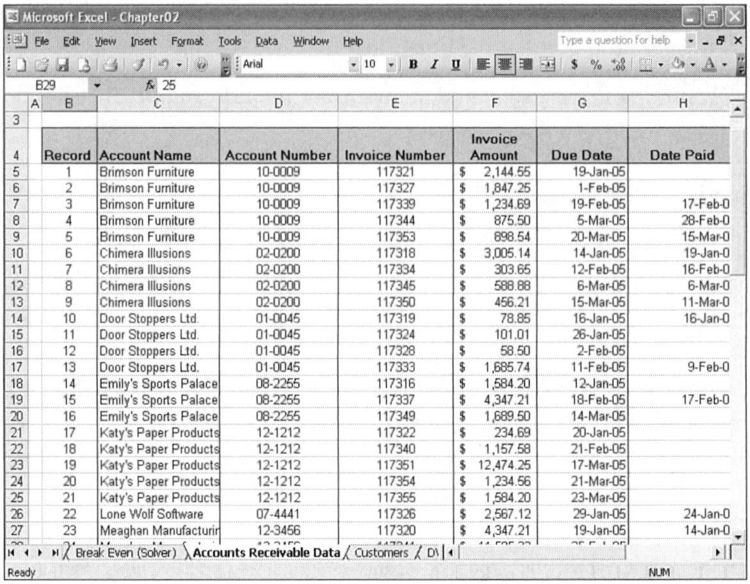

Record	Account Name	Account Number	Invoice Number	Invoice Amount	Due Date	Date Paid
1	Brimson Furniture	10-0009	117321	$ 2,144.55	19-Jan-05	
2	Brimson Furniture	10-0009	117327	$ 1,847.25	1-Feb-05	
3	Brimson Furniture	10-0009	117339	$ 1,234.69	19-Feb-05	17-Feb-0
4	Brimson Furniture	10-0009	117344	$ 875.50	5-Mar-05	28-Feb-0
5	Brimson Furniture	10-0009	117353	$ 898.54	20-Mar-05	15-Mar-0
6	Chimera Illusions	02-0200	117318	$ 3,005.14	14-Jan-05	19-Jan-0
7	Chimera Illusions	02-0200	117334	$ 303.65	12-Feb-05	16-Feb-0
8	Chimera Illusions	02-0200	117345	$ 588.88	6-Mar-05	6-Mar-0
9	Chimera Illusions	02-0200	117350	$ 456.21	15-Mar-05	11-Mar-0
10	Door Stoppers Ltd.	01-0045	117319	$ 78.85	16-Jan-05	16-Jan-0
11	Door Stoppers Ltd.	01-0045	117324	$ 101.01	26-Jan-05	
12	Door Stoppers Ltd.	01-0045	117328	$ 58.50	2-Feb-05	
13	Door Stoppers Ltd.	01-0045	117333	$ 1,685.74	11-Feb-05	9-Feb-0
14	Emily's Sports Palace	08-2255	117316	$ 1,584.20	12-Jan-05	
15	Emily's Sports Palace	08-2255	117337	$ 4,347.21	18-Feb-05	17-Feb-0
16	Emily's Sports Palace	08-2255	117349	$ 1,689.50	14-Mar-05	
17	Katy's Paper Products	12-1212	117322	$ 234.69	20-Jan-05	
18	Katy's Paper Products	12-1212	117340	$ 1,157.58	21-Feb-05	
19	Katy's Paper Products	12-1212	117351	$ 12,474.25	17-Mar-05	
20	Katy's Paper Products	12-1212	117354	$ 1,234.56	21-Mar-05	
21	Katy's Paper Products	12-1212	117355	$ 1,584.20	23-Mar-05	
22	Lone Wolf Software	07-4441	117326	$ 2,567.12	29-Jan-05	24-Jan-0
23	Meaghan Manufacturin	12-3456	117320	$ 4,347.21	19-Jan-05	14-Jan-0

Figure 2.26
The Record field tracks the order in which records are added to a list.

Sorting on Part of a Field

Excel performs its sorting chores based on the entire content of each cell in the field. This method is fine for most sorting tasks, but occasionally you'll need to sort on only part of a field. For example, your list might have a ContactName field that contains a first name and then a last name. Sorting on this field orders the list by each person's first name, which is probably not what you want. To sort on the last name, you need to create a new column that extracts the last name from the field. You can then use this new column for the sort.

Excel's text functions make it easy to extract substrings from a cell. In this case, assume that each cell in the ContactName field has a first name, followed by a space, followed by a last name. Your task is to extract everything after the space, and the following formula does the job (assuming that the name is in cell D2):

```
=RIGHT(D2, LEN(D2) - FIND(" ", D2))
```

Figure 2.27 shows this formula in action. Column D contains the names, and column A contains the formula to extract the last name. I sorted on column A to order the list by last name.

Hiding the Extra Sort Field

If you'd rather not have the extra sort field (column A in Figure 2.27) cluttering the list, you can hide it by selecting a cell in the field and choosing Format, Column, Hide. Fortunately, you don't have to unhide the field to sort on it because Excel still includes the field in the Sort By list.

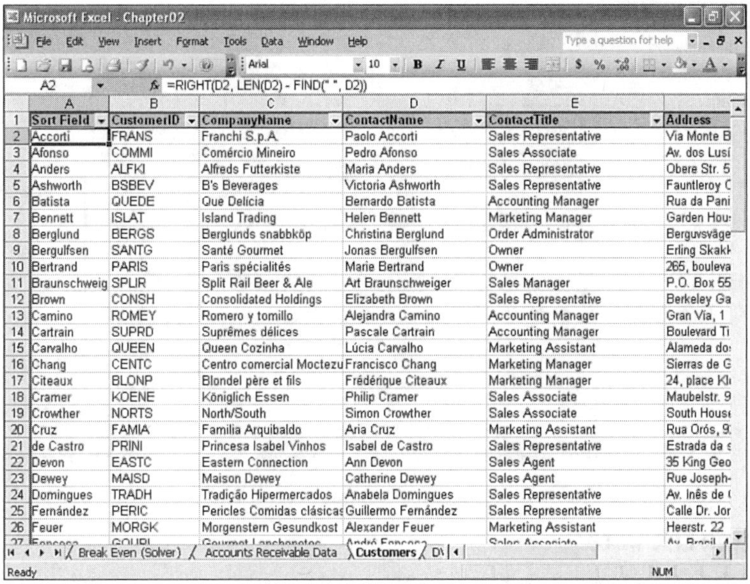

Figure 2.27
To sort on part of a field, use Excel's text functions to extract the string you need for the sort.

Sorting Without Articles

Lists that contain field values starting with articles (*A*, *An*, and *The*) can throw off your sorting. To fix this problem, you can borrow the technique from the preceding section and sort on a new field in which the leading articles have been removed. As before, you want to extract everything after the first space, but you can't just use the same formula because not all the titles have a leading article. You need to test for a leading article using the following OR() function:

```
OR(LEFT(A2,2) = "A ", LEFT(A2,3) = "An ", LEFT(A2,4) = "The ")
```

Here I'm assuming that the text being tested is in cell A2. If the left two characters are A , or the left three characters are An , or the left four characters are The , this function returns TRUE (that is, you're dealing with a title that has a leading article).

Now you need to package this OR() function inside an IF() test. If the OR() function returns TRUE, the command should extract everything after the first space; otherwise, it should return the entire title. Here it is (Figure 2.28 shows the formula in action):

```
=IF( OR(LEFT(A2,2) = "A ", LEFT(A2,3) = "An ", LEFT(A2,4) = "The "),
➥RIGHT(A2, LEN(A2) - FIND(" ", A2, 1)), A2)
```

Figure 2.28
A formula that removes leading articles for proper sorting.

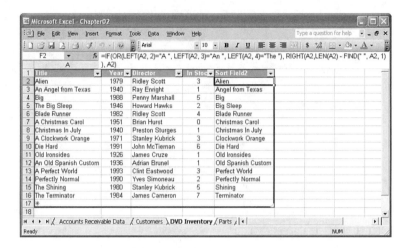

Filtering List Data

One of the biggest problems with large lists is that it's often hard to find and extract the data you need. Sorting can help, but in the end, you're still working with the entire list. What you need is a way to define the data that you want to work with and then have Excel display only those records onscreen. This action is called *filtering* your data. Fortunately, Excel offers several techniques that get the job done.

Using AutoFilter to Filter a List

Excel's AutoFilter feature makes filtering out subsets of your data as easy as selecting an option from a drop-down list. In fact, that's literally what happens. When you convert a range to a list, Excel automatically turns on AutoFilter, which is why you see drop-down arrows in the cells containing the list's column labels. (You can toggle AutoFilter off and on by choosing Data, Filter, AutoFilter.) Clicking one of these arrows displays a list of all the unique entries in the column. Figure 2.29 shows the drop-down list for the Account Name field in an Accounts Receivable database.

If you click an item in one of these AutoFilter lists, Excel takes the following actions:

- It displays only those records that include the item in that field. For example, Figure 2.30 shows the resulting records when the item Brimson Furniture is selected from the list attached to the Account Name column. The other records are hidden and can be retrieved whenever you need them.

Watch for Data Outside the Table

Because Excel hides the rows that don't meet the criteria, you shouldn't place any important data either to the left or to the right of the list.

- It changes the color of the column's drop-down arrow. This indicates which column you used to filter the list.

- It displays `Filter Mode` in the status bar.

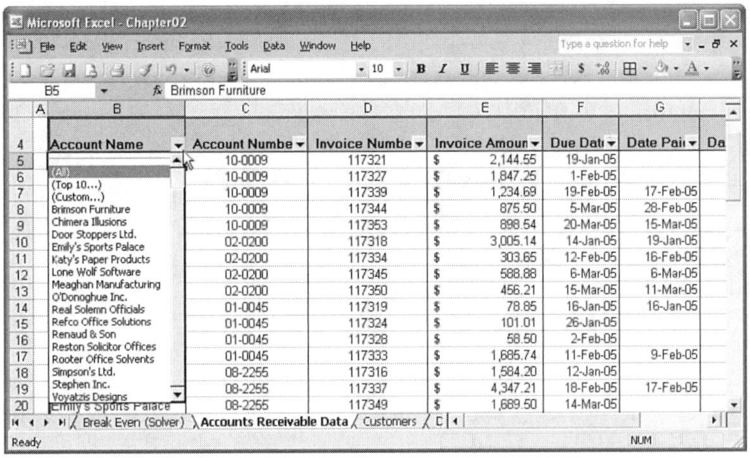

Figure 2.29
For each list field, AutoFilter adds drop-down lists that contain only the unique entries in the column.

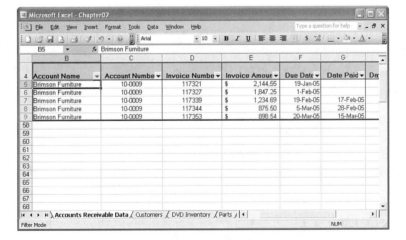

Figure 2.30
Clicking an item in an AutoFilter drop-down list displays only records that include the item in the field.

To continue filtering the data, you can select an item from one of the other lists. For example, you could choose a date from the Due Date list to see only those Brimson Furniture invoices due on that date.

AutoFilter Criteria Options

The items you see in each drop-down list are called the *filter criteria*. Besides selecting specific criteria (such as an account name), you have the following choices in each drop-down list:

- All—Removes the filter criterion for the column. If you've selected multiple criteria, you can remove all the filter criteria and display the entire list by choosing Data, Filter, Show All.

- Top 10—In a numeric or date field, displays the Top 10 AutoFilter dialog box, as shown in Figure 2.31. The left drop-down list has two choices, Top or Bottom. The center spin box enables you to choose a number. The right drop-down list has two choices, Items and Percent. For example, if you choose the default choices (Top, 10, and Items), AutoFilter displays the records that have the 10 highest values in the current field.

Figure 2.31
Use the Top 10 AutoFilter dialog box to filter your records based on values in the current field.

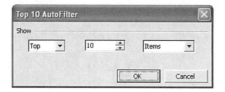

- Custom—Enables you to enter more sophisticated criteria. For details, see the next section.

Setting Up Custom AutoFilter Criteria

In its basic form, AutoFilter enables you to select only a single item from each column drop-down list. AutoFilter's *custom filter criteria*, however, give you a way to select multiple items. In the Accounts Receivable list, for example, you could use custom criteria to display all the invoices with the following:

- An account number that begins with 07
- A due date in January
- An amount between $1,000 and $5,000
- An account name of either Refco Office Solutions or Brimson Furniture

Before you learn the steps required to create a custom AutoFilter criterion, let's go through an overview of what happens. When you click the Custom option in an AutoFilter drop-down list, Excel displays the Custom AutoFilter dialog box, shown in Figure 2.32.

You use the two drop-down lists across the top to set up the first part of your criterion. The list on the left contains a list of Excel's comparison operators (such as Equals and Is Greater Than). The combo box on the right enables you to select a unique item from the field or enter your own value. For example, if you want to display invoices with an amount greater than or equal to $1,000, click the Is Greater Than or Equal operator and enter **1000** into the text box.

Figure 2.32
Use the Custom AutoFilter dialog box to enter your custom criteria.

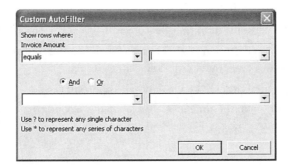

For text fields, you can also use *wildcard characters* to substitute for one or more characters. Use the question mark (?) wildcard to substitute for a single character. For example, if you enter sm?th, Excel finds both Smith and Smyth. To substitute for groups of characters, use the asterisk (*). For example, if you enter *carolina, Excel finds all the entries that end with "carolina."

Including Wildcards

To include a wildcard as part of the criteria, precede the character with a tilde (~). For example, to find OVERDUE?, enter OVERDUE~?.

You can create *compound criteria* by clicking the And or Or buttons and then entering another criterion in the bottom two drop-down lists. Use And when you want to display records that meet both criteria; use Or when you want to display records that meet at least one of the two criteria.

For example, to display invoices with an amount greater than or equal to $1,000 and less than or equal to $5,000, you fill in the dialog box as shown in Figure 2.33.

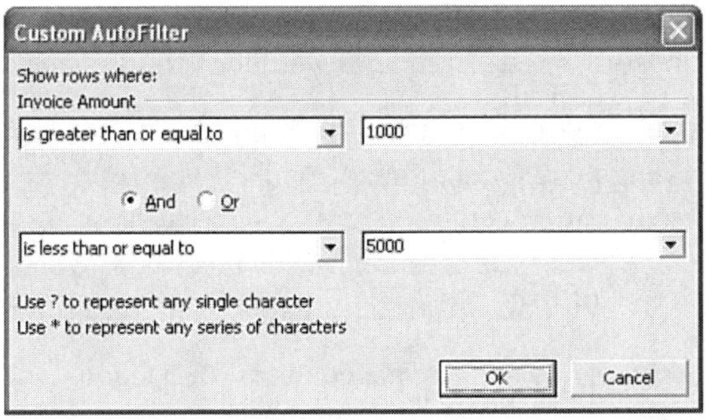

Figure 2.33
A compound criterion that displays the records with invoice amounts between $1,000 and $5,000.

The following procedure takes you through the official steps to set up a custom AutoFilter criterion:

1. Click Custom in the drop-down list attached to the column you want to work with. Excel displays the Custom AutoFilter dialog box.

2. Click a comparison operator and enter a value for the first part of the criterion. If you don't want to create a compound criterion, skip to step 5.

3. Click either the And option or the Or option, as appropriate.

4. Click a comparison operator and enter a value for the second part of the criterion.

5. Click OK. Excel filters the list.

Showing Filtered Records

When you need to redisplay records that have been filtered via AutoFilter, use any of the following techniques:

■ To display the entire list and remove AutoFilter's drop-down arrows, deactivate the Data, Filter, AutoFilter command.

■ To display the entire list without removing the AutoFilter drop-down arrows, choose Data, Filter, Show All.

■ To remove the filter on a single field, display that field's AutoFilter drop-down list and click the All option.

Using Complex Criteria to Filter a List

The AutoFilter should take care of most of your filtering needs, but it's not designed for heavy-duty work. For example, AutoFilter can't handle the following Accounts Receivable criteria:

■ Invoice amounts greater than $100, less than $1,000, or greater than $10,000

■ Account numbers that begin with 01, 05, or 12

■ Days overdue greater than the value in cell J1

To work with these more sophisticated requests, you need to use *complex criteria*.

Setting Up a Criteria Range   Before you can work with complex criteria, you must set up a *criteria range*. A criteria range has some or all of the list field names in the top row, with at least one blank row directly underneath. You enter your criteria in the blank row below the appropriate field name, and Excel searches the list for records with field values that satisfy the criteria. This setup gives you two major advantages over AutoFilter:

■ By using either multiple rows or multiple columns for a single field, you can create compound criteria with as many terms as you like.

■ Because you're entering your criteria in cells, you can use formulas to create *computed criteria*.

You can place the criteria range anywhere on the worksheet outside the list range. The most common position, however, is a couple of rows above the list range. Figure 2.34 shows the Accounts Receivable list with a criteria range. As you can see, the criteria are entered in the cell below the field name. In this case, the displayed criteria will find all Brimson Furniture invoices that are greater than or equal to $1,000 and that are overdue (that is, invoices that have a value greater than 0 in the Days Overdue field).

Figure 2.34
Set up a separate criteria range (B1:D2, in this case) to enter complex criteria.

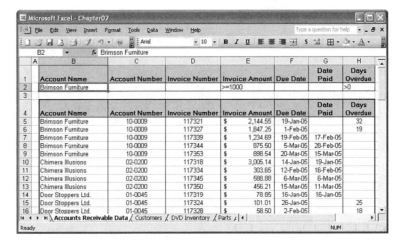

Filtering a List with a Criteria Range After you've set up your criteria range, you can use it to filter the list. The following procedure takes you through the basic steps:

1. Copy the list field names that you want to use for the criteria and paste them into the first row of the criteria range. If you'll be using different fields for different criteria, consider copying all your field names into the first row of the criteria range.

Use Formulas for Criteria Field Name

The only problem with copying the field names to the criteria range is that if you change a field name, you must change it in two places (that is, in the list and in the criteria). So, instead of just copying the names, you can make the field names in the criteria range dynamic by using a formula to set each criteria field name equal to its corresponding list field name. For example, you could enter =**B4** into cell B1 of Figure 2.34.

---

2. Below each field name in the criteria range, enter the criteria you want to use.
3. Select a cell in the list, and then choose Data, Filter, Advanced Filter. Excel displays the Advanced Filter dialog box, shown in Figure 2.35.
4. The List Range text box should contain the list range (if you selected a cell in the list beforehand). If it doesn't, activate the text box and select the list (including the field names).

Figure 2.35
Use the Advanced Filter
dialog box to select your
list and criteria ranges.

5. In the Criteria Range text box, select the criteria range (again, including the field names you copied).

6. To avoid including duplicate records in the filter, activate the Unique Records Only check box.

7. Click OK. Excel filters the list to show only those records that match your criteria (see Figure 2.36).

Figure 2.36
Set up a separate criteria
range (B1:H2, in this
case) to enter complex
criteria.

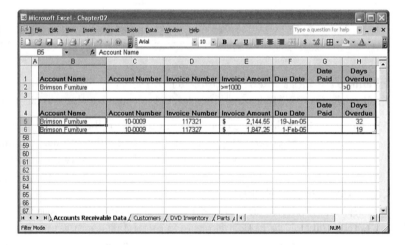

Entering Compound Criteria   To enter compound criteria in a criteria range, use the following guidelines:

- To find records that match all the criteria, enter the criteria on a single row.
- To find records that match one or more of the criteria, enter the criteria in separate rows.

Finding records that match all the criteria is equivalent to activating the And button in the Custom AutoFilter dialog box. The sample criteria shown earlier in Figure 2.34 match records with the account name Brimson Furniture *and* an invoice amount greater than $1,000 *and* a positive number in the Days Overdue field. To narrow the displayed records, you can enter criteria for as many fields as you like.

Using a Field Multiple Times in a Criteria Range
You can use the same field name more than once in compound criteria. To do this, include the appropriate field multiple times in the criteria range and enter the appropriate criteria below each label.

Finding records that match at least one of several criteria is equivalent to activating the Or button in the Custom AutoFilter dialog box. In this case, you need to enter each criterion on a separate row. For example, to display all invoices with amounts greater than or equal to $10,000 or that are more than 30 days overdue, you would set up your criteria as shown in Figure 2.37.

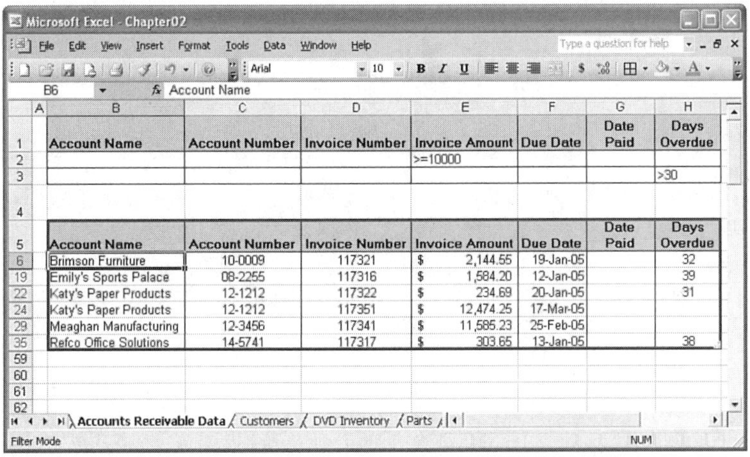

Figure 2.37
To display records that match one or more of the criteria, enter the criteria in separate rows.

Don't Include Blank Rows
Don't include any blank rows in your criteria range because blank rows throw off Excel when it tries to match the criteria.

Entering Computed Criteria

The fields in your criteria range aren't restricted to the list fields. You can create *computed criteria* that use a calculation to match records in the list. The calculation can refer to one or more list fields, or even to cells outside the list, and must return either TRUE or FALSE. Excel selects records that return TRUE.

To use computed criteria, add a column to the criteria range and enter the formula in the new field. Make sure that the name you give the criteria field is different from any field name in the list. When referencing the list cells in the formula, use the first row of the list. For example, to select all records in which the Date Paid is equal to the Due Date in the accounts receivable list, enter the following formula:

```
=G5=F5
```

Note the use of relative addressing. If you want to reference cells outside the list, use absolute addressing.

Creating Compound Computed Criteria

Use Excel's AND, OR, and NOT functions to create compound computed criteria. For example, to select all records in which the Days Overdue value is less than 90 and greater than 31, type the following:

```
=AND(H5<90, H5>31)
```

Figure 2.38 shows a more complex example. The goal is to select all records whose invoices were paid after the due date. The new criterion—named Late Payers—contains the following formula:

```
=IF(ISBLANK(G5), FALSE(), G5 > F5)
```

Figure 2.38
Use a separate criteria range column for calculated criteria.

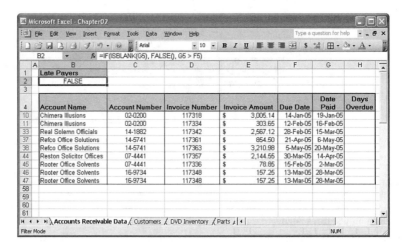

If the Date Paid field (column G) is blank, the invoice hasn't been paid, so the formula returns FALSE. Otherwise, the logical expression G5 > F5 is evaluated. If the Date Paid (column G) is greater than the Due Date field (column F), the expression returns TRUE and Excel selects the record. In Figure 2.38, the Late Payers cell (B2) displays FALSE because the formula evaluates to FALSE for the first row in the list.

Summarizing List Data

Because a list is just a special kind of worksheet range, you can analyze list data using many of the same methods you use for regular worksheet cells. Typically, this task involves using formulas and functions to answer questions and produce results. To make your analysis chores easier, Excel enables you to create *automatic subtotals* that can give you instant subtotals, averages, and more. Excel goes one step further by also offering many list-specific functions. These functions work with entire lists or subsets defined by a criteria range. The rest of this chapter shows you how to use all these tools to analyze and summarize your data.

Creating Automatic Subtotals

Automatic subtotals enable you to summarize your sorted list data quickly. For example, if you have a list of invoices sorted by account name, you can use automatic subtotals to give you the following information for each account:

- The total number of invoices
- The sum of the invoice amounts
- The average invoice amount
- The maximum number of days an invoice is overdue

You can do all this and more without entering a single formula. Excel does the calculations and enters the results automatically. You also can just as easily create grand totals that apply to the entire list.

More Than Just Subtotals

The term *automatic subtotal* is somewhat of a misnomer because you can summarize more than totals. For this topic, at least, think of a subtotal as any summary calculation.

Setting Up a List for Automatic Subtotals

Excel calculates automatic subtotals based on data groupings in a selected field. For example, if you ask for subtotals based on account name, Excel runs down the account name column and creates a new subtotal *each time the name changes*. To get useful summaries, then, you need to sort the list on the field containing the data groupings you're interested in. Figure 2.39 shows the Accounts Receivable database sorted by account name. If you subtotal the Account Name field, you get summaries for Brimson Furniture, Chimera Illusions, Door Stoppers Ltd., and so on.

Subtotals for Filtered Lists

If you want to display subtotals for a filtered list, be sure to filter the list before sorting it (as described earlier in this chapter).

Figure 2.39
A sorted list ready for displaying subtotals.

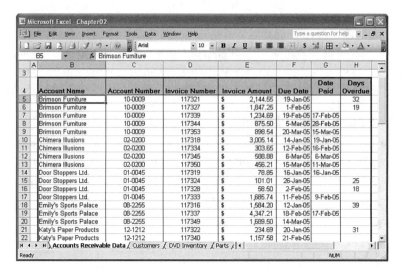

Displaying Subtotals

To subtotal a list, follow these steps:

1. If you haven't already done so, sort your list according to the groupings you want to use for the subtotals.

2. Convert the list to a normal range by choosing Data, List, Convert to Range, and then choosing Yes when Excel asks you to confirm.

3. Choose Data, Subtotals to display the Subtotal dialog box, shown in Figure 2.40.

Figure 2.40
You use the Subtotal dialog box to create subtotals for your list.

4. Enter the options you want to use for the subtotals:

   At Each Change In—This box contains the field names for your list. Click the field you want to use to group the subtotals.

Use Function—Select the function you want to use in the calculations. Excel gives you 11 choices, including Sum, Count, Average, Max, and Min.

Add Subtotal To—This is a list of check boxes for each field. Activate the appropriate check boxes for the fields you want to subtotal.

Replace Current Subtotals—Activate this check box to display new subtotal rows. To add to the existing rows, deactivate this option.

Page Break Between Groups—If you intend to print the summary, activate this check box to insert a page break between each grouping.

Summary Below Data—Deactivate this check box if you want the subtotal rows to appear above the groupings.

5. Click OK. Excel calculates the subtotals and enters them into the list.

Figure 2.41 shows the Accounts Receivable list with the Invoice Amount field subtotaled.

Figure 2.41
A list showing Invoice
Amount subtotals for
each Account Name.

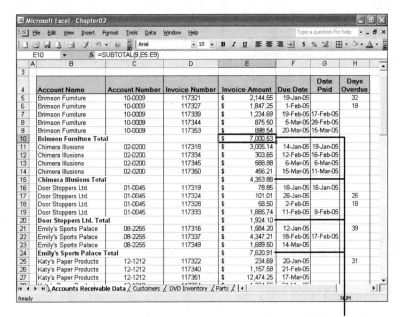

Subtotals for Invoice Amount field

Adding More Subtotals

You can add any number of subtotals to the current summary. The following procedure shows you what to do:

1. Choose Data, Subtotals to display the Subtotal dialog box.

2. Enter the options you want to use for the new subtotal.

3. Deactivate the Replace Current Subtotals check box.

4. Click OK. Excel calculates the new subtotals and adds them to the list.

For example, Figure 2.42 shows the Accounts Receivable list with two new subtotals that count the invoices and display the maximum number of days overdue.

Count of Invoice Number field   Maximum of Days Overdue field

Figure 2.42
You can use multiple subtotals in a list.

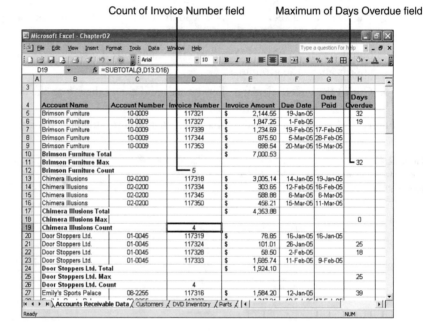

Removing Subtotals

To remove the subtotals from a list, choose Data, Subtotals to display the Subtotal dialog box, and then click Remove All.

Excel's List Functions

To get more control over your list analysis, you can use Excel's *list functions*. These functions are the same as those used in subtotals, but they have the following advantages:

- You can enter the functions into any cell in the worksheet.
- You can specify the range the function uses to perform its calculations.
- You can enter criteria or reference a criteria range to perform calculations on subsets of the list.

About List Functions

To illustrate the list functions, consider an example. If you want to calculate the sum of a list field, for instance, you can enter SUM(*range*), and Excel produces the result. If you want to sum only a subset of the field, you must specify as arguments the particular cells to use. For lists containing hundreds of records, however, this process is impractical. (It's also illegal, for two reasons: Excel allows a maximum of 30 arguments in the SUM() function, and it allows a maximum of 255 characters in a cell entry.)

The solution is to use DSUM(), which is the list equivalent of the SUM() function. The DSUM() function takes three arguments: a list range, a field name, and a criteria range. DSUM() looks at the specified field in the list and sums only records that match the criteria in the criteria range.

The list functions come in two varieties: those that don't require a criteria range and those that do.

List Functions That Don't Require a Criteria Range

Excel has two list functions that enable you to specify the criteria as an argument rather than a range: COUNTIF() and SUMIF().

Using COUNTIF()   The COUNTIF() function counts the number of cells in a range that meet a single criterion:

COUNTIF(*range*, *criteria*)

    range   The range of cells to use for the count.

    criteria   The criteria, entered as text, that determines which cells to count. Excel applies the criterion to *range*.

For example, Figure 2.43 shows a COUNTIF() function that calculates the total number of invoices that are more than 30 days overdue.

Figure 2.43
Use COUNTIF() to count the cells that meet a criterion.

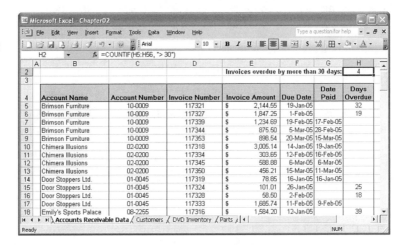

Using `SUMIF()` The `SUMIF()` function is similar to `COUNTIF()`, except that it sums the range cells that meet its criterion:

`SUMIF(`*`range`*`, `*`criteria`*` [, `*`sum_range`*`])`

`range`	The range of cells to use for the criterion.
`criteria`	The criteria, entered as text, that determines which cells to sum. Excel applies the criteria to *`range`*.
`sum_range`	The range from which the sum values are taken. Excel sums only those cells in *`sum_range`* that correspond to the cells in *`range`* and meet the criterion. If you omit *`sum_range`*, Excel uses *`range`* for the sum.

Figure 2.44 shows a Parts database. The `SUMIF()` function in cell F16 sums the total cost (F7:F14) for the parts where Division (A7:A14) is equal to 3.

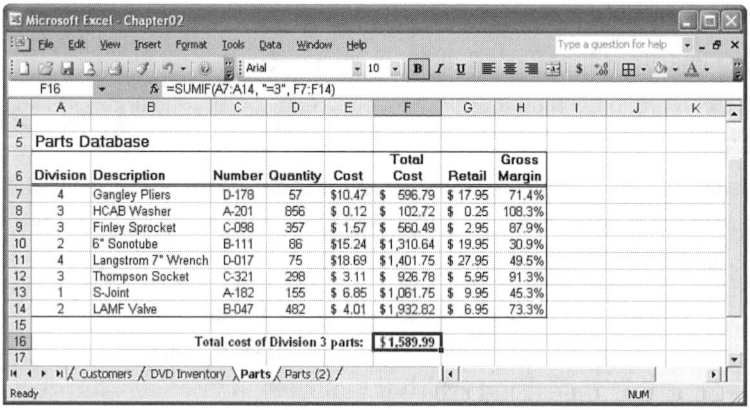

Division	Description	Number	Quantity	Cost	Total Cost	Retail	Gross Margin
4	Gangley Pliers	D-178	57	$10.47	$ 596.79	$ 17.95	71.4%
3	HCAB Washer	A-201	856	$ 0.12	$ 102.72	$ 0.25	108.3%
3	Finley Sprocket	C-098	357	$ 1.57	$ 560.49	$ 2.95	87.9%
2	6" Sonotube	B-111	86	$15.24	$1,310.64	$ 19.95	30.9%
4	Langstrom 7" Wrench	D-017	75	$18.69	$1,401.75	$ 27.95	49.5%
3	Thompson Socket	C-321	298	$ 3.11	$ 926.78	$ 5.95	91.3%
1	S-Joint	A-182	155	$ 6.85	$1,061.75	$ 9.95	45.3%
2	LAMF Valve	B-047	482	$ 4.01	$1,932.82	$ 6.95	73.3%
				Total cost of Division 3 parts:	$1,589.99		

Figure 2.44
Use `SUMIF()` to sum cells that meet a criterion.

List Functions That Require a Criteria Range

The remaining list functions require a criteria range. These functions take a little longer to set up, but the advantage is that you can enter compound and computed criteria.

All these functions have the following format:

`Dfunction(database, field, criteria)`

`Dfunction`	The function name, such as `DSUM` or `DAVERAGE`.
`database`	The range of cells that make up the list you want to work with. You can use either a range name, if one is defined, or the range address.
`field`	The name of the field on which you want to perform the operation. You can use either the field name or the field number as the argument (in which the leftmost field is field number 1, the next field is field

number 2, and so on). If you use the field name, enclose it in quotation marks (for example, `"Total Cost"`).

criteria   The range of cells that hold the criteria you want to work with. You can use either a range name, if one is defined, or the range address.

Operating on Every Record

To perform an operation on every record in the list, leave all the `criteria` fields blank. This causes Excel to select every record in the list.

Table 2.1 summarizes the list functions.

Table 2.1   Excel's List Functions

Function	Description
DAVERAGE()	Returns the average of the matching records in a specified field.
DCOUNT()	Returns the count of the matching records.
DCOUNTA()	Returns the count of the nonblank matching records.
DGET()	Returns the value of a specified field for a single matching record.
DMAX()	Returns the maximum value of a specified field for the matching records.
DMIN()	Returns the minimum value of a specified field for the matching records.
DPRODUCT()	Returns the product of the values of a specified field for the matching records.
DSTDEV()	Returns the estimated standard deviation of the values in a specified field if the matching records are a sample of the population.
DSTDEVP()	Returns the standard deviation of the values of a specified field if the matching records are the entire population.
DSUM()	Returns the sum of the values of a specified field for the matching records.
DVAR()	Returns the estimated variance of the values of a specified field if the matching records are a sample of the population.
DVARP()	Returns the variance of the values of a specified field if the matching records are the entire population.

You enter list functions the same way you enter any other Excel function. You type an equal sign (=) and then enter the function—either by itself or combined with other Excel operators in a formula. The following examples all show valid list functions:

```
=DSUM(A6:H14, "Total Cost", A1:H3)

=DSUM(List, "Total Cost", Criteria)
```

```
=DSUM(AR_List, 3, Criteria)
```

```
=DSUM(1993_Sales, "Sales", A1:H13)
```

The next two sections provide examples of the DAVERAGE() and DGET() list functions.

Using DAVERAGE()   The DAVERAGE() function calculates the average *field* value in the *database* records that match the *criteria*. In the Parts database, for example, suppose that you want to calculate the average gross margin for all parts assigned to Division 2. You set up a criteria range for the Division field and enter **2**, as shown in Figure 2.45. You then enter the following DAVERAGE() function (see cell H3):

```
=DAVERAGE(A6:H14, "Gross Margin", A2:A3)
```

Figure 2.45
Use DAVERAGE() to calculate the field average in the matching records.

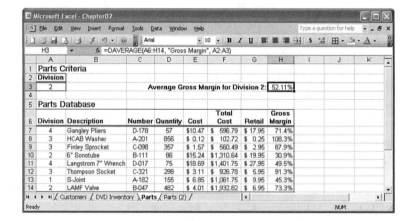

Using DGET()   The DGET() function extracts the value of a single *field* in the *database* records that match the *criteria*. If there are no matching records, DGET() returns #VALUE!. If there is more than one matching record, DGET() returns #NUM!.

DGET() typically is used to query the list for a specific piece of information. For example, in the Parts list, you might want to know the cost of the Finley Sprocket. To extract this information, you would first set up a criteria range with the Description field and enter Finley Sprocket. You would then extract the information with the following formula (assuming that the list and criteria ranges are named Database and Criteria, respectively):

```
=DGET(Database, "Cost", Criteria)
```

A more interesting application of this function would be to extract the name of a part that satisfies a certain condition. For example, you might want to know the name of the part that has the highest gross margin. Creating this model requires two steps:

1. Setting up the criteria to match the highest value in the Gross Margin field.
2. Adding a DGET() function to extract the description of the matching record.

Figure 2.46 shows how this is done. For the criteria, a new field called Highest Margin is created. As the text box shows, this field uses the following computed criteria:

```
=H7 = MAX($H$7:$H$14)
```

Figure 2.46
A `DGET()` function that extracts the name of the part with the highest margin.

	A	B	C	D	E	F	G	H
1	Parts Criteria							
2	Highest Margin							
3	FALSE				Part with Highest Gross Margin:			HCAB Washer
4								
5	Parts Database							
6	Division	Description	Number	Quantity	Cost	Total Cost	Retail	Gross Margin
7	4	Gangley Pliers	D-178	57	$10.47	$ 596.79	$ 17.95	71.4%
8	3	HCAB Washer	A-201	856	$ 0.12	$ 102.72	$ 0.25	108.3%
9	3	Finley Sprocket	C-098	357	$ 1.57	$ 560.49	$ 2.95	87.9%
10	2	6" Sonotube	B-111	86	$15.24	$1,310.64	$ 19.95	30.9%
11	4	Langstrom 7" Wrench	D-017	75	$18.69	$1,401.75	$ 27.95	49.5%
12	3	Thompson Socket	C-321	298	$ 3.11	$ 926.78	$ 5.95	91.3%
13	1	S-Joint	A-182	155	$ 6.85	$1,061.75	$ 9.95	45.3%
14	2	LAMF Valve	B-047	482	$ 4.01	$1,932.82	$ 6.95	73.3%
15								

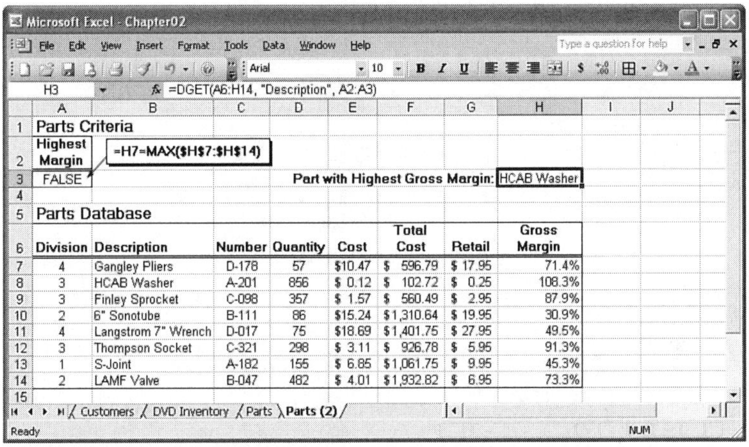

The range $H$7:$H$14 is the Gross Margin field. (Note the use of absolute references.) Excel matches only the record that has the highest gross margin. The `DGET()` function in cell H3 is straightforward:

```
=DGET(A6:H14, "Description", A2:A3)
```

This formula returns the description of the part that has the highest gross margin.

From Here

- If you need more powerful data tools, Microsoft Access should be your Office database program of choice. See Chapter 4, "Taming Access Data."
- If you decide to use Access, you can still analyze the data in Excel. In Chapter 6, see the section titled "Analyzing Access Data in Excel."
- To learn how to share Excel files with other users, see the section titled "Sharing Excel Workbooks" in Chapter 7.
- For information on putting an Excel worksheet on the Web, see the section titled "Publishing an Excel Range, Sheet, or Workbook to the Web" in Chapter 8.
- For a few useful Excel VBA macros, see the section "Excel Macros" in Chapter 12.
- To learn about workbook protection, see the section "More Options for Protecting Excel Workbooks" in Chapter 14.

Constructing Knockout Presentations in PowerPoint

3

Among all the documents that you can create with the Microsoft Office Suite, PowerPoint presentations are unique in that they are the only ones that are regularly critiqued by other people. If someone sends us a Word document or an Access database, we rarely begin by casting a critical eye on the layout and formatting. Among spreadsheet jockeys, there is a worksheet aesthetic that looks for a certain amount of elegance in model building, but the main concern is getting the right answer. A PowerPoint presentation, on the other hand, must first meet a certain standard of visual appeal before we even consider the information it is trying to impart. Why? Perhaps it's because presentations seem to be just one small step removed from entertainment: We sit in a darkened room looking at text and pictures on a screen while a person tells us a story about what we're seeing. Or perhaps it's because we've all seen more than our fair share of PowerPoint presentations, and the idea of sitting through another lackluster series of slides is just too much to bear.

Whatever the reason, if you create PowerPoint presentations for your job, you need to know what Office gurus know: that your presentations—every one of them—must be knockouts. That doesn't mean you need to create something that has your audience cheering and on their feet at the end of the show. Rather, it means having your audience look forward to seeing your presentation and actually learning something from it.

This chapter shows you how to create such presentations. You'll concentrate on the three main areas that compose any knockout presentation: organization, formatting and design, and animation. The focus will be on avoiding so-called *PowerPointlessness*—those fancy formats, transitions, sounds, and other effects that have no discernible purpose, use, or benefit. Instead, you get practical tricks and techniques that serve the goal of creating a knockout presentation.

Organizing Your Presentation

All great documents—a persuasive memo, an illuminating worksheet, a cogent email message—have one thing in common: excellent organization. Content and formatting are important, to be sure, but their effectiveness is diminished or even nullified if the document has a slipshod or poorly thought-out organization. On the other hand, even a document with only so-so content and negligible formatting can get its point across if it's organized coherently and sensibly.

Organization: Telling a Story

Why is organization so important? Probably because research has shown—and poets and storytellers have known for thousands of years—that humans have an innate hunger for narrative. We like to hear stories, and we learn better and take in data more effectively when it's presented in narrative format. This doesn't mean that every letter, email, or worksheet model must begin with "Once upon a time…" Rather, it means that you should apply the basic principles of storytelling to any document. Here are a few ideas to consider:

- Are you proposing a solution to a problem? Use the beginning-middle-end story structure. In the beginning you introduce the problem, in the middle you explain why the problem needs to be solved, and in the end you propose and explain your solution.

- Are you arguing a position? Use the thesis-arguments-conclusion story structure. You state your position up front, marshal the facts and arguments that support your position, anticipate counterarguments, and then return to your now well-buttressed position.

- Are you announcing something interesting or important? Use the exposition-building action-climax-denouement structure. The exposition gives the background and basic information that your listeners require to understand and appreciate the underlying problem. The building action might outline the ongoing efforts and the increasingly desperate need to solve the problem. The climax is the announcement itself, the resolution of the building action; and the denouement is the aftermath of the announcement and what it means to the overall story.

All these potential document types are also potential PowerPoint presentation topics, so it's easy to organize your presentations along narrative lines. In particular, think about the central ideas that you want to impart in your presentation, and with a story structure in mind, think about the text, images, charts, sounds, and other presentation objects that will illuminate your ideas. Be ruthless. If something doesn't further the story, don't use it.

Finally, the preliminary work on your presentation-as-narrative isn't complete until you've thought long and hard about your audience. All storytellers customize their tales depending on their audience. After all, in most cases you wouldn't give the same version of a story to children that you'd give to adults. In your case, you need to know who your audience is. Are they insiders who won't mind jargon and industry gossip? Are they technical types who revel in minutiae and closely reasoned arguments? Are they managers who prefer the big picture or customer service reps who need the details? Do they already know the basics of your topic and so require a shorter background or exposition? Asking yourself these and similar questions is all part of creating a well-thought-out narrative for your presentation and organizing it accordingly.

Organizing Your Presentation with an Outline

As a writer, I'm continually amazed at the power of the humble outline. All my articles, essays, and book chapters start off as a jumbled mess of ideas; all too many of them merely half-baked. As I research the topic, the core ideas that I want to discuss start to crystallize and organize themselves into related groups. After much rearranging and pruning, the ideas coalesce into a neat and tidy hierarchical structure: the outline. This text skeleton details exactly what I'm going to write about and in what order. With that in place, a metaphorical burden lifts from my shoulders and the piece practically writes itself.

You may think outlines are useful only for word processing documents, but they can be an essential part of building a presentation, as well. In PowerPoint, outlines offer a convenient way of organizing the content of your presentation hierarchically:

■ The top level of the outline hierarchy consists of the slide titles.

■ The second level of the outline hierarchy consists of the subtitle in the first slide and the main bullet points in subsequent slides.

■ Lower levels of the outline hierarchy consist of the lower levels of bullet points in subsequent slides.

Using PowerPoint's Outline pane, you can build your presentation from scratch by entering outline text as you would in a Word outline, for instance. You can promote or demote items to different levels with just a keystroke or mouse click. Best of all, because the Outline pane gives you a big-picture view of your presentation, you can adjust the overall organization by cutting and pasting or clicking and dragging outline text.

Viewing the Outline Pane and Outlining Toolbar

The two tools you need to create a PowerPoint outline are the Outline pane and the Outlining toolbar (see Figure 3.1):

■ To display the Outline pane, click the Outline tab.

■ To display the Outlining toolbar, right-click any toolbar and then click Outlining.

Outline tab   Slide icon

Figure 3.1
The PowerPoint tools you
need to create and edit
your presentation outline.

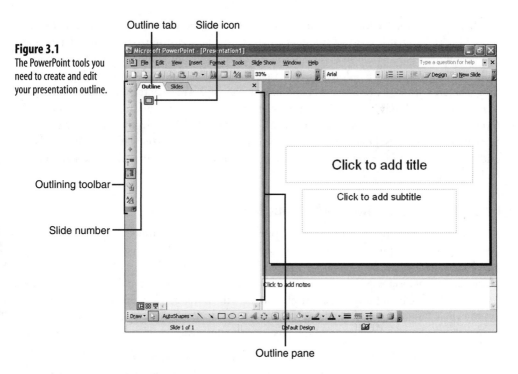

Outlining toolbar

Slide number

Outline pane

Creating a Presentation Outline

For a new presentation, the Outline pane shows the number 1 and an icon. The number is the slide number and the icon represents a slide; together they're the outline equivalent of the initial (empty) slide added to each new presentation. This is the top level of the outline hierarchy and, as I mentioned earlier, it consists of the slide titles. Remember that each item in the outline corresponds to a text object on a slide: title, subtitle, bullet point, and so on.

Creating the Top Level   The best way to begin the outline is to create and title the slides to complete the top-level hierarchy. Here are the steps to follow:

1. Type the slide's title.
2. Press Enter. PowerPoint creates a new slide.
3. Repeat steps 1 and 2 until you've created all your slides.

Figure 3.2 shows a presentation with the slide titles entered into the Outline pane.

Viewing Slide Formatting

 By default, the Outline pane shows all text in a standard font (bold for slide titles; regular text for everything else). If you prefer to see the text formatted as it will appear in the slide, activate the Show Formatting button in the Outlining toolbar.

The title you type here...   ...corresponds to the slide title that appears here

Figure 3.2
Begin the presentation outline by creating the slides and entering the slide titles in the Outline pane.

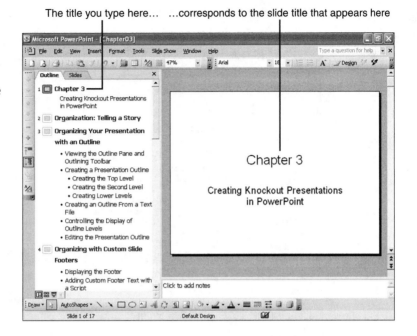

Creating the Second Level   The second-level outline consists of items such as slide subtitles and the main bullet points that compose the bulk of your presentation. Following are the steps to create the second level:

1. In the Outline pane, move the cursor to the end of the title of the slide you want to work with.
2. Press Ctrl+Enter. The outline item created by PowerPoint depends on the slide's text layout:
   - For a Title Slide layout, the new outline item corresponds to the subtitle text box placeholder.
   - For any of the text layouts, the new outline item corresponds to a bullet in the text box placeholder.
3. Type the item text.
4. To create another item on the same level, move the cursor to the end of the current item and press Enter.
5. Repeat steps 1–4 until you've completed the second level.

Figure 3.3 shows an outline with some second-level items added.

Third-level items

Figure 3.3
The outline with some
second-level outline
items.

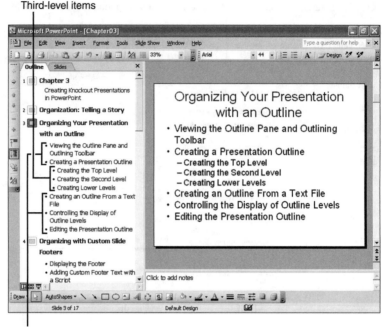

Second-level items

Creating Lower Levels　Figure 3.3 also shows several third-level items. To create the third
and lower levels of the outline, use the Outlining toolbar, as follows:

1. Follow the steps from the previous section to create a new second-level item.

 2. Click the Demote button in the Outlining toolbar.

 3. If you need to toggle the item between regular text and bulleted text, click the Bullets
   button in the Formatting toolbar.

4. Repeat steps 1–3 until you've completed the outline.

Converting a Second-Level Item to a Slide Title

You might add a second-level outline item and then decide you'd prefer that item to be the title of a new slide. To convert the item, place the cursor inside the item and then click the Promote button in the Outlining toolbar. PowerPoint
creates a new slide and uses the outline item as the slide title. Note that all subsequent outline items in the original slide
are copied to the new slide.

Creating an Outline from a Text File

If you've already sketched out the slide titles and headings for your presentation in a text file, you can import the text file and have PowerPoint convert it automatically to an outline. Before you do that, you may need to modify the text file as follows:

- Each slide title must be flush left in the text file.
- First-level headings must begin with a single tab.
- Second-level headings must begin with two tabs.

For example, Figure 3.4 shows a text document that uses these guidelines to specify several slides and headings.

Figure 3.4
Use tabs in a text document to specify outline levels for a PowerPoint presentation.

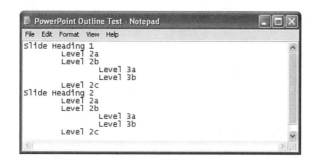

To convert the text to a PowerPoint presentation outline, you have two choices:

- Select File, Open to display the Open dialog box. In the Files of Type list, select All Outlines. Select the text file and then click Open.
- Start a new presentation or open an existing presentation. In the Outline pane, move the cursor to where you want the text file outline to appear. Select Insert, Slides from Outline, select the text file, and then click Insert.

Figure 3.5 shows a new PowerPoint presentation created by opening the text file shown in Figure 3.4.

Importing Outlines from Word

You can create an outline in Word and then import it into PowerPoint where the headings are converted into outline items. For the details, see the section in Chapter 6 titled, "Converting a Word Outline into a PowerPoint Presentation."

Figure 3.5
The PowerPoint presentation outline created by opening the text document shown in Figure 3.4.

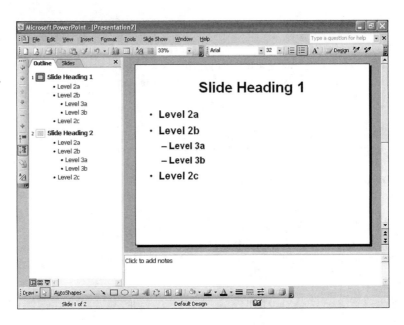

Controlling the Display of Outline Levels

If you're working with a long presentation, the Outline pane might show only a small number of the slides. To keep the big picture in view, you can tell PowerPoint to show less outline detail. Here are the Outlining toolbar techniques to use to expand and collapse the outline levels:

 To hide the levels for a single slide—Click inside the slide and then click Collapse.

 To display the levels for a single slide—Click the slide title and then click Expand.

 To hide the levels for all the slides—Click Collapse All.

 To display the levels for all the slides—Click Expand All.

Editing the Presentation Outline

The Outline pane's forest-instead-of-the-trees view not only lets you easily see the overall organization of your presentation, it makes it easy to modify that organization. That is, by editing the outline, you also edit the organization. Besides editing the text itself, editing the outline falls into two main categories: changing levels and moving items.

Changing levels means moving items down or up within the outline hierarchy. To *demote* an item means to move it lower in the hierarchy (for example, from second level to third); to *promote* an item means to move it higher in the hierarchy (for example, from second level to top level). Here are the techniques to use to change an item's level:

 To demote an item—Click Demote or press Tab.

 To promote an item—Click Promote or press Shift+Tab.

Inserting a Tab Character

If you want to insert a Tab character in an outline item, press Ctrl+Tab. (Alternatively, right-click the position within the item where you want to insert the tab and then click Insert Tab.)

Moving items means changing their physical position within the outline. For example, you might need to change the position of a slide or change the order of bullets within a slide. Here are the techniques to use to move an outline item:

 To move an item up—Click the item and then click Move Up. Alternatively, move the mouse pointer to the left of the item (the pointer changes to the four-headed arrow) and then click and drag the item up to the position you want.

 To move an entire slide up—Collapse the slide, click the slide, and then click Move Up. Alternatively, move the mouse pointer over the slide icon (the pointer changes to the four-headed arrow) and then click and drag the icon up to the position you want.

 To move an item down—Click the item and then click Move Down. Alternatively, move the mouse pointer to the left of the item (the pointer changes to the four-headed arrow) and then click and drag the item down to the position you want.

 To move an entire slide down—Collapse the slide, click the slide, and then click Move Down. Alternatively, move the mouse pointer over the slide icon (the pointer changes to the four-headed arrow) and then click and drag the icon down to the position you want.

Organizing with Custom Slide Footers

In a large presentation, it's often easy to lose track of what slide number you're working with or viewing. Similarly, if you work with a lot of presentations, it can get confusing as to which presentation you're currently working on. To help overcome these and other organizational handicaps, take advantage of the footers that PowerPoint enables you to display on a presentation's slides.

Displaying the Footer

By default, PowerPoint doesn't display the footer in each slide. (Or, more accurately, it displays a blank footer in each slide.) To display the footer, you need to activate the footer content, as follows:

1. Select View, Header and Footer. PowerPoint displays the Header and Footer dialog box. (Figure 3.6 shows a completed version of the dialog box.)

Figure 3.6
Use the Header and Footer dialog box to specify the data that you want to appear in the slide's footer.

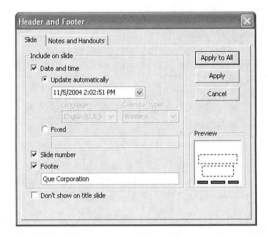

Adding Headers to Notes and Handouts

The "header" part of the Header and Footer dialog box doesn't apply to slides, which can't have headers. Instead, it applies to notes and handouts. To add a header to your presentation's notes and handouts, select the Notes and Handouts tab and type your text into the Header text box.

---

2. To display the date and time in the lower-left corner of the slide, make sure the Date and Time check box is activated and then choose one of the following options:

   Update Automatically—Choose this option to always display the current date and time. Use the list provided to choose the format of the date and time display.

   Fixed—Choose this option to specify a fixed date and time. Note, however, that you can enter any text you like into the Fixed text box.

3. To display the current slide number in the lower-right corner of the slide, activate the Slide Number check box.

4. To display text in the lower middle of the slide, make sure the Footer check box is activated and then type your text into the box provided.

5. If you don't want the footer text to appear on the presentation's title slide, activate the Don't Show on Title Slide check box.

6. To display the footer, click one of the following:

   Apply to All—Displays the footer to every slide in the presentation.

   Apply—Displays the footer on just the current slide.

Changing the Starting Slide Number

If your presentation is a continuation of another presentation, you might prefer to have a different starting slide number appear in the footer. To change the number of the first slide, select File, Page Setup, and then use the Number Slides From spin box to set the starting number.

Figure 3.7 shows a presentation with the slide footer data from Figure 3.6.

Figure 3.7
You can add the date and time, slide number, and custom text to the slide footer.

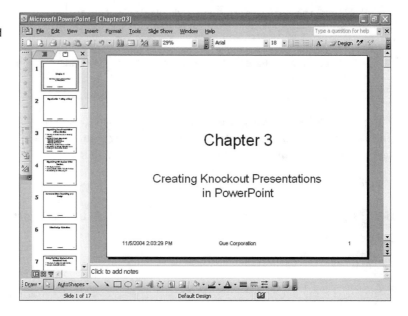

Adding Custom Footer Text with a Script

The Footer text box in the Slide tab of the Header and Footer dialog box enables you to add static text that appears in the placeholder in the lower middle of each slide. That's handy for things such as your company's name, your own name, a project reference, and so on. However, you might prefer something more dynamic, such as the full pathname of the presentation file. You can do this with a relatively simple VBA script that modifies the Footer object's Text property.

Listing 3.1 shows one such script.

This Chapter's Examples

You'll find the PowerPoint file used for the examples in this chapter on my website at www.mcfedries.com/OfficeGurus.

Listing 3.1   A Script That Inserts a Presentation's Pathname into the Footer Placeholder

```
Sub AddPathToFooter()
    Dim txtPath As String

    With ActivePresentation
        '
        ' Build the presentation's pathname
        txtPath = .Path & "\" & .Name
        '
        ' Add the pathname to the Slide Master's footer
        .SlideMaster.HeadersFooters.Footer.Text = txtPath
        '
        ' Add the pathname to all the existing slides
        .Slides.Range.HeadersFooters.Footer.Text = txtPath
    End With
End Sub
```

This procedure stores the active presentation's folder path (the Path property) and filename (the Name property) in the txtPath variable. This string is then stored in the Footer object's Text property for both the slide master and the existing slides.

Listing 3.2 shows another example.

Listing 3.2   A Script That Inserts the String `Slide X of Y` into the Footer Placeholder

```
Sub AddSlideXOfYToFooter()
    Dim s As Slide
    With ActivePresentation
        '
        ' Loop through all the slides
        For Each s In .Slides
            '
            ' Add the "Slide X of Y" text
            s.HeadersFooters.Footer.Text = "Slide " & s.SlideNumber & _
                                " of " & .Slides.Count
        Next 's
    End With
End Sub
```

This procedure loops through all the slides in the active presentation. For each slide s, the Footer object's Text property changes to Slide X of Y, where x is given by the Slide object's SlideNumber property, and Y is given by the Presentation object's Slides.Count property.

Adding Text to the Date and Time Placeholder

If you also want to add custom text to the date and time placeholder, modify the DateAndTime object's Text property:

```
s.HeadersFooters.DateAndTime.Text = "Text"
```

Customizing the Footer Layout

By default, PowerPoint configures the footer with the date and time placeholder in the lower left of the slide, the slide number in the lower right, and the footer text in the lower middle. You can move these placeholders around by first selecting View, Master, Slide Master (you can also hold down Shift and click the Slide Master View icon). Figure 3.8 shows the Slide Master view that appears.

Figure 3.8
Use the Slide Master view to customize the footer layout for the presentation's slides.

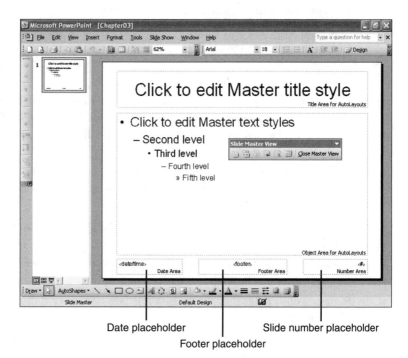

Date placeholder

Footer placeholder

Slide number placeholder

Here are the basic techniques you can use to customize the footer:

- To select a placeholder, click it.
- To delete a placeholder, select it and then press Delete.

Restoring a Deleted Footer Placeholder
If you accidentally delete a footer placeholder, you can restore it by selecting Format, Master Layout. In the Master Layout dialog box, activate the check box for the deleted placeholder and then click OK.

Deleting a Placeholder from a Single Slide

When you delete placeholders from the Slide Master, PowerPoint deletes the placeholder from all the slides. However, in some circumstances you might want to delete the placeholder only from a single slide. For example, you might need extra room to display a chart or picture. You can use VBA to delete any of the three footer placeholders by setting the DateAndTime, Footer, or SlideNumber object's `Visible` property to `False`. For example, following is some code that hides all three placeholders for slide number 2 of the active presentation:

```
With ActivePresentation.Slides(2).HeadersFooters
    .DateAndTime.Visible = False
    .Footer.Visible = False
    .SlideNumber.Visible = False
End With
```

- To size a placeholder, position the mouse pointer over one of the placeholder's sizing handles (the circles that appear at the corners and border midpoints). The pointer changes to a two-headed arrow. Click and drag the sizing handle to the position you want.

- To move a placeholder, position the mouse pointer over one of the placeholder borders (but not over a sizing handle). The pointer changes to a four-headed arrow. Click and drag the placeholder to the position you want.

- To format a placeholder's lines and colors, select the placeholder and then select Format, Placeholder.

- To format the placeholder text, select the text and then select Format, Font. Use the Font dialog box to set the font options you want.

- To display an object—such as clip art or a text box—on every slide, insert the object into the footer area.

Advanced Slide Formatting and Design

Getting the organization of your entire project as well as the individual slides is crucial for any successful PowerPoint presentation. But we live in an age where we ignore image at our peril. Chances are your audience expects at least nice-looking slides, so in your quest for a knockout presentation, you should spend some time on the formatting and design aspects.

Slide Design Guidelines

Getting the slide design right is no easy task because you must strike a balance between giving your audience the eye candy they expect and not overwhelming your message with too many formatting bells and design whistles. With this balance as the goal, here are some design guidelines to bear in mind when constructing your knockout presentation:

- Consider your audience, because some designs will suit certain audiences better than others. For example, if you're presenting to children, a bright, happy design with kid-friendly images will work, whereas a plain, text-heavy design will induce naptime.

On the other hand, if you're presenting to managers or the board of directors, you'll need a design that gets straight to the point and has little in the way of design frills.

- Consider your company's image. I mean this in two ways: First and most obviously, if your company has a set color scheme or style, your presentation should reflect that. Second, if your company is known as one that's staid or bold, serious or fun, your presentation should not conflict with that image.

- Be consistent across all your slides. This means using the same typeface and type size for all your titles, using consistent bullet styles throughout the presentation, using the same or similar background images on all slides, and having the company logo in the same place on each slide. The more consistent you are, the less work your audience has interpreting the formatting for each slide, so the more they'll concentrate on your content.

- However, don't use the same layout on every slide. To help keep your audience interested, vary the layout from slide to slide: Title Only, Text and Title, Text and Content, Content Only, and so on.

- For the typeface, use sans serif fonts (the ones without the little "feet" at the letter tips), such as Arial, Comic Sans MS, Microsoft Sans Serif, and Verdana. These typefaces are easier to read than serif typefaces (the ones with the little "feet") and are a much better choice than fancy, decorative typefaces, which are very difficult to decipher from a distance.

Embedding TrueType Fonts

If you use a nonstandard TrueType typeface in your presentation, and you're either going to send the presentation to another user or run it on another machine, your formatting will be thrown off if the other computer doesn't have the typeface installed. To prevent this problem, embed your TrueType fonts with the presentation when you save it. Select File, Save As, click Tools, and then click Save Options. In the Save Options dialog box, activate the Embed TrueType Fonts check box. If the presentation will be edited on the other computer, also activate the Embed All Characters option, which embeds all the font's characters, even those you didn't use. If you prefer to keep the file size to a minimum, activate the Embed Characters In Use Only option, instead.

- For the type size of your slide content, don't use anything smaller than the default sizes. In particular, never use a type size smaller than 20 points because it will be nearly impossible for your audience to read. If your audience is older, or if you're presenting in a large hall, consider using type sizes even larger than the PowerPoint defaults.

PowerPoint's Default Type Sizes

By default, PowerPoint uses a 44-point type for the slide titles, 32-point type for top-level items, 28-point type for second-level items, 24-point type for third-level items, and 20-point type for fourth- and fifth-level items. Footer text uses only 14-point type, but that's not as much of a concern unless you really want your audience to be able to read the footer data.

- For maximum readability, there should be significant contrast between the text color and the slide's background color. Dark text on a light background is best for overhead presentations; if you'll be presenting using onscreen slides of 35mm slides, use light text on a dark background, instead. Finally, don't use a background image unless it's relatively faint and the text stands out well against it.

- Always use the landscape (horizontal) orientation for your slides. The portrait (vertical) orientation reduces the available width, so each bullet point takes up more vertical space, which makes the slides look overcrowded.

- Finally, and perhaps most important, design your slides so that they don't include too much information. Each slide should have at most four or five main points; anything more than that and you're guaranteed to lose your audience by making them work too hard.

Using the Slide Master to Get a Consistent Look

One of PowerPoint's templates might be just right for your presentation. If so, great! Your presentation's design will be one less thing to worry about on your way to an effective presentation. Often, however, a template is just right *except* for the background color or title alignment or font. Or perhaps you need the company's logo to appear on each slide. Using the template as a starting point, you can make changes to the overall presentation so that it's just right for your needs.

However, what do you do if your presentation already has a number of slides? Isn't it a lot of work to change the background or alignment or font on *every* slide? Well, yes, it is. Fortunately, PowerPoint offers a much easier way: the Slide Master, which is available for every presentation. The Slide Master acts as a kind of "design center" for your presentation. The Slide Master's typefaces, types sizes, bullet styles, colors, alignment options, line spacing, and more are used on each slide in your presentation. Not only that, but any object you add to the Slide Master—a piece of clip art, a company logo, and so on—also appears in the same position on each slide.

Viewing and Editing the Slide Master

The beauty of the Slide Master is that any change you make to this one slide, PowerPoint propagates to *all* the slides in your presentation. Need to change the background color? Just change the background color of the Slide Master. Prefer a different type size for top-level items? Change the type size for the top-level item shown on the Slide Master.

Earlier, you saw how to use the Slide Master to modify the footer layout (see "Customizing the Footer Layout"). Here's a review of the methods you can use to open the Slide Master, shown in Figure 3.9:

- Select View, Master, Slide Master.

 - Hold down Shift and click the Slide Master View icon.

Figure 3.9
Each presentation comes with its own Slide Master, which acts as a "design center" for the slides.

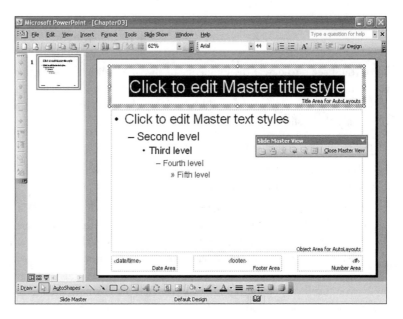

With the Slide Master open, you can format the text, background, bullets, and colors as though you were working in a regular slide.

Editing the Title Master

If your presentation has multiple slides that use the Title Slide layout, you can change the formatting or design for all of them by editing the Title Master. If the template on which you based your presentation doesn't come with a Title Master, switch to the Slide Master view and then select Insert, New Title Master.

Note, however, that the title font is ultimately controlled by the Slide Master. That is, if you change the title typeface in the Title Master, for instance, and then set a different typeface for the title in the Slide Master, the latter typeface will be applied to the Title Master, as well.

Using Multiple Slide Masters

Although having a consistent look among your slides should be a prime design goal for any knockout presentation, that doesn't mean you have to use precisely the same formatting and design on every slide. Some of the most effective presentation designs I've seen are ones that apply a particular design to groups of related slides. Why would you need to do this? Here are some examples:

- For a budget presentation, you might use a green color scheme on income-related slides and a red color scheme on expense-related slides.

- In a presentation that includes both sensitive and nonsensitive material, you could add a "For Internal Use Only" graphic to the slides with sensitive material.

- If your presentation has multiple authors, you might want to display the author's name, signature, or picture on each of the slides he or she created.

This would seem to defeat the efficiency of the Slide Master, except that PowerPoint allows you to have more than one Slide Master in a presentation. You can then apply one of the Slide Masters to the appropriate slides, and any changes you make to that Slide Master will affect only those slides.

To create another slide master, you have two choices:

- To create a default Slide Master, open the Slide Master view and then select Insert, New Slide Master (or press Ctrl+M).

- To create a duplicate of an existing Slide Master, click the Slide Master and then select Insert, Duplicate Slide Master. This technique is useful if your new Slide Master is similar to an existing Slide Master. By duplicating it and then tweaking the new Slide Master as required, you avoid having to create the new Slide Master from scratch.

When you display the Slide Design task pane (select Format, Slide Design), you see in the top part of the pane a section titled Used in This Presentation. This section includes the Slide Masters that you created. To apply one of these Slide Masters, select the slides you want to work with and then click the Slide Master.

Ensuring Good and Consistent Design

Despite your best efforts to follow design guidelines and ensure a consistent look throughout your presentation, you may make a design faux pas or two. These things happen to the best of us. To help you avoid or catch these small mistakes, you can enable PowerPoint's style checker. This feature works something like a spelling or grammar checker—it examines your presentation and looks for style errors and inconsistencies:

- Inconsistent use of uppercase and lowercase letters in title and body text.
- Inconsistent use of "end" punctuation, such as not having a period at the end of each paragraph.
- Using too many fonts.
- Using title or body type sizes that are too small.
- Using too many bullets on a single slide.
- Using too many lines in titles or bullets.

This is a list of many small things that contribute mightily to the large goal of consistent and proper design that is the trademark of any knockout presentation.

To turn on style checking and customize its options, follow these steps:

1. Select Tools, Options.

2. In the Spelling and Style tab, activate the Check Style check box.

3. Click Style Options to display the Style Options dialog box, shown in Figure 3.10.

Figure 3.10
In the Style Options dialog box, use the Case and End Punctuation tab to check for uppercase and lowercase letter style and the punctuation used to end paragraphs.

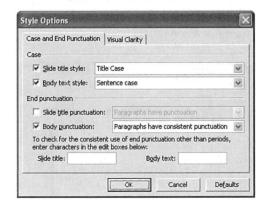

4. Use the lists in the Case group to determine the style of uppercase and lowercase letters to use in slide titles and body text.

5. Use the lists in the End Punctuation group to specify whether title and body paragraphs use punctuation (such as a period) at the end. If you choose Paragraphs Have Consistent Punctuation in either list, and you end your paragraphs with a character other than a period, enter that character in either the Slide Title or Body Text text box.

6. Select the Visual Clarity tab, shown in Figure 3.11.

Figure 3.11
In the Style Options dialog box, use the Visual Clarity tab to set limits on the fonts, text sizes, bullets, and lines used in your presentation.

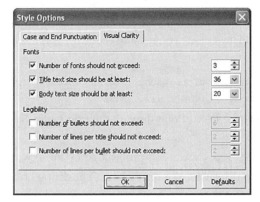

7. Use the controls in the Fonts group to set the maximum number of fonts and the minimum type size for titles and body text.

8. Use the controls in the Legibility group to set maximum values for bullets, lines per title, and lines per bullet.

9. Click OK.

Creating a Custom Color Scheme

If you want to avoid the drudgery of getting your text, line, background, and fill colors to match, PowerPoint comes with a dozen predefined color schemes that do the hard work for you. To select a color scheme, click Slide Design, Color Schemes in the Task pane, and then click the color scheme you want (see Figure 3.12).

Figure 3.12
Select Slide Design, Color Schemes in the Task pane to see PowerPoint's predefined color schemes.

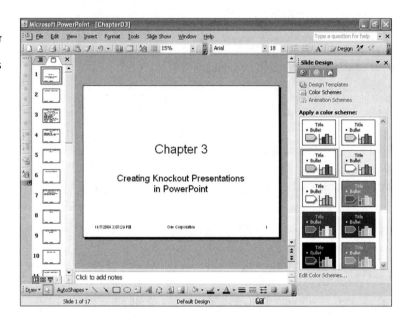

If a particular color scheme isn't quite right for your needs, or if you want to create a color scheme to match your company colors, you need to create a custom scheme. Follow these steps:

1. If you want to base your custom color scheme on an existing design, click the color scheme in the Slide Design, Color Schemes pane.

2. Click Edit Color Schemes. PowerPoint displays the Edit Color Scheme dialog box, shown in Figure 3.13.

3. In the Scheme Colors group, click the slide object you want to work with.

4. Click Change Color to display a color dialog box. (The dialog box that appears depends on the object you're working with.)

5. Choose your color and then click OK.

6. Repeats steps 3–5 to modify the colors of the other slide objects, as needed.

7. If you want your custom scheme to appear in the Slide Design, Color Schemes pane, click Add as Standard Scheme.

8. Click Apply to apply the color scheme to your presentation.

Figure 3.13
Use the Edit Color Scheme dialog box to create your own custom color scheme.

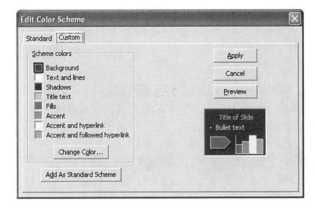

Replacing Fonts

3

I mentioned earlier that it's an important design guideline to use typefaces consistently throughout your presentation. Sometimes, however, typefaces can become inconsistent. For example, you might insert some slides from another presentation that uses a different font; you might collaborate on a presentation and the other person might use some other typeface; or you might start using Verdana or Helvetica instead of Arial.

Whatever the reason, going through the entire presentation and replacing the wrong fonts with the correct ones isn't why they're paying you the big bucks. Fortunately, you can avoid this drudgery by using PowerPoint's Replace Font feature. Here's how it works:

1. Select Format, Replace Fonts. The Replace Font dialog box appears, as shown in Figure 3.14.

Figure 3.14
Use the Replace Font feature to replace all instances of one typeface with another.

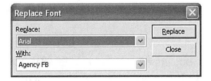

2. Use the Replace list to select the typeface you want to replace.
3. Use the With list to select the typeface to use as the replacement.
4. Click Replace.
5. If you have other typefaces you want to replace, follow steps 2–4 for each one.
6. Click Close.

Changing a Picture's Colors

It's a common source of presentation frustration: you find the perfect piece of clip art for a slide, but the picture's colors don't go with your color scheme. Rather than rejecting the picture outright, you can use PowerPoint's Recolor feature, which enables you to change one or more of the picture's colors for something more complementary to your presentation design. Here are the steps to follow:

1. Click the picture.

 2. In the Picture toolbar, click Recolor Picture. (Alternatively, double-click the picture, select the Picture tab, and then click Recolor.) The Recolor Picture dialog box appears, as shown in Figure 3.15.

Figure 3.15
Use the Recolor Picture feature to change a picture's colors to ones more suitable to your presentation's color scheme.

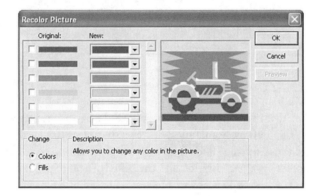

3. In the Original column, click the color you want to change.

4. In the New column, click the list beside the color you chose in step 3 and click the new color you want.

5. Repeat steps 3 and 4 to change any other colors you need.

6. Click OK.

Some AutoShape Tricks

PowerPoint's AutoShapes are handy objects that can add design flair to a presentation without getting in the way of the content. If you use AutoShapes frequently, the next few sections present some tips that you should find useful.

Drawing Circles and Squares

To draw a perfect circle instead of an oval, click the Oval tool, hold down Shift, and then draw the shape. To draw a perfect square instead of a rectangle, click the Rectangle tool, hold down Shift, and then draw the shape.

Drawing Shapes Quickly

Rather than clicking a shape tool and then drawing the tool on your slide, PowerPoint offers a faster way to get a default shape: hold down Ctrl and click the shape tool. PowerPoint adds a default shape in the center of the slide. You can then move, size, and format the shape as needed. You can also hold down Ctrl and Shift and then click Oval or Rectangle to get a quick circle or square.

Setting the Default Formatting for an AutoShape

If you find yourself constantly applying the same fills, line or arrow styles, or colors to a specific AutoShape, you can set that formatting as the default for the shape. There are two ways to do this:

- In the Format AutoShape dialog box, select the Colors and Lines tab, choose the formatting options, and activate the Default for New Objects check box.
- In the slide, right-click the shape and then click Set AutoShape Defaults.

Copying Object Formatting

 If you want to copy the formatting from one shape to another, the easiest method is to click the shape with the formatting, click the Format Painter tool, and then click the other object. To apply the formatting to multiple objects, double-click the Format Painter tool, click each object, and then click the Format Painter tool to deactivate it.

That works well enough, but PowerPoint also has a tool that "remembers" an object's formatting indefinitely, which is handy if you want to apply a particular shape's formatting to different objects over time. Select View, Toolbars, Customize, select the Commands tab, and then click Format in the Categories list. Drag the following tools to a toolbar:

 Pick Up Object Style—Click an object and then click the icon to have PowerPoint "remember" the formatting of the object.

 Apply Object Style—Click an object and then click the icon to apply the "remembered" formatting to the object.

Duplicating Shapes at Evenly Spaced Intervals

You can create effective designs by duplicating a particular shape multiple times. Although it's not hard to copy a shape (hold down Ctrl and drag the shape), it's quite difficult to get the same distance between the duplicates. Happily, PowerPoint can do this for you. Click the shape and press Ctrl+D to create the first duplicate. Use your mouse to drag the duplicate to the correct position. This tells PowerPoint how far away you want each duplicate and in which direction. Press Ctrl+D again and PowerPoint creates a third shape that uses the same spacing as the second. Keep pressing Ctrl+D to create more duplicates, as shown in Figure 3.16.

Figure 3.16
After you establish the spacing between the first and second shapes, press Ctrl+D to create duplicates with the same spacing.

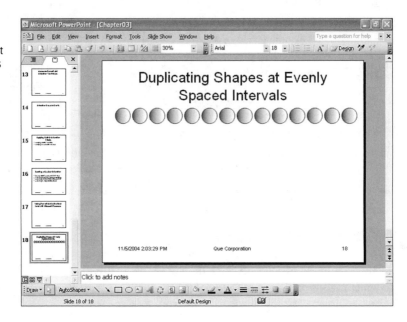

Setting the Default Font for Shape Text

By default, PowerPoint uses 18-point Arial for the text you type in a shape. You can format the text in a specific shape, but what if you want *all* your shapes to use the same font? You can set this default font by first clicking any shape that includes text. (If you don't want to apply the new font formatting to an existing shape, click an empty section of any slide so that no placeholder or object is selected.) Then select Format, Font, and make your choices in the Font dialog box. Activate the Default for New Objects check box and click OK.

Wrapping Text Within a Shape

If you want to display a shape such as an oval or rectangle with text inside, you don't need a separate text box. Instead, draw your shape and then type the text. PowerPoint automatically centers the text within the shape. To prevent the text from spilling over the shape borders, right-click the shape and then select Format AutoShape. Select the Text Box tab and activate the Word Wrap Text in AutoShape check box. If you prefer that the shape expand to accommodate the text, activate the Resize AutoShape to Fit Text check box.

Hiding Slide Master Shapes in a Slide

If you add a shape to the Slide Master, it will appear on all the presentation's slides. If there is a particular slide in which you don't want the shape to appear, you can hide it. First, right-click the shape, and then click Format AutoShape. In the Colors and Lines tab, pull down the Color list in the Fill group and select the Background option. This gives the shape the same background as the portion of the slide background that lies underneath the shape. You should also pull down the Color list in the Line group and select No Line.

Advanced PowerPoint Animation Techniques

For many people, a presentation just isn't complete until they've added slide transitions and other animated effects. These can certainly pump up the "wow" factor in your work, and any presentation that seeks the "knockout" adjective had better incorporate some animation into its design. But animation is a complex business, and without a few tricks up your sleeve, even an Office guru can ruin his or her presentation by blowing the animation stage. This section helps you prevent that fate by showing you a number of advanced but very useful tricks and techniques not only for doing animation well, but for getting the most out of this powerful PowerPoint feature.

Animation Do's and Don'ts

Before you get to the tricks and techniques, it's worth taking a second to put this animation business into some perspective. After all, advanced knowledge of animation is one thing, but putting that knowledge to good use is quite another. Here are some do's and don'ts to bear in mind when adding the animation touches to your presentations:

- Do use transitions. They add visual interest, give the audience a short break between slides, and help you control the pacing of your presentation.

- Don't overuse transitions. Nobody will object to fade-ins, dissolves, and other simple transitions, but don't have multiple objects flying in from all corners of the screen.

- Do keep your audience in mind when planning your animations. In a flashy presentation for sales and marketing types, you can probably get away with more elaborate animations; in a no-nonsense presentation to board members, animations and transitions should be short and sweet.

- Don't use a number of different transitions and animations in a single presentation. Just as your slide text looks awful if you use too many fonts, your presentations will look amateurish if you throw every effect in the book at your audience.

- Do keep your animations snappy, particularly transition effects. It may not seem like a long time, but if your slide transitions are taking 10 or 15 seconds or longer, your audience's mood will soon degenerate from frustration to anger to outright hostility. Unless you're presenting to kids (who, naturally, prefer elaborate animations), the transition from one slide to another should never take more than a few seconds.

- Don't overshadow your content. The goal of any animation should always be to either highlight a slide element or to keep up your audience's interest. If you start adding effects just for fun, I guarantee your audience will *stop* having fun and will start looking for the nearest exit.

Applying Built-In Animation Effects

PowerPoint comes with an extensive library of built-in animations, which often means that you can apply your slide transitions and other effects with just a few mouse clicks. PowerPoint gives you two ways to apply built-in animations:

- Apply a slide transition.
- Apply an animation scheme.

Applying a Slide Transition

Here are the steps to follow to apply a slide transition to one or more slides:

1. Use the Slides pane or Slide Sorter to select the slides you want to work with.

2. Select Slide Show, Slide Transition. The Slide Transition pane appears, as shown in Figure 3.17.

Figure 3.17
Use the Slide Transition pane to apply a built-in slide transition to the selected slides.

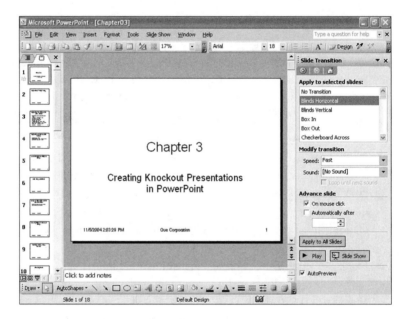

3. Use the Apply to Selected Slides list to select the transition effect you want.

Automatically Previewing Transitions
Be sure to leave the AutoPreview check box activated. This tells PowerPoint to display a preview of the transition as soon as you click it.

---

4. In the Modify Transition group, customize the transition with the following lists:

   Speed—Select the transition speed: Slow, Medium, or Fast.

   Sound—Select the sound that you want to play during the transition.

5. In the Advance Slide group, choose the method by which you want to move to the next slide:

On Mouse Click—Activate this check box to advance the slide when you click the mouse.

Automatically After—Activate this check box to advance the slide after the minutes and/or seconds that you specify in the spin box.

6. If you decide you want to use the transition for all the slides in the presentation, click Apply to All Slides. (If you don't click this option, the transition applies to only the selected slides.)

Applying an Animation Scheme

I've been using the term animation rather loosely up to this point, so this is a good time to tighten up our terminology. In the PowerPoint lexicon, a *transition* is a visual (and sometimes auditory) effect that plays during the switch from one slide to another; an *animation* is a visual effect applied to a specific slide element, such as the slide title or bullet text.

An *animation scheme* is a preset collection of animations that apply to the slide text, including the title, bullets, and paragraphs. Here are the steps to follow to apply an animation scheme to one or more slides:

1. Use the Slides pane or Slide Sorter to select the slides you want to work with.

2. Select Slide Show, Animation Scheme. The Slide Design, Animation Schemes pane appears, as shown in Figure 3.18.

Figure 3.18
Use the Slide Design, Animation Schemes pane to apply a preset animation scheme to the text of the selected slides.

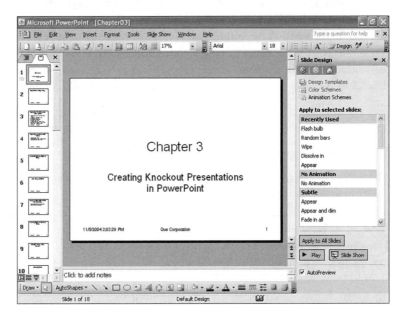

3. Use the Apply to Selected Slides list to select the animation scheme you want.

Stick with the Subtle Schemes

The list of animation schemes is divided into five sections. Besides the Recently Used and No Animation sections at the top, the schemes themselves are listed in three categories: Subtle, Moderate, and Exciting. For most presentations, you're best to stick with the Subtle schemes, because they're the least likely to turn off your audience. Not that you need to ignore the Moderate and Exciting schemes completely, just use them judiciously. For example, if you have a slide with an important or interesting announcement or result, it's okay to highlight the fact with a special animation. As long as you don't use more than one or two of these wilder schemes, your presentation won't suffer.

Automatically Previewing Transitions

Be sure to leave the AutoPreview check box activated. This tells PowerPoint to display a preview of the scheme as soon as you click it.

4. If you decide you want to use the scheme for all the slides in the presentation, click Apply to All Slides. (If you don't click this option, the scheme applies only to the selected slides.)

Creating a Custom Animation

The prefab animation schemes look great and save you tons of time, but they have one very large drawback: you can't customize them directly. For example, you can't change properties such as the speed and direction of the animation. Also, some of the schemes don't work the way you might want. For example, one highly requested visual effect is to display bullet points one at a time. There is an animation scheme named Fade In One by One, but it's not particularly useful because you can't control when each bullet appears, and second- and third-level items appear along with their corresponding top-level item.

To solve all these problems, and to create unique and visually appealing animations, you need to design them yourself using PowerPoint's Custom Animation pane.

Following are the general steps for creating a custom animation:

1. Select the slide you want to work with. (You can work with only one slide at a time for a custom animation.)

Animating the Slide Master

If you want to apply a custom animation to a specific object in all your slides, select View, Master, Slide Master, and then apply the animation to an object on the Slide Master.

Working from a Preset Animation

If one of PowerPoint's preset animations gives you an effect that's close to what you want, don't start your custom animation from scratch. Instead, apply the preset animation and then display the Custom Animation pane. The settings from the preset animation will appear in the Custom Animation pane, and you can then customize them to suit your needs.

For example, another often-requested animation effect is to display scrolling credits on the last slide. PowerPoint comes with a Credits Animation scheme (it's in the Exciting category) that does a good job of this. However, after you apply this scheme, display the Custom Animation pane and then use the Speed list to control the pace of the credit.

2. Select Slide Show, Custom Animation. The Custom Animation pane appears, as shown in Figure 3.19.

Figure 3.19
Use the Custom Animation pane to apply a custom animation effect to the objects on the selected slide.

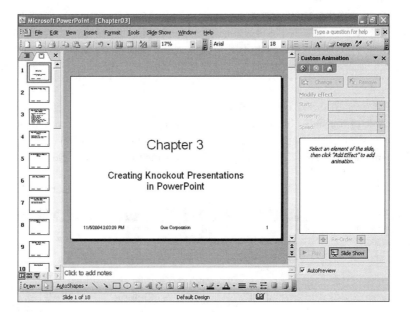

3. Click the slide object you want to animate. Note that you can apply animations to any object, including the title and text placeholders, individual bullets or paragraphs (select the bullet or paragraph text), and drawing layer objects such as text boxes, AutoShapes, clip art, and pictures.

4. Click Add Effect and then select one of the following effects categories:

   Entrance—These effects control how the object comes onto the slide when the slide first appears.

   Emphasis—These effects alter various text properties, including boldface, italic, size, and color.

   Exit—These effects control how the object goes off the slide when you move to the next slide.

Motion Paths—These effects control the path that the object follows when it comes onto and goes off the slide.

5. Modify the effect. The available modifications vary with the chosen effect.

6. To change the order in which the animations occur, select the object and then use the Re-Order arrows to move the object up or down in the animation order.

7. To view the animation, you have two choices:

- Click Play to play all the animations without interaction.
- Click Slide Show to start the slide show and play the animations with interaction.

Copying Custom Animations

Custom animations apply to only one slide. If you've created a complex animation for an object such as a slide title, PowerPoint doesn't have a direct way to apply the animation to a title on a different slide. You can work around this limitation by selecting Insert, Duplicate Slide. The duplicate slide contains a copy of the custom animation. Now copy the text from the slide that you want to animate, paste it on the duplicate slide, and then delete the original.

Figure 3.20 shows a slide with a custom animation applied. Notice the numbers attached to some of the slide objects. These numbers represent the slide's animation order. That is, when you click once, the animation effect runs for the objects with a 1 beside them; when you click a second time, the animation runs for the objects labeled with 2, and so on.

Expand contents

Figure 3.20
A slide with a custom animation added.

These numbers represent the slides animation order

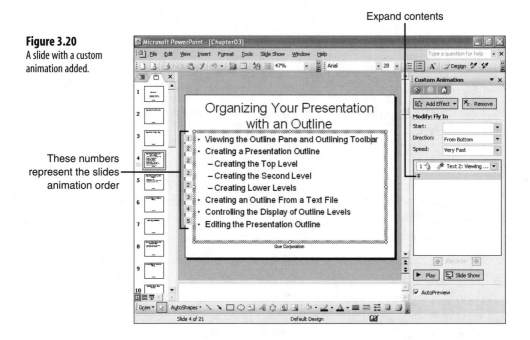

The sections that follow take you through some specific examples of custom animations.

Showing Animations on the Web

By default, PowerPoint doesn't include any animations when you save your presentation for the Web. To include the animation, select Tools, Options, select the General tab, and then click Web Options. Activate the Show Slide Animation While Browsing check box, and then click OK.

Making Bullets Appear One at a Time

I mentioned earlier that one of the animations I'm asked about most often is making bullets appear individually, usually in response to a mouse click. This is a very useful presentation trick because it gives you full control over the display of your bullets. By animating bullets individually, you can

- Prevent your audience from being distracted by bullets beyond the one you're currently discussing.
- Hide bullets that contain "surprise" results until you're ready to present them.
- Place extra emphasis on the individual bullets because they don't enter the slide individually as a group.
- Add pizzazz by giving each bullet a different animation effect. (Although, of course, you want to be careful here that you don't induce animation overload on your audience.)

With the Custom Animation pane displayed, follow these steps to animate your bullets individually:

1. Select the placeholder that contains the bullets.
2. Select Add Effect, Entrance, and then click the animation effect you want to use. PowerPoint applies the effect to all the bullets and displays the animation order numbers beside each bullet.
3. Click the expand contents button (two downward pointing arrows; see Figure 3.20). PowerPoint displays all the bullets, as shown in Figure 3.21.
4. Click the bullet you want to work with.
5. To change the animation effect for the bullet, select Change, Entrance, and then select the effect you want.
6. If you want the bullet to appear only when you click the mouse, change the Start option to On Click. PowerPoint renumbers the animation order.
7. Customize the other effect settings, as needed.
8. Repeat steps 3–6 to configure the animation for each bullet.

Objects with a mouse icon are animated
one by one when you click the mouse

Figure 3.21
After you apply an effect
to the entire placeholder,
expand the contents to
see each bullet.

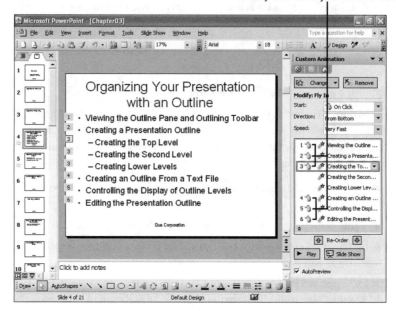

Applying Animations One By One

It's usually easiest to apply an effect to the entire placeholder and then modify each bullet. However, if you want to use quite different animations for each bullet, it might be easier to work with the bullets one by one from the start. To apply a custom animation to a bullet, select the bullet text, click Add Effect, and then select the effect you want.

Animating a Chart by Series or Category

If you use charts in your presentations—either charts imported from Excel or created with Microsoft Graph—you can animate the components of the chart. Depending on the chart, you have up to five animation possibilities:

- As one object—Adds the entire chart.

- By series—Adds each data series to the chart one series at a time. For example, if you have a bar chart that shows quarterly sales figures by region, you could display the bars one quarter at a time.

- By category—Adds each data category to the chart one category at a time. For example, if you have a bar chart that shows quarterly sales figures by region, you could display the bars one region at a time.

- By element in series element—Adds each data marker in each series to the chart one marker at a time. For example, if you have a bar chart that shows quarterly sales figures by region, you could display the bars for each region one quarter at a time.

- By element in category—Adds each data marker in each category to the chart one marker at a time. For example, if you have a bar chart that shows quarterly sales figures by region, you could display the bars for each quarter one region at a time.

Here are the steps to follow to animate a PowerPoint chart object:

1. Insert the chart into a PowerPoint slide.
2. Select the chart object.
3. Select Slide Show, Custom Animation.
4. Click Add Effect, Entrance, and then select the animation effect you want.

Not All Effects Support Chart Animation

Be careful when choosing the animation effect for your chart because not all effects support separate animations for chart series, categories, and elements. For example, you can use the Fly In and Crawl In effects to animate only the entire chart. If you want to use a particular effect that doesn't support the animation of chart components, you need to ungroup the chart and work with its components directly. See the next section, "Animating Individual Chart Components."

---

5. In the animation list, drop down the chart animation's menu and then select Effect Options, as shown in Figure 3.22. PowerPoint displays a dialog box of options for the effect.

Figure 3.22
To animate the chart, select Effect Options.

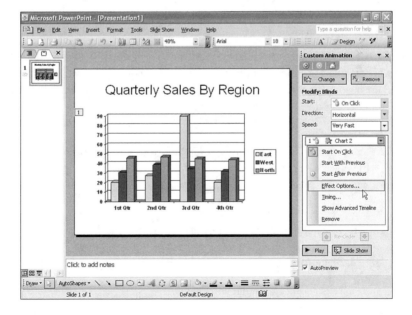

6. Display the Chart Animation tab.
7. In the Group Chart list (see Figure 3.23), select the animation option you want.

Figure 3.23
Use the list in the Chart Animation tab to select the chart components to animate.

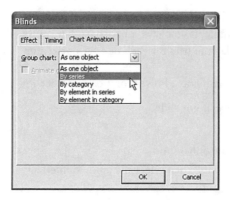

8. If you want to include the chart's gridlines and legend in the animation (these appear first), activate the Animate Grid and Legend check box.

9. Click OK.

Animating Individual Chart Components

The chart animation is slick, to be sure, but it has some limitations. The most glaring is that it doesn't work with certain effects, such as Fly In and Crawl In. Also, you can't tie the animation of the legend and the data series together. For example, if you're animating the chart by series, it might be nice sometimes to have the corresponding legend text enter along with its series.

To work around these problems, you need to drill down to another level so that you work with the chart components directly. To do that, you need to *ungroup* the chart so that the chart becomes a series of graphical objects, each of which you can animate individually. Follow these steps to ungroup a chart:

1. Right-click the chart.

2. Select Grouping, Ungroup. PowerPoint asks you to confirm that you want to convert the chart to a group.

3. Click Yes. PowerPoint converts the chart to a group.

4. Right-click the chart.

5. Select Grouping, Ungroup. PowerPoint ungroups the chart's components.

Figure 3.24 shows an ungrouped chart with each component selected.

Figure 3.24
Ungroup the chart to animate its components individually.

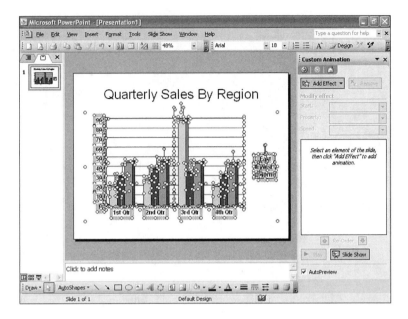

You're now ready to animate the components:

1. Select Slide Show, Custom Animation.

2. Click an empty part of the slide to ensure that no components are selected.

3. Select the chart components you want to work with. For example, Figure 3.25 shows the ungrouped chart with 14 objects selected:

   - For each data marker, the three visible sides are selected. (2D charts are much easier to animate because you have to select only a single "side" for each data marker.)

   - In the legend, the North text and its bullet are selected.

Selecting Multiple Objects

The easiest way to select multiple objects is to click the first object and then hold down Ctrl as you click the other objects.

---

4. Right-click any of the selected objects and then select Grouping, Group. PowerPoint converts the selected objects to a single group. This enables you to easily select the objects later if you need to make changes to the animation.

5. Click Add Effect, Entrance, and then select the animation effect you want.

6. Customize the other effect settings, as needed.

7. Repeat steps 2–6 to configure the animation for other components.

Figure 3.25
Select the individual
objects that you want to
animate.

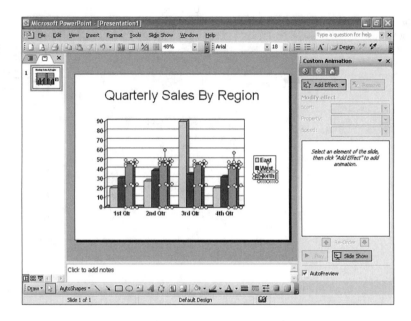

Animating an Organization Chart

If you use organization charts in your presentations, you can animate the charts to display
the hierarchy in various ways:

- As one object—Adds the entire chart.

- All at once—Adds all the positions to the chart at once, with slightly different timings
  for each position.

- Each branch, shape by shape—Adds each position in each branch to the chart one position at a time.

- Each level, shape by shape—Adds each position in each level to the chart one position
  at a time.

- Level by level—Adds all the positions in each level to the chart, one level at a time.

Here are the steps to follow to animate a PowerPoint organization chart object:

1. Insert the organization chart into a PowerPoint slide.
2. Select the organization chart object.
3. Select Slide Show, Custom Animation.
4. Click Add Effect, Entrance, and then select the animation effect you want.
5. In the animation list, drop down the organization chart animation's menu and then
   select Effect Options. PowerPoint displays a dialog box of options for the effect.
6. Display the Diagram Animation tab.
7. In the Group Diagram list (see Figure 3.26), select the animation option you want.

Figure 3.26
Use the list in the
Diagram Animation tab to
select the organization
chart components to ani-
mate.

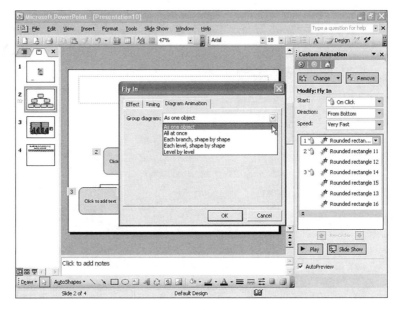

8. Click OK.

Taking PowerPoint to the Next Level with Microsoft Producer

PowerPoint is a complex, powerful program that has enough bells and whistles to satisfy
most users. However, have you ever wished PowerPoint could do any of the following?

- Capture, edit, and display high-quality audio and video.
- Create a rich playback experience for users of web presentations, even with browsers
  other than Internet Explorer.
- Set up presentations so that they play properly on a Mac.
- Capture and synchronize narration.

All these tasks and many more are doable using Microsoft Producer, a PowerPoint add-in.
You can download Producer at this site:

`http://www.microsoft.com/office/powerpoint/producer/prodinfo/overview.mspx`

From Here

- You can create an outline in Word and then import it into PowerPoint, where the
  headings are converted into outline items. For the details, see the section titled
  "Converting a Word Outline into a PowerPoint Presentation" in Chapter 6.

- You can also use Word to create professional-looking handouts. See the section titled "Using Word to Custom Format PowerPoint Handouts" in Chapter 6.

- To learn how to put your presentations online, see the section titled "Publishing a PowerPoint Presentation to the Web" in Chapter 8.

3

Taming Access Data

Microsoft Access is the data powerhouse of the Office suite. It's a full-fledged relational database management system, but it offers easy-to-use features for storing, viewing, and manipulating data. However, Office gurus want to go far beyond these simple data tasks, and they know that Access has the tools that are powerful and flexible enough to handle just about any need. Running through all of these tools would require several books of this size. However, I have a few favorite tools, tricks, and techniques that I find are the most useful for bringing Access data down to size, and I tell you about these features in this chapter. You learn how to create a totals query, how to create queries that make decisions, how to run action queries, how to set up form validation features, how to use controls to improve form data entry, how to create multiple-column reports, how to use calculations in report fields, and how to control the output of your reports.

Creating a Totals Query

A totals query includes a column that performs an aggregate operation—such as summing or averaging—on the values of a particular field. A totals query derives either a single value for the entire dynaset or several values for the records that have been grouped within the dynaset. Table 4.1 outlines the aggregate operations you can use for your totals queries.

4

Operation	Purpose
Group By	Groups the records according to the unique values in the field.
Sum	Sums the values in the field.
Avg	Averages the values in the field.
Min	Returns the smallest value in the field.
Max	Returns the largest value in the field.
Count	Counts the number of values in the field.
StDev	Calculates the standard deviation of the values in the field.
Var	Calculates the variance of the values in the field.
First	Returns the first value in the field.
Last	Returns the last value in the field.
Expression	Returns a custom total based on an expression in a calculated column.
Where	Tells Access to use the field's criteria to filter the records before calculating the totals.

Table 4.1   Aggregate Operations Available for Totals Queries

The next few sections show you how to use these operations in your queries.

More Info

I adapted some of the material in this chapter from my book *Microsoft Access 2003, Forms, Reports, and Queries* (Que Publishing, 2004). If you need more detail about queries, forms, or reports, you can check out the book at your local store or online at www.mcfedries.com/AccessForms/.

Displaying the Total Row in the Design Grid

Before you can work with the aggregate operations, you need to do one of the following in the query design window:

- Choose View, Totals.
- Click the Totals button in the toolbar.

As shown in Figure 4.1, Access adds the Total row to the design grid, and each Total cell contains a list of the aggregate operations.

Downloading This Chapter's Examples

You'll find the database file that contains this chapter's examples at www.mcfedries.com/OfficeGurus/.

Totals

Figure 4.1
Choose View, Totals to
display the `Total` row
in the query design grid.

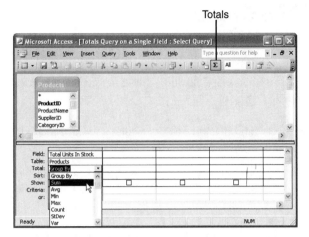

Setting Up a Totals Query on a Single Field

In the simplest totals query case, you can apply one of the mathematical aggregate operations to a single field. Access will then display the mathematical result for that field. The following steps are required to create a totals query on a single field:

1. Display the `Total` row, if it's not already displayed.

2. In the field's `Total` cell, use the drop-down list to click the function you want to use.

3. If you want to restrict the records involved in the aggregate operation, enter the appropriate expression in the field's `Criteria` cell.

4. (Optional) In the dynaset, Access displays *OperationOfFieldName* in the field header, where *Operation* is the aggregate operation you chose in step 2 and *FieldName* is the name of the field you're working with. If you'd rather see a more readable name, change the `Field` cell to the following, where *FieldName* is the name you want to use:
   Field Alias:FieldName

5. Run the query.

Figure 4.2 shows the result when the `Sum` aggregate operation is applied to the UnitsInStock field of Northwind's Products table. As you can see, the datasheet consists of a single cell that shows the result of the aggregate operation.

Figure 4.2
The datasheet shows
only the result of the calculation applied to the
single field.

Setting Up a Totals Query on Multiple Fields

If you want to see more data in the totals query, you can add more fields:

- Add other fields and apply any mathematical aggregate operation to each field.
- Add other copies of the same field and apply different mathematical aggregate operations to each field.

Note, however, that you can only add fields to which you want to apply an aggregate operation; you can't add nonaggregate fields to the query.

Figure 4.3 shows a query with five columns. These include a Count of the ProductID field, Sum of the UnitsInStock field, and three operations on the UnitPrice field—Max, Min, and Avg. Figure 4.4 shows the result.

Figure 4.3
A totals query showing five aggregate operations on three fields.

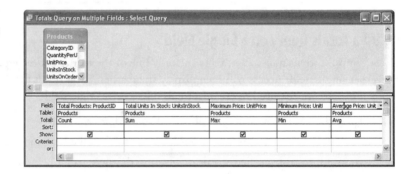

Figure 4.4
The result of the totals query shown in Figure 4.3.

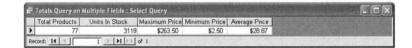

Filtering the Records Before Calculating Totals

I mentioned earlier that you can add criteria to any of the aggregate columns, and Access will perform the operation only on the records that match the criteria. What if you want to filter the table based on a field that isn't part of any aggregate operation? You can't include a nonaggregate field in the query results, but it *is* possible to use a nonaggregate field to filter the records. Here are the steps to follow:

1. Add the nonaggregate field to the query design grid.
2. Clear the field's Show check box.
3. In the field's Total cell, drop down the list and click Where.
4. Add the required expression to the field's Criteria cell.

In this case, Access filters the records based on the criteria and *then* performs the aggregate operation.

For example, in the query shown earlier in Figure 4.3, suppose you want to run the aggregate operations on only those products in the Beverages category. To do this, you add the Categories table to the query and then set up the CategoryName field with the Where operation and the criteria "Beverages," as shown in Figure 4.5. Figure 4.6 shows the results for the filtered records.

Figure 4.5
A totals query that uses the Where operation to filter the records before performing the other aggregate operations.

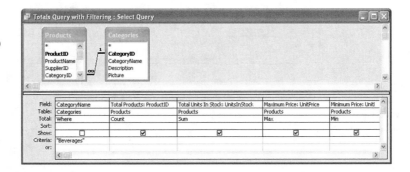

Figure 4.6
The result of the totals query shown in Figure 4.5.

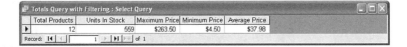

Creating a Totals Query for Groups of Records

In its basic guise, a totals query shows a single total for all the records in a table (or all the records in a subset of the table, depending on whether the query includes criteria). Suppose, however, that you prefer to see that total broken out into subtotals. For example, instead of a simple sum on the UnitsInStock field, how about seeing the sum of the orders grouped by category?

Grouping your totals requires just two steps:

1. Add the field you want to use for the groupings to the design grid.
2. In the field's Total cell, drop down the list and click Group By.

Figure 4.7 shows the query from Figure 4.5 changed so that the CategoryName field is now set up with the Group By operation. Running this query produces the result shown in Figure 4.8. As you can see, Access groups the entries in the Category Name column and displays subtotals for each group.

Grouping on Multiple Fields

You can extend this technique to derive totals for more specific groups. The general idea is that as you apply the Group By operation to more fields, Access groups the records from left to right.

Figure 4.7
To group your totals, add the field used for the grouping and click `Group By` in the `Total` cell.

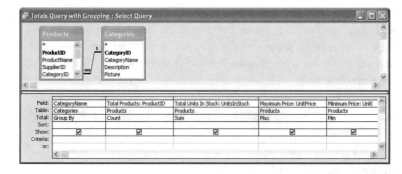

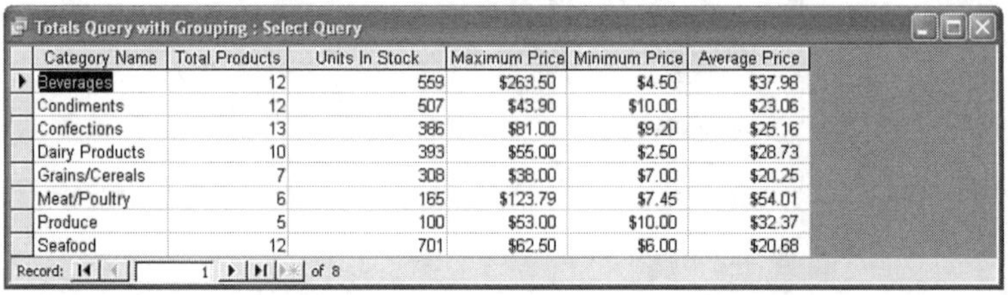

Figure 4.8
Access groups the records and displays subtotals for each group.

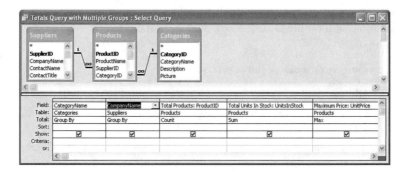

For example, suppose you want to see subtotals for each supplier within the categories. You can do this by adding the Suppliers table to the query, adding the SupplierName field to the right of the CategoryName field, and clicking `Group By` in the `Total` cell. Figure 4.9 shows the revised query, and Figure 4.10 shows the result. Access creates the groups from left to right, so the records are first grouped by Category and then by Supplier.

Figure 4.9
You can refine your groupings by applying the `Group By` operation to more fields, where the grouping occurs from left to right.

Creating a Totals Query Using a Calculated Field

So far you've seen aggregate operations applied to regular table fields. However, you can also apply them to calculated fields. For example, you've seen how to use the following expression in the Northwind Order Details table to calculate the extended price of an item given its unit price, quantity, and discount percentage:

```
[UnitPrice] * [Quantity] * (1 - [Discount])
```

Figure 4.10
The dynaset produced by the query in Figure 4.9.

Category Name	Company Name	Total Products	Units In Stock	Maximum Price	Minimum Price	Average P ▲
Beverages	Aux joyeux ecclésiastiques	2	86	$263.50	$18.00	$140
Beverages	Bigfoot Breweries	3	183	$18.00	$14.00	$15
Beverages	Exotic Liquids	2	56	$19.00	$18.00	$18
Beverages	Karkki Oy	1	57	$18.00	$18.00	$18
Beverages	Leka Trading	1	17	$46.00	$46.00	$46
Beverages	Pavlova, Ltd.	1	15	$15.00	$15.00	$15
Beverages	Plutzer Lebensmittelgroßmärkte AG	1	125	$7.75	$7.75	$7
Beverages	Refrescos Americanas LTDA	1	20	$4.50	$4.50	$4
Condiments	Exotic Liquids	1	13	$10.00	$10.00	$10
Condiments	Forêts d'érables	1	113	$28.50	$28.50	$28
Condiments	Grandma Kelly's Homestead	2	126	$40.00	$25.00	$32
Condiments	Leka Trading	1	27	$19.45	$19.45	$19
Condiments	Mayumi's	1	39	$15.50	$15.50	$15
Condiments	New Orleans Cajun Delights	4	133	$22.00	$17.00	$20 ▼

Record: 14 ◀ 1 ▶ ▶I ▶* of 49

This gives you the total charge per product, but what if you want to know the total charge for the entire invoice? You can calculate this by applying the Sum operation to the calculated field that's based on the previous expression. Also, because Order Details usually includes a number of records for each invoice, you need to group the records by the unique OrderID field to get the per-invoice total. Figure 4.11 shows a query with this setup, and Figure 4.12 shows the results. (For good measure, the query also displays the customer and order date from the joined Orders table and displays the total units in each order.)

Figure 4.11
To calculate the total charge for each invoice, apply the Sum operation to the calculated Extended Price field and group the Order Details records by OrderID.

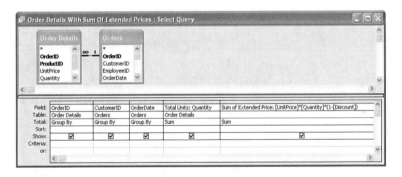

4

Figure 4.12
The dynaset produced by the query in Figure 4.11.

Order ID	Customer	Order Date	Total Units	Sum of Extended Price
10248	Wilman Kala	04-Jul-1996	27	$440.00
10249	Tradição Hipermercados	05-Jul-1996	49	$1,863.40
10250	Hanari Carnes	08-Jul-1996	60	$1,552.60
10251	Victuailles en stock	08-Jul-1996	41	$654.06
10252	Suprêmes délices	09-Jul-1996	105	$3,597.90
10253	Hanari Carnes	10-Jul-1996	102	$1,444.80
10254	Chop-suey Chinese	11-Jul-1996	57	$556.62
10255	Richter Supermarkt	12-Jul-1996	110	$2,490.50
10256	Wellington Importadora	15-Jul-1996	27	$517.80
10257	HILARIÓN-Abastos	16-Jul-1996	46	$1,119.90
10258	Ernst Handel	17-Jul-1996	121	$1,614.88
10259	Centro comercial Moctezuma	18-Jul-1996	11	$100.80
10260	Old World Delicatessen	19-Jul-1996	102	$1,504.65
10261	Que Delícia	19-Jul-1996	40	$448.00

Record: 14 ◀ 1 ▶ ▶I ▶* of 830

Access Converts the Query

If you apply an aggregate operation to a calculated field in the manner shown in Figure 4.11 and then close and reopen the query, you'll see that Access has changed the calculated field by "moving" the aggregate operation into the field's expression and changing the `Total` cell to `Expression`. Access has converted the totals query so that it uses an aggregate *function*. See the next section for an explanation of the aggregate functions.

Creating a Totals Query Using Aggregate Functions

The collection of Access built-in functions also includes a category called *SQL Aggregate* that includes all the mathematical aggregate operations. There are nine aggregate functions in all, as shown in Table 4.2.

Table 4.2   Aggregate Functions Available for Totals Queries

Function	Returns
`Avg(field)`	The average of the values in `field`.
`Sum(field)`	The sum of the values in `field`.
`Min(field)`	The smallest value in `field`.
`Max(field)`	The largest value in `field`.
`Count(field)`	The number of values in `field`.
`StDev(field)`	The standard deviation of the values in `field`, where those values are a sample of a larger population.
`StDevP(field)`	The standard deviation of the values in `field`, where those values represent the entire population.
`Var(field)`	The variance of the values in `field`, where those values are a sample of a larger population.
`VarP(field)`	The variance of the values in `field`, where those values represent the entire population.

The most straightforward way to use an aggregate function is to apply it to a single field using an expression in the `Field` cell instead of entering an operation in the `Total` cell. For example, instead of clicking `Sum` in the `Total` cell of the UnitsInStock field, you can use the expression in the `Field` cell (see Figure 4.13):

`Sum([UnitsInStock])`

The advantage here is that you don't need to display the `Total` row, so your query is a little less cluttered. (In fact, you *must* turn off the totals to use this method; otherwise, Access will convert the `Sum` function to a `Sum` aggregate operation.)

Figure 4.13
This query uses the Sum function to calculate the sum of the UnitsInStock field without using the Total row.

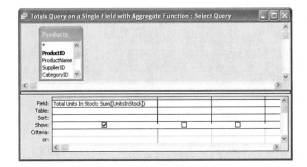

You can also include in the query other calculated fields that use aggregate functions. For example, if you also want to know the maximum unit price, you can create a second calculated field that uses the following aggregate expression:

```
Max([UnitPrice])
```

Combining Aggregate Functions and Totals

The problem with using the aggregate functions without the Total row is that there's no function that's equivalent to the Group By operation, so you can't group the records. If you need to use the Group By operation, or if you want to filter the records before the aggregate calculation by using the Where operation, you need to use the Totals feature.

This means you can't apply the aggregate functions on a single field, because Access will just convert the function to an operation in the Total row. However, it does mean that you're free to create *custom totals*. These are totals that you create yourself by building expressions that combine one or more aggregate functions with the other query operators and operands. This is a calculated field, so you enter the expression in the Field cell. Note, too, that you must also choose Expression in the Total cell. Figure 4.14 shows the query from Figure 4.11 converted to use the following aggregate function expression:

```
Sum([UnitPrice] * [Quantity] * (1 - [Discount]))
```

Figure 4.14
The Sum of Extended Price calculated field uses the Sum function in the Field cell and Expression in the Total cell.

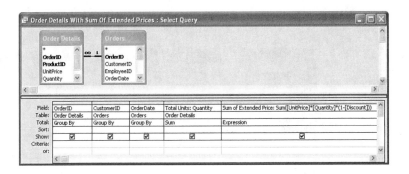

Calculating Units Left In Stock

If you manage inventory, you always need to know how many units of each product you have left in stock. You might take a physical inventory once or twice a year, but in between these counts you still need to keep tabs on the stock in case you need to reorder. The easiest way to do that is to take the existing number of units in stock and subtract the day's order quantities. The result is the number of units left in stock. Figure 4.15 shows a query set up to make this calculation using the Northwind sample database.

Figure 4.15
This query uses a custom total to calculate the number of units left in stock after subtracting a day's orders from the current inventory.

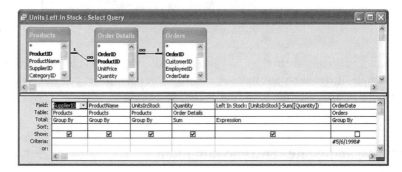

Following are some features of this query to note:

- In case a reorder is necessary, the records are grouped first by SupplierID and then by ProductName (both from the Products table).
- The query also includes the UnitsInStock field and the Sum of the Quantity field from Order Details.
- The Left In Stock calculated field is set up with the Expression operation in the Total cell and uses the following expression in the Field cell to create a custom total:
  `[UnitsInStock] - Sum([Quantity])`
- The records are filtered to include only those orders from a specific date, using the Where operation applied to the nonaggregate OrderDate field.

Figure 4.16 shows the results.

Figure 4.16
The dynaset produced by the query in Figure 4.15.

Supplier	Product Name	Units In Stock	SumOfQuantity	Left In Stock
Exotic Liquids	Aniseed Syrup	13	4	9
Exotic Liquids	Chang	17	34	-17
New Orleans Cajun Delights	Chef Anton's Cajun Seasoning	53	1	52
New Orleans Cajun Delights	Louisiana Hot Spiced Okra	4	1	3
Grandma Kelly's Homestead	Grandma's Boysenberry Spread	120	21	99
Grandma Kelly's Homestead	Northwoods Cranberry Sauce	6	2	4
Grandma Kelly's Homestead	Uncle Bob's Organic Dried Pears	15	1	14
Tokyo Traders	Ikura	31	1	30
Cooperativa de Quesos 'Las Cabras'	Queso Manchego La Pastora	86	2	84
Mayumi's	Konbu	24	4	20
Mayumi's	Tofu	35	21	14
Pavlova, Ltd.	Pavlova	29	16	13
Specialty Biscuits, Ltd.	Sir Rodney's Marmalade	40	1	39
Specialty Biscuits, Ltd.	Teatime Chocolate Biscuits	25	10	15

Record: 14 ◄ 1 ► ►I ►* of 27

Creating Queries That Make Decisions

Besides the usual tasks of sorting, filtering, and calculating, queries are also useful for analyzing data. For example, the query from the previous section returned the number of units left in stock. If you see a negative number returned, obviously a product is going to be back-ordered, so you need to contact the supplier right away. However, some products also have a specified *reorder level*, which is the minimum number of units that need to be in stock before the product is reordered. So rather than waiting for the stock to get to 0 (or less), you might reorder when it gets down to 25 units or 10 units, for instance.

A logical approach here would be to add the ReorderLevel field to the query and then compare the Units Left In Stock calculation with the reorder level. If the number of units remaining is less than or equal to the reorder level, you need to reorder the product; otherwise, you do nothing.

This approach will work, but it suffers from two drawbacks:

- It can be tedious and time-consuming if you have a lot of products.
- It's easy to make a mistake one way or the other (that is, to reorder a product that has sufficient stock or to miss reordering a product that is below the reorder threshold).

Making Decisions with the `IIf` Function

The solution to both problems is to get Access to make the decision for you. One of the secrets to this is a very handy function called `IIf` (which you read as "Inline If"). Here's the syntax:

```
IIf(logical_test, value_if_true, value_if_false)
```

`logical_test`	A logical expression; that is, an expression that returns `True` or `False`.
`value_if_true`	The value returned by the function if `logical_test` evaluates to `True`.
`value_if_false`	The value returned by the function if `logical_test` evaluates to `False`.

Let's start with a simple example:

```
IIf([UnitsInStock]) = 0, "Reorder", "Don't reorder")
```

The logical test is the expression `[UnitsInStock] = 0`. If this returns `True`, the function returns the string value `"Reorder"`; otherwise, it returns the string value `"Don't reorder"`. The idea is that you use this function as the expression for a calculated field, as shown in Figure 4.17. This creates a field that, when you run the query, displays either `"Reorder"` or `"Don't reorder"` for each product, as shown in Figure 4.18.

4

Figure 4.17
This query uses the `IIf` function to test whether the UnitsInStock field is 0.

Simple Products Reorder Check : Select Query

Supplier	Product Name	Units In Stock	Reorder Product
Exotic Liquids	Chai	39	Don't reorder
Exotic Liquids	Chang	17	Don't reorder
Exotic Liquids	Aniseed Syrup	13	Don't reorder
New Orleans Cajun Delights	Chef Anton's Cajun Seasoning	53	Don't reorder
New Orleans Cajun Delights	Chef Anton's Gumbo Mix	0	Reorder
Grandma Kelly's Homestead	Grandma's Boysenberry Spread	120	Don't reorder
Grandma Kelly's Homestead	Uncle Bob's Organic Dried Pears	15	Don't reorder
Grandma Kelly's Homestead	Northwoods Cranberry Sauce	6	Don't reorder
Tokyo Traders	Mishi Kobe Niku	29	Don't reorder
Tokyo Traders	Ikura	31	Don't reorder
Cooperativa de Quesos 'Las Cabras'	Queso Cabrales	22	Don't reorder
Cooperativa de Quesos 'Las Cabras'	Queso Manchego La Pastora	86	Don't reorder
Mayumi's	Konbu	24	Don't reorder
Mayumi's	Tofu	35	Don't reorder
Mayumi's	Genen Shouyu	39	Don't reorder
Pavlova, Ltd.	Pavlova	29	Don't reorder
Pavlova, Ltd.	Alice Mutton	0	Reorder

Record: 1 of 77

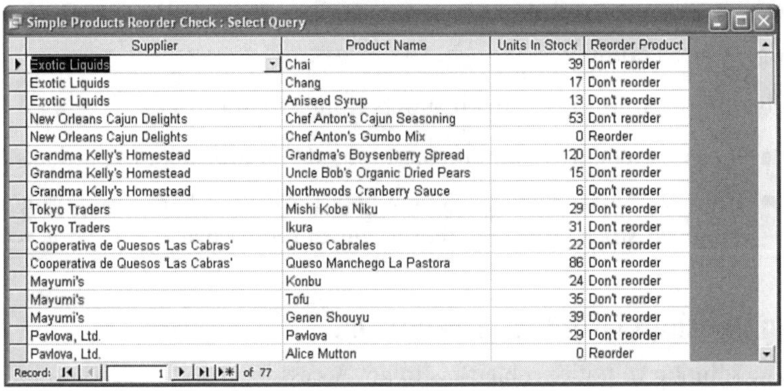

Figure 4.18
The dynaset produced by the query in Figure 4.17.

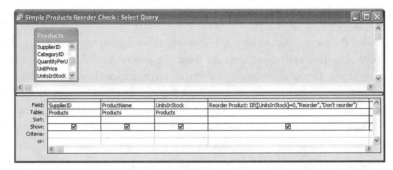

Determining Whether Stock Needs to Be Reordered

A more realistic example takes into account the day's orders by subtracting them from the current stock and then comparing the result with the product's reorder level:

```
IIf([UnitsInStock] - Sum([Quantity]) <= [ReorderLevel], "Yes", "No")
```

If the units left in stock are less than or equal to the reorder level, the function returns the string `"Yes"`; otherwise, it returns `"No"`. As you can see in Figure 4.19, I've used this expression as the basis for the calculated Reorder field, and I've also set the field's criteria to `"Yes"` so that the query returns the records for only those products that need ordering, as shown in Figure 4.20.

Making Decisions with the `Switch` Function

The `IIf` function is certainly very useful, but it's limited by the fact that it can perform only a single logical text. You can get around that to a certain extent by using the `And` or `Or` operators. For example, suppose an order qualifies for a bonus discount only if the total quantity is at least 50 units *and* the order total is at least $1,000. Here's a simplified version of the required logical test:

```
If Quantity >= 50 And Total >= 1000
```

Figure 4.19
This query uses the IIf function to test whether the number of units left in stock is at or below the reorder level.

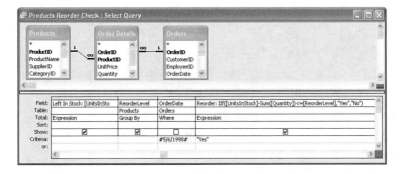

Figure 4.20
The dynaset produced by the query in Figure 4.19.

Here's an actual IIf function that tests for this:

```
IIf(Sum([Quantity]) >= 50 And
➡Sum([UnitPrice] * [Quantity] * (1 - [Discount])) >= 1000, 0.05, 0)
```

Similarly, suppose an order qualifies for a bonus discount only if the total quantity is at least 50 units *or* the order total is at least $1,000. Here's an IIf function that tests for this:

```
IIf(Sum([Quantity]) >= 50 Or
➡Sum([UnitPrice] * [Quantity] * (1 - [Discount])) >= 1000, 0.05, 0)
```

This is a powerful idea, but you're still performing only a single logical test and then returning one of two values depending on whether the result is True or False.

For more complex situations, you need a tool that can run multiple tests and return multiple values depending on the result. Fortunately, Access comes with just the thing—the Switch function:

```
Switch(test1, value1 [, test2, value2, ...])
```

test1	A logical expression; that is, an expression that returns True or False.
value1	The value returned by the function if *test1* evaluates to True.
test2	A logical expression; that is, an expression that returns True or False.
value2	The value returned by the function if *test2* evaluates to True.

For example, Northwind's Shippers table lists three shipping companies: Speedy Express (ShipperID = 1), United Package (ShipperID = 2), and Federal Shipping (ShipperID = 3). Suppose that each company charges based on the total value of an order, and the charges are 5%, 10%, and 15%, respectively. The freight charge formula will look something like this:

```
Total * Shipping Charge
```

Calculating the Shipping Charge portion is a perfect task for the Switch function:

```
Switch([ShipperID] = 1, .05, [ShipperID] = 2, .1, [ShipperID] = 3, .15)
```

If ShipperID is 1 (Speedy Express), the function returns .05; if ShipperID is 2 (United Package), the function returns .1; if ShipperID is 3 (Federal Shipping), the function returns .15.

Running Action Queries

All the queries you've worked with to date have been *select queries*. A select query is one in which Access uses the query criteria to select the matching rows from a table or join. However, Access has several other query types that are designed to perform actions on the data, such as changing values, adding records, deleting records, and writing records to a new table. These so-called *action queries* are the subject of the next four sections.

Modifying Table Data with an Update Query

Access, like many programs, has a Replace command that enables you to substitute one piece of text for another either in certain records or throughout a table. Although this command often comes in handy, there are some jobs it simply can't handle. For example, what if you want to replace the contents of a field with a new value, but only for records that meet certain criteria? Or what if your table includes price data and you want to increase all the prices by 5%?

For these tasks, you need a more sophisticated tool: an *update query*. Unlike a select query, which only displays a subset of the table, an update query actually makes changes to the table data. The idea is that you select a field to work with, specify the new field value, set up some criteria (this is optional), and then run the query. Access flashes through the table and changes the field entries to the new value. If you enter criteria, only records that match the criteria are updated.

To create and run an update query, follow these steps:

1. Create a select query that includes the field (or fields) you want to update and the field (or fields) you'll need for the criteria. (Remember, criteria are optional for an update query. If you leave them out, Access updates every record in the table.)

2. When the select query is complete, run it to make sure the criteria are working properly.

Handle with Care

Update queries can save you a great deal of time, but they must be approached with caution. After you run an update query, Access offers no direct method for undoing the operation. Therefore, *always* start off with a select query to make sure your criteria are doing what they're supposed to do. If your data is particularly precious, consider making a temporary copy of the table before running the update query. (To copy a table, click it in the database window, press Ctrl+C, and then press Ctrl+V. In the Paste Table As dialog box, enter a name for the backup table, make sure the Structure and Data option is clicked, and then choose OK.)

3. Convert the query to an update query by choosing Query, Update Query. (Alternatively, on the toolbar's Query Type drop-down list, click Update Query.) Access changes the query window's title bar to Update Query, removes the Sort and Show rows from the design grid, and replaces them with an Update To row (see Figure 4.21).

Query Type

Figure 4.21
When you convert a select query to an update query, Access replaces the design grid's Sort and Show rows with an Update To row.

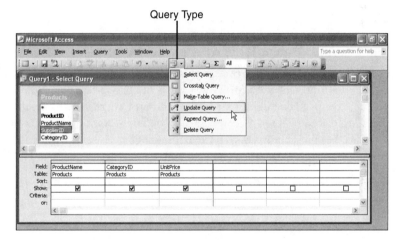

4. In the Update To cell for the field you want to change, enter the new value.

5. Run the query. Access displays a dialog box to tell you how many rows (records) will be updated.

6. Choose Yes to perform the update.

After you see what update queries can do, you'll wonder how you ever got along without them. For example, one common table chore is changing prices and, in a large table, it's a drudgery most of us can live without. However, if you're increasing prices by a certain percentage, you can automate the whole process with an update query.

In Northwind's Products table, suppose you want to increase each value in the UnitPrice field by 5%. To handle this in an update query, you add the UnitPrice field to the design grid and then enter the following expression in the Update To cell:

```
[UnitPrice] * 1.05
```

This expression tells Access that you want every UnitPrice field entry increased by 5%. You can also set up criteria to gain even more control over the update. Figure 4.22 shows an update query that raises the UnitPrice field by 5%, but only for those records where the CategoryID field is 1.

Figure 4.22
This update query increases the UnitPrice values by 5% for those products where CategoryID equals 1.

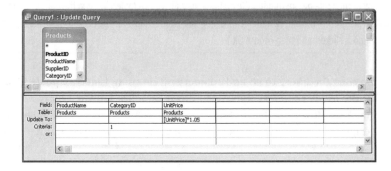

Removing Records from a Table with a Delete Query

If you need to delete one or two records from a table, it's easy enough to select each record and choose Edit, Delete Record. But what if you have a large chunk of records to get rid of? For example, you might want to clean out an Orders table by deleting any old orders that were placed before a certain date. Or you might want to delete records for products that have been discontinued. In both examples, you can set up criteria to identify the group of records to delete. You then enter the criteria in a delete query and Access will delete all the matching records.

Follow these steps to create and run a delete query:

1. Create a select query that includes the asterisk "field" (the asterisk represents the entire table) and any field you need for your deletion criteria.

2. Enter the criteria and then run the select query to make sure the query is picking out the correct records.

3. Convert the select query to a delete query by choosing Query, Delete Query. (You can also use the toolbar's Query Type list to click Delete Query.) The title bar changes to Delete Query and Access replaces the design grid's Sort and Show lines with a Delete line. The asterisk field will display From in the Delete cell and each criteria field will display Where in the Delete cell. Figure 4.23 shows a delete query for the Products table that removes all the records where the Discontinued field is set to True.

4. Run the query. Access analyzes the criteria and then displays a dialog box telling you how many records you'll be deleting.

5. Choose Yes to proceed with the deletion.

Figure 4.23
A delete query uses the asterisk field and any fields you need for your criteria.

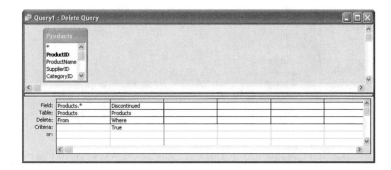

Delete Carefully!
If anything, the delete query is even more dangerous than the update query because the records you delete are gone for good and nothing can bring them back. Again, setting up and running a select query first is an easy way to avoid wiping out anything important. (Remember, too, that you can always make a temporary copy of any table that contains particularly important data.)

Creating New Tables with Make-Table Queries

The results of select queries are called *dynasets* because they're dynamic subsets of the table data. When I say "dynamic," I mean that if you edit the query records, the corresponding records in the table also change. Similarly, if you edit the table, Access changes the query records automatically.

This is usually welcome behavior because at least you know you're always working with the most up-to-date information. However, there might be the odd time when this is not the behavior you want. For example, at the end of the month or the end of the fiscal year, you might want some of your tables to be "frozen" while you tie things up at month's or year's end (this applies particularly to tables that track invoices).

Instead of letting the new work pile up until the table can be released, Access lets you create a table from an existing one. You can then use the new table for your month-end duties, so the old table doesn't need to be held up. You do this using a *make-table* query.

Here are the steps to follow to create and run a make-table query:

1. Create a select query that includes the fields you want to include in the new table as well as the field (or fields) you need for the criteria. (The criteria are optional for a make-table query. If you leave them out, Access includes every record in the new table.)
2. When the select query is complete, run it to make sure the criteria are working properly.
3. Convert the query to a make-table query by choosing Query, Make-Table Query. (Alternatively, on the toolbar's Query Type drop-down list, click Make-Table Query.) Access displays the Make Table dialog box, shown in Figure 4.24.

Figure 4.24
Use the Make Table dialog
box to define your new
table.

4. Use the Table Name text box to enter the name you want to use for the new table.

5. To create the table in the same database, click Current Database. If you prefer to add the table to an external database, click Another Database and enter the path and file-name of the database in the File Name text box.

6. Click OK.

7. Run the query. Access displays a dialog box to tell you how many rows (records) will be added to the new table.

8. Choose Yes to create the new table.

Adding Records to a Table with an Append Query

Instead of creating an entirely new table, you might prefer to add records from one table to an existing table. You can accomplish this with an *append query*.

Follow these steps to create and run an append query:

1. Create a select query that includes the fields you want to include in the appended records as well as the field (or fields) you need for the criteria. (The criteria are optional for a make-table query. If you leave them out, Access appends every record to the other table.)

2. When the select query is complete, run it to make sure the criteria are working prop-erly.

3. Convert the query to an append query by choosing Query, Append Query. (Alternatively, on the toolbar's Query Type drop-down list, click Append Query.) Access displays the Append dialog box, which is identical to the Make Table dialog box shown in Figure 4.24.

4. Use the Table Name text box to enter the name of the table to which you want the records appended.

5. If the other table is in the same database, click Current Database. If the other table is in an external database, click Another Database and enter the path and filename of the database in the File Name text box.

6. Click OK. Access adds an Append To row to the design grid.

7. For each field in the design grid, use the Append To cell to choose the field in the other table to use for the append operation.

Using the Asterisk Field

If you add the asterisk field to the design grid, its `Append To` cell will show the name of the other table. In this case, if you add other fields for criteria purposes, make sure these fields have their `Append To` cells blank.

---

8. Run the query. Access displays a dialog box to tell you how many rows (records) will be appended to the table.

9. Choose Yes to append the records.

Preventing Form Errors by Validating Data

If, as the cooks say, a recipe is only as good as its ingredients, a database is only as good as its data. Viewing, summarizing, and analyzing the data are meaningless if the table you're working with contains erroneous or improper data. For basic data errors (for example, entering the wrong date or transposing a number's digits), there's not a lot you can do other than exhorting yourself or the people who use your forms to enter data carefully. Fortunately, you have a bit more control when it comes to preventing improper data entry. By "improper," I mean data that falls into either of the following categories:

- Data that is the wrong type. For example, entering a text string in a cell that requires a number.

- Data that falls outside of an allowable range. For example, entering 200 in a cell that requires a number between 1 and 100.

The next few sections show you several techniques that can help you reduce these types of errors.

Helping Users with Text Prompts

You can prevent improper entries to a certain extent by adding text that provides details on what is allowable inside a particular cell. You have two choices:

- Add status bar text—This is a string that appears in the Access status bar when users enter the field. You specify this text by opening the field's property sheet, displaying the Other tab, and then entering the string in the Status Bar Text property.

- Add a label—Place a Label control near the field and use it to enter text that describes the field's data requirements or shortcut keys. For example, if the field requires a date, the label might say `Press Ctrl+; to enter today's date`.

For instance, Figure 4.25 shows a form used as a Mortgage Calculator. Notice the labels added beside the Interest Rate and Term text boxes that specify to the users that they must enter the interest rate per annum and the term in years. Note, too, the status bar text that appears when the users enter the Interest Rate field.

Figure 4.25
Use form labels and status bar text to give the users text prompts about the data they must enter.

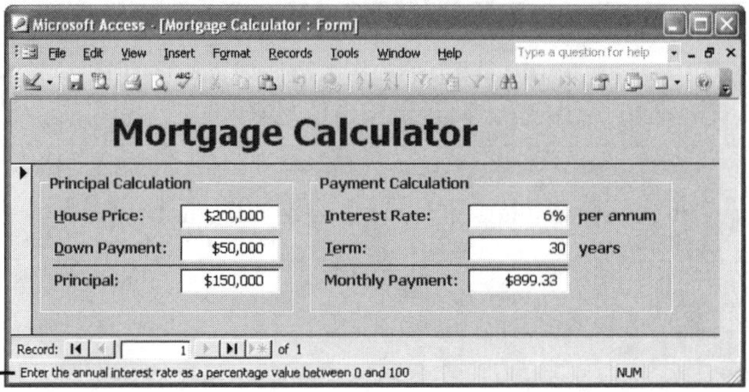

Status bar prompt

Preventing Errors with Data Validation Expressions

The problem with text prompts is they require other people to both read *and* act on the text. The better solution for preventing data-entry errors is the Access data validation feature. With data validation, you create rules that specify exactly what kind of data can be entered and in what range that data can fall. You can also specify pop-up input messages that appear when a cell is selected, as well as error messages that appear when data is entered improperly.

Follow these steps to define the settings for a data validation rule:

1. Display the property sheet of the field to which you want to apply the data validation rule.

2. Display the Data tab.

3. Click inside the Validation Rule property.

4. Enter a formula that specifies the validation criteria. You can either enter the formula directly into the property box or you can click the ellipsis (…) button and enter the formula using the Expression Builder.

5. If you want a dialog box to appear when the users enter invalid data, click inside the Validation Text property and then specify the message that appears.

6. Close the property sheet to apply the data validation rule.

For example, suppose you want the users to enter an interest rate. This should be a positive quantity, of course, but it should also be less than 1. (That is, you want to users to enter 6% as 0.06 instead of 6.) Figure 4.26 shows the property sheet for a field named InterestRate that meets these criteria by defining the following expression in the Validation Rule property:

```
>0 And <1
```

Figure 4.26
Use the Validation Rule property to enter a data validation expression for a field.

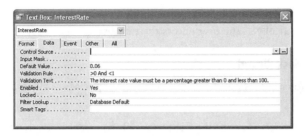

Figure 4.26 also shows a string in the Validation Text property. If the users enter invalid data (that is, any value for which the Validation Rule expression returns False), the Validation Text appears in a dialog box, as shown in Figure 4.27.

Figure 4.27
If the users enter invalid data in the field, Access displays a dialog box such as this one, which uses the string entered into the Validation Text property.

Using Input Masks for Consistent and Accurate Data Entry

One of the major headaches that database administrators have to deal with is data entered in an inconsistent way. For example, consider the following phone numbers:

```
(123)555-6789
(123)  555-6789
(123)5556789
123555-6789
1235556789
```

These kinds of inconsistencies might appear trivial, but they can cause all kinds of problems, from other users misreading the data, to improper sorting, to difficulties analyzing or querying the data. And it isn't just phone numbers that cause problems. You also see them with social security numbers, ZIP Codes, dates, times, account numbers, and more.

One way to avoid such inconsistencies is to add a label or status bar message that specifies the correct format to use. As with data validation, however, these prompts are not guaranteed to work every time (or even most of the time).

A better solution is to apply an *input mask* to the field. An input mask is a kind of template that shows users how to enter the data and prevents them from entering incorrect characters (such as a letter where a number is required). For example, here's an input mask for a phone number:

```
(___)___-____
```

Each underscore (_) acts as a placeholder for (in this case) a digit, and the parentheses and dash appear automatically as the user enters the number.

Using the Input Mask Wizard

The easiest way to create an input mask is to use the Input Mask Wizard. Here are the steps to follow:

1. Display the property sheet of the field to which you want to apply the input data.
2. Display the Data tab.
3. Click inside the Input Mask property.
4. Click the ellipsis (...) button to start the Input Mask Wizard, shown in Figure 4.28.

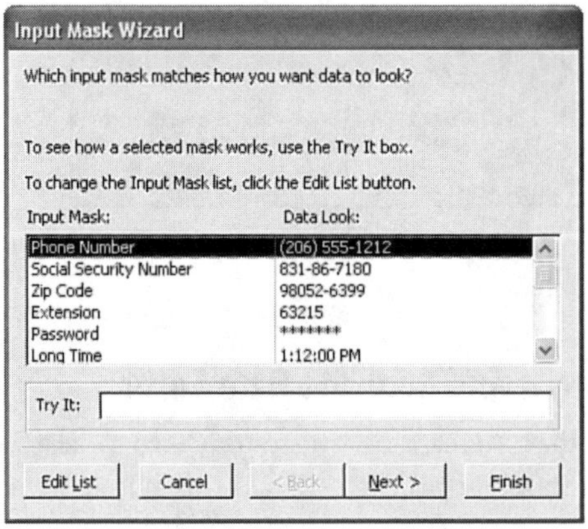

Figure 4.28
Use the Input Mask Wizard to choose a predefined input mask or to create your own input mask.

5. In the Input Mask list, click the input mask you want (or one that's close to what you want) and then click Next.
6. Use the Input Mask box to make changes to the mask (see "Creating a Custom Input Mask Expression" in the next section, for the specifics of which symbols to use), use the Placeholder Character list to choose the character you want to appear in the input mask as a placeholder, and then click Next.
7. Click the option that matches how you want the field data stored in the table (click Next after you've made your choice):
   - With the Symbols in the Mask—Click this option if you want the extra symbols (such as the parentheses and dash in a phone number mask) stored along with the data.
   - Without the Symbols in the Mask—Click this option to store only the data.
8. Click Finish.

Creating a Custom Input Mask Expression

If your data doesn't fit any of the predefined input masks, you need to create a custom mask that suits your needs. You do this by creating an expression that consists of three kinds of characters:

- Data placeholders—These characters are replaced by the actual data typed by the users. The different placeholders specify the type of character the users must enter (such as a digit or letter) and whether the character is optional or required.
- Modifiers—These characters aren't displayed in the mask; instead, they're used to modify the mask in some way (such as converting all the entered characters to lowercase).
- Literals—These are extra characters that appear in the mask the same as you enter them in the expression. For example, you might use parentheses as literals to surround the area code portion of a phone number.

Table 4.3 lists the data placeholders you can use to build your input mask expressions.

Table 4.3   Data Placeholders to Use for Custom Input Masks

Placeholder	Data Type	Description
0	Digit (0–9)	The character is required; the users are not allowed to include a plus sign (+) or a minus sign (–).
9	Digit or space	The character is optional; the users are not allowed to include a plus sign (+) or a minus sign (–).
#	Digit or space	The character is optional; the users are allowed to include a plus sign (+) or minus sign (–).
L	Letter (a–z or A–Z)	The character is required.
?	Letter (a–z or A–Z)	The character is optional.
a	Letter or digit	The character is required.
A	Letter or digit	The character is optional.
&	Any character or space	The character is required.
C	Any character or space	The character is optional.

Table 4.4 lists the modifiers and literals you can use to build your input mask expressions.

Table 4.4   Modifiers and Literals to Use for Custom Input Masks

Modifier	Description
\	Displays the following character as a literal; for example, \(is displayed as (.
"*text*"	Displays the string *text* as a literal; for example, "MB" is displayed as MB.

continues

Table 4.4	Continued
Modifier	**Description**
.	Decimal separator.
,	Thousands separator.
: ; - /	Date and time separators.
<	Displays all the following letters as lowercase.
>	Displays all the following letters as uppercase.
!	Displays the input mask from right to left when you have optional data placeholders on the left.
Password	Displays the characters as asterisks so that other people can't read the data.

You can enter your input mask expressions directly into the Input Mask property, or you can modify a predefined input mask using the Input Mask Wizard.

For example, suppose your company uses account numbers that consist of four uppercase letters and four digits, with a dash (–) in between. Here's an input mask suitable for entering such numbers:

```
>aaaa\-0000
```

Note, too, that input masks can contain up to three sections separated by semicolons (;):

```
first;second;third
```

> *first*—This section holds the input mask expression.
>
> *second*—This optional section specifies whether Access stores the literals in the table when you enter data. Use 0 to include the literals; use 1 (or nothing) to store only the data.
>
> *third*—This optional section specifies the placeholder character. The default is the underscore (_).

For example, following is an input mask for a ZIP Code that stores the dash separator and displays dots (.) as placeholders:

```
00000\-9999;0;.
```

Using Form Controls to Limit Data-Entry Choices

Data entry always trips over two unfortunate facts of life: humans are fallible creatures and typing is an error-prone activity. Expert data-entry operators can't achieve 100% accuracy (although some come remarkably close), and the rest of us can only hope for the best. In short, if your form relies on other people (or yourself, for that matter) typing in field values, it's death-and-taxes certain that your table will end up with errors.

It stands to reason, then, that you can greatly reduce the number of errors by greatly reducing the amount of typing. The best way to do that is by taking advantage of controls to generate field values automatically. Here are some examples:

- If you have a Yes/No field that uses a text box, the users must enter the unintuitive values –1 (for Yes) and 0 (for No). A more intuitive approach is to use a check box (or toggle button) that the users either activate (for Yes) or clear (for No).

- Suppose you have a field that can take only one of a small set of values (say, two to five). For example, an invoice form might offer the users three choices for freight or four choices for credit cards. Again, rather than having the users type the freight choice or credit card name, you can populate the form with option buttons representing the choices.

- Suppose you have a field that can take one of a relatively large set of values (more than five). For example, the field might hold a customer name or a product name. Rather than making the users look up (time-consuming) and then type (inaccurate) the value, it's both faster and more accurate to place all the possible values into a drop-down list.

This section shows you how to use check boxes, toggle buttons, option buttons, lists, and other controls to build faster and more accurate forms. In each case, the idea is to move the users away from typing values and toward selecting them via a familiar and easily used control.

4

Avoid Form Complacency

This is as good a place as any to warn you against what I call "form complacency." This is the attitude (which I've succumbed to myself on many an occasion) that assumes that after *you* are happy with your form's layout, format, and data validation, other people will automatically be happy with those things, too. Probably not! Other people will almost certainly approach the form differently, and they'll almost always have trouble figuring out how it works and what's expected of them. In other words, *always* "test drive" your form by letting other users take their best shots at it. It takes only a little extra time, and the suggested changes they come up with (and there *will* be suggestions, believe me) will save you time in the long run. Better yet, ask your future users in advance (that is, while you're contemplating the form's design) what features and layout they prefer.

Working with Yes/No Fields

Use Yes/No fields in tables when you have a quantity that you can represent in one of two states: on (Yes, True, or –1) or off (No, False, or 0).

When you create a Yes/No field in the table's Design view, the Display Control property (it's in the Lookup tab) defaults to Check Box. This means that when you add a Yes/No field to a form, Access automatically represents the field with a check box control (along with a label that displays the name of the field or the field's Caption property). However, it's possible that the Display Control property has been set to Text Box, either by design or by accident. As I mentioned earlier, you want to avoid users having to enter –1 or 0 into a text box, so you should never use a text box for a Yes/No field on your forms. Instead, you have two choices:

- If you have access to the table's design, change the Yes/No field's Display Control property to Check Box. After you've done that, return to the form, delete the Yes/No field's text box and label (if they're already on the form), and then add the field back to the form to get the check box version.
- If you can't change the table design, use a check box or toggle button control bound to the Yes/No field. The next two sections show you how to do this.

Using Check Boxes

Here are the steps to follow to insert a check box and bind it to a Yes/No field:

1. Click the Check Box button in the Toolbox.
2. Draw the check box on the form.
3. Edit the text of the label control that Access adds to the right of the check box. (For clarity, it's best to use the name of the Yes/No field.)
4. Click the check box and then click View, Properties.
5. In the Data tab, use the Control Source property to choose the name of the Yes/No field you want bound to the check box.
6. In the Default Value property, enter the initial value for new records: Yes, True, or –1; or No, False, or 0.

Option Groups and Check Boxes

Many form designers like to use an option group as a way of "framing" a number of related controls. This is often a good idea, but you need to be careful: If you add the option group and then insert the check boxes within the group, Access treats the check boxes as mutually exclusive options. That is, the users can activate only one check box at a time. To avoid this, add the check boxes to the frame first, and then draw the option group around them.

It's worth pointing out here that check boxes (and toggle buttons, discussed next) can insert only one of two values into a field: –1 or 0. You can't use a check box for other two-state choices, such as "male" and "female" or "Pepsi" and "Coke". For fields that can take only one of two values other than 0 and –1, use option buttons, instead (as described later in this chapter).

Using Toggle Buttons

A toggle button is a cross between a check box and a command button: Click it once and the button stays pressed; click it again and the button returns to its normal state. The button can either display a caption or a picture. Here are the steps to follow to insert a toggle button and bind it to a Yes/No field:

1. Click the Toggle button in the Toolbox.
2. Draw the toggle button on the form.
3. Click View, Properties to display the toggle button's property sheet.
4. In the Format tab, you have two choices that determine what appears on the face of the button:

   Caption—Use this property to specify text that appears on the face of the button. (For clarity, it's best to use the name of the Yes/No field.)

   Picture—Use this property to specify an image that appears on the button face. Click the ellipsis button (...) to display the Picture Builder dialog box, shown in Figure 4.29. Either use the Available Pictures list to click an image, or click Browse to choose an image from the Select Picture dialog box.

Figure 4.29
Use the Picture Builder dialog box to choose an image to appear on the face of the toggle button.

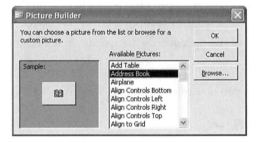

5. In the Data tab, use the Control Source property to choose the name of the Yes/No field you want bound to the toggle button.
6. In the Default Value property, enter the initial value for new records. For the "pressed" state, use Yes, True, or –1; for the "unpressed" state, use No, False, or 0.

Using Option Buttons to Present a Limited Number of Choices

Option buttons are a good choice if the underlying field accepts only a limited number of possible numbers: at least two, but no more than about five or six. (If you have more possible values, use a list box or combo box, discussed later in this chapter.)

How does having multiple option buttons on a form enable you to store a single value in a field? There are two components to consider:

- The option buttons—You assign each option button a value from among the list of possible values that the field can take.

Numeric Fields Only
Option button values must be numeric. Therefore, you can use only option groups and option buttons with numeric fields.

- The option group—This is a separate control that you use to organize the option buttons. That is, if you insert multiple option buttons inside a group, Access allows the users to activate only one of the options at a time. (You can also use check boxes or toggle buttons, but option buttons are best because most users are familiar with them and know how to operate them.)

The option group is bound to the field in the underlying table. Therefore, when you activate an option button, the value assigned to that button is stored in the field. This form of data entry brings many advantages to the table (literally!):

- It's quick—The users don't have to look up the possible values elsewhere.
- It's accurate—The field value is stored "behind the scenes," so the users can't enter the wrong value.
- It's intuitive—The option button captions can be as long as you like (within reason), so you can provide users with a helpful description or title for each option.
- It's familiar—All Windows users know how to operate option buttons, so no extra training is required.

The next two sections show you how to create option buttons using a wizard and by hand.

Running the Option Group Wizard

The easiest way to create an option group and its associated option buttons is to use the Option Group Wizard, as described in the following steps:

1. Make sure the Control Wizards button is activated and then click the Option Group button in the Toolbox.
2. Draw the option group on the form. Access launches the Option Group Wizard.
3. For each option button you want, enter the label in the Label Names list and press Tab. When you're done, click Next.
4. To select a default choice (the option that is activated automatically when the users start a new record), leave the Yes, the Default Choice Is option activated and then choose the option label from the list. Click Next.
5. Use the Values column to assign a numeric value for each option, as shown in Figure 4.30. Note that each value must be unique. Click Next when you're done.
6. Specify where you want the option group value stored (click Next when you're done):

   Save the Value for Later Use—Click this option to have Access save the option group value.

   Store the Value in This Field—Click this option and then select a field from the list to have Access store the option group value in the field.
7. Click the type of control you want to use in the option group: Option Buttons, Check Boxes, or Toggle Buttons. You can also select the special effect used by the option group border (Etched, Flat, and so on). Click Next to continue.

Figure 4.30
Use this Option Group
Wizard dialog box to
assign a unique numeric
value to each option.

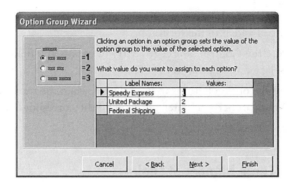

8. Edit the option group caption (the text that the users see along the top border of the option group frame—use the field name or something similar) and then click Finish to complete the wizard.

Handling an "Unframed" Option Button

If you already have an "unframed" option button on your form, you can still insert it into an option group. Just select the button, cut it to the Clipboard, select the option group (by clicking its frame), and paste. Access adds the button to the option group.

Creating an Option Group by Hand

If you'd rather create the option group yourself, here are the steps to follow:

1. Make sure the Control Wizards button is deactivated and then click the Option Group button in the Toolbox.
2. Draw the option group on the form.
3. Click Option Button in the Toolbox.
4. Draw the option button inside the option group.
5. Click View, Properties to display the option button's property sheet.
6. In the Data tab, use the Option Value property to specify the numeric value associated with the option.
7. Use the drop-down list to choose the label associated with the option button. (It's the control that is one number greater than the option button. For example, if the option button name assigned by Access is Option10, the associated label would be named Label11.)
8. In the Format tab, use the Caption property to specify text that appears alongside the option button.
9. Repeat steps 3–8 for the other option buttons you want to add to the option group.

10. Use the drop-down list to choose the option group (it's named Frame*n*, where *n* means it was the *n*th control added to the form).

11. In the Data tab, use the Control Source property to choose the field in which you want the value of the selected option button stored.

12. If you want one of the option buttons to be activated when the users start a new record, use the Default Value property to enter the value of the corresponding option button.

13. Close the property sheet.

Using Lists to Present a Large Number of Choices

Option buttons have three main disadvantages:

- If a field can take more than about five or six values, option buttons become too unwieldy and confusing for the users.

- Option buttons can't work with non-numeric values.

- Users can't enter unique values. This is normally a good thing, but there might be instances where you want to give the users the flexibility to choose either a predefined value or to enter a different value.

To solve all these problems, Access offers two list controls that enable you to present the users with a list of choices:

- A list box presents a list of choices. These choices are static, meaning that users can't enter any different values.

- A combo box enables users to either select a value from a drop-down list or (optionally) to enter a different value using the associated text box.

Consider the Size of the List Control

Another consideration you need to bear in mind when deciding between a list box and a combo box is the size of each control on the form. A list box is usually large enough to show at least three or four items in the list, whereas a combo box always shows only a single item (the users clicks the list to choose another). Therefore, the list box always takes up quite a bit more room than the combo box, so keep that in mind when designing your form. If you don't have much room, but you don't want the users to be able to add different values to the field, you'll see later that it's possible to restrict the combo box to only the values in the list.

In both cases, the item the users choose from the list (or the item the users enter in the combo box) is the value that gets stored in the bound field. This means that you can use list and combo boxes for any type of value, including numeric, string, and date values.

It's important to note that Access defaults to a combo box when you add to the form a field that is used as part of a relationship with another table. Specifically, if the relationship is one-to-many and the current table is the "many" side, adding the field that corresponds to the common field on the "one" side creates a list that contains all the values from that field.

For example, the Products table has a one-to-many relationship with the Order Details table via the common ProductID fields. If you're putting together a form based on the Order Details table and you add the ProductID field, Access creates a combo box list and populates it with the values from the Products table's ProductName field. (Why ProductName and not ProductID? Because in the design for the Order Details table, the ProductID field's Row Source property [in the Lookup tab] specifies an SQL statement that selects the ProductName field from the Products table.)

The next few sections show you various ways to work with both controls.

Starting the List Box or Combo Box Wizard

The List Box Wizard and Combo Box Wizard make it easy to create a bound list control. Here are the steps to follow to get started with these wizards:

1. Make sure the Control Wizards button is activated in the Toolbox.

2. Click one of the following controls in the Toolbox:

   • Combo Box

   • List Box

3. Draw the box on the form. Access starts either the List Box Wizard or the Combo Box Wizard.

These wizards work identically, but the steps you take vary dramatically depending on which option you choose in the initial dialog box. The next three sections take you through the details of each option.

Getting List Values from a Table or Query Field

The most common list scenario is to populate the list box or combo box with values from a field in a specified table or query. For example, if you're putting together an orders form, you'll probably want to include a list that contains all the customer names, so you'll populate the list with the values from the Customers table's CustomerName field.

The following steps show you how to continue with the List Box or Combo Box Wizard to populate a list with values from a table or query field:

1. In the first wizard dialog box, select the I Want the List Box to Look Up the Values in a Table or Query option and then click Next.

2. Select the table or query that contains the field you want to use for the list, and then click Next.

3. In the Available Fields list, select the field you want to use and then click > to add it to the Selected Fields list. Click Next.

4. If you want the list sorted, use the drop-down list to choose the field you selected, click the Ascending (or Descending) toggle button, and then click Next.

5. Click and drag the right edge of the column header to set the width of the list column, and then click Next.

6. To create a bound list box or combo box, select the Store That Value in This Field option, choose the field you want to use from the drop-down list, and then click Next.

7. In the final wizard dialog box, use the text box to edit the label text that appears above the list, and then click Finish.

Specifying Custom List Values

If the items you want to appear in your list exist in another table or query, you need to specify them by hand. Here are the steps to follow to continue with the List Box or Combo Box Wizard and populate a list with custom values:

1. In the first wizard dialog box, select the I Will Type in the Values That I Want option and then click Next.

2. For each value you want to add, type the item text and press Tab. Click Next when you're done.

3. To create a bound list box or combo box, select the Store That Value in This Field option, choose the field you want to use from the drop-down list, and then click Next.

4. In the final wizard dialog box, use the text box to edit the label text that appears above the list, and then click Finish.

Getting List Values from the Current Table

Sometimes the values you want in your list already exist in the form's underlying table or query. For example, if your form uses the Customers table, you might want to set up a list for the ContactTitle field and use the unique values in that to populate the list. (This is a good example of when you might want to use a combo box, because a new customer contact could have a title other than the ones in the list.)

The following steps show you how to continue with the List Box or Combo Box Wizard to populate a list with values from a field in the form's current data source:

1. In the first wizard dialog box, select the Find a Record on My Form Based on the Value I Selected in My Combo Box option, and then click Next.

2. In the Available Fields list, select the field you want to use and then click > to add it to the Selected Fields list. Click Next.

3. Click and drag the right edge of the column header to set the width of the list column, and then click Next.

4. In the final wizard dialog box, use the text box to edit the label text that appears above the list, and then click Finish.

Creating a Multiple-Column List

At times, displaying a single column of values in a list isn't enough. For example, if you're working with data from the Northwind Employees table, displaying only the ProductName field might not give the users enough information. Instead, you might also want to show the users the corresponding Category or Supplier value (using an inner join query) for each product.

You can do this by adding one or more columns to the list and then specifying which of those columns contains the value you want to store in your form's bound field. Here are the steps to follow:

1. Draw a list box or combo box on the form to launch the List Box or Combo Box Wizard.
2. In the first wizard dialog box, select the I Want the List Box to Look Up the Values in a Table or Query option and then click Next. (Note that you can also display multiple columns using the Find a Record on My Form Based on the Value I Selected in My Combo Box option.)
3. Select the table or query that contains the field you want to use for the list, and then click Next.
4. In the Available Fields list, for each field you want to display in the list, select the field and then click > to add it to the Selected Fields list. Click Next.
5. Sort the list on multiple fields by using separate drop-down lists to choose each field and its sort order. Click Next.
6. Click and drag the right edge of each column header to set the width of the list columns. Note, too, that you can also change the column order by clicking and dragging the column headers to the left or right. Click Next.
7. To create a bound list box or combo box, select the Store That Value in This Field option, choose the field you want to use from the drop-down list, and then click Next.
8. In the final wizard dialog box, use the text box to edit the label text that appears above the list, and then click Finish.

Figure 4.31 shows a form that uses a two-column combo box to display both the ProductName field and the CategoryName field from an inner join query of the Products and Categories tables.

Figure 4.31
By using an inner join query of the Products and Categories tables, this combo box displays both the ProductName field and the corresponding CategoryName field.

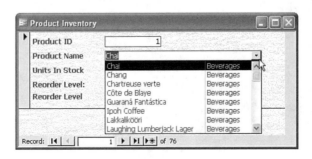

Using Text Boxes as Calculated Form Controls

In a query, you can use an expression to build a calculated column that, when you run the query, displays the result of the expression for each record in the query dynaset. You can do something similar in your forms by setting up a text box to display the results of an expression. This expression can use any of the Access operators, operands, and functions, and it can use the values in both bound and unbound controls.

Here are the steps to follow to create a calculated text box control:

1. Click the Text Box button in the Toolbox.
2. Draw the text box on the form. Access adds the text box and an associated label.
3. Click the text box to select it.
4. Choose View, Properties (or press Alt+Enter) to display the control's property sheet.
5. Choose the Data tab.
6. Enter the expression in the Control Source property.
7. Close the property sheet.

For example, Figure 4.32 shows the property sheet for a text box that has the expression =Date() as its Control Source property. In the Form view in Figure 4.33, you can see that the text box displays the current date. (Note that I entered the format string mmmm d, yyyy in the text box's Format property to get the date format shown in Figure 4.33.)

Calculated Text Cannot Be Edited

Users can't edit the text in a calculated text box. They can move the insertion point cursor within the control and then can select and copy the control text, but if they try to edit the text, Access beeps the speaker and displays the following in the status bar (where *expression* is the expression in the Control Source property):

```
Control can't be edited; it's bound to the expression 'expression'.
```

Calculated text box

Figure 4.32
To create a calculated control, enter an expression into a text box's Control Source property.

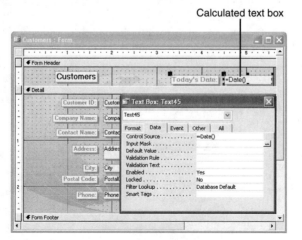

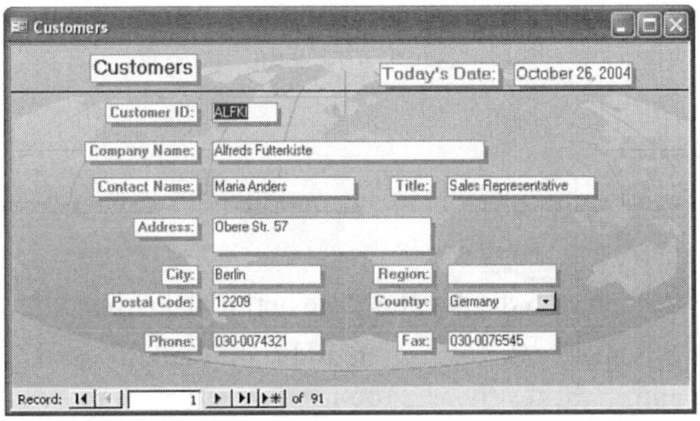

Figure 4.33
In the Form view, the text box displays the current date.

Creating a Multiple-Column Report

Access reports come in two flavors: tabular, which uses a datasheet-like layout with fields in columns and records in rows; and columnar, which uses a form-like layout with the fields arranged in a single, vertical column for each record. For this reason, the columnar layout is also called the *single-column* layout.

The single-column format is useful when you have wide fields, because each field can use up to the entire width of the page. If your fields aren't all that wide, however, the columnar layout is wasteful because you end up with a great deal of whitespace to the right of the fields. The tabular layout can get rid of the whitespace, but it's not as nice looking as the columnar layout.

Instead of compromising, it's possible to get the efficiency of the tabular layout combined with the attractive look of the columnar layout. You can do this by creating a *multiple-column* report that takes the basic columnar format and bends the records so that they now snake through two or more columns. (This is sometimes called a *snaked-column* layout.)

Setting Up the Report

The multiple-column effect appears only when you preview or print the report. In other words, it's not something that you set up within the report Design window (that is, by manipulating the position of the fields and field labels). However, that doesn't mean that you can apply the multiple-column layout to any report. When you're building your report, bear in mind that the page is going to be divided into columns and that the width of each column is the width of the page divided by the number of columns, less the margins and the amount of space you want between each column.

For example, suppose you want two columns a half-inch apart on a page 8.5 inches wide. Assuming the left and right margins are one inch, that leaves six inches for the two columns, or three inches each. Therefore, when building the report, you need to make sure that no part of the report is wider than three inches. (Use the horizontal ruler to monitor the width of the report. If you don't see the ruler, choose the View, Ruler command.)

Finally, after your controls are set to the proper width, change the width of the report itself so that it's no wider than the column width you want.

Tweaking the Page Setup

You set up a report to use multiple columns by modifying the Page Setup options. Here are the steps to follow:

1. Choose File, Page Setup to display the Page Setup dialog box.

2. In the Margins tab, make note of the left and right margin widths, as given by the values in the Left and Right text boxes. You need these values to calculate the optimal column width.

3. Display the Columns tab.

4. In the Grid Settings group, use the Number Of Columns text box to enter how many columns you want to use in your report. As shown in Figure 4.34, when you enter a value greater than 1, Access enables the Column Layout group.

Figure 4.34
Use the Columns tab to set up your report to use multiple columns.

5. If you want to include extra space between each record, add the spacing value (in inches) in the Row Spacing text box.

6. Use the Column Spacing text box to specify the amount of space (in inches) to allow between each column.

7. In the Column Size group, the Width text box should already be set to the width of your report (assuming the Same as Detail check box is activated). If not, use the Width text box to enter the width you want to use for each column. You can also use the Height text box to specify the height of each record.

8. Use the Column Layout group to choose one of the following options:

   Down, Then Across—With this option, the records are printed down each column, and the columns run across the page.

Across, Then Down—In this case, the records are printed across each row, and the rows run down the page.

9. Click OK.

10. Preview the report to make sure your columns look the way you want.

Cross-Reference

You can force Access to start a section at the beginning of a column (or row). For the details, see "Starting Sections at the Top of a Row or Column," later in this chapter.

Figure 4.35 shows a two-column report with data from the Northwind Customers table.

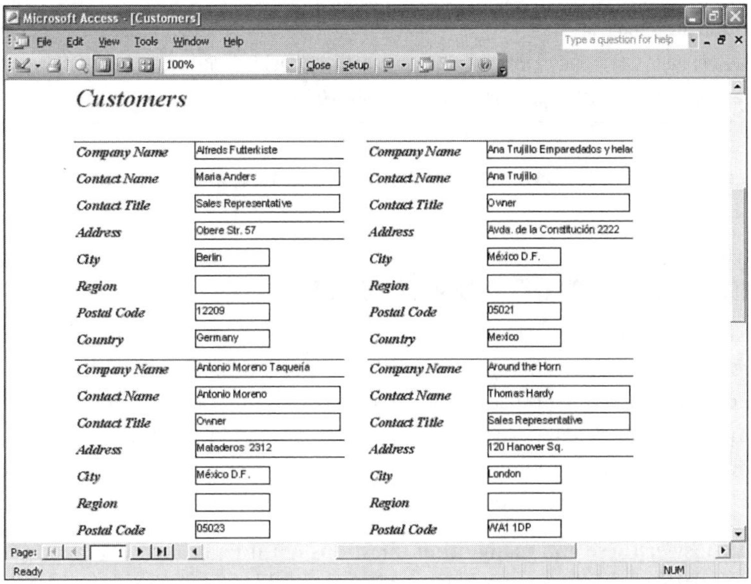

Figure 4.35
An example of a two-column report.

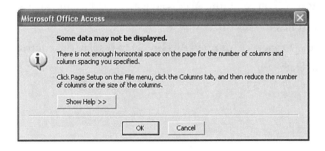

Troubleshooting Multiple Columns

If your columns don't all fit on the page, Access displays the dialog box shown in Figure 4.36.

Figure 4.36
Access displays this dialog box if your columns don't all fit the width of the page.

Here are some solutions to try:

- Reduce the number of columns. For example, if three columns won't fit on the page, trying using only two.

- Reduce the width of each column. In the Columns tab of the Page Setup dialog box, reduce the value of the Width text box in the Column Size group.

- Reduce the width of your report by reducing the width of the controls and the report itself. If this prevents a field text box from displaying all its data, try increasing the height of the text box to compensate.

- In the Margins tab of the Page Setup dialog box, reduce the Left and Right values accordingly. The smaller your margins, the more room Access can devote to the columns.

Watch the Margin Size

Most printers don't support margins much smaller than about 0.25 inches. Also, some older printers (such as the HP LaserJet Series II) don't support margins smaller than 0.5 inches.

- In the Page tab of the Page Setup dialog box, choose Landscape instead of Portrait.

Adding Calculations to a Report

Reports are often used just to display data. For example, it might be enough that an inventory report displays the in-stock, reorder level and on-order values for all a company's products. But anyone who uses a report as part of a decision-making process probably wants more than mere data. Such a person likely also needs to *analyze* the data in some way, and most data analysis requires one or more calculations. What were the total sales last quarter? How many days overdue are the unpaid invoices? How many records are in this report?

To answer these and many other questions within a report, you need to add one or more calculations. In the report Design view, you add calculations by adding text boxes, which you can use as unbound controls that display calculated results.

Here are the steps to follow to create a calculated text box control:

1. Click the Text Box button in the Toolbox.
2. Draw the text box on the form. Access adds the text box and an associated label.
3. Click the text box to select it.
4. Choose View, Properties (or press Alt+Enter) to display the control's property sheet.
5. Choose the Data tab.

6. Enter the expression in the Control Source property; be sure to begin the expression with an equal sign (=). (If you want to use the Expression Builder, click the ellipsis (…) button beside the Control Source property.)

7. Close the property sheet.

A Faster Way

You can also enter the expression directly into the text box.

Calculations in the Headers and Footers

If you enter a calculation in the report header or report footer, Access performs the calculation over the entire report. Similarly, if the calculation is in the page header or page footer, Access uses only those records included in the page. If the calculation is in the group header or group footer, Access applies the expression to only those records included in the group.

For example, the report in Figure 4.37 contains a number of calculated text box controls.

Figure 4.37
To create a calculated control, enter an expression into an unbound text box (or into its Control Source property).

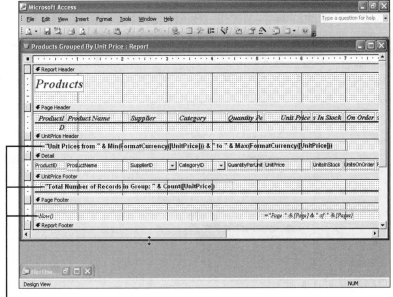

Calculated text boxes

Two of the controls deal with the report grouping. The first, in the group header section (named UnitPrice Header in the figure), uses the following expression:

```
="Unit Prices from " & Min(FormatCurrency([UnitPrice])) & " to " &
➥Max(FormatCurrency([UnitPrice]))
```

Because this control resides in the group header, the expression applies only to those records in each grouping. In this case, the expression uses the Min and Max functions to specify the range of values within each group.

The second grouping-related calculated text box control in Figure 4.37 is in the group footer section (named UnitPrice Footer in the figure); it uses the following expression:

```
="Total Number of Records in Group: " & Count([UnitPrice])
```

This expression uses the Count function to display the number of records in the group.

The report in Figure 4.37 also includes two calculated text box controls in the Page Footer section. The text box on the left displays the current date and time using the following expression:

```
=Now()
```

On the right of the page footer, a text box displays page number data using the following expression:

```
="Page " & [Page] & " of " & [Pages]
```

Here the [Page] identifier displays the current page number, and the [Pages] identifier displays the total number of pages in the report.

Figure 4.38 shows a preview of the report.

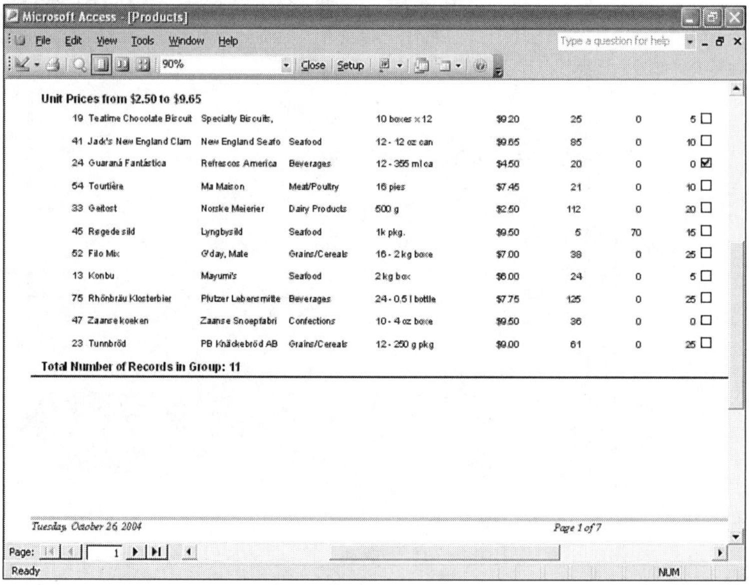

Figure 4.38
The preview of the form shown in Figure 4.37.

Creating a Shadow Effect for Report Text

Access comes with a palette of six special effects that enable you to display control borders in various interesting ways. The six choices are Flat, Raised, Sunken, Etched, Shadowed, and Chiseled. However, the Shadowed effect applies only to control borders. What if you want the same effect with the text in a label? You can do this by following these steps:

1. Add the label to the report, edit the text, and set up the text formatting as needed.
2. With the label selected, pull down the Formatting toolbar's Line/Border Color palette and click Transparent.
3. Select Edit, Duplicate to create a copy of the label.
4. Move the copy of the label so that it is offset slightly from the original (slightly below and slightly to the right is the usual shadow position).

Nudging the Shadow's Position

If you need to fine-tune the position of the copy, hold down the Ctrl key and press the arrow keys to nudge the label in the direction of the selected key.

---

5. Use the Formatting toolbar's Font/Fore Color palette to choose a relatively light color for the shadow label (such as light gray or white).

4

Controlling Report Output

Let's conclude this look at advanced Access features by looking at three properties that give you more control over how Access displays a report, particularly at the section level.

Adding Page Breaks After Sections

To make reports more readable, it's often a good idea to start a particular section (such as a grouping) on a new page. Rather than adding a Page Break control, you can force Access to add automatic page breaks by modifying a section's Force New Page property. Follow these steps:

1. Open the report in Design view.
2. Select the section you want to work with.
3. Choose View, Properties to display the section's property sheet.
4. Display the Format tab.
5. Use the Force New Page list to choose one of the following values:

   Before Section—Choose this option to force a page break before the section. This ensures that the section begins at the top of a new page.

   After Section—Choose this option to force a page break after the section. This ensures that the next section begins at the top of a new page.

Before & After—Choose this option to force page breaks before and after the section. This ensures that the section appears on a page by itself.

6. Close the property sheet.

7. Print preview the report to confirm that each section is formatted the way you want.

Starting Sections at the Top of a Row or Column

You saw earlier that it's possible to configure a report to use multiple columns, where the fields are arranged down and then across (in columns) or across and then down (in rows). It's possible to force Access to start a section at the beginning of a column or row by modifying the section's New Row or Col property. Follow these steps:

1. Open the report in Design view.

2. Select the section you want to work with.

3. Choose View, Properties to display the section's property sheet.

4. Display the Format tab.

5. Use the New Row or Col list to choose one of the following values:

Before Section—Choose this option to force the section to begin at the top of a new row or column.

After Section—Choose this option to force the next section to begin at the top of a new row or column.

Before & After—Choose this option to force the section to appear in a new row or column by itself.

6. Close the property sheet.

7. Print preview the report to confirm that each section is formatted the way you want.

Avoiding Widowed Records

A *widow* is a control or field that appears at the top of a new page by itself. In most cases, the report is more readable if you avoid widows and force all the elements of a section to appear together on the page. You can do this by modifying the section's Keep Together property, as shown in the following steps:

1. Open the report in Design view.

2. Select the section you want to work with.

3. Choose View, Properties to display the section's property sheet.

4. Display the Format tab.

5. In the Keep Together property, choose Yes.

6. Close the property sheet.

7. Print preview the report to verify that each section is formatted the way you want.

From Here

- To learn how to export Access data to Excel for analysis, see the section titled "Analyzing Access Data in Excel" in Chapter 6.

- To learn how to export Access data to Word for publishing within a document, see the section titled "Publishing Access Data in Word" in Chapter 6.

- To learn how to export Access data to Word for a mail merge, see the section titled "Merging Data from Access, Excel, and Outlook" in Chapter 6.

- To learn how to import a Word table to Access, see the section titled "Exporting a Word Table to Access" in Chapter 6.

- To learn how to create Access macros, see Chapter 13, "Taking Advantage of Access Macros."

- For information on database security, see the section titled "Protecting Access Data with Passwords and Permissions" in Chapter 14.

4

Getting the Most Out of Outlook

5

If you're a writer, a financial analyst, or a database administrator, you probably spend the bulk of your work day using Word, Excel, or Access. The rest of us dip into and out of these programs (and PowerPoint) throughout the day. However, there's one member of the Office family that most of us leave open and use all day long: Outlook. Whether it's handling our ever-growing email load, organizing our calendar, or managing our contacts, Outlook gets a real workout in a typical business day.

With that in mind, this chapter presents a number of techniques designed to help you get the most out of Outlook's Inbox, Calendar, and Contacts features to help you take Outlook to the Office guru level.

Getting the Most Out of Email

You're probably too busy reading, composing, and managing your email to give much thought to what your life was like just a few short years ago when most of us had barely heard of email or rarely used it beyond sending out the odd internal message to a colleague or two. Now email is, hands down, the most often used and, arguably, the most important business tool in the modern day business arsenal. It's so important that I think it's a crime if you don't become an expert email user, particularly an expert on Outlook's prodigious email capabilities. Taking a few minutes now to learn the ins and outs of the Outlook Inbox will save you *hours* of time every week because your email work will be faster and more efficient. The first part of this chapter shows you quite a few techniques that will get you well on your way to becoming an Outlook expert.

Customizing the Inbox Message Fields

The default fields in Outlook's Inbox tell you the basic information you need for any message. Much more information is available, however. For example, you might want to know the date and time the message was sent, the number of lines in the message, and the first few words of the message. All of these items and many more can be displayed as columns in the message list.

Moving the Reading Pane

In Outlook's default layout, the message list appears in the middle of the window and the Reading pane appears on the right. This brain-dead layout makes *both* the message list and the Reading pane practically useless. A much better arrangement is to have the Reading pane below the message list. You can set this up by selecting View, Reading Pane, Bottom.

 To customize Outlook's fields, right-click any field header and then select Field Chooser (or click Field Chooser in the Advanced toolbar). Outlook displays the Field Chooser dialog box, shown in Figure 5.1. The drop-down list at the top of this dialog box contains various categories of message fields, so you should first select the category that contains the field you want to add. (If in doubt, you can select the All Mail fields item to see all the available fields.) After the field is displayed, you add it to the Outlook window by dragging it from the Field Chooser and dropping it inside the field headers at the point where you want the field to appear.

Figure 5.1
Use the Field Chooser dialog box to customize the fields displayed in the message list.

Here's a rundown of a few other field customization chores you can perform:

- Outlook has a "big picture" method of customizing columns. To try it, select View, Arrange By, Custom, and then click Fields. In the Show Fields dialog box that appears, the Select Available Fields From list contains the various categories of message fields. You also see two lists: the Available Fields list shows the field headings you can use, and the Show These Fields in This Order list shows the current field headings. Use the

Add and Remove buttons to customize the field selection. You can also use the Move Up and Move Down buttons to adjust the field order.

- To move a field, drag its header left or right within the column header area.

- To size a field, drag the right edge of the field's header to the left or right. If you want a field to be as wide as its widest entry, right-click the field header and then select Best Fit.

- To change how text is aligned within a field, right-click the field's header, select Alignment, and then select Align Left, Align Right, or Center.

Creating a Custom Field

Outlook also enables you to create custom fields where the displayed value is based on a formula that you build. Display the Field Chooser dialog box and click New. (Alternatively, display the Show Fields dialog box and click New Field.) Enter a name for the field and then use the Type list to select Formula. Type the formula into the Formula text box or click Edit to use the Formula Field dialog box, which offers lists of the available fields and functions. For example, suppose you create a field named "Conference" and you want it to display "Yes" if the message subject contains the word "Conference." Here's the formula to use:

```
IIf(Instr([Subject],"Conference") <> 0, "Yes", "")
```

This formula uses the `Instr` function to see if the `[Subject]` field contains the word `Conference`. If so, the word `Yes` is returned; otherwise, a blank string is returned. After you create the field, it appears in the User-Defined Fields in Inbox category, and you can add it to the Inbox fields from there.

Changing the Folder View

You'll often need to work with multiple, related messages. For example, you might want to see all the messages from a particular correspondent, or you might want to work with all messages that have the same Subject line (even if there's a RE: tacked on to the beginning). Outlook is particularly strong in this area because, as you'll see in the next few sections, it provides you with a seemingly endless number of methods for manipulating a message list.

We'll begin this section by looking at *views*. A view is just another way of looking at a message list. For example, the Unread Messages view tells Outlook to display only those messages that you haven't opened.

Displaying Multiple Views of the Same Folder

Instead of switching from one view to another, you can tell Outlook to display the same folder using multiple views. Begin by right-clicking the folder name in the All Mail Folders list and then selecting Open in New Window. This creates a second window for the folder so you can display one view in the first window and another view in the second window.

Outlook's default view is Messages, which displays each message on a single line showing only the header information. There are five other predefined views that you might want to try out:

5

- Messages with AutoPreview—Displays each unread message by showing the header information (From, Subject, Received) followed by the first three lines of the message body.

- Last Seven Days—Displays only those messages that you've received in the last week. This is an example of a message *filter*. See "Filtering the Messages" later in this chapter for more information on filters.

- Unread Messages in This Folder—Filters the messages to show only those that haven't yet been read (or marked as read).

- Sent To—Sorts the messages by the name of the person to whom each message was sent.

- Message Timeline—This unique view displays a timeline that lists the messages you received underneath the date you received them. The View menu has three commands—Day, Week, and Month—that you can use to customize the timeline.

To change the view, Outlook gives you three methods:

- Select View, Arrange By, Current View, and then select the view you want from the menu that appears.

- Select View, Arrange By, Show Views in Navigation Pane. This displays a collection of option buttons for the view in the Outlook Navigation pane. Click the view you want.

- Use the Current View drop-down list in the Advanced toolbar.

AutoPreview in Other Views

You can access the AutoPreview feature in any of the views, not just Messages by AutoPreview. Either activate the View, AutoPreview command, or click the AutoPreview button in the Advanced toolbar.

Creating Custom Views

Outlook also lets you define your own views. I'll tell you how to do this after I show you how to sort, filter, and group messages (see the later section "Defining a Custom View").

Sorting the Messages

By default, Outlook sorts the Inbox messages in descending order according to the values in the Received column. Similarly, messages in the Sent Items folder are sorted by the values in the Sent column. But you're free to sort the messages based on any displayed column. Following are the techniques you can use:

- Click the header for the field you want to use for the sort. An arrow appears beside the column name to tell you the direction of the sort (an up arrow for ascending and a down arrow for descending; clicking the header toggles the sort direction).

- Right-click the header of the field you want to use and then select either Sort Ascending or Sort Descending from the context menu.

- Select View, Arrange By, and then select the field on which you want to sort.

- Select View, Arrange By, Custom, and then click Sort to display the Sort dialog box, shown in Figure 5.2. Use the Sort Items By list to choose the first field you want to use for the sort, use Then By to select a second field, and so on. In each case, activate either Ascending or Descending. Click OK to put the sort order into effect.

Figure 5.2
Use the Sort dialog box
to sort your messages.

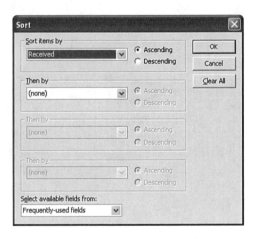

Sorts Are Unique to Folders
The sort order you choose is unique to the current folder. This is convenient because it lets you set up different sort orders for different folders.

5

Grouping the Messages

Outlook can group a folder's messages based on the current sort order. Select View, Arrange By, Show in Groups. For example, if you have your messages sorted according to the Received field, grouping the messages by the date combines today's messages in one group, yesterday's in another, last week's in a third, and so on. As you can see in Figure 5.3, the resulting display is reminiscent of the outline views in Word or Excel:

- To expand a group, click its plus sign (+) or select View, Expand/Collapse Groups, and then select either Expand This Group or Expand All Groups.

- To collapse a group, click its minus sign (–) or select View, Expand/Collapse Groups, and then select either Collapse This Group or Collapse All Groups.

The big advantage of working with grouped messages is that Outlook treats them as a unit. This means that you can open, move, or delete all the messages in the group with a single operation.

Collapse group

Figure 5.3
The message list grouped by the date portion of the Received field.

Expand group

Defining a New Grouping

Rather than the default grouping based on the current sort order, Outlook enables you to set up groupings on any field and even on multiple fields. Just follow these steps:

1. Select View, Arrange By, Custom.
2. Click Group By to display the Group By dialog box, shown in Figure 5.4.

Figure 5.4
Use the Group By dialog box to define a new grouping for the messages.

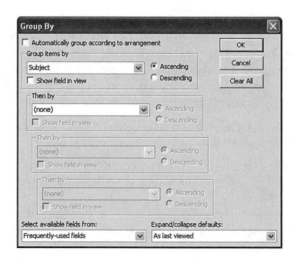

3. Deactivate the Automatically Group According to Arrangement check box. (When this check box is activated, Outlook groups the folder according to the current sort order.)

4. Use the Group Items By list to choose the first field you want to use for the grouping and then activate either Ascending or Descending. (If you don't see a field you want, use the Select Available Fields From list to select All Mail Fields.)

5. Use the Then By list to choose the next field you want to use for the grouping and then activate either Ascending or Descending.

6. Repeat step 5 until you've chosen all the grouping fields.

7. The Expand/Collapse Defaults list determines whether the groupings are displayed expanded (each message in each group is shown) or collapsed (only the groups are shown). You can also choose As Last Viewed to display the groups as you previously had them.

8. Click OK to put the grouping into effect.

Easier Groupings with the Group By Box

If you change the grouping frequently, Outlook offers an easy drag-and-drop method for switching from one grouping to another: the Group By box. To display the Group By box, either right-click any field header and then select Group By Box, or click the Group By Box button in the Advanced toolbar. Figure 5.5 shows the Inbox folder with the Group By box. The button inside the Group By box tells you which field is being used for the grouping.

Group By box

Figure 5.5
You can use the Group By box to work with your groups.

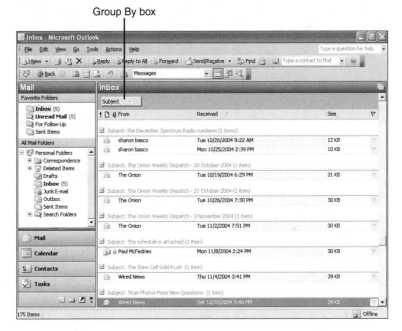

Here's a summary of the various techniques you can use with the Group By box to adjust your groupings:

- Click the field button inside the Group By box to toggle the group sort order between ascending and descending.

- To add an existing message list field to the grouping, drag the field's header into the Group By box.

- To add any other field to the Group By box, right-click any field header, select Field Chooser to display the Field Chooser dialog box, and then drag the field you want to use into the Group By box.

- If you have multiple fields in the Group By box, you can change the subgroupings by dragging the field buttons left or right.

- To remove the grouping, either drag the field button outside the group box or right-click the field button and choose Don't Group by This Field.

Filtering the Messages

Grouping messages often makes them easier to deal with, but you're still working with *all* the messages inside the folder. To really knock a message list down to size, you need to *filter* the messages. When we looked at views earlier, we saw that certain views displayed only selected messages. For example, choosing the Last Seven Days view reduced the message list to only those missives that were received in the last week.

As with groups, Outlook makes it easy to design your own filters. You'll soon see that filtering is one of Outlook's most powerful (and potentially complex) features. Yes, you can perform simple filters on field values, but Outlook can take you far beyond these basic filters. For example, you can filter messages based on words or phrases in the subject or body.

To get started, select View, Arrange By, Custom, and then click Filter. The Filter dialog box that appears, shown in Figure 5.6, contains four tabs:

- Messages—Use the controls in this tab to set message-based criteria. For example, you can enter a word or phrase in the Search for the Word(s) text box and select an item from the In drop-down list (for example, Subject Field Only). Outlook will filter messages that contain the word or phrase in the chosen item.

- More Choices—This tab lets you fine-tune your filter. For example, you can set up a case-sensitive filter by activating the Match Case check box. You can also filter based on categories, read status, attachments, priority, importance, flag status, and size.

- Advanced—This tab lets you set up sophisticated criteria for your filter. Use the Field list to choose a field; use the Condition list to select an operator (such as Contains or Is Empty); and use the Value list to enter a criteria value. Click Add to List to add the criteria to the filter.

- SQL—This tab displays the Structured Query Language (SQL) command created by the choices you made in the other three tabs. You can edit the SQL statement directly, but you're better off working with the controls in the other tabs to generate the SQL automatically.

Figure 5.6
Use the Filter dialog box
to set up a custom mes-
sage filter.

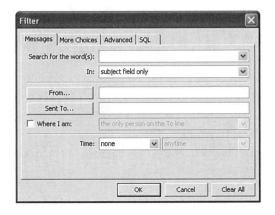

Defining a Custom View

If you go to a lot of work to set up a sort order, grouping, or filter, it seems a shame to have to repeat the process each time you want to use the same view. Happily, Outlook saves you that drudgery by letting you save custom sorts, groupings, or filters. In fact, Outlook goes one better by letting you save *combinations* of these views. In other words, you can define a view that includes a sort order, a grouping, and a filter. And, for added convenience, these views are available along with Outlook's predefined views, so they're easy to implement.

Here are the steps to follow to create a custom view:

1. If you want to apply the view to a specific folder, select the folder.
2. Select View, Arrange By, Current View, Define Views to display the Custom View Organizer dialog box.
3. Click New. Outlook displays the Create a New View dialog box.
4. In the Name of New View text box, enter a name for the view you'll be creating, and use the Type of View list to choose the view type. (For a mail folder, this will probably be Table, but feel free to try out some of the others.) Also, use the Can Be Used On group to select the folders to which the view will apply. Click OK to continue.
5. The Custom View dialog box contains the buttons that you've seen in the past few sections: Fields, Group By, Sort, and Filter, plus three other buttons that we didn't cover:

   Other Settings—Enables you to change the row and column fonts, grid line styles, AutoPreview fonts, Reading pane location, and more.

   Automatic Formatting—Enables you to change the font that Outlook applies automatically to things such as unread messages and expired messages.

5

Format Columns—Enables you to change the column display for each visible field. For example, you could change the Attachment field from showing an icon (the paperclip) to showing Yes/No or True/False.

6. Click OK to return to the Custom View Organizer.

7. If you'd like to switch to the new view right away, click Apply View. Otherwise, click Close to return to Outlook.

Don't Create New Views from Scratch

If another view exists that's similar to the custom view you want to create, there's a method you can use to save some time. Rather than creating the new view from scratch, highlight the existing view in the Custom View Organizer and then click Copy. In the Copy View dialog box that appears, enter a name for the new view and click OK. Outlook will then display the Customize View dialog box so that you can make your adjustments.

Incoming Message Tricks

Whether you receive several dozen messages a day or several hundred, handling incoming messages probably takes up more time than you'd like. To help out, this section takes you through a few tricks for knocking those incoming messages down to size so that you have extra time for more productive pursuits.

Using Rules to Process Messages Automatically

With email now fully entrenched on the business (and even home) landscape, email chores probably take up more and more of your time. And I'm not just talking about the three R's of email: reading, 'riting, and responding. Basic email maintenance—flagging, moving, deleting, and so on—also takes up large chunks of otherwise-productive time.

To help ease the email time crunch, Outlook lets you set up "rules" that perform actions in response to specific events. Here's a list of just a few of the things you can do with rules:

- Move an incoming message to a specific folder if the message contains a particular keyword in the subject or body, or if it's from a particular person.
- Automatically delete messages with a particular subject or from a particular person.
- Flag messages based on specific criteria (such as keywords in the subject line or body).
- Have Outlook notify you with a custom message if an important message arrives.
- Have copies of messages you send stored in a specific folder, depending on the recipient.

Creating a Rule from Scratch   Clearly, rules are powerful tools that shouldn't be wielded lightly or without care. Fortunately, Outlook comes with a Rules Wizard that makes the process of setting up and defining rules almost foolproof. Here are the steps to follow:

1. Select Tools, Rules and Alerts to display the Rules and Alerts dialog box.

2. Click New Rule to launch the Rules Wizard.

3. You can use one of the displayed templates, but to get the most out of rules, you need to create them from scratch, so activate the Start From a Blank Rule option.

4. Select one of the following and then click Next:

   Check Messages When They Arrive—Select this item to apply the rule to incoming messages.

   Check Messages After Sending—Select this item to apply the rule to outgoing messages.

5. The next step is to define the criteria that will cause Outlook to invoke this rule. In other words, what conditions must a message meet to apply the rule to that message? In the Select Condition(s) list, activate the check box for a condition you want to use.

6. In the Edit the Rule Description box, if the condition requires more information from you, you'll see underlined placeholder text. For example, if you activated the With Specific Words in the Subject condition, you'll see the phrase Specific Words underlined. Click that phrase and then, in the dialog box that appears, enter the word or words that satisfy your criteria, as shown in Figure 5.7.

Figure 5.7
If a condition needs more information, click the placeholder text to define the criteria.

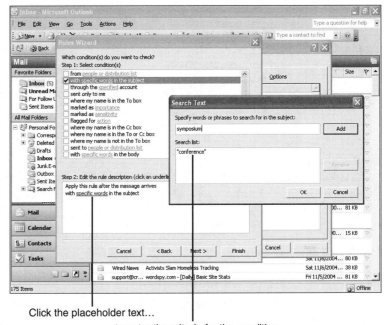

Click the placeholder text…

…to enter the criteria for the condition

7. Repeat steps 5 and 6 to add more conditions to your rule, as necessary.

8. Click Next.

9. Now you specify the action that you want Outlook to take for messages that meet the conditions you specified. In the Select Action(s) list, activate the check box for an action you want to apply to the messages.

10. If the action requires more information from you, click the placeholder text and enter the information.

11. Repeat steps 9 and 10 to specify other actions, as necessary.

12. Select your exceptions to the rule, if any, and click Next.

13. Enter a name for the rule.

14. Click Finish.

Your new rule is added to the E-mail Rules tab, as shown in Figure 5.8.

Figure 5.8
The rules you've defined appear in the E-mail Rules tab.

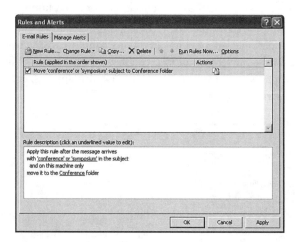

Rule Maintenance
You can use the E-mail Rules tab to maintain your rules. For example, each rule you've defined has a check box beside it that toggles the rule on and off. You can change a rule by highlighting it and clicking Change Rule. To get rid of a rule, highlight it and click Delete.

Creating a Rule from a Message   You'll often find yourself creating a rule because of a message you've received. It might be a particular sender whose messages you want moved to a specific folder or a particular subject line that you want to be alerted about. For a limited set of conditions and actions, Outlook enables you to create a new rule based on one or more properties of an existing message. Here's how:

1. Right-click the message from which you want to create the rule.

2. Select Create Rule. Outlook displays the Create Rule dialog box, shown in Figure 5.9.

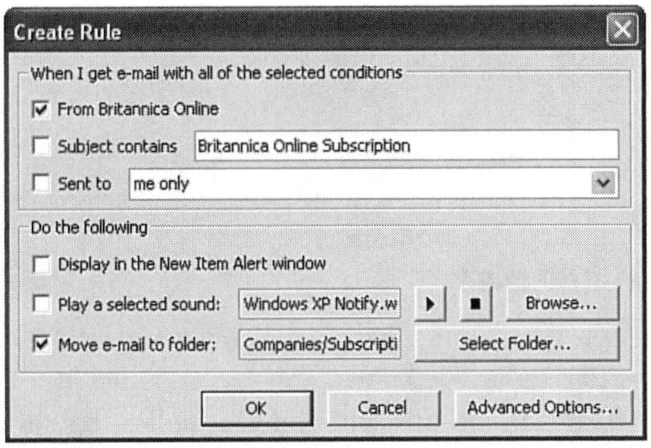

Figure 5.9
Use the Create Rule dialog box to create a new rule from the properties of an existing message.

3. In the When I Get E-mail with All of the Selected Conditions group, activate the check boxes that specify the conditions: sender's email address (often shown as just the sender's display name), subject line, or the address to whom the message was sent.

4. In the Do the Following group, activate the check boxes beside the actions you want to take, and use the associated controls to specify the action. (For example, if you activate Move E-mail to Folder, click Select Folder.)

5. If the Create Rule dialog box doesn't have the exact conditions or actions you want, click Advanced Options to use the Rules Wizard to complete the rule. Otherwise, click OK.

Applying Colors to Messages from Specific Senders

If you're interested in email from a particular person, keeping an eye out for that person's messages can be tricky, particularly if you receive a large number of messages each day. One way to solve this problem is to set up an incoming message rule where the person's address is the condition and the action is to display an alert or move the person's messages to a special folder. This works well, but Outlook offers a simpler alternative: coloring the person's messages, which really makes them stand out. Here are the steps to follow:

1. Click a message from the person you want to work with.

2. Select Tools, Organize.

3. Click Using Colors to display the pane shown in Figure 5.10.

Figure 5.10
Use the Using Colors pane to apply a color to a sender's messages.

4. Use the Color Messages…In list to choose the color you want to use for the person's messages.

5. Click Apply Color.

6. Click X to close the pane.

Setting a Message Follow-Up Reminder

Outlook enables you to flag a selected message for follow-up by selecting Actions, Follow Up, and then selecting the flag color you want. (You can also click the Flag field in the message list to set the default flag.) Despite the fact that Outlook offers several flag colors, these flags are of limited value because people tend to get used to them, and the follow-up percentage tends to drop over time. If you have a message that requires an important follow-up, you can take things to the next level by setting a reminder. Here's how it works:

1. Select the message you want to work with.

2. Select Actions, Follow Up, Add Reminder. Outlook displays the Flag for Follow Up dialog box, shown in Figure 5.11.

Figure 5.11
Use the Flag for Follow Up dialog box to set a message follow-up reminder.

3. In the Flag To list, select the reason for the flag (Call, Forward, Reply, and so on).

4. In the Due By lists, select the date and time by which the follow-up must occur.

5. Use the Flag Color list to set the flag.

6. Click OK.

Cutting Your Mailbox Down to Size

The busier your email life is, the larger your Outlook mailbox gets. Having a massive mailbox not only makes it hard to find the messages you want, it also slows down Outlook's performance. To avoid these problems, use the Mailbox Cleanup tool to delete old or large items, archive items, and clean out the Deleted Items folder. To display this tool, select Tools, Mailbox Cleanup. Outlook displays the Mailbox Cleanup dialog box, shown in Figure 5.12.

Figure 5.12
Use Mailbox Cleanup to reduce the size of your Outlook mailbox and improve performance.

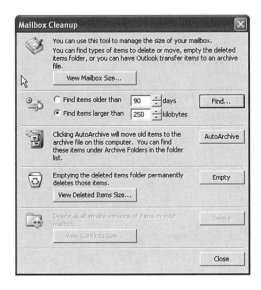

Here's how to use this tool:

- Click View Mailbox Size to keep track of the size of the Outlook mailbox. The Folder Size dialog box that appears tells you the overall size of the mailbox as well as the size of each folder. Click Close when you're done.

- To find old messages, activate Find Items Older Than X Days and then click Find. The messages are displayed in the Advanced Find, and from there you can delete or move the messages.

- To find large messages, activate Find Items Larger Than X Kilobytes and then click Find. Again, the messages are displayed in the Advanced Find, and from there you can delete or move them.

- To archive messages, click AutoArchive.

Setting AutoArchive Options
To configure the default settings for AutoArchive, select Tools, Options, select the Other tab, and then click AutoArchive. The dialog box that appears enables you to turn archived items on and off, set the AutoArchive frequency, and more. If you want special AutoArchive settings for a particular folder, right-click the folder, click Properties, and then select the AutoArchive tab.

- To clean out the Deleted Items folder, click Empty.

Using the Inbox Repair Tools

If you have problems opening Outlook or working with your email, your Personal Folders data file may have become corrupted. You can often fix this problem by using the Inbox Repair Tool, which you can launch by selecting Start, Run and entering the following address in the Run dialog box (include the quotation marks):

```
"C:\Program Files\Common Files\System\MSMAPI\1033\SCANPST.exe"
```

Enter the path and name of your Personal Folders data file. If you're not sure, here's the default location (replace *User* with your Windows username):

```
C:\Documents and Settings\User\Local Settings\Application Data\Microsoft\
➥Outlook\Outlook.pst.
```

If Outlook is running, shut it down. Click Start to begin the repair.

Checking the Same Account from Different Computers

In today's increasingly mobile world, we often find ourselves needing to check the same email account from multiple devices. For example, you might want to check your business account not only using your work computer, but also using your home computer or your notebook while traveling, or using a PDA or other portable device while commuting.

Unfortunately, after you download a message, the message is deleted from the server and you can't access it from any other device. If you need to check mail on multiple devices, the trick is to leave a copy of the message on the server after you download it. That way, the message will still be available when you check messages using another device. Follow these steps to adjust your account to leave a copy of each message on the server:

1. Select Tools, E-mail Accounts.

2. Activate the View or Change Existing E-mail Accounts option and click Next. The E-mail Accounts dialog box appears.

3. Select the account you want to work with and click Change.

4. In the Outgoing Mail Server (SMTP) text box, enter the domain name of the third-party host's SMTP server.

5. Click More Settings. The Internet E-mail Settings dialog box appears.

6. Select the Advanced tab.

7. Activate the Leave a Copy of Messages on the Server check box.

8. You can also activate the following options:

   Remove from Server After X Days—If you activate this check box, Outlook automatically deletes the message from the server after the number of days specified in the spin box.

   Remove from Server When Deleted from 'Deleted Items'—If you activate this check box, Outlook deletes the message from the server only when you permanently delete the message.

9. Click OK to return to the E-mail Accounts dialog box.

10. Click OK.

Here's a good strategy to follow:

- On your main computer, activate the Leave a Copy of Messages on the Server check box *and* the Remove from Server After *X* Days check box. Set the number of days long enough so that you have time to download the messages using your other devices.

- On all your other devices, activate only the Leave a Copy of Messages on the Server check box.

This strategy ensures that you can download messages on all your devices, but it prevents messages from piling up on the server.

Outgoing Message Tricks

Handling incoming messages is, unfortunately, only half the email battle. We also have to send replies, forward messages, and compose new messages from scratch. If you send a lot of email, you should find the tricks I outline in this section helpful.

Creating an Email Shortcut for a Recipient

When you need to send a message, if you don't leave Outlook open all day, it can seem like a lot of work to start the program, compose the new message, send it, and then close Outlook. You can save yourself a couple of steps by creating an email shortcut on your desktop or in a folder such as Quick Launch for a particular recipient. When you open the shortcut, a new email message window appears, already addressed to the recipient. You then fill in the rest of the message and send it, all without starting Outlook.

Follow these steps to create an email shortcut:

1. Display the desktop or open the folder in which you want to create the shortcut.

2. Right-click the desktop or folder and then select New, Shortcut. The Create Shortcut dialog box appears.

3. In the text box, type the following (where *address* is the email address of the recipient; see the example in Figure 5.13):
   ```
   mailto:address
   ```

4. Click Next.

5. Enter a title for the shortcut (such as the person's name or email address).

6. Click Finish.

5

Figure 5.13
Enter
`mailto:address` to
create an email shortcut
for an email recipient.

Having Replies Sent to a Different Address

If you have multiple accounts, when you compose a new message or reply to or forward an incoming message, you can click Accounts in the toolbar to choose from which account the message is sent. Normally, any replies to your message are sent to that account. However, that might not be convenient for you. For example, you might be sending the message from an account that is scheduled to be deleted soon and you want replies to go to your new account. Or you might prefer that replies go to your assistant or someone else in your department. Similarly, you might be sending a business message from home and prefer that replies go to your business address.

For these situations, you can specify an alternative address to which replies will be sent:

1. In the message window, click Options to display the Message Options dialog box, shown in Figure 5.14.

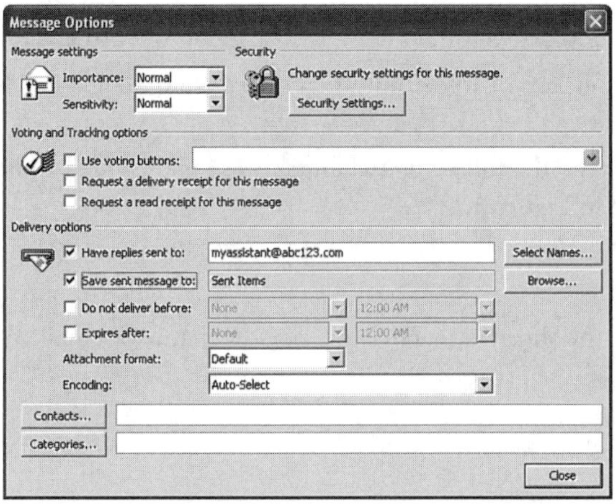

Figure 5.14
Use the Message Options
dialog box to specify an
alternative address for
replies to the message.

2. Activate the Have Replies Sent To check box.

3. In the text box, enter the address you want to use. To choose an address from your Contacts list, click Select Names, choose the recipient, and click OK.

4. Click Close.

Using a Different SMTP Port

For security reasons, some Internet service providers (ISPs) insist that all their customers' outgoing mail must be routed through the ISP's Simple Mail Transport Protocol (SMTP) server. This usually isn't a problem if you're using an email account maintained by the ISP, but it can lead to problems if you're using an account provided by a third party (such as your website host):

■ Your ISP might block messages sent using the third-party account because it thinks you're trying to relay the message through the ISP's server (a technique often used by spammers).

■ You might incur extra charges if your ISP allows only a certain amount of SMTP bandwidth per month or a certain number of sent messages, whereas the third-party account offers higher limits or no restrictions at all.

■ You might have performance problems, with the ISP's server taking much longer to route messages than the third-party host.

You might think that you can solve the problem by specifying the third-party host's SMTP server in the account settings. However, this doesn't usually work because outgoing email is sent by default through port 25; when you use this port, you must also use the ISP's SMTP server.

To work around this, many third-party hosts offer access to their SMTP server via a port other than the standard port 25. Here's how to configure an email account to use a nonstandard SMTP port:

1. Select Tools, E-mail Accounts.

2. Activate the View or Change Existing E-mail Accounts option and click Next. The E-mail Accounts dialog box appears.

3. Select the account you want to work with and click Change.

4. In the Outgoing Mail Server (SMTP) text box, enter the domain name of the third-party host's SMTP server.

5. Click More Settings. The Internet E-mail Settings dialog box appears.

6. Select the Advanced tab.

7. In the Outgoing Server (SMTP) text box, enter the port number specified by the third-party host, as shown in Figure 5.15.

Figure 5.15
Change the Outgoing Server (SMTP) value to the port number used by your third-party host.

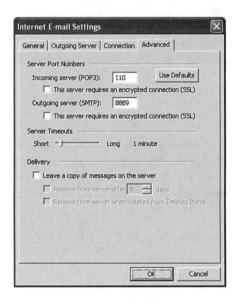

8. Click OK to return to the E-mail Accounts dialog box.
9. Click OK.

Activating SMTP Authentication

Another security feature commonly implemented by email hosts is SMTP Authentication, which authenticates the sender of each message. If you're having trouble getting messages through, you may need to adjust your account for SMTP Authentication. In the Internet E-mail Settings dialog box, select the Outgoing Server tab and activate the My Outgoing Server (SMTP) Requires Authentication. Most SMTP authentication uses your account username and password, so leave the Use Same Settings as My Incoming Mail Server option activated. If your host uses a separate outgoing logon, activate Log On Using, instead, and fill in your User Name and Password.

Getting the Most Out of the Calendar

It seems almost redundant to describe modern life as "busy." Everyone is working harder, cramming more appointments and meetings into already-packed schedules, and somehow finding the time to get their regular work done between crises. As many a management consultant has advised over the years (charging exorbitant fees to do so), the key to surviving this helter-skelter, pell-mell pace is *time management*. And although there are as many theories about time management as there are consultants, one of the keys is that you should always try to make the best use of the time available. Although that often comes down to self-discipline and prioritizing your tasks, an efficient scheduling system can sure help.

That's where Outlook's Calendar feature comes in. At first glance, Calendar just looks like an electronic version of your day planner. You move around from day to day and month to month, entering tasks and appointments at their scheduled times. But Calendar goes far beyond this simple time-keeping function. For example, you can use it to schedule meetings via email and, depending on the responses, update your schedule automatically. You can put your Calendar on a public network folder so that others can see when you're available and set up appointments with you based on this information.

In other words, Calendar helps you spend less time scheduling, which gives you more time to do real work. This section takes you through the full spectrum of Calendar's features and functions, including setting up appointments, meetings, and events.

Starting Outlook in the Calendar Folder

By default, Outlook opens with the Inbox folder displayed, which makes sense because most people use Outlook primarily for email. If most of your Outlook time is spent in the Calendar, instead, you might prefer to display the Calendar folder automatically at startup. Here's how to do it:

1. Select Tools, Options to display the Options dialog box.
2. Select the Other tab.
3. Click Advanced Options.
4. Beside the Startup in this Folder box, click Browse.
5. Select the Calendar folder.
6. Click OK until you exit all the open dialog boxes.

Using the Calendar Folder

When you display the Calendar folder, Outlook displays a window similar to the one shown in Figure 5.16. As you can see, Calendar is laid out more or less like a day planner or desk calendar. Here are two items to note right up front:

- Calendar—This takes up the bulk of the Calendar folder and it shows one day at a time, divided into half-hour intervals. The appointments and meetings you schedule appear in this area.

- Date Navigator—This part of the Navigation pane shows six weeks of dates, including the current month, the last few days from the previous month, and the first few days from the next month. As its name suggests, you use the Date Navigator to change the date shown in the Calendar area. Dates for which you have already scheduled appointments or meetings are shown in bold type. Note that today's date always has a red square around it.

Today's date

Figure 5.16
Outlook's Calendar folder.

Date Navigator

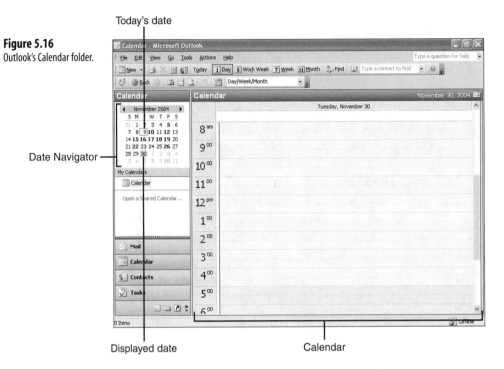

Displayed date

Calendar

Using the Date Navigator

Calendar always opens with today's date displayed. However, if you want to work with a different day, the Date Navigator makes it easy. All you have to do is click a date, and Outlook will display it in the Calendar. If the month you need isn't displayed in the Date Navigator, use either of the following techniques to pick a different month:

- Click the left-pointing arrow in the month header to move backward one month at a time. Similarly, click the right-pointing arrow in the month headers to move forward one month at a time.

- Move the mouse pointer over the month header, then press and hold down the left mouse button. A pop-up menu displays seven months—the month you clicked and the three months before and after. Drag the mouse to the month you want and release the button. For later or earlier months, drag the mouse pointer off the bottom or the top of the list and Outlook scrolls through the months.

Displaying Two Months at a Time

If you liked the old Outlook Date Navigator that showed two months at once, you can get the same view in Outlook 2003. Move your mouse pointer over the border that separates the Navigation pane and the Calendar so that the horizontal resize pointer appears. Drag the border to the right to roughly double the size of the default Navigation pane. When you release the mouse, Outlook displays two months in the Date Navigator.

Changing the Number of Days Displayed

Calendar's default view is the Day calendar, which shows a single day's worth of appointments and meetings. However, Calendar is quite flexible and is happy to show two days, three days, a week, or even a month at a time.

Changing the Time Scale

By default, the Day view displays time in half-hour blocks. If that doesn't work for you, you can change the time scale by right-clicking the time display and then clicking the interval you prefer (60, 30, 15, 10, 6, or 5 minutes). If the time is not displayed in the current view, right-click the Calendar and then click Other Settings. Use the Time Scale list to select the interval you prefer.

The easiest way to change the view is to use Calendar's Day, Work Week, Week, and Month commands:

- For the Work Week calendar, select View, Work Week, or click the Work Week toolbar button.

- For the Week calendar, select View, Week, or click the Week toolbar button (you can also press Alt+hyphen).

- For the Month calendar, select View, Month, or click the Month toolbar button (you can also press Alt+=).

- To return to the Day calendar, select View, Day, or click the Day toolbar button.

Besides these predefined views, Outlook also lets you view however many days you want. Move the mouse pointer into the Date Navigator and drag the pointer over the days you'd like to see. When you release the button, Outlook displays the selected days. For example, in Figure 5.17, I dragged the mouse over the 9, 10, and 11. You can also use the following techniques:

- To view multiple consecutive dates, click the first date, hold down Shift, and click the last date.
- To view multiple, nonconsecutive dates, click the first date, then hold down Ctrl and click the other dates.
- To view an entire week (Sunday through Saturday), move the mouse pointer to the left of the week and click.
- To view multiple consecutive weeks, move the mouse pointer to the left of the first week and then click and drag down or up to select the weeks.
- To view multiple nonconsecutive weeks, move the mouse pointer just to the left of the first week and then click; hold down Ctrl and then for each of the other weeks, move the mouse pointer to the left of the week and click.

5

Drag the mouse over the days you want to show

Figure 5.17
Outlook can display any
number of days in the
Calendar.

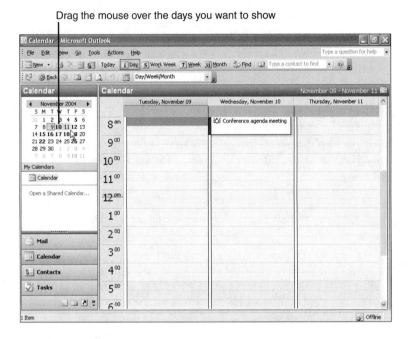

Quickly Displaying Any Number of Days

You can also display *x* number of days by pressing Alt+*x*. For example, pressing Alt+3 displays the three days beginning with the currently selected day. Press Alt+0 for 10 days.

Giving Weekends Extra Space

Outlook assumes you use the Calendar less on weekends, so it compresses the Saturday and Sunday fields in the Week and Month views. If you need more space on the weekends, right-click the Calendar and then click Other Settings. Deactivate the Compress Weekend Days check box and then click OK.

You can also include Saturday and/or Sunday in the Work Week view. Select Tools, Options, and in the Preferences tab click Calendar Options. In the Calendar Work Week group, activate the check boxes for the days you want to include in the Work Week view (such as the Sat and Sun check boxes).

Working with Calendar's Views

As with all of Outlook's folders, you can view your calendar in several ways. For example, you can set up the Calendar folder to show only the events you've scheduled.

The Day, Week, and Month calendars are part of Calendar's default Day/Week/Month view. To look at your appointments, events, and meetings in a new light, try one of Calendar's five other predefined views:

- Active Appointments—Displays a tabular list of all the items you've scheduled, sorted by date.

- Events—Displays a tabular list of scheduled events, sorted by the event's start date.

- Annual Events—Displays a tabular list of all the events you've scheduled with an annual recurrence.

- Recurring Appointments—Displays a tabular list of all the recurring appointments you've created.

- By Category—Groups the appointments by category.

Outlook gives you two methods for changing the view:

- Select View, Arrange By, Current View, and then choose the view you want from the menu that appears.

- Use the Current View drop-down list in the toolbar.

Custom Calendar Views

You can also create your own views of the Calendar folder. See "Defining a Custom View," earlier in this chapter, to learn how to create custom views. Note, too, that when you use any of the tabular views, Outlook lets you modify the columns that are displayed in the table, as well as sort, filter, and group the appointments.

Other Navigation Techniques

To complete your look at Calendar's navigation aids, here are a few more techniques you can use:

- To move to today's date, select Go, Today, or click the Today button on the toolbar.

- To move to a specific date, select Go, Go to Date, or press Ctrl+G to display the Go To Date dialog box shown in Figure 5.18. Enter the date you want in the Date text box, or drop down the box to display a calendar and click the date. You can also use the Show In list to select the calendar view you want: Day Calendar, Week Calendar, Month Calendar, or Work Week Calendar. Click OK to display the date.

Figure 5.18
Use the Go To Date dialog box to navigate to a specific date.

- Use the keyboard shortcuts summarized in Table 5.1.

Table 5.1 Calendar's Navigation Keys

Press	To Select...
Day Calendar	
Up arrow	The previous block of time
Down arrow	The next block of time
Left arrow	The previous day
Right arrow	The next day
Tab	The next appointment
Shift+Tab	The previous appointment
Home	The beginning of the workday
End	The end of the workday
Ctrl+Home	The beginning of the day
Ctrl+End	The end of the day
Alt+Up arrow	The same day in the previous week
Alt+Down arrow	The same day in the next week
Alt+Page Up	The first day of the current month
Alt+Page Down	The last day of the current month
Week Calendar	
Up arrow	The previous day
Down arrow	The next day
Home	The first day of the week
End	The last day of the week
Page Up	The same day of the week in the previous week
Page Down	The same day of the week in the next week
Alt+Page Up	The first day of the current month
Alt+Page Down	The last day of the current month
Month Calendar	
Left arrow	The previous day
Right arrow	The next day
Home	The first day of the week
End	The last day of the week
Up arrow	The same day of the week in the previous week

5

Press	To Select...
Month Calendar	
Down arrow	The same day of the week in the next week
Alt+Page Up	The first day of the current month
Alt+Page Down	The last day of the current month

Displaying a Second Time Zone

If you have colleagues on the opposite coast, clients in Europe, or if you can never figure out what the time is in Indiana, Outlook allows you to display a second time zone in the Day and Work Week views. Here's how:

1. Right-click the time display and then click Change Time Zone to display the Time Zone dialog box. (Figure 5.19 shows a completed version of this dialog box.)

Figure 5.19
Use the Time Zone dialog box to select a second time zone to display in the Calendar's Day and Work Week views.

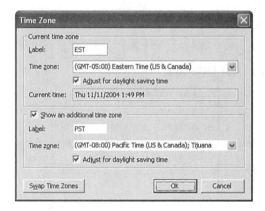

2. In the Current Time Zone group, use the Label text box to enter a label that appears at the top of the current time zone. (Labeling the time zones makes it easy to know which one you're working with.)

3. Activate the Show an Additional Time Zone check box.

4. Use the Label text box to enter a label that appears at the top of the second time zone.

5. Use the Time Zone list to select the time zone you want to add.

6. If the time zone supports daylight saving time (DST) and you want Outlook to adjust the time zone for DST automatically, activate the Adjust for Daylight Saving Time check box.

7. Click OK.

Figure 5.20 shows the Day Calendar with two time zones displayed.

Figure 5.20
Outlook's Day Calendar with the Eastern Time (EST) and Pacific Time (PST) zones displayed.

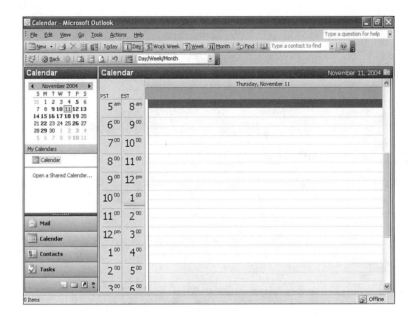

Adding Custom Holidays to Your Calendar

Outlook comes with a list of holidays for more than 80 countries, and you can add the holidays for one or more countries to your Calendar. You probably need the holidays only for your own country, but adding those of another country is a good idea if you regularly deal with people from that country or are planning a trip there. Here are the steps to follow:

1. Select Tools, Options.
2. Click Calendar Options.
3. Click Add Holidays. The Add Holidays to Calendar dialog box appears.
4. Activate the check box for each country's holidays that you want to add. (Note that the check box for United States is activated by default.)
5. Click OK. Outlook adds the holidays.
6. Click OK to exit all dialog boxes.

This works well if all your holidays are covered by one or more of the default holidays supported by Outlook. However, you might have nonstandard holidays to deal with: special company dates (picnics, the owner's birthday, and so on), personal dates (birthday, anniversary), or religious holidays. For these nonstandard holidays, you can add all-day events by hand, but that could be quite time-consuming, particularly if you need to enter multiple years' worth of dates.

A better solution is to customize Outlook's holiday file to include your own dates. To do this, first open the holiday file in Notepad by selecting Start, Run and then enter the following command into the Run dialog box (change the path if you installed Microsoft Office in a different location):

```
notepad "C:\Program Files\Microsoft Office\Office11\1033\outlook.hol"
```

Figure 5.21 shows a portion of the Outlook.hol file.

Figure 5.21
Edit the Outlook.hol file to add your own custom holidays to Outlook.

```
[United States] 120
Administrative Professionals Day,2003/4/23
Administrative Professionals Day,2004/4/21
Administrative Professionals Day,2005/4/27
Administrative Professionals Day,2006/4/26
Administrative Professionals Day,2007/4/25
Christmas Day,2003/12/25
Christmas Day,2004/12/25
Christmas Day,2005/12/25
Christmas Day,2006/12/25
Christmas Day,2007/12/25
Christmas Eve,2003/12/24
Christmas Eve,2004/12/24
Christmas Eve,2005/12/24
Christmas Eve,2006/12/24
Christmas Eve,2007/12/24
Columbus Day,2003/10/13
Columbus Day,2004/10/11
Columbus Day,2005/10/10
Columbus Day,2006/10/9
Columbus Day,2007/10/8
Easter Day,2003/4/20
Easter Day,2004/4/11
Easter Day,2005/3/27
Easter Day,2006/4/16
Easter Day,2007/4/8
Election Day,2003/11/4
Election Day,2004/11/2
Election Day,2005/11/8
Election Day,2006/11/7
Election Day,2007/11/6
Father's Day,2003/6/15
Father's Day,2004/6/20
Father's Day,2005/6/19
Father's Day,2006/6/18
Father's Day,2007/6/17
Flag Day,2003/6/14
Flag Day,2004/6/14
Flag Day,2005/6/14
```

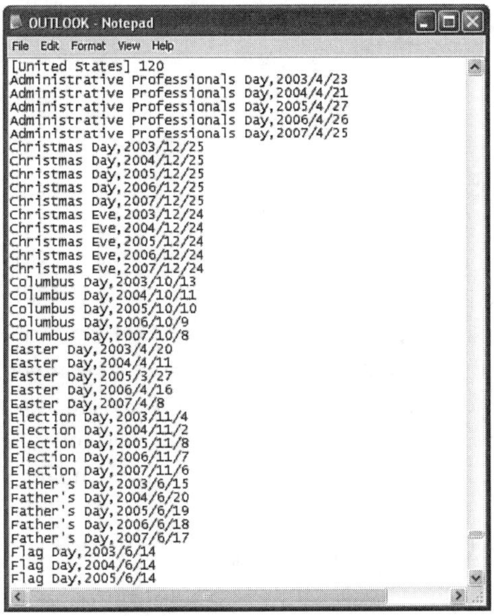

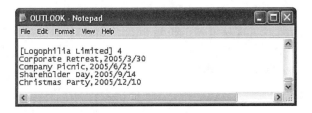

For each country, the holiday list uses the following general form:

```
[Country] Holidays
Name,yyyy/m/d
```

Here, `Country` is the name of the country (this is the check box text that appears in the Add Holidays to Calendar dialog box), `Holidays` is the number of holidays listed, `Name` is the name of the holiday, and `yyyy/m/d` is the date of the holiday. Instead of a country name, you can use your company name, family name, or whatever is appropriate. Figure 5.22 shows a custom holiday list for a company.

Figure 5.22
The Outlook.hol file with a custom holiday list.

```
[Logophilia Limited] 4
Corporate Retreat,2005/3/30
Company Picnic,2005/6/25
Shareholder Day,2005/9/14
Christmas Party,2005/12/10
```

When you open the Add Holidays to Calendar dialog box after customizing the holiday list, you see your company name (or whatever you added) in the list, as shown in Figure 5.23.

Figure 5.23
After you customize Outlook.hol, the "country" name you entered appears in the Add Holidays to Calendar dialog box.

Printing a Blank Calendar

It's often handy to print out a blank calendar for a particular month. For example, you might want to pin the calendar to a company bulletin board so that people can write in appointments or events. Unfortunately, it's likely you won't be able to print a blank monthly calendar directly from your Outlook Calendar because it's probably filled with appointments and events. However, it's possible to create a second Calendar folder and then print directly from that.

First, here's how you create the blank Calendar folder:

1. Switch to Month view and display the month you want to print. (For a blank day or week calendar, switch to the appropriate view and display the day or week you want to print.)
2. Select File, New, Folder (or press Ctrl+Shift+E). The Create New Folder dialog box appears.
3. Enter a name for the new folder.
4. Click OK.

Outlook adds the new Calendar folder to the My Calendars list in the Navigation pane.

Now follow these steps to print the blank calendar:

1. Activate the blank calendar's check box in the My Calendars list.
2. Close the main Calendar by deactivating the Calendar check box in the My Calendars list.
3. Select File, Page Setup, Monthly Style.
4. Click Print.
5. Adjust the Start and End dates to print only those dates you want in the blank calendar.
6. Click OK.

Taking Advantage of AutoDate

One of Outlook's most interesting features is its capability to accept natural-language entries in date and time fields and to convert those entries into real dates and times. If today is November 9, for example, entering next week in a date field will cause Outlook to enter November 16 as the date. Similarly, you can enter noon in a time field, and Outlook "knows" that you mean 12:00 p.m.

This slick feature is called *AutoDate*, and after you understand its ways, you'll find that it saves you lots of time when entering dates and times for appointments, events, and meetings. I won't give you a full description of what AutoDate understands, but a few examples should give you an idea of what it can do, and you can experiment from there.

Here are some notes about entering natural-language dates:

- AutoDate will convert yesterday, today, and tomorrow into their date equivalents.
- You can shorten day names to their first three letters: sun, mon, tue, wed, thu, fri, and sat. (Notice, too, that case isn't important.) You can also shorten month names: jan, feb, mar, apr, may, jun, jul, aug, sep, oct, nov, and dec.
- To specify a date in the current week (Calendar's weeks run from Sunday through Saturday), use the keyword this (for example, this fri).
- To specify a date from last week or last month, use the keyword last (for example, last aug).
- To specify a date in the next week or month, use the keyword next (for example, next sat).
- If you want to use the first day of a week or month, use the keyword first. For example, first mon in dec will give you the first Monday in December. Similarly, use last to specify the last day of a week or month.
- To get a date that is a particular number of days, weeks, months, or years from some other date, use the keyword from (for example, 6 months from today).
- To get a date that is a particular number of days, weeks, months, or years before some other date, use the keyword before (for example, 2 days before Christmas).

AutoDate's Built-In Holidays

Yes, AutoDate also recognizes a number of holidays that fall on the same date each year, including the following: Boxing Day, Cinco de Mayo, Christmas, Christmas Day, Christmas Eve, Halloween, Independence Day, Lincoln's Birthday, New Year's Day, New Year's Eve, St. Patrick's Day, Valentine's Day, Veterans Day, and Washington's Birthday.

- To get a date that is a particular number of days, weeks, months, or years in the past, use the keyword **ago** (for example, 4 weeks ago).
- AutoDate also accepts spelled-out dates, such as August 23rd and first of January. These aren't as useful because they probably take longer to spell out than they do to enter the date in the usual format.

5

For time fields, keep the following points in mind:

- AutoDate will convert noon and midnight into the correct times.
- AutoDate understands military time. So if you enter 9, AutoDate converts it to 9:00 a.m. However, if you enter 21, AutoDate changes it to 9:00 p.m.
- Use **now** to specify the current time.
- You can specify time zones by using the following abbreviations: CST, EST, GMT, MST, and PST.

Color-Coding Appointments

If you have a lot of appointments, consider taking advantage of Outlook's capability to color code—or *label*—important appointments. This means that you apply a particular background color to the appointment. Each of the available colors is associated with a particular label, such as Important, Business, and Personal.

 To set the label for an existing appointment, right-click the appointment, click Label (or click the Calendar Coloring toolbar button), and then select the label. If you're creating a new label, select the label you want from the Label list.

If you don't like Outlook's default labels, you can change them by selecting Edit, Label (or clicking the Calendar Coloring toolbar button) and then selecting Edit Labels. In the Edit Calendar Labels dialog box that appears, edit the labels you want to change and then click OK. Note, however, that you should think twice about editing the labels if you plan on sharing your calendar with other users—because those users won't be familiar with your custom labels.

Getting the Most Out of Contacts

Outlook's contact management module—called, appropriately enough, *Contacts*—gives you amazing flexibility for dealing with your ever-growing network of colleagues, clients, friends, and family. So, yes, you can use Contacts to store mundane information such as phone numbers and addresses, but with more than 140 predefined fields available, you can preserve the minutiae of other people's lives: their birthdays and anniversaries, the names of their spouses and children, and even their nicknames.

The rest of this chapter takes you through a few useful tricks and techniques that will help you take your work in the Contacts folder to the next level.

Working with the Contacts Folder's Views

As with all of Outlook's folders, you can view your contacts in several ways. For example, you can set up the Contacts folder to group items by Company or Location. Outlook has seven predefined views for the Contacts folder:

- Address Cards—Displays the Contacts folder as a kind of Rolodex, with each contact given its own "card" showing basic information.

- Detailed Address Cards—This view is similar to Address Cards, but it shows more fields for each contact, including home data, web page, and notes. Also, multiline entries are displayed in full.

- Phone List—Displays the contacts in a table format with the fields as columns. You see the full name, company name, and phone numbers for each contact.

- By Category—Groups the contacts on the Categories field and displays them in a table format. Within each category, contacts are sorted by the File As field.

- By Company—Groups the contacts on the Company field and displays them in a table format. Within each company, contacts are sorted by the File As field.

- By Location—Groups the contacts on the Country/Region field and displays them in a table format. Within each country, contacts are sorted by the File As field.

- By Follow-Up Flag—Groups the contacts on the Flag Status field and displays them in a table format. Within each Flag type, contacts are sorted by the File As field.

Outlook gives you three methods of changing the Contacts view:

- Click a view option in the Current View section of the Navigation pane.

- Select View, Arrange By, Current View, and then choose the view you want from the menu that appears.

- Use the Current View drop-down list in the toolbar.

Custom Contacts Views

You can also create your own views of the Contacts folder. See "Defining a Custom View," earlier in this chapter, to learn how to create custom views. Note, too, that when you use any of the Table views, Outlook lets you modify the columns that are displayed in the table, as well as sort, filter, and group the appointments.

Editing Data for Multiple Contacts

If you work with a large Contacts list, it's common to have many Contacts with the same data in a particular field. For example, you might have a number of Contacts from the same company, in which case they'd all have the same Company field. Similarly, you might have a number of Contacts from a particular department, in which case the contacts would all have the same Department field. This is fine until this common data changes. For example, if the name of the company or department changes, you need to edit the appropriate field for all the affected Contacts.

You can avoid this tedious procedure by taking advantage of grouping. Here's how it works:

1. Group the Contacts according to the field you want to change. You have two choices:

   • Select an existing view. For example, if you want to modify the Company field, select the By Company view.

   • Customize the view. Click Customize Current View, click Group By, select the field you want to work with, and click OK. (If the Group By button is disabled, it means the current view doesn't support grouping. Switch to a view—such as Phone List—that supports grouping.)

2. Select View, Expand/Collapse Groups, Collapse All Groups.

3. Find the group that corresponds to the Contacts you want to edit, and then expand that group by clicking its plus sign (+).

4. Edit the field in the group's first Contact. Outlook immediately adds a new group for the edited data and moves the first Contact to that group.

5. Drag the group header for the rest of the Contacts with the old data and drop it on the group header for the new data. Outlook updates all the Contacts with the new field data.

Phoning a Contact

You can have Outlook dial your phone automatically via an attached modem. To use this feature, you need to arrange your phone cables appropriately:

- Run one phone cable from your phone to the "Phone" jack on your modem.
- Run a second phone cable from your modem's "Line" jack to the phone jack on your wall.

With that out of the way, select the contact you want to phone, and then do either of the following:

- Select Actions, Call Contact.
- Drop down the Dial button on the toolbar.

Either way, you'll see a list of commands that includes the phone number (or numbers) for the contact. Select the number you want to dial. Outlook displays the New Call dialog box, shown in Figure 5.24. Before starting your call, you can use the following options in this dialog box:

- Open Contact—Click this button to open the Contact window for the current contact.
- Dialing Properties—Click this button to select or change the dialing properties for Windows.
- Dialing Options—Use this button to set up speed-dial numbers. See the next section for details.

- Create New Journal Entry When Starting New Call—Activate this check box to create an entry in Outlook's Journal for this call.

Figure 5.24
Use the New Call dialog box to set dialing properties and initiate the call.

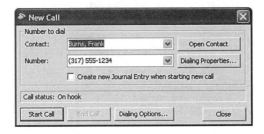

When you're ready to dial, click Start Call. When the Call Status reads Connected, pick up the phone and proceed with your call. When you're done, click End Call.

Redialing Recent Calls
Outlook keeps track of the last seven calls you dialed. To redial one of these numbers, select Actions, Call Contact, Redial, or drop down the Dial button and then click Redial. Select the number to redial from the cascade menu that appears.

On-the-Fly Dialing
Besides phoning specific contacts, you can also use Outlook to dial numbers on-the-fly. Select Actions, Call Contact, New Call (or press Ctrl+Shift+D) to display the New Call dialog box. Enter the phone number into the Number text box and then click Start Call.

Quick Connections with Speed Dial

If you have several contacts that you dial regularly, you can save a few steps by setting up their phone numbers in Outlook's Speed Dial feature. This places the numbers on the Speed Dial menu so that they're only a few clicks away.

To create a Speed Dial number, display the New Call dialog box. (It doesn't matter how you do this. Unfortunately, Outlook doesn't give you a direct method for defining a specific number as a Speed Dial number. It would be nice if we had an Add to Speed Dial command, but there isn't one.) Now click the Dialing Options button to display the Dialing Options dialog box, shown in Figure 5.25. Enter a name into the Name text box, enter the phone number into the Phone Number text box, and then click Add. You can add up to 20 entries.

To place a call using Speed Dial, select Actions, Call Contact, Speed Dial, or drop down the Dial button and choose Speed Dial. In the menu that appears, choose the number you want to call.

Figure 5.25
Use the Dialing Options dialog box to define your Speed Dial numbers.

Adding a Picture for a Contact

With digital cameras all the rage, sharing photos is as easy as emailing or, in the case of camera phones, making a phone call. This means it's possible you may have a picture of one or more of your contacts. If so, you can add that picture to the person's contact data. Here's how:

1. Open the person's contact data.
2. Select Actions, Add Picture, or click the Add Contact Picture button shown in Figure 5.26. The Add Contact Picture dialog box appears.

Add Contact Picture

Figure 5.26
You can replace the Add Contact Picture button with an actual picture of your contact.

3. Select the picture you want to use.

4. Click OK. Outlook replaces the Add Contact Picture button with the picture you selected, as shown in Figure 5.27.

Figure 5.27
The contact with a picture added.

Displaying Contact Activity

The integrated nature of Outlook means that we often deal with people in a number of ways: read their email, send them email, have meetings with them, or include them in journal entries, notes, and tasks. Multiply all this by the dozens of other people we deal with, and finding, for instance, a particular meeting with a particular person can kill a lot of precious time.

If the person you're working with is set up as a contact, however, Outlook offers an often-overlooked method for filtering out other people and items and drilling down to the specific item you're looking for. It's called the Activities tab, and you use it as follows:

1. Open the contact you want to work with.

2. Display the Activities tab shown in Figure 5.28.

3. Use the Show list to choose the specific items you want to see.

5

Figure 5.28
Use the Activities tab to see all the email messages, appointments, meetings, and other items associated with the current contact.

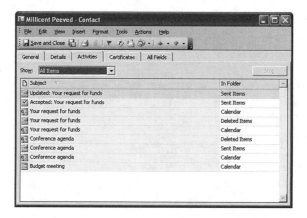

From Here

- To learn how to use Outlook email to send Office documents to other users, see the section in Chapter 7 titled "Sharing Office Documents via Email."

- For information on sharing calendars and performing other Outlook collaborative chores, see the section in Chapter 7 titled "Collaborating via Outlook."

- To learn how to collaborate on documents using SharePoint, see the section in Chapter 7 titled "Using SharePoint to Collaborate on Office Documents."

- To put your calendar on the Web for others to view, see the section in Chapter 8 titled "Publishing an Outlook Calendar to the Web."

- To learn how to use a digital pen to create an email, see the section in Chapter 9 titled "Inking an Email Message."

- For a few Outlook-related VBA macros, see the section in Chapter 12 titled "Outlook Macros."

- To learn how to protect your Outlook data files, see the section in Chapter 14 titled "Assigning a Password to Your Outlook Personal Folders."

- To get full details on the rest of Outlook's email security and privacy features, see Chapter 15, "Enhancing Outlook Email Security and Privacy."

Office 2003 Sharing and Collaboration Tricks

II

Office in Overdrive: Sharing Data Between Applications

6

It's getting hard to remember the days when applications operated in splendid isolation. In those bygone days, if you needed to write a memo, you'd fire up your word processor program and start hunting and pecking. If you then realized you needed a spreadsheet to complement the text, you'd shut down the word processor, crank up your spreadsheet program, and start crunching numbers. The only tools you had at hand to connect these two documents were a paper clip and a "See attached" message.

Now, thanks to wonders such as multitasking, cut-and-paste techniques, and linking and embedding, applications have gone from isolation to collaboration. Not only can you have Word and Excel running at the same time, but you can easily share data between them, to the point where you can actually place, for example, an entire worksheet inside a Word document.

This willingness to share data between its applications is one of the best features of Office, and it's the subject of this chapter. I'll show you the full gamut of data-sharing tools, from simple cut-and-paste Clipboard techniques to sophisticated linking and embedding operations to the powerful integration tools that come with each Office application.

Using the Office Clipboard

When you cut or copy data in a non-Office program, Windows stores the data in a special memory location called the *Clipboard*. When you run the Paste command, Windows grabs the data from the Clipboard and adds it to the document. This has worked well for Windows users for many years, but all of us have run into the Clipboard's glaring weakness: it can hold only one item at a time. If you cut or copy something else, the previous data is discarded.

The Office programmers have been trying to fix this weakness since Office 2000 by implementing a Clipboard replacement called the Office Clipboard that's capable of storing multiple cut or copied items. Early incarnations of the Office Clipboard were clunky and barely usable, so they were ignored by most users. The Office 2003 version of the Office Clipboard is the best one yet, but it's still a relatively limited tool.

Like its Windows cousin, at its most basic level the Office Clipboard is a don't-reinvent-the-wheel device. In other words, if you've created something that works—whether it's a bit of polished prose, an attractive graphic, or a complex worksheet formula—and you'd like to reuse it, don't waste time re-creating the data from scratch. Instead, you can send the existing data to the Office Clipboard and then insert a copy of it into a different document or even into a different application altogether.

Unlike its Windows cousin, the Office Clipboard can store up to 24 items at a time, even items cut or copied from non-Office programs. The Office Clipboard is implemented as part of the Task pane and it appears in the following circumstances:

- When you cut or copy two items in a row without pasting
- When you select Edit, Office Clipboard
- When you select Clipboard from the Task pane menu
- When you press Ctrl+C twice

Figure 6.1 shows an example of the Office Clipboard with several items stored. The items are listed with the most recently added at the top of the list.

Figure 6.1
The Office 2003 version of the Office Clipboard can store up to 24 items.

Moving Multiple Items in Word

If you want to move multiple items in a Word document, you could cut each one and then paste them from the Office Clipboard. However, Word also offers a special AutoText entry called Spike that's a bit easier to use. For each item you want to move, select it and press Ctrl+F3. In each case, Word removes the item from the document and appends it to the Spike. To paste everything from the Spike, type `spike` and press Enter (or press Ctrl+Shift+F3).

Here are the techniques to use to work with items on the Office Clipboard:

- To paste the top item, select Edit, Paste, or press Ctrl+V. (The top item in the Office Clipboard corresponds to the current item in the Windows Clipboard.)
- To paste any item, click it.

Paste Is Office Only

Although you can add items to the Office Clipboard from any application, you can paste Office Clipboard items only to Office applications.

- To paste all the items stored in the Office Clipboard, click Paste All.

Paste All Is Disabled

If the Paste All button is disabled, it means the Office Clipboard contains a mix of data formats, at least one of which can't be pasted into the document you're working with. For example, in Access you can't paste any nontext data into a text-only field.

- To remove an item from the Office Clipboard, right-click it and then click Delete.
- To remove all the items from the Office Clipboard, click Clear All.

Closing Office Clears the Office Clipboard

When you shut down all your running Office programs, the Office Clipboard gets cleared out. If you have data you want to preserve, you must keep at least one Office program running at all times.

Setting Office Clipboard Options

If you plan to use the Office Clipboard regularly, it comes with a few options that enable you to control some aspects of its behavior. To see these settings, click the Options button:

- Show Office Clipboard Automatically—When you activate this option, the Office Clipboard appears automatically when you cut or copy two items in a row without pasting.
- Show Office Clipboard Automatically When Ctrl+C Pressed Twice—When you activate this option, you can display the Office Clipboard by pressing Ctrl+C twice in succession.

■ Collect Without Showing Office Clipboard—When you activate this option, the Office Clipboard remains active, but it doesn't appear until you display the Clipboard taskbar. If you deactivate this option and you deactivate Show Office Clipboard Automatically, then the Office Clipboard is active only when the Clipboard task pane is displayed in at least one Office application.

Deactivating the Office Clipboard

In other words, if you don't want to use the Office Clipboard at all, you must do three things: deactivate the Show Office Clipboard Automatically option, deactivate the Collect Without Showing Office Clipboard option, and turn off the Clipboard task pane in all Office applications.

■ Show Office Clipboard Icon on Taskbar—When you activate this option, an icon for the Office Clipboard appears in the taskbar's notification area.

■ Show Status Near Taskbar When Copying—When you activate this option, balloon text appears near the Office Clipboard's notification area icon. This text tells you the number of items on the Office Clipboard and whether the collection was successful.

Pasting Data in a Different Format

If the Office Clipboard has a glaring weakness of its own, it's that it can't paste data in different formats. You can occasionally use the Paste Options smart tag to select the paste format, but this aspect of Office 2003 is inconsistent and poorly implemented. If you want to control the format, you need to return to the Windows Clipboard.

Clipboard data usually has a default format that's used when you select the Paste command. For example, if you send a piece of a Paint image to the Clipboard and then paste it into Word, the image is inserted using the bitmap format. However, there are often multiple formats for a given data type. An Excel worksheet range can be copied as RTF text, a bitmap, HTML, a Worksheet object, and more.

If you'd like to use a different format when you paste data, the Office applications all have a Paste Special command on the Edit menu. Selecting this command displays a dialog box similar to the one shown in Figure 6.2. Here, the As box lists the various formats that are available. You select the one you want and click OK. (However, you need to be careful that you don't *embed* the data. In many cases, the first item shown in the As list is an Object format. If you select this item, Windows pastes the data as an embedded object. I'll discuss this in more detail when I talk about linking and embedding later in this chapter.)

6

Figure 6.2
The Paste Special dialog box gives you access to the other formats available with the data you're pasting from the Clipboard.

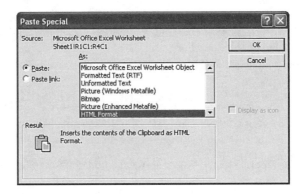

Using the Clipboard Contents in a Replace Operation

The Replace command that appears on the Edit menu of the Office application is normally used to replace text or formatting. However, you can also use it to replace text with an image or just about any other data by using the Clipboard. For example, you might want to replace all instances of the word "Time" with an image of a clock; or you may want to replace some instances of your company name with your company logo. Here are the steps to follow:

1. Copy the data that you want to use to replace the text.
2. In the Office document containing the text, select Edit, Replace.
3. In the Find What text box, type the text you want to replace.
4. In the Replace With text box, type ^c (that's the caret symbol (^) followed by the letter *c*). This symbol represents the contents of the Clipboard.
5. For each instance you want to replace, click Find Next and then click Replace. (Alternatively, click Replace All to replace all the instances.)
6. Click Close.

Inserting an Object from Another Application

Using the Office or Windows Clipboard to copy data from one application to another is simple, but both methods suffer from three major problems. First, if the data gets changed in the original application, the document containing the copy will become out of date. This has two consequences:

- If you know that the data needs to be updated, you have to repeat the whole copy-and-paste procedure to get the latest version of the data.
- If you don't know that the data needs to be updated (for example, if someone else changes the original data without telling you), you'll be stuck with an old version of the info.

Second, what if you want to make changes to the copied data? You might be able to edit the data directly (if it's just text, for example), but more often than not, you'll need to fire up the original application, change the data there, and then copy the data again. However, problems can arise if you're not sure which application to use or if you're not sure which file contains the original data.

Third, copying data between documents is often wasteful because you end up with multiple copies of the same data. You could cut the data from the original application and then paste it, but then there would be no easy way to edit the data using the original application.

It would be nice if you didn't have to worry about the updating of your shared data. It would be nice if there were a system that would accomplish three goals:

- If the data changes in the original application, it updates the copied data automatically.
- If you want to edit the copied data, it makes it easy to find both the original application and the original data file.
- It lets you store non-native data inside a document without having to maintain separate documents for the original data.

Happily, the twin technologies of linking and embedding meet all three goals and add a few extra conveniences to the mix for good measure.

Understanding Compound Documents

A *compound document* is a document that contains, along with its native data, one or more objects that were created using other applications. The key point is that the compound document's native data and its objects can have entirely different data formats. For example, a Word document can include an Excel range object or a sound clip object. The container application doesn't need to know a thing about these alien data formats, either. All it has to know is the name of the server application that created the data and how to display the data. All this information (and more) is included free of charge as part of the object, so it's readily available to the container application.

You create a compound document by either linking objects to the document or embedding objects in the document. The next three sections explain linking and embedding in more depth.

Linking and Embedding in Access

You can't link or embed objects in just any field of an Access table. Instead, you need to create a separate field that's configured for the OLE Object data type. After that's done, you can insert linked or embedded objects in that field.

Understanding Linking

Linking is one of the methods you can use to insert an object into a file from a container application and thus create a compound document. In this case, the object includes only the following information:

- The Registry key needed to invoke the object's server application.
- A metafile that contains instructions on how to display the object. These instructions generate the primitives (lines, circles, arcs, and so on) that create an image of the object. So the container application doesn't have to know a thing about the object itself; it just follows the metafile's instructions blindly, and a perfect replica of the object's image appears.
- A pointer to the server application file (the *source document*) that contains the original data.

Linking brings many advantages to the table, but three are most relevant to our purposes. First, the link lets the container application check the source document for changes. If it finds that the data has been modified, it can use the link to update the object automatically. For example, suppose you insert a linked Excel worksheet object into a Word document. If you revise some of the numbers in the worksheet sometime down the road, the object inside the document is automatically updated to reflect the new numbers. However, this updating is automatic only under certain conditions:

- If the container application is running and has the compound document open, the update is automatic.
- If the compound document isn't open when the data is changed, the object gets updated automatically the next time you open the compound document.
- Most applications let you disable automatic updating either for individual documents or for the application as a whole. In this case, you need to perform the updates manually. (I'll show you how this is done later in this chapter.)

Second, because the object "knows" where to find both the server application and the source document, you can edit the object from within the container application. In most cases, double-clicking the object invokes the server and loads the appropriate source file. You can then edit the original data and exit the server application, and your object is, once again, updated automatically.

Third, because the source data exists in a separate file, you can easily reuse the data in other compound documents, and you can edit the data directly from within the server application.

Understanding Embedding

One of the problems associated with linking is that if you distribute the compound document, you also have to distribute the source document. *Embedding* solves this problem by inserting an object not only with the server's Registry information and the metafile for displaying the object, but also with the object's *data*. This way, everything you need to display

6

and work with the object exists within the object itself. There's no need for a separate source file, so you can distribute the compound document knowing that the recipient will receive the data intact.

In fact, embedding lets you *create* server objects from within the container application. If you're working with Word, for example, you can insert a new Excel worksheet object into your document. Windows will start Excel so that you can create the new object, but when you exit Excel, the object will exist only within the Word compound document. There will be no separate Excel file.

Note that many applications can operate only as servers. This means that they aren't stand-alone applications and therefore have no way to create files on their own. They exist only to create objects for compound documents. Microsoft Office ships with several examples of these applications, including WordArt and Microsoft Graph.

Should You Link or Embed?

Perhaps the most confusing aspect of all this is determining whether you should link your objects or embed them. As you've seen, the major difference between linking and embedding is that a linked object stores only a pointer to its data, whereas an embedded object stores its own data internally.

With this in mind, you should link your objects if any of the following situations apply:

- You want to keep your compound documents small. The information stored in a linked object—the pointers to the server and source document, and the metafile—consume only about 1.5KB, so very little overhead is associated with linking.

- You need to keep the source file as a separate document in case you want to make changes to it later, or in case you need it for other compound documents. You're free to link an object to as many container files as you like. If you think you'll be using the source data in different places, you should link it to maintain a separate file.

- You won't be sending the compound document via email or floppy disk. Again, OLE expects the linked source data to appear in a specific place. If you send the compound document to someone else, he or she might not have the proper source file to maintain the link.

Similarly, you should embed your objects if any of the following situations apply:

- You don't care how big your compound documents get. Embedding works best in situations in which you have lots of hard disk space and lots of memory.

- You don't need to keep the source file as a separate document. If you need to use the source data only once, embedding it means you can get rid of the source file (or never have to create one in the first place) and reduce the clutter on your hard disk.

■ You'll be sending the compound documents and you want to make sure the object arrives intact. If you send a file containing an embedded object, the other person will see the data complete and unaltered. If the recipient wants to edit the object, however, he or she will need to have the server application installed.

Linking an Object

If you have data you'd like to share between applications, and you think that linking is the best way to go, Windows gives you two methods: linking via the Clipboard and inserting a linked file. The next two sections discuss each method. Then I'll show you how to work with and maintain your links.

Linking via the Clipboard

After you've placed the data on the Clipboard, switch to the container application and position the cursor where you want the data to be pasted. Now select Edit, Paste Special to display the Paste Special dialog box, shown in Figure 6.3.

Figure 6.3
Use the Paste Special dialog box to paste Clipboard data as a linked object.

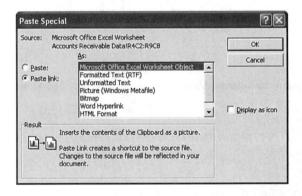

The As box lists the various formats available for the data, but you can ignore most of them. To establish a link between the container and the server, you need to do two things:

■ Activate the Paste Link option.

■ Select the "Object" format (for example, Microsoft Office Excel Worksheet Object).

If you'd like the data to appear as an icon in the container document, activate the Display as Icon check box. When you're ready, click OK to paste the linked object into the container. Figure 6.4 shows an Excel range pasted normally and as an icon.

6

Figure 6.4
A linked Excel worksheet object displayed normally and as an icon.

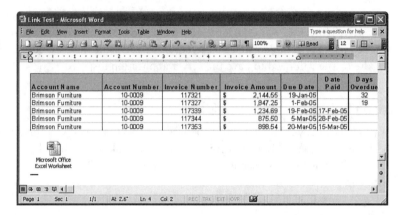

Inserting a File as a Linked Object

Instead of pasting part of a document as a linked object, you might prefer to insert an entire file as a linked object. For example, if you insert a linked Excel workbook into a Word document, the container object will reflect *any* changes made to the original file, including data added or removed, global formatting adjustments, and so on. (Note, however, that in this case only the first worksheet is inserted.)

Also, in certain situations you have no choice but to insert a file. For example, you can't insert part of a bitmap as a linked object; instead, you have to insert the entire file.

Here are the basic steps to follow to insert a file as a linked object:

1. In the container application, position the cursor where you want the file inserted.
2. Select Insert, Object to display the Object dialog box.
3. Select the Create from File tab, shown in Figure 6.5. (In some applications—such as PowerPoint and Access—you activate the Create from File option, instead.)

Figure 6.5
Use the Create from File tab to insert a file object in the container.

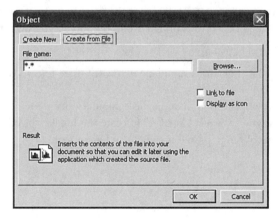

6

4. Enter the filename of the file you want to link. You can also click the Browse button to choose the file from a dialog box.

5. Activate the Link to File check box. (In PowerPoint and Access, activate the Link check box, instead.)

6. If you want the linked file to appear as an icon, activate the Display as Icon check box.

7. Click OK to insert the linked file object.

Managing Links

All container applications that support object linking also give you some kind of method to manage document links. This involves updating a link so that the container displays the most recent changes, changing a link's source, determining how links are updated in the container, and breaking links you no longer need to maintain.

In most container applications, you manage links by selecting Edit, Links to display the Links dialog box, which should be similar to the one shown in Figure 6.6 (this is the Links dialog box from Word).

Figure 6.6
Container applications that support object linking have a Links dialog box that you can use to maintain the links.

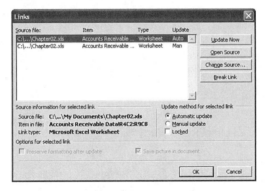

Following is a rundown of the basic link management chores you can perform:

- Changing the link update method—By default, links are updated automatically. In other words, if both the source and the container are open, whenever the source data changes, the data in the container also changes. If you would prefer to update the container document by hand, select the link and activate the Manual option.

- Updating the link—If you've set a link to Manual, or if the server document isn't open, you can make sure a link contains the latest information by selecting it and clicking the Update Now button.

- Changing the link source—If you move the source document, you might need to modify the link so that it points to the new location. You can do this by selecting the appropriate link and clicking the Change Source button.

6

- Breaking a link—If you no longer want to maintain a link between the source and the container, you can break the link. This will leave the data intact, but changes made to the original data will no longer be reflected in the container. To break a link, highlight it and click the Break Link button.

Embedding an Object

If you prefer to embed an object instead of linking it, Windows gives you three methods to choose from (depending on the server application): the Clipboard, inserting a new embedded object, and inserting an embedded file.

Embedding via the Clipboard

To embed data that's been placed on the Clipboard, switch to the container application, position the cursor where you want the data to be pasted, and select Edit, Paste Special. In the Paste Special dialog box that appears, you embed the data by doing two things:

- Activate the Paste option.
- Select the Object format (for example, Microsoft Office Excel Worksheet Object).

Also, if you'd like the data to appear as an icon in the container document, activate the Display as Icon check box. When you're ready, click OK to embed the object in the container.

Inserting a New Embedded Object

If the object you want to embed doesn't exist, and you don't need to create a separate file, Windows lets you insert the new object directly into the container application. Here's how it works:

1. In the container application, move the cursor to where you want the new object to appear.
2. Select Insert, Object to display the Object dialog box as shown in Figure 6.7. Make sure the Create New tab is selected.

Figure 6.7
In the Object dialog box, use the Create New tab to select the type of embedded object you want to create.

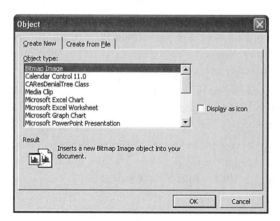

3. The Object Type list displays all the available objects on your system. Select the type of object you want to create.

4. Click OK. Windows starts the server application for the object type you selected. The server will appear either in place or in a separate window.

5. Create the object you want to embed.

6. Exit the server application. If you were working with the server using visual editing, click outside the object. Otherwise, select File, Exit and Return to *document*, where *document* is the name of the active document in the container application.

Inserting an Embedded File

You can insert an entire existing file (in contrast to an object within a file) as an embedded object. This is useful if you want to make changes to the file from within the container without disturbing the original. Follow these steps:

1. In the container document, position the cursor where you want to embed the object.

2. Select Insert, Object to display the Object dialog box.

3. Select the Create from File tab. (In some applications—such as PowerPoint and Access—you activate the Create from File option instead.)

4. Enter the filename of the file you want to link. You can also click the Browse button to choose the file from a dialog box.

5. If you want the embedded file to appear as an icon, activate the Display as Icon check box.

6. Click OK to insert the embedded file object.

Editing a Linked or Embedded Object

If you need to make some changes to a linked or embedded object, you can use the container application to launch the server application and load the object automatically. (Remember, too, that for a linked object, you can always run the server application and work with the object directly.) How you do this depends on the application, but here are a few methods that work for most containers applications:

- Double-click the object.

- Select the object, pull down the Edit menu, and then select either Linked *ObjectType* Object (for a linked object) or *ObjectType* Object (for an embedded object). In both cases, *ObjectType* is the type of object you selected (for example, Bitmap Image or Worksheet). In the menu that appears, select Edit. If the server application supports visual editing, this will launch the object in place.

- Select the object, pull down the Edit menu, and then select either the Linked *ObjectType* Object command (for a linked object) or the *ObjectType* Object command (for an embedded object). In the cascade menu that appears, select Open. For servers that support the Open verb, this will launch the object in a separate window.

■ Right-click the object, select either Linked *ObjectType* Object or *ObjectType* Object, and select either Edit or Open.

Edit Isn't Always the Default

Sometimes, when you double-click an object (such as a PowerPoint presentation or a sound file), Windows will play the object instead of editing it. In this case, you can edit the object only by using the appropriate Edit command.

More Office Tools for Sharing Data

Besides the Office and Windows Clipboards and linking and embedding, Office 2003 comes with a number of other tools and techniques for sharing data between the Office applications. The next few sections take you through the most useful of these tools.

Converting a Word Outline into a PowerPoint Presentation

In Chapter 3, "Constructing Knockout Presentations in PowerPoint," you learned how to convert a simple text file into a presentation (see the section titled, "Creating an Outline from a Text File"). Given the hierarchical structure of a PowerPoint outline, you may not be surprised to hear that you can convert Word's own outline hierarchy—the styles Heading 1, Heading 2, and so on—into a PowerPoint outline. Here are the details:

■ PowerPoint interprets a Heading 1 style as a top-level item in a presentation outline. In other words, each time PowerPoint comes across Heading 1 text, it starts a new slide and the text associated with the Heading 1 style becomes the title of the slide.

■ PowerPoint interprets a Heading 2 style as a second-level item in a presentation outline. So each paragraph of Heading 2 text becomes a main bullet (or subtitle) in the presentation.

■ PowerPoint interprets the styles Heading 3, Heading 4, and so on as lower-level items in the presentation outline.

To convert a Word outline into a PowerPoint presentation, follow these steps:

1. In PowerPoint, select File, Open to display the Open dialog box.
2. In the Files of Type list, select All Outlines.
3. Select the Word file containing the outline you want to convert.

Close the Word Document

PowerPoint won't convert the Word document if it's open elsewhere, so be sure to close it before following these steps.

---

4. Click OK. PowerPoint converts the Word outline to a presentation.

Sending the Outline from Word to PowerPoint

Another technique you can use is to open the outline in Word and then select File, Send To, Microsoft Office PowerPoint. This launches PowerPoint and creates a new presentation with the converted outline.

Converting a Web Page to a PowerPoint Outline

If you know HTML, you might be wondering if you can convert the heading tags—<H1>, <H2>, and so on—into a PowerPoint presentation outline. You can, but only if you first open the page in Word. Then select File, Send To, Microsoft Office PowerPoint to create the presentation outline. Note that <H1> tags are converted to top-level items (slide titles), <H2> tags are converted to second-level items (main bullets and slide subtitles), and so on.

Figure 6.8 shows a Word outline and Figure 6.9 shows the document converted to a PowerPoint presentation outline.

Figure 6.8
You can convert Word outlines such as this one to PowerPoint presentation outlines.

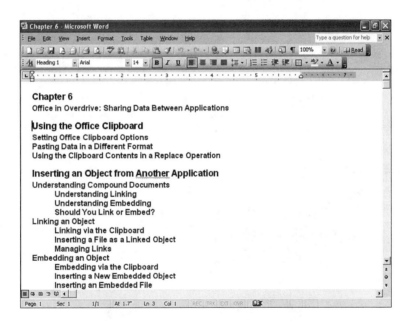

Using Word to Custom Format PowerPoint Handouts

You can create simple handouts in PowerPoint to go along with your presentations. However, if you want to spruce up the handouts, you need the more powerful text and paragraph formatting available in Word. Here are the steps to follow to export your presentation to Word so that you can format the handout text:

1. In PowerPoint, select File, Send To, Microsoft Word. The Send to Microsoft Office Word dialog box appears.

2. Select the page layout you want to use.

6

3. Activate the Paste Link option.

4. Click OK. The presentation appears in Word.

5. Add, edit, and format your handout text.

Figure 6.9
The PowerPoint presentation outline created by converting the Word outline shown in Figure 6.8.

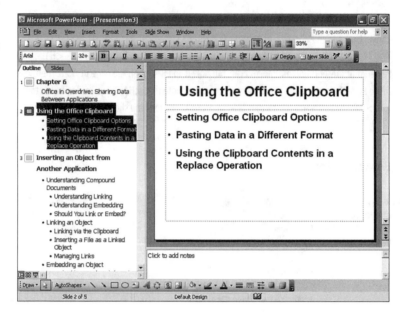

Importing Excel Data into Access

As you saw in Chapter 2, "Analyzing Data with Excel," you can perform some fairly sophisticated flat-file database analysis within Excel (see the section titled, "Analyzing Data with Lists"). However, Excel's database prowess is limited, and you may find you need the relational database power of Access to get the most out of your data. In that case, you need to import the Excel data into Access.

The easiest way to import worksheet data is via simple cut and paste:

1. In Excel, select the range that you want to import.

2. Select Edit, Copy (or press Ctrl+C).

3. Switch to Access.

4. Select Edit, Paste (or press Ctrl+V). Access asks if the first row of your data contains column headings.

5. Click Yes or No, as appropriate. Access pastes the data into a new table and lets you know if the operation was successful.

6. Click OK.

The resulting table is given the same name as the worksheet from which you copied your data, and Access assigns default data types and sizes to each field based on the data in each column.

If you want more control over the import, you need to use the Import Spreadsheet Wizard. Follow these steps:

1. In Excel, close the workbook you'll be importing if it's currently open.

2. In Access, select File, Get External Data, Import. Access displays the Import dialog box.

3. In the Files of Type list, select Microsoft Excel.

4. Select the workbook you want to import and then click Import. Access starts the Import Spreadsheet Wizard.

5. Either activate the Show Worksheets option and select the worksheet you want to import, or activate the Show Named Ranges option and select the named range you want to import. When you're done, click Next.

6. If the first row of the worksheet or range contains the field names you want to use, activate the First Row Contains Column Headings check box, and then click Next.

7. In the next Wizard dialog box, activate In a New Table if you want to import the data to a new table. Otherwise, activate In an Existing Table and choose the table from the list provided. When you're done, click Next to display the Import Spreadsheet Wizard dialog box shown in Figure 6.10.

Figure 6.10
Use this Import Spreadsheet Wizard dialog box to specify information about each field you're importing.

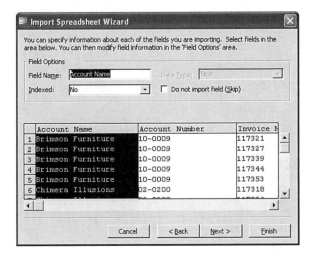

8. For each field (column), edit the field name and specify whether the field should be indexed. If you want the wizard to bypass a field, activate the Do Not Import Field (Skip) check box. To select a different field, click the field's header. When you're done, click Next to move to the next dialog box.

9. The next Wizard dialog box lets you specify a primary key for the new table. You have three choices (click Next when you've made your choice):

Let Access Add Primary Key—Choose this option to tell Access to create a new field (called ID) to use as the primary key.

Choose My Own Primary Key—Choose this option to select a primary key from one of the existing fields (which you select from the associated drop-down list).

No Primary Key—Choose this option if you don't want to specify a primary key for the new table.

10. In the final Import Spreadsheet Wizard dialog box, edit the name for the new table in the Import to Table text box. If you'd like the wizard to analyze the structure of the table (to look for data redundancies and other relational issues), activate the I Would Like a Wizard to Analyze check box. When you're ready, click Finish. Access creates the new table and displays a dialog box to let you know.

11. Click OK to return to the database.

Importing Outlook Data

Access also has an Import Exchange/Outlook Wizard that enables you to import data from an Outlook folder (or an Exchange folder, if you're on an Exchange Server network). Select File, Get External Data, Import to display the Import dialog box. In the Files of Type list, select Outlook to launch the wizard.

Exporting a Word Table to Access

If you have data in a Word table that you want to export to Access, the process isn't as straightforward as the Excel-to-Access route. In particular, you must create in advance a table in Access to hold the Word table data. The Access table must follow these guidelines:

- There should be at least as many fields as there are columns in your Word table.
- The data type of the fields must match the data in the Word table. For example, if your Word table contains text in the first column, the first field in the Access table must use the Text data type. (This also implies that your Word table must use data types consistently. For example, if the first column contains a mixture of text and numbers, the data won't export to Access properly.)

With that done, follow these steps to export the Word table:

1. In Word, select the table (or part of a table) you want to export.
2. Select Edit, Copy (or press Ctrl+C) to place the table data on the Clipboard.
3. In Access, open the table you created to hold the Word data.
4. Select the entire table.
5. Select Edit, Paste (or press Ctrl+V). Access pastes the Word table data.

Analyzing Access Data in Excel

In the same way that Excel is only an adequate database tool, Access is only an adequate data analysis tool. If you want to apply the more robust data analysis capabilities of Excel to the data in an Access table, you need to export the table records to a worksheet.

Transferring table records from Access to Excel can be done in one of three ways: with the Clipboard, the Access Analyze It with Microsoft Office Excel feature, or Excel's Get External Data feature.

Transferring Records via the Clipboard

Here's a rundown of the Clipboard method:

1. In Access, open the table or run the query and select the records you want to export (see Figure 6.11).

Figure 6.11
Select the table or query records you want to export to Excel.

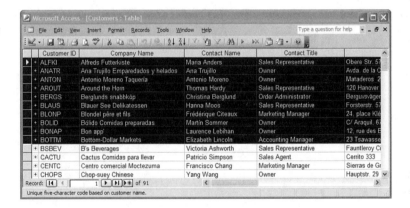

2. Select Edit, Copy (or press Ctrl+C) to place the records on the Clipboard.
3. In Excel, select the destination cell for the records. (This cell will hold the name of the first table field.)
4. Select Edit, Paste (or press Ctrl+V).

Excel pastes the field names in the current row and the records in separate rows below, as shown in Figure 6.12. As you can see, you might need to adjust column widths and row heights, and there may be formula error smart tags to deal with.

Using Analyze It with Microsoft Office Excel

The Analyze It with Microsoft Office Excel feature can convert an Access object into an Excel worksheet and open the new sheet in Excel, all in one step. To try this out, first open the object you want to send to Excel. Then select Tools, Office Links, Analyze It with Microsoft Office Excel. As you can see in Figure 6.13, the resulting worksheet is a bit neater than the one created via the Clipboard.

6

Figure 6.12
The Access records from Figure 6.11 pasted into an Excel worksheet.

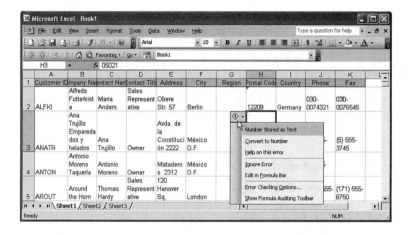

Figure 6.13
Records imported into Excel using the Access tool Analyze It with Microsoft Office Excel.

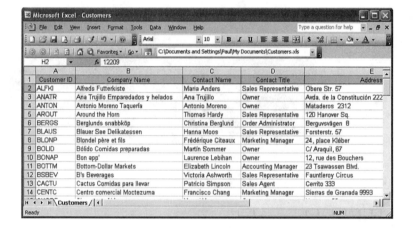

Using Excel's Get External Data Feature

The problem with both the Clipboard and the Analyze It with Microsoft Office Excel tool is that the data is "live" in the sense that if it changes in Access, the version on your worksheet is not updated. However, it is possible to set up a one-way link to the data. That is, if the data changes in the underlying Access table, the data is updated in Excel. (The link is one way because changing the data in Excel doesn't affect the data in Access.) You do this by importing the data into Excel using the Import Data command. Here's how it works:

1. In Excel, select Data, Import External Data, Import Data. The Select Data Source dialog box appears.

2. In the Files of Type list, select Access Databases.

3. Select the Access database and click Open. The Data Link Properties dialog box appears.

4. If the database requires you to log on with a password, deactivate the Blank Password check box and enter the required User Name and Password. (To ensure the log on data is correct, click Text Connection.)

5. Click OK. The Select Table dialog box appears, as shown in Figure 6.14.

Figure 6.14
Use the Select Table dialog box to select the query or table you want to import.

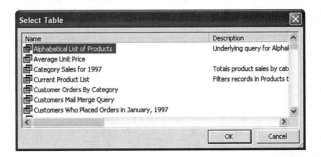

6. Select the query or table you want to import and then click OK. The Import Data dialog box appears.

7. To import to an existing worksheet, activate the Existing Worksheet option and then select the destination cell. Otherwise, activate the New Worksheet option.

8. Click OK. Access imports the data.

To refresh the data, select Data, Refresh Data.

Refreshing Data Automatically
Rather than refreshing the external data by hand, you can have Excel refresh it for you automatically. Select Data, Import External Data, Data Range Properties. In the External Data Range Properties dialog box, activate the Refresh Every check box and enter the refresh interval, in minutes, in the spin box. If you also want Excel to refresh the data automatically each time you open the workbook, activate the Refresh Data on File Open check box.

Publishing Access Data in Word

Access has a Publish It with Microsoft Office Word feature that copies an Access object such as a table or a report to a Word document in Rich Text Format. This enables you to use Word's formatting tools to spruce up the table or report for publishing.

To try this out, open the Access object you want to publish and then select Tools, Office Links, Publish It with Microsoft Office Word. The look of the resulting RTF document depends on the Access object:

- If the object is a table or query, the data appears in an unformatted Word table.

- If the object is a form, the data appears in a Word table with formatting based on the form's appearance.

- If the object is a report, the data appears as regular text formatted to look like the report output.

Merging Data from Access, Excel, and Outlook

I've never liked the term *mail merge* because the "mail" part makes everyone think about form letters and mass mailings (read: junk mail). A better term might have been *data merge*, because that's really what mail merge is all about: It takes data from a source file—an Access table or query, an Excel list, or the Outlook Contacts folder—and merges it with a special Word document populated with fields that specify where each piece of data goes. There are no restrictions on how you lay out the Word document, so the merged result can be not only customized form letters and envelopes, but just about anything you want: customized broadcast email messages, labels, name tags, phone directories, catalogs, parts lists, invoices, and much more.

This section introduces you to Word's mail-merge capabilities and shows you a few tricks for getting the most out of this powerful feature.

To use mail merge successfully, you need to understand only a few basic concepts:

- Data source—This is the object that contains the data you want to use. For our purposes in this section, the data sources can be an Access table or query, an Excel list, or the Outlook Contacts folder. However, Word also supports a number of other data source types, including SQL Server, Oracle, ODBC, Microsoft Works, Lotus 1-2-3, Paradox, and dBase. In this section, I assume you've already created the data source you want to use.

- Main document—This is the Word document that acts as a kind of boilerplate for the merge operation. The main document (also called the *starting document*) includes the text that you want to appear in the merge, as well as the data source fields that serve to customize the merge.

- Recipient—This is Word's term for the merge result when you apply a single data source record to the starting document. The recipient can be a separate document (such as a customized form letter), an email message, or an item in a directory.

After you have these concepts down, running a mail merge couldn't be simpler because Word has a Mail Merge task pane (Tools, Letters and Mailings, Mail Merge) that takes you through the steps that are required. However, as an Office guru, you should know how to build a mail merge from scratch using the powerful Mail Merge toolbar, so that's what we'll do here. The next few sections discuss the steps you have to follow. For now, display the Mail Merge toolbar by selecting Tools, Letters and Mailings, Show Mail Merge Toolbar.

Step 1: Opening the Main Document

You begin the mail-merge process by opening or creating the main document that Word uses to hold the mail-merge fields and boilerplate text. You have three choices:

- Use the existing document.
- Create a new document using either the Normal template or some other template.
- Open a document that you used with a previous mail-merge operation.

Step 2: Selecting the Mail-Merge Document Type

 You continue the mail merge by specifying the type of document you want Word to create as the main document. Click the Main Document Setup button to display the Main Document Type dialog box, shown in Figure 6.15.

Figure 6.15
Use the Main Document Type dialog box to specify the type of mail-merge document you want to create.

You have six document types to choose from (click OK when you've made your choice):

The Faxes Document Type

The Faxes document type is disabled unless you have a fax program installed that supports the Merge to Fax feature. Early versions of Microsoft Fax supported Merge to Fax, but Outlook 2003 does not work with Microsoft Fax, so the Faxes document is disabled in most Office 2003 installations.

- Letters—Personalized letters, memos, or other correspondence meant to be printed. The address, salutation, and specified fields within the text are personalized based on the information in the data source. Word creates a single document where the letter for each recipient is in its own section, separated by a page break.
- Email messages—Personalized messages sent via Outlook email. Word creates separate email messages for each recipient.

Email Addresses Must Be in the Data Source

If you plan to merge email messages, your data source must include a field that holds the recipients' email addresses.

- Envelopes—Personalized envelopes meant to be printed. The recipient's name and address on the envelope are personalized using the data source fields. Usually (but not always), each envelope has a corresponding letter. If you choose this type, Word displays the Envelope Options dialog box, which you use to select your envelope size, address fonts, and printing options.

6

Cross Reference

If you're creating form letters and corresponding envelopes for printing, there's a trick you can use to avoid running separate mail merges for the letters and envelopes. See "Creating Letters and Envelopes at the Same Time," later in this chapter.

- Labels—Personalized labels meant to be printed. The recipient's name and address on the label are personalized using the data source fields. If you choose this type, Word displays the Label Options dialog box, which you use to specify the label and printer information. If more than one label fits on a page, the document then shows several <<Next Record>> fields, which serve to separate the labels on each page. See "Inserting Word Fields" later in this chapter for more information on the <<Next Record>> field.

- Directory—A list of the source data, such as a phone directory, catalog, parts list, and so on. Each item in the list (which Word stills calls a "recipient") is personalized from the source data. Word creates a single document that contains the entire list.

- Normal Word document—A regular Word document that you personalize by adding fields from the data source.

Step 3: Opening the Data Source

 The next mail-merge step is to open the data source that you want to use to personalize the main document. Click the Open Data Source button in the Mail Merge toolbar. The Select Data Source dialog box appears, as shown in Figure 6.16.

Figure 6.16
Use the Select Data Source dialog box to choose the data source you want to use with your mail merge.

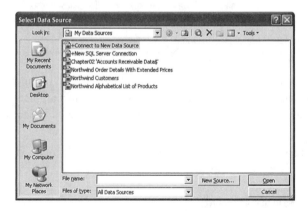

If you have already defined the data source you want to use (see "Defining a New Data Source," later in this chapter), select it and click Open.

Otherwise, use the Files of Type list to select the source type, such as Access Databases or Excel Files and then click Open. Word displays the Select Table dialog box, from which you select the query or table (for an Access data source) or named range (for an Excel data source) that you want to use, and then click OK.

Selecting the Outlook Contacts Folder as the Data Source

If you use the Mail Merge task pane to set up your mail merge, the Select Recipients pane has a Select from Outlook Contacts option that enables you to use Outlook's Contacts folder as the data source. It's frustrating, but Word offers no way to choose the Contacts folder as the data source using the Select Data Source button or any other Mail Merge toolbar button. There are two ways you can work around this bizarre limitation.

Here's the first workaround:

1. In Outlook, select the Contacts folder.
2. If you want to limit the number of contacts included in the data source, either select the contacts you want or customize the view with a filter to display only the contacts you want.
3. If you want to limit the number of fields included in the data source, customize the view to display only the fields you want.
4. Select Tools, Mail Merge to display the Mail Merge Contacts dialog box.
5. Specify the contacts by activating either All Contacts in Current View or Only Selected Contacts.
6. Specify the fields by activating either All Contact Fields or Contact Fields in Current View.
7. Specify the main document by activating either New Document or Existing Document. If you choose the latter, type the document path or click Browse.
8. Use the Document Type list to select the merge document type.
9. Click OK.

The second workaround uses a short VBA macro:

```
Sub SelectContactsAsDataSource ()
    With ActiveDocument
        .MailMerge.OpenDataSource _
            Name:="", _
            SubType:=wdMergeSubTypeOutlook
    End With
End Sub
```

When you run this macro, Word displays the Select Contact List Folder dialog box. Select the Contacts folder you want to use and then click OK. (If the Select the Contact List Folder dialog box appears again, select the folder again and click OK.)

Defining a New Data Source

If you have an Access or Excel data source that you use often, you should define it as a data source file that appears in the My Data Sources folder for easy access. Here are the steps to follow:

6

1. Click the Open Data Source button in the Mail Merge toolbar. The Select Data Source dialog box appears.

2. Click New Source to start the Data Connection Wizard.

3. Select ODBC DSN and then click Next.

4. Select MS Access Database or Excel Files and then click Next.

5. Select the Access or Excel file that contains the data source and click OK.

6. Select the Access query or table or Excel named range that you want to use as the data source and then click Next.

7. (Optional) Type a Description of the data source.

8. Click Finish.

Step 4: Selecting, Sorting, and Filtering the Recipients

With your data source set, you can use it to select which recipients (records) you want to include in the mail merge. If you've already done this in advance using an Access query or an Excel named range, you can skip this step.

Selecting Recipients

Click the Mail Merge Recipients button in the Mail Merge toolbar to display the Mail Merge Recipients dialog box, shown in Figure 6.17.

Figure 6.17
Use the Mail Merge Recipients dialog box to select, sort, and filter the mail-merge recipients.

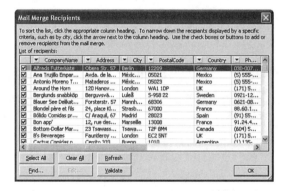

To select the mail-merge recipients, use the following techniques:

- To remove a recipient, deactivate its check box.

- To select a recipient, activate its check box.

- To remove all recipients, click Clear All. (This is handy if you want to select only a few recipients from a large list. Remove all the recipients and then select the ones you want.)

- To select all recipients, click Select All.

Finding a Recipient

If you have a large data source and you're having trouble locating a recipient, click Find to open the Find Entry dialog box. Type your search string into the Find text box. To search only a specific field, activate the This Field option and select the field from the list.

Filtering Recipients

Rather than activating and deactivating recipient check boxes, you might prefer to filter the recipients based on the data in one or more fields. To filter the recipients, first notice that each column header has a drop-down arrow. Clicking that arrow in the column you want to work with displays a list with four values:

- (All)—Displays all the recipients.
- (Blanks)—Displays only those recipients for which the current field is blank.
- (Nonblanks)—Displays only those recipients for which the current field is not blank.
- (Advanced)—Displays the Filter and Sort dialog box. In the Filter Records tab, shown in Figure 6.18, use the Field list to select the field you want to use for the filter; use the Comparison list to select an operator such as Equal To or Contains; use the Compare To text box to enter the comparison value. To create compound filter criteria, fill in as many rows as you need, choosing And or Or for each.

Figure 6.18
Select (Advanced) in any column's drop-down list to display the Filter and Sort dialog box.

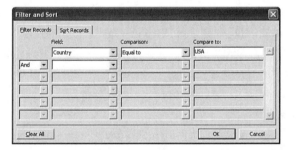

Sorting Recipients

In mail-merge operations, the sort of the recipients is often crucial. For example, if you're sending out a mass mailing, putting the recipients in postal code order can help you get a reduced rate. Also, if you'll be creating both letters and corresponding envelopes or labels, you must ensure that both merge operations use the same sort order.

In the Mail Merge Recipients dialog box, you can use two methods to sort the entries:

- Click a column header. This sorts the recipients based on the data in that column. Clicking the same column header toggles between an ascending and descending sort. To sort on multiple fields, click the column headers in reverse order of priority. For

6

example, suppose you want to sort customers by the City field, and then within each city you want to sort by the CompanyName field. To do this, first click the CompanyName header and then click the City header.

■ Use the Filter and Sort dialog box. Click any column's drop-down arrow and then click (Advanced). In the Sort Records tab (see Figure 6.19), use the Sort By list to choose the main sort field, and then activate either Ascending or Descending. To sort on multiple fields, use the Then By lists.

Figure 6.19
Use the Sort Records tab to sort the recipients on up to three fields.

Step 5: Adding Text and Merge Fields

You're now ready to start building the main document, which requires the bulk of your mail-merge efforts. You add two things to the document:

■ Boilerplate text (and perhaps other elements such as lines and clip art)—This is the text that remains constant in each letter, email message, envelope, and so on.

■ Merge fields—These are the items that personalize the mail merge for each recipient. The next few sections show you how to add the various types of merge fields.

Inserting an Address Block

Recipient addresses are a common mail-merge feature. They appear on envelopes and labels, of course, but they're also found at the top of form letters, as well as in directory list-ings, invoices, purchase orders, and many other applications. Unfortunately, addresses can also be time-consuming to work with because they require you to add separate fields for name, company name, street address, city, region, and so on. Having to do this repeatedly in different mail merges is a recipe for tedium and frustration. Fortunately, the Word pro-grammers took pity on poor mail mergers and came up with an efficient solution: the address block. This is a single field that includes the standard address items and is customiz-able to suit your address style.

To add an address block, follow these steps:

1. Position the cursor where you want the address block field to appear.

 2. Click the Insert Address Block button on the Mail Merge toolbar. Word displays the Insert Address Block dialog box, shown in Figure 6.20.

Figure 6.20
Use the Insert Address Block dialog box to configure the address block for your mail merge.

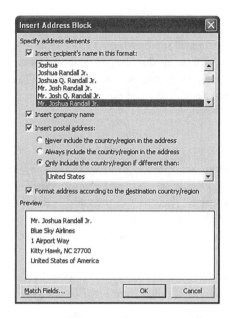

3. Use the following check boxes to configure the address fields (watch the Preview box to see the effect on the resulting address block):

Insert Recipient's Name in This Format—Toggles the recipient's name on and off. If you include the name, use the list to select the name format you prefer.

Insert Company Name—Toggles the company name on and off.

Insert Postal Address—Toggles the postal address on and off. If you include the postal address, use the option buttons to determine whether the country/region field is included.

Format Address According to the Destination Country/Region—Configures the address according to the address standards used in the recipient's country.

4. Click OK.

Word inserts the address block, which appears in the document as follows:

`<<AddressBlock>>`

6

The `AddressBlock` Field

The `<<AddressBlock>>` code is a front end for Word's `{ADDRESSBLOCK}` mail-merge field. To see the full field syntax, click `<<AddressBlock>>` and then press Shift+F9. (For more about Word's fields, see Chapter 1, "Building Dynamic Documents in Word.")

Working with Labels

If you're creating a label mail merge, you need to insert an address block for each label. If you have multiple labels per page, place the first address block in the first label. For the other labels, you can insert the address blocks by hand between the `<<Next Record>>` fields. However, Word offers an easier method: Click the Propagate Labels button in the Mail Merge toolbar. This copies the layout of the first label to all the other labels.

Matching Fields

If when you preview the mail merge (see "Step 6: Previewing the Results," later in this chapter) the address block doesn't include one or more of your address items, that's probably because Word didn't recognize those fields as part of the address. For example, to include a person's name in an address block, Word looks for a separate first name and last name with the names FirstName and LastName. If your data source has the entire name in a field named ContactName, Word won't recognize it.

To solve this problem, you need to tell Word which fields in your data source correspond with the fields that Word expects. This is called *matching fields* and it works like this:

1. Click the Match Fields button in the Mail Merge toolbar. (You can also click Match Fields in the Insert Address Block dialog box.) The Match Fields dialog box appears, as shown in Figure 6.21.

Figure 6.21
Use the Match Fields dialog box to match your data source address fields with the fields expected by Word.

2. The list on the left contains the items that Word expects. Find the item that corresponds to one of your missing address fields.

3. On the right, use the associated list to select the corresponding field from your data source.

4. Repeat steps 2 and 3 for all your nonstandard address fields.

5. Click OK.

Creating Letters and Envelopes at the Same Time

If you're creating a form letter for printing, you almost certainly want to also create envelopes in which to mail those letters. Normally, this means running a form letter mail merge, then a separate envelope mail merge, and then collating the two jobs. If that sounds like a lot of work, you're right, it is. You can simplify your life by creating the form letters and envelopes within a single mail merge. Follow these steps:

1. Select Tools, Letters and Mailings, Envelopes and Labels.

2. Display the Envelopes tab.

3. Enter the Return Address you want to use on the envelopes, as well as any other envelope options you require. Be sure to leave the Delivery Address blank.

4. Click Add to Document. Your merge document now has two pages: page 1 is the envelope you just created and page 2 is the form letter.

5. In the envelope page (page 1), double-click at the point where you want the recipient address to appear, and then insert an Address Block field.

6. Build the rest of your form letter and complete the mail merge as discussed later in this chapter.

When you print the mail merge, for each recipient the envelope prints first, followed by the form letter.

Inserting a Greeting Line

If you merge a lot of form letters, you know the greeting is another common merge item, and it can be problematic not only because you have to insert multiple fields (usually the courtesy title and last name), but you also have to deal with invalid names (such as using a generic greeting such as "Dear Sir or Madam"). Happily, you can avoid all of this by inserting a *greeting line*, a single field that displays the salutation and name the way you want and also handles invalid names automatically. Follow these steps to insert a greeting line:

1. Position the cursor where you want the greeting line to appear.

2. Click the Insert Greeting Line button on the Mail Merge toolbar. Word displays the Greeting Line dialog box, shown in Figure 6.22.

3. In the Greeting Line Format section, use the lists to select the salutation, the name format, and the punctuation mark.

4. Use the Greeting Line for Invalid Recipient Names list to select the greeting to use for invalid names in the data source.

5. Click OK.

6

Figure 6.22
Use the Greeting Line dialog box to configure the greeting line for your mail merge.

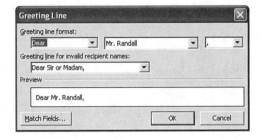

Word inserts the greeting line, which appears in the document as the following merge field:

<<GreetingLine>>

The GreetingLine **Field**
The <<GreetingLine>> code is a front end for Word's {GREETINGLINE} mail-merge field. To see the full field syntax, click <<GreetingLine>> and then press Shift+F9.

Inserting Data Source Fields

If you're creating an envelope or label mail merge, the address block may be all you need. For letters, email messages, and directories, however, you probably also need to insert non-address fields from the data source, as well as individual address fields. Here's how it's done:

1. Position the cursor where you want the field to appear.

 2. Click the Insert Merge Fields button in the Mail Merge toolbar. The Insert Merge Field dialog box appears, as shown in Figure 6.23.

Figure 6.23
Use the Insert Merge Field dialog box to insert any field from your data source.

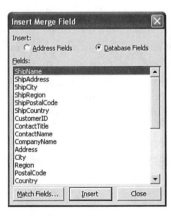

3. Activate the Database Fields option. (You use the Address Fields to insert individual fields from the address block.)

4. Select the field you want to insert.

5. Click Insert.

6. Repeat steps 4 and 5 to insert any other fields you need.

7. Click Close.

 Figure 6.24 shows a Word document with some text and various fields added, including an address block, a greeting line, and several data source fields. To view the fields highlighted, click the Highlight Merge Fields button in the Mail Merge toolbar.

Using MergeField

If you prefer to enter your fields manually (by pressing Ctrl+F9), you can insert a data source field by using MergeField, which is one of Word's mail-merge fields:

    {MERGEFIELD FieldName}

Here, replace FieldName with the name of the data source field.

Adding Formatting Switches

If you want to format text, dates, times, or numbers, you need to add Word's field formatting switches (see "Understanding Field Code Syntax" in Chapter 1). To add a switch to a field, click the field and then press Shift+F9 to see the underlying Word field. Add your switch at the end of the field, before the closing brace (}).

Figure 6.24
A Word mail-merge document with text and merge fields.

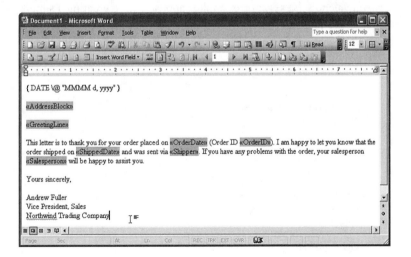

Inserting Word Fields

Besides the AddressBlock and GreetingLine fields you've seen so far, Word has a number of other merge fields that you can use to control the merge. You can insert one of these fields by clicking Insert Word Field in the Mail Merge toolbar and then clicking the field you want. There are nine fields available:

- Ask—Prompts the user for input and stores the result in a bookmark. The field equivalent is {ASK}.

- Fill-in—Prompts the user for input and stores the result in the merge document. See "Personalizing Mail Merges with Fill-In Fields," later in this chapter.

- If...Then...Else—Inserts text into the document based on the result of a conditional expression. See "Intelligent Merging I: The If Field," later in this chapter.

- Merge Record #—Displays the record number for each record in the mail merge. The field equivalent is {MERGEREC}. For example, you could use this field to generate automatic invoice numbers (in this case, 101, 102, and so on):

  `Invoice Number: {=Sum(100,{MERGEREC})}`

- Merge Sequence #—Displays the record number from the original data source for each record in the mail merge. This will be different from the Merge Record # value if the mail-merge records are a subset of the original data source. For example, suppose the original data source has 100 records and the mail merge is filtered to include only records 50 through 100. The Merge Record # field assigns 1 to the first mail-merge record; the Merge Sequence # field assigns 50 to the first record. The field equivalent is {MERGESEQ}.

- Next Record—Moves to the next record in the data source. This is most often used in directory-type merges where you have multiple records in a single document. The field equivalent is {NEXT}. For example, suppose you're creating a simple phone list that consists of a person's first name, last name, and phone number. If you want only five records to appear per page, you'd set up the main document like so:

```
<<FirstName>> <<LastName>>
<<PhoneNumber>>

<<Next Record>>
<<FirstName>> <<LastName>>
<<PhoneNumber>>

<<Next Record>>
<<FirstName>> <<LastName>>
<<PhoneNumber>>

<<Next Record>>
<<FirstName>> <<LastName>>
<<PhoneNumber>>

<<Next Record>>
<<FirstName>> <<LastName>>
<<PhoneNumber>>
```

- Next Record If—Moves to the next record in the data source, but applies a conditional expression to determine whether the record appears in the current document. This is the same as filtering out the record based on the condition, so it's always easier to use the Filter and Sort dialog box. See "Filtering Recipients," earlier in this chapter.

- Set Bookmark—Sets the value of a bookmark. The field equivalent is {SET}.

- Skip Record If—Skips the current merge record if the record satisfies a conditional expression. Again, this is the same as filtering the records, so see "Filtering Recipients," earlier in this chapter.

Personalizing Mail Merges with Fill-In Fields

By definition, the mail-merge results are personalized documents, because the information in each one is at least partly based on whatever information is in its data source record. However, a document may require personalized data that doesn't come from the data source. For example, you might want to put the current date at the top of each letter, which is easily done with the Date field.

For personalized items that have no field equivalent, you can still insert them into your mail merge by prompting the user for the appropriate value, either once for the entire merge or for each recipient. In a letter, for example, you might want to personalize the complimentary close based on whether you know the person.

You can prompt for personalized information by using a Fill-in field:

1. In the Mail Merge toolbar, pull down the Insert Word Field list and select Fill-in. The Insert Word Field: Fill-in dialog box appears, as shown in Figure 6.25.

Figure 6.25
Use a Fill-in field to prompt the user for data to insert into the mail-merge documents.

2. Use the Prompt box to enter the text that appears in the dialog box that prompts the user to enter the data.

3. Use the Default Fill-in Text box to enter a default value for the field.

4. If you want the prompt to appear only once at the beginning of the mail merge (so the field value applies to every document), activate the Ask Once check box.

6

Prompt with Care on Large Data Sources

One of the most common—and most frustrating—`Fill-in` field errors is to leave the Ask Once check box deactivated in a merge that uses a data source with hundreds or even thousands of records. This means, of course, that Word will dutifully prompt you hundreds or thousands of times. If your data source is a big one, either activate the Ask Once check box or forget about using a `Fill-in` field.

---

5. Click OK. Word displays the prompt (for the main document), as shown in Figure 6.26.

Figure 6.26
An example of a `Fill-in` field prompt dialog box.

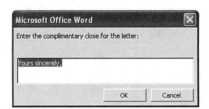

6. Enter the value and click OK.

Intelligent Merging I: The `If` Field

In some merge operations, you might want to customize a portion of the text based on some aspect of the data in the current record. For example, in a letter thanking people for donations, you might want to check the size of the donation: if it's over a certain amount, insert the word "generous" before each instance of the word "donation." Similarly, if your data source has a courtesy title field that contains "Mr.," "Miss," "Mrs.," or "Ms.," you could customize the greeting to display "Dear Sir" for recipients with "Mr." as the courtesy title, and "Dear Madam" for all the others.

You can do this by inserting an If…Then…Else field, which is the same as an `If` Word field (in Chapter 1, see the section titled "Creating Decision-Making Fields"). This field evaluates a conditional expression and then, depending on the result, inserts into the document one of two text values. Follow these steps to set up such a field:

1. In the Mail Merge toolbar, pull down the Insert Word Field list and select If…Then…Else. The Insert Word Field: IF dialog box appears, as shown in Figure 6.27.

2. Use the Field Name list to choose the field you want to use in the conditional expression.

3. Use the Comparison list to choose a conditional operator (such as Equal To or Is Blank).

4. Use the Compare To text box to enter the value to which you want the field compared. (You don't need to enter a value if you chose either Is Blank or Is Not Blank as the comparison operator.)

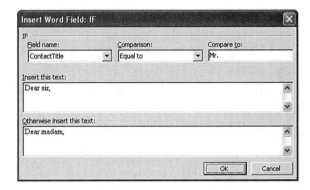

Figure 6.27
Use an If field to insert one of two text values based on the result of a conditional expression.

5. Use Insert This Text box to enter the text you want to insert into the document if the comparison returns a True result.

6. Use Otherwise Insert This Text box to enter the text you want to insert into the document if the comparison returns a False result.

7. Click OK.

Step 6: Previewing the Results

 When you've completed your main document—or even if the document is only partially complete—you can preview the merge to make sure things look the way you want. You switch to preview mode by clicking the View Merged Data button in the Mail Merge toolbar. Figure 6.28 displays a preview of the merge document shown earlier in Figure 6.24.

Go to Record

Figure 6.28
A preview of the merge document from Figure 6.24.

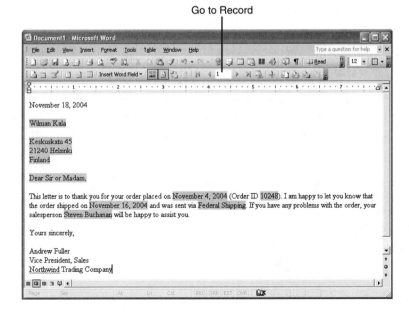

6

When the preview mode is active, use the following Mail Merge toolbar techniques to navigate the records:

- Click First Record to display the first record in the data source.

- Click Previous Record to display the previous record in the data source.
- To go to a specific record number, type the number into the Go to Record text box (see Figure 6.28) and press Enter.

- Click Next Record to display the next record in the data source.

- Click Last Record to display the last record in the data source.

- To locate a record, click Find Entry and use the Find Entry dialog box to enter your search criteria.

This is also a good time to check the mail merge for errors. Click the Check for Errors button in the Mail Merge toolbar to display the Checking and Reporting Errors dialog box shown in Figure 6.29. Activate the Simulate the Merge and Report Errors in a New Document option and then click OK. Word runs through a simulated version of the merge. If it finds any errors, it displays them in a new document.

Figure 6.29
Use the Checking and Reporting Errors dialog box to run a simulated merge that checks for errors.

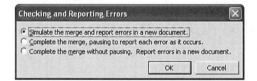

Step 7: Completing the Mail Merge

You're now ready to complete the merge. Word gives you three choices:

- Merge to New Document—Click to display the merge results in a new document. In the Merge to New Document dialog box that appears (see Figure 6.30), specify the records you want to include in the merge: All, Current Record only, or the range of record numbers that you enter in the From and To text boxes.

Figure 6.30
Use the Merge to New Document dialog box to specify the range of records to include in the merge.

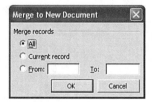

■ Merge to Printer—Click to send the merge results directly to your printer. Use the Merge to Printer dialog box (it has the same layout as the Merge to New Document dialog box) to specify the range of records you want to include in the merge. Click OK to display the Print dialog box and choose your print options.

 ■ Merge to E-mail—Click to send the merge results as email messages. The Merge to E-mail dialog box not only lets you choose the records to include in the merge, it also lets you select the data source field that includes the recipient email addresses, the Subject line, and the message format (Attachment, Plain Text, or HTML). When you click OK, Word sends the results to Outlook.

From Here

■ To get the details on using fields in Word, see the section in Chapter 1 titled "Using Fields to Insert Dynamic Data."

■ For more information on using lists in Excel, see the section in Chapter 2 titled "Analyzing Data with Lists."

■ You'll find information on creating Access queries in Chapter 4, "Taming Access Data."

Working as a Team: Collaborating with Other Users

Long gone are the days when computer users worked in what used to be known, somewhat quaintly, as "splendid isolation." *Collaboration* is the watchword for the modern user, whether he or she works in a large corporation (where everyone works in "teams" these days), a small business (where everyone pitches in to help everyone else), or as a freelancer (where feedback from clients, editors, lawyers, and others is the norm).

Fortunately, Microsoft Office 2003 was built with collaboration in mind. The suite is loaded with tools and options that enable you and your colleagues to work on documents together, share files, schedule meetings, and have conversations. This chapter takes you through the most useful and powerful of these Office collaboration features.

Collaborating on a Word Document

Working with other people on a Word document is one of the most common collaborative tasks in business. Whether it's adding your two cents' worth with a comment, editing text with tracking activated, or parceling out subdocuments for others to create, Word has a powerful suite of collaboration tools, which I describe in this section.

Inserting Comments

The most basic collaborative tasks are to critique existing text or make suggestions for new text. In Word, these tasks fall under the rubric of *comments*, and Word implements them as a kind of electronic version of sticky notes. That is, a comment doesn't change the original text, and when you display the comment, it appears "above" the text in a balloon (with, appropriately, a yellow background reminiscent of the original sticky notes).

To insert a comment, first select the text you want to comment on. (If you want to comment on a particular word, you can position the cursor within or immediately to the left or right of the word.) Now either select Insert, Comment, or click the Insert Comment button in the Reviewing toolbar. (If you don't see the Reviewing toolbar, right-click any toolbar or menu and then click Reviewing.) Word highlights the selected text to indicate that it has an associated comment.

How you type the comment depends on what view you're using:

- If you're using Normal or Outline view, Word adds your initials after the selected text, followed by an integer representing the comment number. For a user with the initials KH, the first comment is marked as KH1, the second as KH2, and so on. You also see the Reviewing pane, as shown in Figure 7.1. Type your comment into the Reviewing pane.

Changing the Comment Color

The color Word applies to the background of the commented-on text and your initials is user dependent. (That is, your comments might be red, another person's might be blue, and so on.) That's useful because if you have a number of people commenting on a document, you can use the colors to easily pick out a person's comments. However, if you want all the comments to appear with the same color, select Tools, Options, display the Tracking tab, and use the Comment Color list to select the color you prefer.

Toggling the Reviewing Pane

You can toggle the Reviewing pane on and off by clicking the Reviewing Pane button in the Reviewing toolbar. To see a comment in Normal view with the Reviewing pane turned off (or on, for that matter), hover the mouse over the highlighted text. Word displays a banner with the reviewer name, the date and time he or she inserted the comment, and the comment text.

- If you're using the Web or Print view, you see a comment balloon, as shown in Figure 7.2. Type your comment into the balloon.

To make changes to a comment, edit the comment text directly in the Reviewing pane or the comment balloon. If you don't have the Reviewing pane or balloons displayed, you have two choices:

- Right-click the associated document text and then select Edit Comment.
- Click the associated document text and then click the Edit Comment button in the Reviewing toolbar.

Figure 7.1
If you insert a comment in Normal or Outline view, Word displays the Reviewing pane.

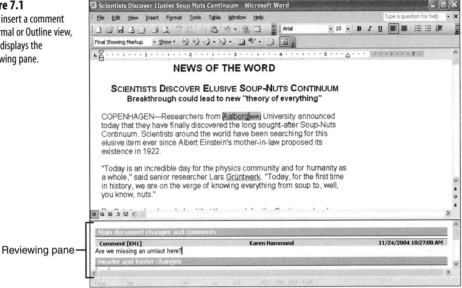

Reviewing pane

Figure 7.2
If you insert a comment in Web or Print view, Word displays a Comment balloon.

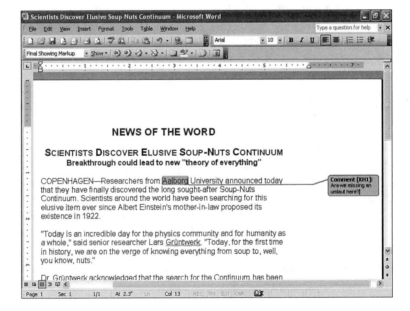

7

Extra Reviewing Buttons

It's likely that your Reviewing toolbar doesn't display the Edit Comment button. To add this and a number of other useful Reviewing buttons, click the Toolbar Options button on the right edge of the Reviewing toolbar, select Add or Remove Buttons, Reviewing, and then click the buttons you want to add.

Inserting a Voice Comment

 Another choice in the extra Reviewing toolbar buttons is Insert Voice, which you use to insert a voice comment if you have a microphone attached to your sound card. Clicking this button displays the Sound Object in *Document* window (where *Document* is the name of your document). Click the red Record button, record your comment, and then click Stop. Voice comments are represented in the Reviewing pane and balloons by a sound icon; double-click the icon to hear the voice comment. Note, too, that you can also add text to the same comment.

Tracking Word Document Changes

Inserting comments is a relatively passive strategy for reviewing a document because comments don't change the original document text. Contrast this with making changes to the original text without telling your colleagues, which is surely a decidedly aggressive strategy for reviewing a document (and is a major faux pas in collaborative circles).

Between these two techniques lies a third strategy that is ideal for many projects: tracking changes. This means that you make changes to the original text—including adding, editing, deleting, and formatting the text—but Word keeps track of the changes and shows not only what changes were made, but who made them and when.

To turn on Word's Track Changes feature, use either of the following techniques:

- Click the Track Changes button in the Reviewing toolbar.
- Double-click the TRK button in Word's status bar (the TRK text changes from gray to black to indicate that Track Changes is activated).

As with comments, how Word displays reviewers' changes depends on which view you're using:

- If you're using Normal or Outline view, as shown in Figure 7.3, new text appears in a user-specific color. Deleted text appears in a user-specific color formatted with the strikethrough effect, and lines that include any changes (including formatting changes) appear with a vertical bar in the left margin. If you want to see which reviewer made the change and when, hover the mouse pointer over the change to display a banner similar to the one shown in Figure 7.3. You can also review the changes by activating the Reviewing pane.
- If you're using the Web or Print view, you see the changes in balloons, as shown in Figure 7.4.

7

Figure 7.3
If you insert a comment in Normal or Outline view, Word displays brackets around the document text as well as the reviewer's initials.

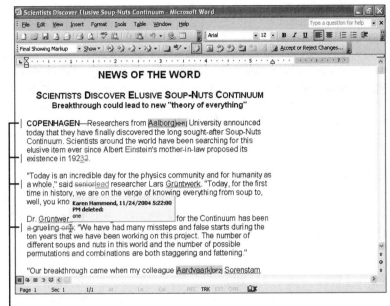

Vertical bars indicate lines that include reviewer changes

Figure 7.4
If you track changes in Web or Print view, Word displays the changes in balloons.

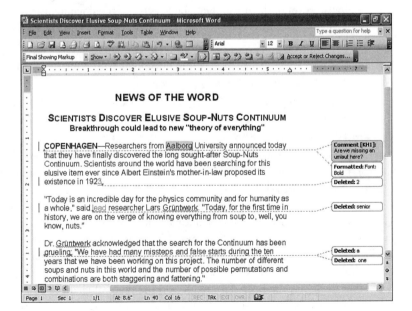

Commenting with Highlighted Text

 If you don't like the Reviewing pane or the balloons, comments become difficult to use because you can view them only by hovering over the associated text with your mouse. If you'd prefer to put your comments in the text, you can use a combination of highlighted text and tracked changes. First, select the text you want to comment on and then click the Highlight button in the Reviewing toolbar (or drop down the list and click the highlight color you want). Now, either before or after the paragraph with the highlighted text, start a new paragraph and insert your comment. Be sure to refer to the highlighted text specifically (for example, "For the text highlighted below…").

Working with Comments and Changes

If you use Word's Comments and Track Changes features often, you need to know the ins and outs of working with comments and changes, including controlling the display of, navigating, and accepting or rejecting comments and changes. The next few sections give you the details.

Viewing Comments and Changes

Word 2003 offers a welcome variety of options for controlling the display of comments and changes. For starters, the Reviewing toolbar's Display for Review list offers four choices:

- Final Showing Markup—This is the view I described with Figures 7.3 and 7.4. It shows the final version of the document (the version of the document if you accept all the current changes) with the *markup*—the font changes and balloons that indicate the changes.

- Final—This is the final version of the document with none of the markup showing (all the changes have been accepted).

- Original Showing Markup—In Web or Print view, this shows the original document text, with deletions marked as strikethrough, and comments, additions, and formatting changes shown in balloons.

- Original—This is the original version of the document, before any changes were made (or, more precisely, either before Track Changes was turned on or after the last time all the changes were accepted).

Word also has the capability to filter out particular types of changes, and even changes made by particular reviewers. You can find these filters by clicking the Show button on the Reviewing toolbar to drop down the list. The Final and Original options are the same as the Final Showing Markup and Original Showing Markup option in the Display for Review list. The other display options serve to toggle specific types of changes on and off: Comments, Ink Annotations, Insertions and Deletions, and Formatting. To toggle the display of changes made by a particular reviewer, select Reviewers and then click the reviewer you want to work with.

→ For the details on ink annotations and other Tablet PC features, see Chapter 9, "Collaborating with a Tablet PC and OneNote," p. 321

Navigating Comments and Changes

Depending on the view you're using, you can see a document's comments and changes either by scrolling through the items in the Reviewing pane or by scrolling through the document itself. However, if you want to ensure that you don't miss any markup, or if you want to accept or reject comments or changes, you need to use Word's reviewing navigation tools:

 ■ Click Next to move to the next comment or change.

 ■ Click Previous to move to the previous comment or change.

 ■ Click Next Change to move to the next change.

 ■ Click Previous Change to move to the previous change.

 ■ Click Next Comment to move to the next comment.

 ■ Click Previous Comment to move to the previous comment.

Accepting or Rejecting Comments and Changes

After you've navigated to some markup, you can either accept it (changes only) or reject it (comments and changes). Word gives you a variety of choices for both options.

To accept changes, you have four choices:

 ■ To accept the current change, click the Accept Change button in the Reviewing toolbar.

■ To accept all the changes in the current document, drop down the Accept Change list and select Accept All Changes in Document.

■ To accept only certain types of changes (such as formatting or insertions and deletions), first use the Show list to turn off the markup for all the changes except the ones you want to work with; then drop down the Accept Change list and select Accept All Changes Shown.

■ To accept only the changes made by a particular reviewer, first use the Show list to turn off the markup for all reviewers except the one you want to work with, then drop down the Accept Change list and select Accept All Changes Shown.

To delete comments or reject changes, you have six choices:

 ■ To delete or reject the current comment or change, click the Reject Change/Delete Comment button in the Reviewing toolbar.

■ To delete all the comments in the current document, drop down the Reject Change/Delete Comment list and select Delete All Comments in Document.

- To reject all the changes in the current document, drop down the Reject Change/Delete Comment list and select Reject All Changes in Document.

- To delete comments made by a particular reviewer, first use the Show list to turn off the markup for all reviewers except the one you want to work with, then drop down the Reject Change/Delete Comment list and select Delete All Comments Shown.

- To reject only certain types of changes (such as formatting or insertions and deletions, or changes made by a particular reviewer), first use the Show list to turn off the markup for all the changes except the ones you want to work with. Then drop down the Reject Change/Delete Comment list and select Reject All Changes Shown.

- To delete all ink annotations, drop down the Reject Change/Delete Comment list and select Delete All Ink Annotations in Document.

Customizing Markup

The markup that Word uses to indicate insertions, deletions, formatting changes, and changed lines is all fully customizable. To see the options you have, select Tools, Options and display the Tracking tab. (Another route to the Tracking tab is to click Show in the Reviewing toolbar and then select Options.)

In the Markup section, you have three lists for the text markup: Insertions, Deletions, and Formatting. In each case, you have half a dozen format choices: Color Only, Bold, Italic, Underline, Double Underline, and Strikethrough. The Deletions list also includes three extra choices: Hidden (which doesn't display the deletions) and the characters ^ and # (which Word displays in place of the deleted text). Use the Changed Lines list to choose where you want the border displayed: Left Border, Right Border, or Outside Border.

Note, too, that each markup item also has an associated Color list that determines the color Word uses to display the markup. For Insertions, Deletions, and Formatting, the default color option is By Author, which means Word applies user-specific colors to each change. (I discussed the Comment Color option earlier; see "Inserting Comments.")

User Colors Are Both Static and Random

The way Word applies user colors is frustrating to any guru who wants full control over the program. First, the colors that Word applies for any given user are not customizable through program options, VBA code, or even Registry entries. Second, the way Word applies those colors is more or less random, particularly on documents with multiple reviewers.

If you use the Web or Print layout, you can also customize how Word displays the changes in balloons. For example, you can change the width of margin used by the balloons, move them to the left margin, and even turn them off if you prefer the Reviewing pane. In the Balloons section of the Tracking tab, you can work with the following options:

- Use Balloons (Print and Web Layout)—Select Always (the default) to force Word to show balloons for all changes. Select Only for Comments/Formatting to show balloons only for comment and format changes. Select Never to turn off the balloons.

Another Way to Toggle Balloons

If you just want to work with the Use Balloons options, you don't need to display the Options dialog box. Instead, click Show in the Reviewing toolbar and then select Balloons. The commands in the submenu that appear are the same as the options in the Use Balloons list.

- Preferred Width—Use this spin box to set the width, in inches, of the margin in which the balloons appear. If you prefer to set the margin as a percentage of the window width, select Percent in the Measure In list.

- Margin—Select Right to show the balloons to the right of the text; select Left to show the balloons to the left of the text.

- Show Lines Connecting to Text—Leave this check box activated to show a line running from the balloon to the changed text. In sections where there are many changes, the lines can get confusing, so you can turn them off by deactivating this check box.

- Paper Orientation—If you're printing the balloons, use this list to choose the orientation of the paper. The Preserve option uses the document's specified orientation. The Force Landscape option prints the document in landscape orientation to ensure that the balloons fit on the page. Select Auto to let Word choose the orientation that fits the balloons.

Working with Document Versions

If you've made substantial changes that have messed up a document, you might be able to revert to a good version of the document using any of the following techniques:

- If you have Track Changes activated, reject the changes you've made.

- Undo some or all of your work from the current document session.

- If you've shared the document with other people, ask them if they have a copy of the good version of the document.

However, anyone who has used Word long enough has come across situations where none of these techniques are available—you've already accepted the changes; you've closed and reopened the document; other people have only recent versions.

To avoid this unpleasant and frustrating problem, use Word's Versions feature. With Versions, Word keeps track of different versions of the document, and you can open a version at any time. This feature is particularly useful in collaborative environments because it enables you to save in various situations:

- Before you send the document to a reviewer

- After you receive the document back from a reviewer

- After you accept or reject the reviewer's changes

7

Word also keeps track of which user saved the version (and when), so you could also ask reviewers to save a version when they have completed their work with a document.

Here are the steps to follow to save a version of a document:

1. Select File, Versions. Word displays the Version in *Document* dialog box (where *Document* is the name of your document).

2. Click Save Now to display the Save Version dialog box.

3. Use the Comments on Version box to enter a description of the version (such as "First draft" or "Copyedited version").

4. Click OK.

To view a version, select File, Versions to open the Versions in *Document* dialog box, select the version you want, and then click Open. Word opens the version in a new window and tiles the current version and the selected version horizontally so you can compare them.

Delete Unneeded Versions

Word stores each version in the document. This doesn't substantially increase the file size if you have just a few versions because Word just stores what's *different* about each version, not the entire document. However, a large document with many changes and many versions can get quite large in a hurry. To keep the file size under control, you should delete old versions that you no longer need. Select File, Versions, select the version you want to get rid of, and then click Delete.

Automatic Versions

If you don't want to rely on yourself or reviewers to remember to save versions, have Word do it for you. Select File, Versions, and then activate the Automatically Save a Version on Close check box. This tells Word to save a version each time you or someone else closes the document.

Creating a Master Document and Subdocuments

So far we've talked about two types of collaboration in Word: commenting on a document and making changes to a document. In this section, we'll talk about the third type of collaboration: sharing the work of creating a new document among multiple users. This isn't practical with small documents, but if you're collaborating on a large project, it's a good idea to split up the work. For example, if you're putting together an annual report, you could divide the report by department and have a person in each department create a portion of the report. Similarly, if you're managing a multiple-author book, you could assign one or more chapters to different authors.

The problem with large projects is coordinating the workload. How do you organize the project? How do you keep track of each contributor's progress? How do you put everything together? The answer to these questions is a powerful Word feature called a *master document*. This is a document that, although it can have its own text, really acts as a kind of binder that holds together the various pieces of a large project. These pieces are called *sub-documents*, and they exist as separate files. The master document contains links to each of these subdocuments. Here's how the master document/subdocument strategy solves the big project problems:

- You use the master document to organize the project. As you'll see, the master document is really an outline of the project, so you can use the outline to see the big project picture as well as to rearrange the project elements as needed. Also, Word applies the master document template to each subdocument, so you always have consistent formatting throughout the project.

- The subdocuments are separate files. By storing them on a shared network folder, other users can access them easily, and you can view the documents at any time to see the progress.

- The master document contains links to the subdocuments. However, you can "expand" the links to view the subdocument text. Therefore, putting together the final project is as easy as expanding all the subdocuments.

Word gives you two basic ways to create master documents and subdocuments: from an outline and from existing documents.

Creating a Master Document and Subdocuments from an Outline

The easiest way to work with master documents and subdocuments is to create them from scratch using an outline. There are various ways to do this, but the following technique is one that I've found leads to the fewest problems down the road. First, create the master document outline:

1. Create a new, blank document.
2. Save the document to an empty folder. If you'll be collaborating with other network users, be sure to share the folder with the network.
3. Select View, Outline to switch to Word's Outline view.
4. Create the outline for your project. In particular, be sure to follow these guidelines:
   - Use the Heading 1 style to define the beginning of each subdocument. (You can use any heading style you want, but Heading 1 makes sense because, presumably, the subdocuments compose the major sections of your project.)
   - In each Heading 1 paragraph, enter the filename (without the extension) that you want to use for each subdocument.

7

Punctuation Interferes with Subdocument Names

When Word names the subdocument files, it uses the Heading 1 text. However, Word stops as soon as it encounters any punctuation marks in the text. For example, if your Heading 1 text is "Chapter 1—Building Dynamic Documents in Word," the resulting subdocument filename would be Chapter 1.doc. If this isn't what you want, remove any punctuation from the Heading 1 text. Remember, you can always edit the Heading 1 text after you've created the subdocuments.

5. When your outline is complete, save your work.

Converting an Existing Document to a Master

If you have an existing document that you want to use as a master, you need to convert it to the master document format. This means applying the Heading 1 style to the paragraphs that define the beginning of each subdocument. You might also consider moving the document to an empty shared folder so that you can easily keep track of the subdocuments that Word creates.

 You're now ready to create the subdocuments. Begin by clicking the Master Document View button in the Outlining toolbar. This expands the toolbar to display the buttons related to master documents and subdocuments.

 Select the portion of the master document that you want to turn into subdocuments. Then click the Create Subdocuments button in the Outlining toolbar. Word identifies the subdocuments and displays a border around each one, as shown in Figure 7.5. If all looks well, save the master document. Word saves the document and then creates the documents as separate files in the same folder that you used to save the master document.

Figure 7.5
When you click the Create Subdocuments button, Word displays a border around each subdocument in the master document.

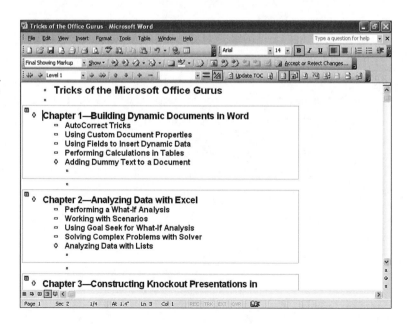

Don't Move or Rename Subdocuments

After you've created the subdocuments, never move or rename them, or else you'll break the link in the master document.

Creating Subdocuments from Existing Documents

If you have existing documents that you want to use in your project, follow these steps to convert the existing documents to subdocuments:

1. Create a new, blank document.

2. Save the document to an empty folder. If you'll be collaborating with other network users, be sure to share the folder with the network.

3. Select View, Outline to switch to Word's Outline view.

 4. If you don't see the master document buttons in the Outlining toolbar, click the Master Document View button.

5. Position the insertion point where you want to insert the existing document.

 6. Click the Insert Subdocument button in the Outlining toolbar. Word displays the Insert Subdocument dialog box.

7. Select the document you want to insert and then click Open. Word inserts the subdocument.

8. Repeats steps 6 and 7 to insert all the documents you require.

Working with Subdocuments

Here are a few techniques you need to know for working with subdocuments from the master document:

 ■ To edit a subdocument, either work with the text directly in the master document or open the subdocument by double-clicking the subdocument icon in the upper-left corner of the subdocument.

 ■ To prevent anyone from editing a subdocument, select it in the master document and then activate the Lock Document button in the Outlining toolbar. (A lock icon appears beneath the subdocument icon.)

 ■ To combine two or more subdocuments into a single subdocument, select the subdocuments in the master document and then click the Merge Subdocument button in the Outlining toolbar.

 ■ To split a subdocument into two subdocuments, first position the insertion point where you want the split to occur. Then click the Split Subdocument button in the Outlining toolbar.

7

- To convert a subdocument to text in the master document, position the insertion point inside the subdocument and then click the Remove Subdocument button in the Outlining toolbar.
- To delete a subdocument, select it and press Delete.

Delete the Subdocument File

After you've converted a subdocument to master document text or deleted a subdocument (because you no longer need the subdocument file), you must delete it by hand.

Embedding Fonts in Shared Documents

If you use some unusual TrueType fonts in a shared document, your formatting efforts will be wasted if the other user doesn't have those fonts installed. To solve this problem, save your document with the TrueType fonts embedded, which ensures that the other user will see your document exactly as you designed it. Here are the steps to follow:

1. Select Tools, Options As to display the Options dialog box.
2. Select the Save tab.
3. Activate the Embed TrueType Fonts check box.
4. To reduce the size of the document, you can force the application to embed only the characters used in the document by activating the Embed Characters In Use Only check box.
5. Click OK.
6. Click Save.

Sharing Excel Workbooks

As with Word, Excel offers three levels of collaboration: comments, tracking changes, and sharing a file among multiple users. Although these features are implemented slightly differently in Excel, the underlying concepts are basically the same, as you'll see in this section.

Inserting Comments in Cells

The simplest level of collaboration with an Excel workbook is the comment that doesn't change any worksheet data, but offers notes, suggestions, and critiques of the worksheet content. In Excel, you associate comments with individual cells (not ranges) by following these steps:

1. Select the cell in which you want to insert the comment.
2. Select Insert, Comment, or click the New Comment button in the Reviewing toolbar. Excel displays an empty comment balloon.

3. Type the comment text.

4. When you're done, click outside the comment balloon.

Excel indicates the inserted comment by adding a small red triangle to the upper-right corner of the cell. To view the comment, hover the mouse pointer over the cell.

Removing the Comment Indicator

If you don't want to see the comment indicators, you can turn them off by selecting Tools, Options, displaying the View tab, and activating the None option in the Comments section.

After you've added one or more comments to a worksheet, use the following Reviewing toolbar techniques to navigate, display, and work with the comments:

 ■ Click Next Comment to move to the next comment.

 ■ Click Previous Comment to move to the previous comment.

 ■ Click Show/Hide Comment to toggle the comment in the current cell on and off.

 ■ Click Show All Comments to toggle all the worksheet's comments on and off.

Showing All Comments

Activating the Show All Comments button is the same thing as selecting Tools, Options, displaying the View tab, and activating the Comment and Indicator option in the Comments section.

 ■ Click Delete Comment to remove the comment from the current cell.

Tracking Worksheet Changes

If you want other people to make changes to a workbook, it's a good idea to keep track of those changes so you can either accept or reject them. Like Word, Excel has a Highlight Changes feature that enables you to do this. When you turn on Highlight Changes, Excel monitors the activity of each reviewer and stores their cell edits, row and column additions and deletions, range moves, worksheet insertions, and worksheet renames. You can also filter the changes by date, reviewer, or worksheet location.

Highlight Changes Limitations

When you activate Highlight Changes, Excel doesn't track formatting changes. Also, Excel doesn't allow a number of operations, including the insertion and deletion of ranges and the deletion of worksheets. For a complete list of disallowed operations, see "Sharing a Workbook," later in this chapter.

7

Here are the steps to follow to activate and configure Highlight Changes:

1. Select Tools, Track Changes, Highlight Changes to display the Highlight Changes dialog box.

2. Activate the Track Changes While Editing check box, as shown in Figure 7.6. (The check box text mentions that this also shares the workbook. See "Sharing a Workbook," later in this chapter.)

Figure 7.6
Use the Highlight Changes dialog box to activate revision tracking for the current workbook.

3. Use the following controls to specify which changes Excel displays:

When—Use this list to filter the displayed changes by time. To specify a date, select Since Date and then edit the date that Excel displays (the default is the current date).

Who—Use this list to filter the displayed changes by reviewer. At first, this list contains Everyone and Everyone but Me. Later, when other users have made changes, the list will include the name of each reviewer.

Where—Use this range box to select the range in which you want changes displayed.

4. Click OK. Excel displays a dialog box letting you know that it will save your workbook.

5. Click OK.

Now, when you make changes to the workbook, Excel displays a blue triangle in the upper-left corner of the cell. (If you delete a row or column, Excel displays a blue line between the cells where the row or column used to be.) Hover the mouse pointer over the cell to see the change, as well as who made it and when, as shown in Figure 7.7.

Figure 7.7
With change tracking turned on, hover the mouse pointer over any cell that shows the change indicator to see a balloon specifying the change.

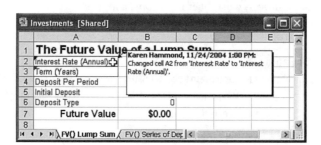

If you want to review the history of changes to the workbook, select Tools, Track Changes, Highlight Changes, activate the List Changes on a New Sheet check box, and click OK. Excel adds a History tab to the workbook and adds data about all the tracked changes.

Modifying the Change History Length

By default, Excel keeps track of changes made for the past 30 days. (The exception is if you turn off change tracking; in that case, Excel deletes the history of changes.) To change the number of days of history that Excel tracks, select Tools, Share Workbook, display the Advanced tab, and then change the Keep Change History for *X* Days spin box.

To accept or reject the workbook changes, follow these steps:

1. Select Tools, Track Changes, Accept or Reject Changes. (If Excel tells you it will save the workbook, click OK.) Excel displays the Select Changes to Accept or Reject dialog box.

2. Use the When, Who, and Where controls to filter the changes, as needed.

3. Click OK. Excel displays the Accept or Reject Changes dialog box and displays a change.

4. Click Accept or Reject. (You can also click Accept All or Reject All to take care of all the changes at once.) Excel moves to the next change.

Multiple Cell Changes

If the reviewers made two or more changes to a cell, the Accept or Reject Changes dialog box displays the Select a Value for cell *Cell* list (where *Cell* is the address of the cell), which shows the original value and the changes. Select the value you want to keep and then click Accept.

---

5. Repeat step 4 until you have reviewed all the changes.

Sharing a Workbook

As you saw in the previous section, activating change tracking also activates *workbook sharing*, the Excel feature that enables two or more users to collaborate on a workbook at the same time. This is a powerful tool because it enables you to share the burden of building a workbook. For example, if you're coordinating a budget model, you might want to share the workbook and assign a different tab to a user in each department.

I should point out here that although turning on change tracking also turns on workbook sharing, the opposite is not the case. That is, you can share a workbook without also displaying changes. Follow these steps to share a workbook:

1. If another person is currently using the workbook, ask that person to close the file.

2. Select Tools, Share Workbook. Excel displays the Share Workbook dialog box.

3. Activate the Allow Changes by More Than One User at the Same Time check box, as shown in Figure 7.8.

Figure 7.8
Use the Share Workbook dialog box to activate workbook sharing and allow multiple users to collaborate on the workbook at the same time.

4. Click OK. Excel tells you it will save the workbook.

5. Click OK.

Excel displays [Shared] in the document title bar to remind you that the workbook is shared. You and your collaborators are now free to work on the file at the same time. Note, however, that Excel doesn't allow the following operations while a workbook is shared:

- Inserting and deleting ranges (although you can insert and delete entire rows and columns)
- Merging cells
- Creating lists
- Creating or modifying PivotTables
- Deleting or moving worksheets
- Applying conditional formatting
- Working with scenarios
- Subtotaling, validating, grouping, and outlining data
- Inserting charts, symbols, pictures, diagrams, objects, and hyperlinks
- Checking for formula errors

Updating a Shared Workbook

To ensure that you're always working with the most up-to-date version of the file, save the workbook. This tells Excel to display other reviewers' changes in your view of the workbook. If any changes were added, Excel displays a dialog box to let you know. Note, too, that you can also see other users' changes by clicking the Update File button in the

Reviewing toolbar (although with this method, Excel doesn't let you know if any changes were added to the workbook).

To control when Excel updates a shared workbook, follow these steps:

1. Select Tools, Share Workbook to display the Share Workbook dialog box.

2. Display the Advanced tab.

3. Select one of the following options:

   When File Is Saved—When you activate this option, Excel updates the workbook automatically when you save the file.

   Automatically Every *X* Minutes—When you activate this option, Excel updates the workbook using the interval you specify (the minimum is 5 minutes; the maximum is 1,440 minutes). You can also elect to have Excel save your changes at the same time or just see the changes made by other users.

4. Click OK.

Working with Reviewers

If you want to know who is currently using the workbook besides yourself, select Tools, Share Workbook. As you can see in Figure 7.9, the Who Has This Workbook Open Now list displays all the current users. If you want to prevent a reviewer from using the workbook, click the user and then click Remove User. Note, however, that you should use this technique only as a last resort because it could easily cause the user to lose unsaved changes. It's safer (and friendlier) to ask the person directly to save his or her changes and close the workbook.

Figure 7.9
Select Tools, Share Workbook to see a list of the workbook's current reviewers.

7

Handling Conflicts

What happens if another user changes a cell, saves his or her changes, and then you change the same cell before updating? This creates a conflict in the workbook versions that must be resolved. To do this, Excel displays the Resolve Conflicts dialog box, shown in Figure 7.10. You have two choices: click Accept Mine to accept your change; click Accept Other to accept the other user's change.

Figure 7.10
Use the Resolve Conflicts dialog box to choose between a change made by you and one made by another user.

To control how Excel handles conflicts, follow these steps:

1. Select Tools, Share Workbook to display the Share Workbook dialog box.
2. Display the Advanced tab.
3. Select one of the following options:

   Ask Me Which Changes Win—When you activate this option, Excel displays the Resolve Conflicts dialog box.

   The Changes Being Saved Win—When you activate this option, Excel automatically accepts your changes.

It's Better to Resolve Conflicts

Collaboration is all about cooperation, so it's always good practice to display conflicts in the Resolve Conflicts dialog box so that you can make an intelligent choice about which change to accept. Therefore, only activate The Changes Being Saved Win option as a last resort.

---

4. Click OK.

Collaborating via Outlook

Collaboration is all about communication, so it's no surprise that Outlook—the Microsoft Office communication center—offers the widest variety of collaboration options among the Office applications. You can share documents via email, share your Contacts folder, request face-to-face meetings, conduct online meetings, and share documents using public Exchange folders. This section covers these and other Outlook collaboration strategies.

Sharing Office Documents via Email

The simplest way to collaborate with others using Outlook is to send an Office document through the email system. However, the method you use to do this depends on the type of collaboration you need:

- If you want the other person to see only the document contents (and not the document itself), send the document as an email message.

- If you want to give the other person a copy of the document, send the document as an email attachment.

- If you want the other person to make tracked changes to the document, send the document with a review request.

- If you want to share the document with a large number of people, send the document with a routing slip.

The next few sections take you through the specifics of these methods.

Sending a Document as an Email Message

When you send a document as an email message, Outlook converts the document to HTML format and inserts the HTML code into the body of the message. How you start depends on whether you're sending an existing document or a new document:

- To send an existing document, open the document and select File, Send To, Mail Recipient. (In Publisher, select File, Send E-Mail, Send This Page as Message.)

Sending a Worksheet Range

If you want to send only a portion of an Excel worksheet, select the range and then select File, Send To, Mail Recipient. In the E-mail dialog box that appears, activate the Send the Current Sheet as the Message Body option and click OK. Fill in the email details and click Send This Selection.

- To send a new document, either create the document in the appropriate application or in Outlook, select Actions, New Mail Using, Microsoft Office, and then select the type of document you want to send.

Outlook converts the document to HTML and inserts the HTML code into a new email message. Select your recipients, enter a Subject line, and then click Send a Copy.

Sending a Document as an Attachment

If you prefer that the user receives a copy of the document, you can send the document as an email attachment. Open the document (this can be a Word document, an Excel workbook, a PowerPoint slide show, a Publisher publication, or an Access data page) and select File, Send To, Mail Recipient (as Attachment). (In Publisher, select File, Send E-Mail, Send

7

Publication as Attachment.) In the message window that appears, select your recipients, enter a Subject line, and then click Send.

Shared Attachments

Rather than sending out copies of attachments (which can get confusing), you can instead send out a *shared attachment* that resides in a single location as part of a shared workspace. See "Sending a Shared Attachment," later in this chapter.

Turning Off Reading Layout View

When you open a Word document received as an attachment, Word displays the document in Reading Layout, a pared-down view designed for reviewing and commenting. If you prefer to work with such documents normally, you can turn off the automatic Reading Layout display. Select Tools, Options, display the General tab, and deactivate the Allow Starting in Reading Layout check box.

Sending a Document with a Review Request

A common collaboration task is to email a document to a reviewer, have that person make changes to the document, and then incorporate those changes into the original document. If you want to do this, you need to send the document with a review request. (Yes, there's a method you can use to incorporate a reviewers' changes when you send a document as a regular attachment, but it's convoluted, time-consuming, and unreliable. The review-request method is simple, quick, and robust, so it's the only one I discuss here.) Here are the steps to follow:

1. Open the Word document, the Excel workbook, or the PowerPoint presentation that you want to send.

2. If you're working with an Excel workbook, activate workbook sharing (see "Sharing a Workbook," earlier in this chapter).

3. Select File, Send To, Mail Recipient (for Review). Outlook creates a review request, which is a message window that has the Review flag set, the document attached, and a "Please review" message in the Subject line and message body, as shown in Figure 7.11.

Figure 7.11
When you select the Mail Recipient (for Review) command, Outlook creates a review-request message.

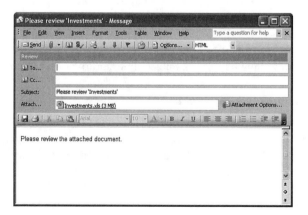

4. Add the recipients and body text, as needed.

5. Click Send. Outlook sends the document.

When the reviewer gets the email, he or she opens the attached document and makes whatever changes are necessary. He or she then clicks the Reply with Changes button in the Reviewing toolbar. (Alternatively, click File, Send To, Original Sender.) This opens an Outlook reply message addressed to the original sender of the document and includes the revised document as an attachment. The reviewer then clicks Send to return the document.

When you receive the reply, check the name of the attached document. If it's the same as your original document, close the original document to avoid an error. Then double-click the attached document. The application recognizes the file and displays a dialog box like the one shown in Figure 7.12, asking if you want to merge the reviewer's changes into the original document. Click Yes to merge the changes; click No to review the changes made by the reviewer.

Figure 7.12
When you open a reviewed document, the program asks whether you want to merge the reviewer's changes into the original.

How Office Tracks Review Documents

Documents returned from the reviewer often have a different name from the original (for example, Investments (2).xls instead of Investments.xls). How does the Office application associate the reviewed copy with the original? The answer is that Outlook adds a custom property called _ReviewCycleID to the document. This is a random 10-digit value uniquely associated with the original document. The association is maintained by a file named review.rcd in the following folder:

```
C:\Documents and Settings\User\Application Data\Microsoft\Office
```

This is a text file that contains entries similar to the following:

```
[3807988912]
Path=C:\Workbooks\Investments.xls
```

This document's _ReviewCycleID property is set to 3807988912, and that doesn't change as the reviewer works with and returns the document. So, no matter the document name, the application always knows where the original file is located.

Don't Pass Around Review Requests

_ReviewCycleID isn't the only custom property that Outlook adds when you send a document with a review request (to see all the custom properties, select File, Properties and display the Custom tab). It also adds _AuthorEmail and _AuthorEmailDisplayName properties that are set to your email address and name, respectively. If you don't want third parties seeing this information, ask your reviewers not to send review request documents to other users.

7

Routing Documents

You can use Office applications (Excel, Word, PowerPoint, and Access) with Microsoft Exchange (or other compatible mail packages) to send an online copy of a document. The recipients can then comment on, revise, or add to the document, and it will be routed back to you via email. You might want to route a document if you have a longer review period or a short list of reviewers. Other advantages of routing a document include the following:

- You automatically receive a routing status message as each recipient forwards your document.

- You ensure that each recipient is reminded to forward the document to the next recipient.

Preparing Documents for Review

The review request method works well if you have a small number of recipients. For larger projects, managing all those attachments can be a daunting task. A better strategy for Word documents and Excel workbooks is to route the document to a number of reviewers, in any order you specify.

When you route a document, you specify a series of recipients on a routing slip. Outlook sends the document to the first person on the routing slip. When that person is done with the document, he or she sends it, and the routing slip automatically addresses the document to the next person on the routing slip. The document eventually finds its way back after each person has reviewed it. (If you want, you can also route the documents to all the reviewers at once.)

Here are the steps to follow to route a document:

1. In Word or Excel, open the file you want to route.
2. Select File, Send To, Routing Recipient. (If you see an Outlook dialog box warning that the program is trying to access Outlook email addresses, click Yes.) The Routing Slip dialog box appears.
3. Click Address to display the Address Book.
4. For each recipient, either select the recipient Name and click To, or type the address directly into the To box. When you're done selecting recipients, click OK to return to the Routing Slip dialog box. Figure 7.13 shows the dialog box with several recipients added.

Changing the Recipient Order
If you want to change the order in which recipients will receive your document, select a recipient's name in the To box and use one of the Move arrows to move the name up or down in the list.

Figure 7.13
Use the Routing Slip dialog box to select recipients and route a document.

5. Adjust the Subject text, if necessary, and enter an explanatory message into the Message Text area.

6. In most cases, you want the document sent to the reviewers sequentially, so leave the One After Another option activated. If you prefer that the reviewers receive the document at the same time, activate All at Once instead.

7. If you want the document returned to you after the last recipient has worked with it, leave the Return When Done check box activated.

8. If you'd like to receive a message each time a recipient routes the document to the next person, leave the Track Status check box activated.

9. If you're routing a Word document, use the Protect For list to set the document protection: Tracked Changes turns on the Track Changes feature, Comments allows only inserted comments, and Forms allows only data entry in forms.

10. When you're ready, click the Route button. (If Outlook displays a warning that a program is trying to send mail, click Yes.) If you want to attach a routing slip and route the document at a later time, click the Add Slip button.

Routing to Groups

If you have group aliases set up in your Address Book, you can select a group alias as the recipient. However, all members of the group alias are considered one recipient, so they will all receive the document at the same time. To route the document to members of a group alias one after another, send it to the individual members, not to the alias.

After a reviewer is done with the document, he or she selects the File, Send To, Next Routing Recipient command. In the Routing Slip dialog box that appears, the reviewer is given the option of routing to the next recipient or sending a copy without a routing slip.

Sharing Your Outlook Folders

If you work in an Exchange Server shop, or if you have an account on a Exchange Server host, you can share any of your folders with other Exchange Server users. You can set up the sharing for specific users, and you can apply permissions that determine what actions each user can perform within the folder. Outlook gives you two ways to share your folders: with permissions and with delegate access.

Sharing Your Folders with Permissions

To share any Outlook folder, follow these steps:

1. Open the folder you want to share.
2. Select File, Folder, Sharing. Outlook opens the folder's Properties dialog box and displays the Permissions tab, shown in Figure 7.14.

Sharing Links

When you open the Calendar, Contacts, Tasks, Notes, and Journal folders, the Navigation pane includes a link for sharing the folder. For example, to share the Calendar, click the Share My Calendar link.

Figure 7.14

Use the Permissions tab to configure a folder for sharing with other users on your Exchange Server system.

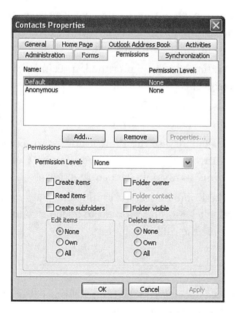

3. Click Add to display the Add Users dialog box.
4. For each user you want to allow to open the folder, select the name and then click Add. When you're done, click OK to return to the Properties dialog box.
5. Select the name of the user to whom you want to assign permissions.

6. Use the Permission Level list to select the permission level for the user:

Owner—User can create, read, edit, and delete all folder items, create subfolders, and change the permission levels for other users.

Publishing Editor—User can create, read, edit, and delete all items, and create subfolders.

Editor—User can create, read, edit, and delete all items.

Publishing Author—User can create and read all items and create subfolders, but can edit and delete only the user's own items.

Author—User can create and read all items, but can edit and delete only the user's own items.

Nonediting Author—User can create and read all items, but can delete only the user's own items.

Reviewer—User can only read items.

Contributor—User can only create items. The contents of the folder do not appear. (Does not apply to delegates.)

None—User can't open the folder.

7. Customize the permission level by activating or deactivating the check boxes and option buttons.

8. Repeat steps 5–7 to set the permission level for each user.

9. Click OK.

Sharing a Contact

If you want to share one of your contacts with another person, it's often easier to email the contact information to that person. To do this, open the contact and pull down the Actions menu. If the recipient has Outlook, select Forward; if the recipient doesn't have Outlook, select Forward as vCard.

Sharing Your Folders with Delegate Access

When you share one of your private folders, the other users access that folder as themselves. For example, if you share a message folder and the user has Create Items permission, that person can send messages from your folder, but the message will be from the user.

That's usually what you'll want, but there may be times when you want to give a user permission to access your folders as *you*. For example, you might have an assistant or deputy that you want to give access to your Inbox folder and then have that person send new messages, replies, and forwards in your name. This is called *send-on-behalf-of* permission, and you set it up by defining a user as a *delegate* and giving that user *delegate access*. As with folder permissions, you need to be part of an Exchange Server network or host for this to work.

7

Here are the steps to follow to set up a user as a delegate:

1. In Outlook, select Tools, Options to display the Options dialog box.
2. Display the Delegates tab.
3. Click Add. Outlook displays the Add Users dialog box.
4. Select the user you want to assign delegate access and click Add.
5. Click OK. Outlook displays the Delegate Permissions dialog box for the user, as shown in Figure 7.15.

Figure 7.15
Use the Delegate Permissions dialog box to specify the permissions for the selected delegate.

6. Use the lists to set the user's permissions for each of your folders. Note that delegates have only three permission types: Editor, Author, and Reviewer (see the previous section for descriptions of these types).
7. If you want to alert the delegate to the permissions you set, activate the Automatically Send a Message to Delegate Summarizing These Permissions check box.
8. If you want the delegate to also see those items that you marked as private, activate the Delegate Can See My Private Items check box.
9. Click OK to return to the Options dialog box.
10. Click OK.

Accessing Shared Folders

Whether you have access to another user's shared folder via folder permissions or as a delegate, follow these steps to display the shared folder:

1. Select File, Open, Other User's Folder. Outlook displays the Open Other User's Folder dialog box.

2. Type the name of the person who shared the folder. If you're not sure of the name, click Name to display the Select Name dialog box, select the user, and then click OK.

3. Use the Folder Type list to select the type of folder you want to access.

4. Click OK.

Opening Shared Nonmessage Folders

For nonmessage folders, you can also click the Open Shared *Type* link in the Navigation pane, where *Type* is the type of folder (for example, Open Shared Contacts).

Outlook displays the shared folder. For a nonmessage folder, Outlook adds the shared folder to the Navigation pane, as shown in Figure 7.16.

Figure 7.16
When you open a shared private folder, Outlook adds the folder to the Navigation pane.

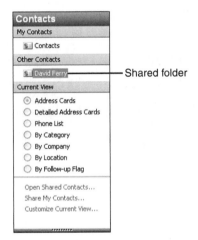

— Shared folder

Working with Another Email Account as a Delegate

If you're a delegate with Editor or Author privileges, you have send-on-behalf-of permission, meaning you can send new messages, replies, and forwards using the folder owner's email account. Although you can do this by displaying a shared message folder, it's much easier if you add the owner's email account to your Exchange Server profile. Here's how it's done:

1. Select Tools, E-Mail Accounts.

2. Select View or Change Existing E-Mail Accounts and click Next.

3. Select your Exchange Server account and click Change. The Exchange Server Settings dialog box appears.

4. Click More Settings.

5. Display the Advanced tab.

7

6. Click Add.

7. Type the owner's name and click OK.

8. Click OK to return to the Exchange Server Settings dialog box.

9. Click Next.

10. Click Finish.

Outlook displays both sets of mail folders, as shown in Figure 7.17.

Figure 7.17
If you're a delegate, add the owner's email account to your profile to access the shared message folders.

To send a message as a delegate on behalf of the owner, start a new message or reply to or forward an existing message in one of the owner's message folders. Make sure the From field is displayed by dropping down the Options list and activating the From command. Type the owner's name into the From field and then fill out and send the message normally. When the recipient receives the message, the From field data will have the following format:

Delegate Name [*Delegate Address*] on behalf of *Owner Name* [*Owner Address*]

Requesting a Meeting

If you've shared your Calendar folder, others on your Exchange Server network can view your appointments and events (at least those that you haven't set up as private). But there might be times when you need to coordinate schedules with other people to arrange a meeting.

The old-fashioned method of doing this involved a phone conversation in which each person consulted his day planner to try to find a mutually free time. This isn't too bad if just two people are involved, but what if there are a dozen? Or a hundred? You could try sending out email messages, but you're still looking at a coordination nightmare for a large group of people.

Outlook solves this dilemma by implementing a couple of time-saving features:

■ Meeting Requests—These are email messages that you use to set up small meetings. They let the invitees respond to your invitation with a simple click of a button.

■ Plan a Meeting—This more sophisticated tool is designed for coordinating larger groups. The Plan a Meeting feature lets you see in advance the schedule of each invitee, so you can schedule a suitable time *before* inviting everyone.

The next two sections show you how to use both features.

Sending Out a New Meeting Request

If you need to set up a simple meeting that involves just a few people, a basic meeting request is all you need. A meeting request is an email message that asks the recipients to attend a meeting on a particular day at a particular time. The recipients can then check their schedules (although Outlook does this for them automatically) and either accept or reject the request by clicking buttons attached to the message.

To start a meeting request, select Actions, New Meeting Request or press Ctrl+Shift+Q. Outlook displays the Meeting form, shown in Figure 7.18. Use the To box to enter the email addresses of the invitees. (Or you can click To and choose the addresses from an address book. Note that you can designate attendees who are required and attendees who are optional.) Fill in the other fields and then click the Send button to mail the request.

Figure 7.18
Use the Meeting form to send out a meeting request.

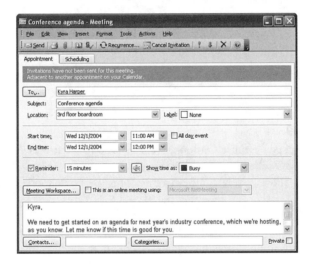

When the recipient gets the message, he or she sees a window similar to the one shown in Figure 7.19. There are two important things to note about this message:

- The toolbar contains four buttons that define the response: Accept, Tentative, Decline, and Propose New Time.

- When Outlook receives a meeting request, it checks your Calendar to see if the request conflicts with any existing appointments. If a conflict is present, Outlook tells you when you view the request.

To respond to this request, the recipient either clicks one of the toolbar response buttons or pulls down the Actions menu and selects a command such as Accept or Decline. Outlook then displays a dialog box with the following options:

- Edit the Response Before Sending—Select this option to display the Meeting Response form, which lets you enter some explanatory text in your response.

7

- Send the Response Now—Select this option if you want to return the response without any explanatory text.
- Don't Send a Response—Select this option to ignore the request (it will be deleted).

Figure 7.19
An example of what the meeting request looks like on the recipient's end.

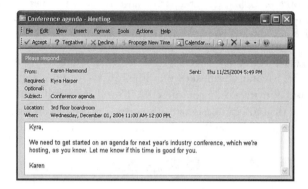

If you Accept or Tentatively Accept the meeting, Outlook adds it to your Calendar automatically.

Planning a Meeting

For larger meetings, you can use Outlook's Plan a Meeting feature to do some advance work. Specifically, you tell Plan a Meeting the names of the invitees, and Outlook queries their schedules and shows you when they're free. This lets you choose a convenient time for the meeting before sending out the request.

To plan a meeting, you have two choices:

- If you've already started a meeting request, activate the Scheduling tab in the Meeting form.

- If you're starting from scratch, either select Actions, Plan a Meeting, or click the Plan a Meeting button on the toolbar.

The first thing you need to do is add all the attendees. You can either type in the person's name under your own in the All Attendees column, or you can click Add Others to select names using an address book. As you add names, Outlook checks their schedules and fills the timeline with blocks that represent each person's existing appointments and meetings, as shown in Figure 7.20.

After you've added all the attendees, you can adjust your meeting time accordingly. There are three methods you can use:

- Enter new values in the Meeting Start Time and Meeting End Time controls.
- In the timeline, use the mouse pointer to drag the meeting selection bars left or right. The green bar represents the meeting start time, and the red bar represents the end time.

■ To have Outlook select an appropriate time automatically, use the AutoPick feature. Click << to choose an earlier time, or click AutoPick Next >> to choose a later time.

Figure 7.20
Use this window to plan a meeting.

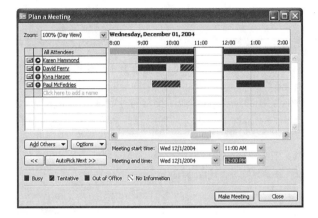

If you're working in the Plan a Meeting window, click Make Meeting to generate the meeting request. Fill in the fields as usual, and then click Send.

To monitor the status of the responses, double-click the meeting in your Calendar and activate the Tracking tab. Outlook displays a list of the attendees and their current status (Accepted, Declined, and so on).

Using SharePoint to Collaborate on Office Documents

If you're on a network and you want to share a document with other users, the easiest way to do that is to place the document in a shared network folder and give those users access to the folder. If you also want to have online discussions with those users and share a calendar and contacts, the easiest route is via an Exchange Server on your network.

However, what if you want to work with people who don't have access to your network? These days, many businesses are "virtual" in the sense that they consist of permanent employees and temporary contract workers, all of whom work or live in separate locations. For these far-flung businesses, you can still use Exchange Server via a hosting service. However, this usually means creating a separate Outlook profile just for the Exchange Server account, which is a hassle if you also have POP or HTTP accounts, for instance.

A better solution for many businesses is a website that runs Windows SharePoint Services, an extension to Windows Server 2003 that enables users to come together online as a virtual "team" for sharing documents, lists, calendars, and contacts and to have online discussions and meetings. Each SharePoint site has at least one administrator who configures the site and sets up users as team members with unique usernames and passwords. (It's also possible to set up a SharePoint site to allow anonymous access.)

7

In this section, I assume that you or someone else has already set up the SharePoint site and that you have your username and password (which the administrator should have emailed to you). Given that, I'll focus on the SharePoint features that enable team members to collaborate on Office documents.

Add SharePoint to Trusted Sites

If you have trouble accessing a SharePoint site, the problem might be that you haven't added it to your list of trusted sites. In Internet Explorer, select Tools, Internet Options, display the Security tab, select Trusted Sites, and then click Sites. If your SharePoint site isn't secure (most aren't), deactivate the Require Server Verification (https:) for All Sites in This Zone check box. Type the SharePoint site address into the Add This Web Site to This Zone text box, click Add, and then click OK.

Sharing Documents in a Document Library

The most basic form of collaboration on a SharePoint site is a *document library*, which is a folder on the site that stores documents added by team members. Each member can open and work with any of these documents (assuming, of course, that the SharePoint administrator has given the member sufficient permission to do so), and the changes are reflected on the site copy, so they're seen by the other team members. A standard SharePoint site comes with a default document library called Shared Documents, as you can see in Figure 7.21.

Figure 7.21
A standard home page for a SharePoint site, which includes a Shared Documents library.

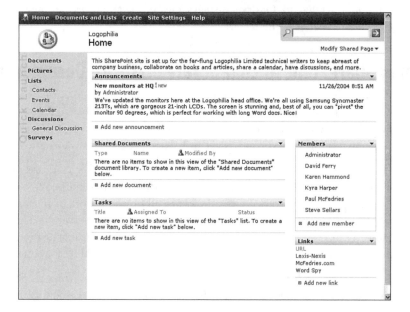

Creating a New Document Library

You can use the default Shared Documents library, or you can create your own libraries. For example, you might want to create separate libraries for individual projects, departments, and so on. Here are the steps to follow to create a new document library:

1. In the SharePoint site's Quick Launch bar, click Documents.

2. Click Create Document Library. The Create Page screen appears.

3. Click Document Library. The New Document Library screen appears, as shown in Figure 7.22.

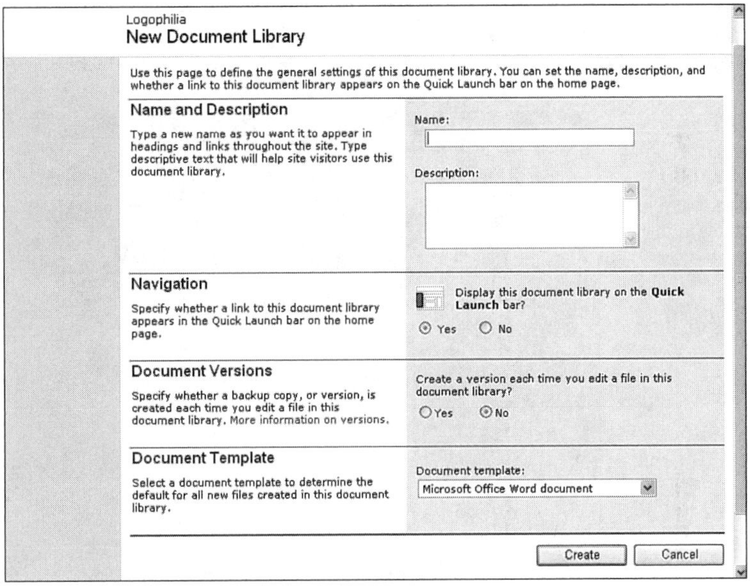

Figure 7.22
Use the New Document Library page to create a new library.

4. Type a Name and Description for the library.

5. In the Navigation section, if you want the library to appear in the Quick Launch bar, select Yes; otherwise, select No.

6. In the Document Versions section, if you want SharePoint to create a version each time you edit a file (see "Working with Document Versions," earlier in this chapter), select Yes; otherwise, select No.

7. In the Document Template section, use the list to select the document type that SharePoint uses as a default template for new documents created in the library.

8. Click Create. SharePoint creates and then displays the new library.

7

Uploading an Existing Document

To upload a document to a library, SharePoint gives you three methods to choose from:

- In any Office program, open the document and then select File, Save As. Click My Network Places, select the network place for your SharePoint site, click Open, and then enter your username and password. A list of the available libraries appears, as shown in Figure 7.23. Open the library you want to use and then click Save.

Creating a SharePoint Network Place

To set up a network place for your SharePoint site, select Start, My Network Places, click Add a Network Place, click Next, select Choose Another Network Location, and click Next. Type the address of the SharePoint site, click Next, and enter your username and password when prompted. Type a name for the site, click Next, and then click Finish.

Figure 7.23
After you open the SharePoint site, select the document library you want to use to store the document.

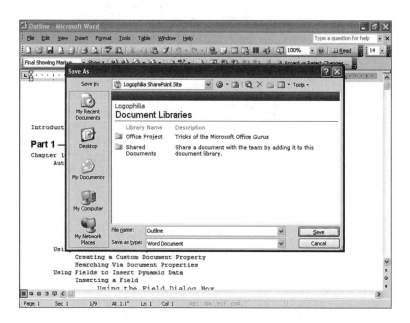

- If you want to use the default Shared Documents library, return to the SharePoint site's home page (click the Home link in the site menu bar). Click Add New Document, click Browse to open the Choose File dialog box, select the document, and then click Open. Click Save and Close to upload the file.

- To use the SharePoint site to upload the document to any library, click Documents in the Quick Launch bar. Click the document library you want to use and then click Upload Document. Click Browse to open the Choose File dialog box, select the document, and then click Open. Click Save and Close to upload the file.

Uploading Multiple Files

If you have a number of documents to upload, it's faster to click the Upload Multiple Files link and then use the Explorer view to open the folder containing the files and activate the check box for each file you want to upload.

Creating a New Document

To create a new document directly in a library, follow these steps:

1. On the SharePoint site, click Documents in the Quick Launch bar.
2. Click the document library you want to use.
3. Click New Document. (If Internet Explorer displays a warning dialog box, click OK.) A new file opens in whatever application supports the default template type you specified when you created the library.
4. Select File, Save to open the Save As dialog box, which displays the contents of the SharePoint document library.
5. Type a filename for the document and click Save.

Opening a Document

When you want to work with a file stored in a SharePoint document library, you can open it either from an Office program or from the SharePoint site.

To open a SharePoint document from an Office application, follow these steps:

1. Select File, Open to display the Open dialog box.
2. Click My Network Places.
3. Select the network place for your SharePoint site and click Open.
4. Enter your username and password.
5. In the list of available libraries that appears, open the library you want to use.
6. Select the document and then click Open.

To open a document directly from the SharePoint site, follow these steps:

1. In the SharePoint site home page, click Documents in the Quick Launch bar.
2. Click the library that contains the document you want to work with.
3. Drop down the list associated with the document, as shown in Figure 7.24.
4. Select Edit In *Program*, where *Program* is the Office application associated with the document's file type.
5. If Internet Explorer displays a warning dialog box, click OK.
6. If another user has the document open, the program might warn you that the file is locked. You can then open a read-only copy, create a local copy, or ask for a notification when the other user is finished with the document.

7

Figure 7.24
In the document library, each document has a list of associated actions that you can perform.

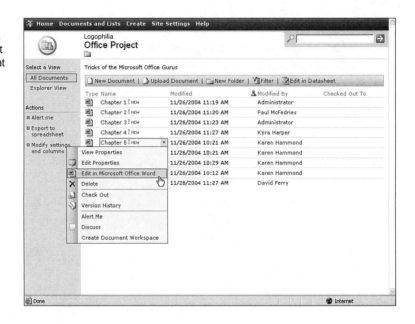

Whichever method you use, the document opens in the Office applications, which also displays the Shared Workspace task pane, as shown in Figure 7.25. This is the shared workspace for the SharePoint site as a whole. To learn more about shared workspaces as well as how to create new ones, see "Collaborating with a Shared Workspace," later in this chapter.

Figure 7.25
When you open a document, the Office program also displays the Shared Workspace task pane.

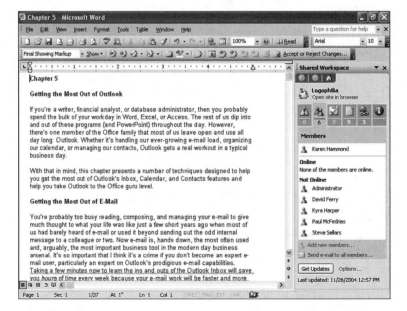

Other Document Actions

The drop-down list associated with each SharePoint document contains a number of actions besides the Edit in *Program* action. Here's a summary:

Permissions Required

You can run many of these actions only if your SharePoint account has the appropriate permissions.

- View Properties—Displays various properties of the document, including its name, title, and the date and time it was created and last modified.
- Edit Properties—Enables you to change the document's Name and Title properties.
- Delete—Deletes the document.
- Check Out—Checks out the document from the library, which means that no other user can make changes to the document. After you select this action, the document library's Check Out To column displays your username.
- Check In (this item appears only when the document is checked out)—Checks the document back in. The page that appears gives you the option of checking the document in, checking in only the changes you made while keeping the document checked out, or undoing your changes.
- Version History—Displays the document's versions, assuming you enabled file versions when you set up the library. You can view versions, restore a document to an earlier version, and delete versions.
- Alert Me—Configures an email alert to be sent to you when the document changes.
- Discuss—Opens the document and adds a Discussions bar that enables you to have an online discussion with other members about the document.
- Create Document Workspace—Creates a new document workspace centered around the document. See the next section for more information about shared workspaces.

Collaborating with a Shared Workspace

A shared workspace is a kind of mini version of a SharePoint site, except that it's usually associated with a document instead of a larger entity such as a project or department. For example, if you have a team working on a budget workbook, you could create a shared workspace for that document, which not only allows members to work on the document, but also allows the team to perform other SharePoint tasks such as discussions, announcements, meetings, and so on.

Assuming you have the appropriate permissions, you can create a shared workspace for a document in Word, Excel, or PowerPoint by following these steps:

1. Open the document you want to share.
2. Select Tools, Shared Workspace to display the Shared Workspace task pane, as shown in Figure 7.26.

7

Figure 7.26
Use the Shared
Workspace task pane to
create the new shared
workspace.

3. Edit the Document Workspace Name, if necessary.

4. In the Location for New Workspace text box, type the address of your SharePoint site.

5. Click Create.

6. If the program asks to save the file, click Yes.

7. Log in to the SharePoint site. The Shared Workspace task pane appears.

8. Click Add New Members.

9. Type the username or email addresses of the people you want to give access to the shared workspace, select a site group, click Next, and then click Finish.

10. When prompted to send an email invitation to the new members, click OK, modify the message as necessary, and then click Send.

Sending a Shared Attachment

When you send a document as an email attachment, each recipient gets a copy of the document. This is inefficient in many cases. For example, if you're sending the document to a number of people, all of whom may make comments or changes, coordinating those edits can be problematic. Even if the document is for information purposes only, you might not want a bunch of copies floating around if the document contains sensitive data.

You can solve these kinds of problems by sending the document as a *shared attachment*. This means that you set up a shared workspace for the document, and the copies you send out are linked to the original in the shared workspace. Here are the steps to follow to send a shared attachment:

1. In Outlook, start a new message and attach the file that you want to work with.

2. Click the Attachment Options button. Outlook displays the Attachment Options task pane.

3. Activate the Shared Attachment option.

4. Use the Create Document Workspace At box to enter the address of your SharePoint site.

5. Press Tab. Outlook confirms the SharePoint site and adds the text shown in Figure 7.27 to the message body.

Figure 7.27
Activate the Shared Attachment option to send a document as part of a shared document workspace.

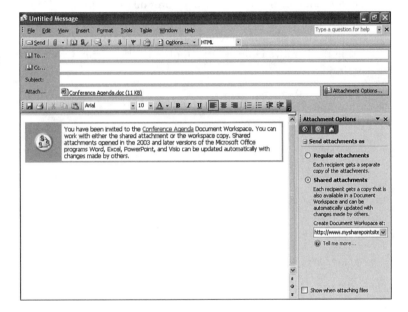

6. Fill in the rest of the email and send it.

Publishing an Excel List to a SharePoint Site

Rather than sharing an entire workbook on a SharePoint site, you can publish just a worksheet list. This enables other people to work on the list through the SharePoint site. After you create a list (see the section in Chapter 2 titled "Analyzing Data with Lists"), select Data, List, Publish List. Enter the SharePoint site address, as well as a Name and Description. If you want changes to the list to automatically appear on the SharePoint list, activate the Link to the New SharePoint List check box. Click Next, check the column data types Excel displays, and if all looks well, click Finish.

7

From Here

- You can also collaborate by publishing documents to the Web. See Chapter 8, "Office Without Borders: Using Office Documents on the Web."

- To learn how to collaborate using ink and other Tablet PC features, see Chapter 9, "Collaborating with a Tablet PC and OneNote."

- Security is an important collaboration issue. In Chapter 14, see the sections "Using File Passwords and Encryption" and "Setting Document Permissions with Information Rights Management."

- When you use many of the Office features discussed in this chapter, you often end up adding lots of hidden data to a document: comments, tracked changes, reviewer names, and more. To learn how to remove this data, see the sections in Chapter 14 titled "Using the Remove Hidden Data Tool" and "Removing Other Private Data."

Office Without Borders: Using Office Documents on the Web

8

Ever since Microsoft's belated 1995 realization that the Internet was something big that ought to factor into the company's plans, they have been cramming the Office suite with Net-friendly features and adding Office-friendly features to Internet Explorer. The goal has always been to blur the previously hard-edged distinction between here—your computer and your LAN—and there—the Web, FTP sites, and other online locations.

In this chapter, you'll see that Microsoft has succeeded for the most part, and that it's easy to move documents from offline to online and back again without losing your data or formatting.

Converting Office Documents to Web Pages

What do you do if you have existing documents, worksheets, and presentations that you want to mount on the Web? Internet Explorer can work in conjunction with Office to display these files, but all your readers might not have that capability. To make sure *anyone* who surfs to your site can access your data, you need to convert your files into the Web's *lingua franca:* HTML. Fortunately, the Office applications make this easy by including features that convert documents from their native format to HTML. This section explains the techniques that you use in each application.

Converting a Word Document to a Web Page

Word does an excellent job of converting existing documents into HTML format. Character formatting (that is, those formats that are compatible with HTML) is carried out flawlessly. Bullets, numbers, and tables remain intact; graphics are preserved; and hyperlinks make the journey without a hitch. You'll need to watch out for your headings, but as long as you've used Word's default heading styles (Heading 1, Heading 2, and so on), these will be transferred correctly to HTML heading tags.

Of course, there will still be a few Word knickknacks that don't survive the trip: text boxes, unusual symbols, columns, and table formulas, to name a few.

The best part is that the conversion is about as painless as these things get. Here are the steps to follow:

First, Choose Your Target Browser

Before you save the document, you might want to tell Word which browser or browsers your users surf with, because this determines the features Word uses to render the web page XML or HTML. For example, if you tell Word that your users browse with Netscape Navigator 4.0 or later, Word disables the MHTML format (described in the steps that follow). Select Tools, Options, display the General tab, click Web Options, and display the Browsers tab. Select a target browser from the People Who View This Web Page Will Be Using list. Note, too, that you can use the check boxes in the Options list to customize the web page features.

---

1. Make sure you've saved your document in Word format.
2. Select File, Save as Web Page. Word displays the Save As dialog box.
3. Use the Save In box to select a location for the new file.
4. If you want to change the page title (the text that appears in the browser's title bar), click Change Title, enter the new Page Title, and click OK.
5. Use the File Name box to change the name of the file if necessary. If you don't, Word just changes the document's extension to .htm.
6. In the Save As Type list, you choose from three possibilities:

   Single File Web Page—This is the MIME Encapsulation of Aggregate HTML Documents (MHTML) format. It combines the HTML and references to external files such as images into a single file that uses the .mht extension. Note that only Internet Explorer supports this file type.

   Web Page—This is a regular HTML web page that uses the .htm file extension. Word also creates a folder named *Filename*_files (where *Filename* is the text in the File Name text box) that includes any supporting files, such as images required by the web page.

   Web Page, Filtered—This is also a regular HTML web page that uses the .htm extension. The difference is that this format also strips out any Office-specific tags that Word uses in the Web Page format to facilitate the conversion of the file back into Word format. If you don't care about converting the document back to Word, choose this format for a smaller size (less than half the Web Page format). Note, too, that this format also creates a folder to hold the page's supporting files.

Bypassing the Supporting Files Folder

The supporting files folder created with the regular HTML web page formats is a convenient way to organize those files, but it might be unnecessary if you're saving the web page in a folder that you upload to a web server. To avoid the supporting files folder and save all the supporting files in the same folder as the web page, select Tools, Options, display the General tab, click Web Options, display the Files tab, and deactivate the Organize Supporting Files in a Folder check box.

7. Click Save.

8. If you chose the Web Page, Filtered format, Word warns you that you'll lose the Office-specific tabs and asks if you want to proceed. Click Yes.

9. Depending on the original format of the file, Word may display a warning that you might lose formatting. Click Continue. Word converts the document and then displays the new web page.

Publishing an Excel Range, Sheet, or Workbook to the Web

Excel's row-and-column format mirrors the layout of an HTML table, so it's natural that you should be able to convert a range into the appropriate HTML table tags. Of course, you can also publish entire workbooks as web pages.

Here are the steps to follow to publish a range or workbook to the Web:

1. Decide what you want to publish:

Choosing a Target Browser

To choose the target browser, select Tools, Options, display the General tab, click Web Options, and display the Browsers tab. Select a target browser from the People Who View This Web Page Will Be Using list. You can also use the check boxes in the Options list to customize the web page features.

- To publish an entire workbook, open the workbook.
- To publish a worksheet, select the entire worksheet.
- To publish a range, select the range.
- To publish a chart, select the chart.

2. Select File, Save as Web Page. Excel displays the Save As dialog box.

3. Use the Save In box to select a location for the new file.

4. Use the File Name box to change the name of the file, if necessary. If you don't, Excel changes the document's extension to .htm.

5. In the Save as Type list, you choose from two possibilities:

Single File Web Page—This is the MIME Encapsulation of Aggregate HTML Documents (MHTML) format. It combines the HTML and references to external files such as images into a single file that uses the .mht extension. Note that only Internet Explorer supports this file type.

8

Web Page—This is a regular HTML web page that uses the .htm file extension. Word also creates a folder named *Filename*_files (where *Filename* is the text in the File Name text box) that includes any external files such as images required by the web page.

Bypassing the Supporting Files Folder

To save all the supporting files in the same folder as the web page, select Tools, Options, display the General tab, click Web Options, display the Files tab, and deactivate the Organize Supporting Files in a Folder check box.

---

6. Click Publish to display the Publish as Web Page dialog box.

7. If the object you want to publish isn't selected in the Choose box, use the drop-down list to select what you want to publish.

8. If your users surf with Internet Explorer 5.1 or later, you can make the web page interactive by activating the Add Interactivity With check box and then selecting either Spreadsheet Functionality or PivotTable Functionality in the list. (Here, *interactive* means the user can add, edit, and delete cell data.)

9. If you want to change the page title (the text that appears in the browser's title bar), click Change, enter the new Title, and click OK.

10. If you want Excel to republish the object automatically, activate the AutoRepublish Every Time This Workbook Is Saved check box.

11. Click Publish. Excel publishes the object to a web page. Figure 8.1 shows a worksheet published as an interactive page.

Appending an Object to an Existing Web Page

Excel has the capability to append new objects to existing pages. Follow the steps in this section, making sure you specify an existing web page as the target. After you click Publish, Excel displays a dialog box asking if you want to replace the file or add to it. Click Add to File to append the new object.

Stopping the AutoRepublish Prompt

If you activate the AutoRepublish Every Time This Workbook Is Saved check box, each time you save the workbook Excel displays a dialog box asking if you want to disable or enable AutoRepublish. To avoid this annoyance, either activate the Disable the AutoRepublish Feature option or activate Enable the AutoRepublish Feature option and also the Do Not Show This Message Again check box.

Publishing a PowerPoint Presentation to the Web

Publishing a PowerPoint presentation to the Web is becoming increasingly common. After a conference, for example, many people make their presentations available online for those who couldn't attend. Also, with business travel budgets tightening, "presenting" online saves the expense of either traveling to the audience or bringing the audience to you.

Figure 8.1
An Excel worksheet published as an interactive web page.

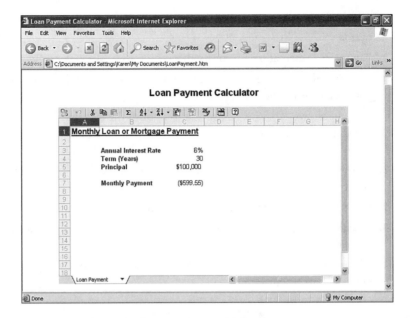

PowerPoint gives you extensive page-publishing options, as the following steps show:

1. Open the presentation you want to publish.

2. Select File, Save as Web Page. PowerPoint displays the Save As dialog box.

3. Use the Save In box to select a location for the new file.

4. Use the File Name box to change the name of the file, if necessary. If you don't, PowerPoint changes the document's extension to .htm.

5. In the Save As Type list, you choose from two possibilities:

   Single File Web Page—This is the MIME Encapsulation of Aggregate HTML Documents (MHTML) format. It combines the HTML and references to external files such as images into a single file that uses the .mht extension. Note that only Internet Explorer supports this file type.

   Web Page—This is a regular HTML web page that uses the .htm file extension. PowerPoint also creates a folder named *Filename*_files (where *Filename* is the text in the File Name text box) that includes any external files such as images required by the web page.

Bypassing the Supporting Files Folder

To save all the supporting files in the same folder as the web page, select Tools, Options, display the General tab, click Web Options, display the Files tab, and deactivate the Organize Supporting Files in a Folder check box.

---

6. Click Publish to display the Publish as Web Page dialog box.

8

7. To determine how much of the presentation you publish, PowerPoint gives you three options:

Complete Presentation—Activate this option to publish every slide in the presentation.

Slide Number *X* Through *Y*—Activate this option to publish only the range of slides you specify using the two spin boxes.

Custom Show—Activate this option to publish the custom slide show you select in the associated list. (PowerPoint disables this option if the presentation has no custom slide shows. To create a custom slide show, select Slide Show, Custom Show.)

8. If you also want to include your speaker notes, leave the Display Speaker Notes check box activated.

9. Use the options in the Browser Support group to set the target browser for your users.

10. To change the page title (the text that appears in the browser's title bar), click Change, enter the new title, and click OK.

11. Click Publish. PowerPoint publishes the presentation to a web page. Figure 8.2 shows a published presentation.

Figure 8.2
A PowerPoint presentation published as a web page.

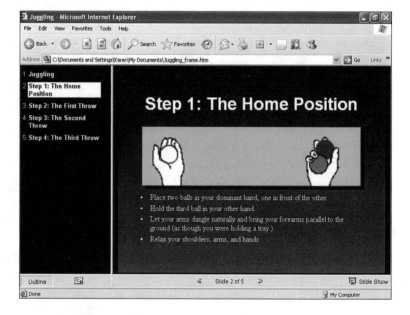

Publishing an Outlook Calendar to the Web

If you don't have access to an Exchange Server, or if you don't want to publish your Free/Busy information on the Web, you can still publish your Outlook Calendar as a web page. Here are the steps to follow:

1. Select the Calendar.

2. Select File, Save as Web Page.

3. Enter the Start Date and End Date for the time frame that you want to publish.

4. Enter a Calendar Title.

5. Specify a File Name and location for the HTML file.

6. Click Save.

Displaying Web Pages in Excel

Excel supports the HTML format. Therefore, if a web page contains data that you need, the easiest way to get at it is to open the page right in Excel. This section shows you how to open web pages, explains Excel's HTML limitations, and outlines the HTML extensions that Excel supports.

Opening a Web Page in Excel

As usual, select File, Open to display the Open dialog box. After this, you have two choices:

- If the page resides on your hard drive or LAN, use the Files of Type drop-down list to choose All Web Pages, select the file, and click Open.

- If the page resides on the Internet or your corporate intranet, use the File Name text box to enter the web page's URL (for example, http://www.our-intranet.com/data.html), and then click Open.

Keep in mind, however, that Excel won't necessarily display the web page in the same way that a browser would. Although Excel's HTML support includes most formatting tags, there are quite a few tags it won't display. Here's a quick rundown of how Excel treats various categories of HTML tags:

- Most character formatting tags are supported, including the tags for bold, italic, underlined, and monospaced text, as well as the `<FONT>` tag's various attributes (`COLOR`, `SIZE`, and `FONT`).

- Heading tags are converted into the equivalent heading styles.

- Links are preserved intact.

- Definition lists are displayed as two-column lists, whereas bulleted and numbered lists are displayed in a single column.

- `<P>` tags convert to blank rows.

- Most table tags and attributes are supported.

Excel's HTML Extension: The `formula` Attribute

The `formula` attribute is an extension of both the `<th>` and `<td>` tags. Recall from the last chapter that you use `<th>` and `<td>` to define a single cell in a table. The `formula` attribute, as its name suggests, defines an Excel formula expression. When you use Excel to view a page that uses `formula`, Excel enters the formula into a cell and proceeds to calculate the result. Thus, with little effort and no programming whatsoever, you can create dynamic, formula-driven web pages.

Here's the syntax to use with the `formula` attribute:

`formula="=expression"`

Here, *expression* is a legal Excel expression, as shown in the following example:

```
<table>
<tr>
<th>Sales
<th>Expenses
<th>Profit
<tr>
<td>100
<td>85
<td formula="=A2-B2">Sales-Expenses
</table>
```

Figure 8.3 shows how Excel displays these tags. Notice how the formula defined by the `formula` attribute has been entered into cell C2. In contrast, Figure 8.4 shows the same page displayed in Internet Explorer. As you can see, the browser ignores the `formula` attribute completely and displays the text after the `<td>` tag.

Figure 8.3
Use the `formula` attribute to work with web page calculations while viewing the page in Excel.

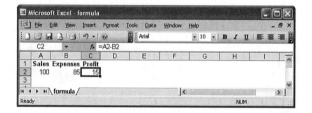

Figure 8.4
Browsers ignore the `formula` attribute.

Adding a Live Stock Price Quote to a Worksheet

If you analyze financial data or maintain a stock portfolio, you can configure an Excel worksheet to display a live, refreshable stock price from MSN MoneyCentral. This is done using the Financial Symbol Smart Tag, which you activate as follows:

1. Select Tools, AutoCorrect Options to display the Options dialog box.
2. Select the Smart Tags tab.
3. In the Recognizes list, activate the Financial Symbol check box.
4. Click OK.

In your worksheet, enter the stock symbol you want to work with (such as MSFT for Microsoft). Point at the cell to display the Smart Tag, click the Smart Tag, and then click Insert Refreshable Stock Price.

Office and FTP

If you regularly exchange Office files with other people via FTP, you're probably best served by using a dedicated FTP client such as CuteFTP (available from www.cuteftp.com). For the occasional file transfer, however, you can use any application that uses the Office Save As or Open dialog boxes. That is, you can download files from FTP sites and upload files to FTP sites all within the comfort of any Office application.

When you display the Open or Save As dialog box and drop down the Look In list (or the Save In list, as it's called in the Save As dialog box), you'll see that it contains an item called FTP Locations. Selecting this item displays a list of the FTP sites that you've defined, as shown in Figure 8.5. (I'll show you how to define FTP sites shortly.) Double-clicking one of these sites logs you in to the FTP server (assuming that you have the appropriate privileges to do so) and displays the files and directories available, as shown in Figure 8.6. From here, you have two choices:

- If you're opening a file, select it and click Open to display it inside the Office application. (I'm assuming, of course, that the application can handle the file type you select.)
- If you're saving a file, select the location, change the name, if necessary, and click Save. This will store the file on the FTP server.

Figure 8.5
Office's Open and Save As dialog boxes let you work with FTP sites.

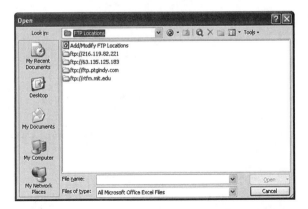

Figure 8.6
Opening an FTP location
displays the files and
directories available.

Here are the steps to follow to define an FTP location:

1. In any Office application, display either the Open dialog box or the Save As dialog box.

2. Use the Look In or Save In list to select FTP locations.

3. Double-click Add/Modify FTP Locations. (You can also select this item directly from the Look In or Save In list.) You'll see the Add/Modify FTP Locations dialog box, shown in Figure 8.7.

Figure 8.7
Use this dialog box to
define FTP sites.

4. In the Name of FTP Site text box, enter the host name of the FTP server (for example, `ftp.domain.com`).

5. Use the Log On as group to enter your login information:

   • If you have an account on the server, activate the User option, enter your username in the text box provided, and enter your password in the Password text box.

- If you don't have an account, but the server accepts anonymous logins, activate the Anonymous option and enter your email address in the Password text box.

6. Click Add. The site is added to the FTP Sites list.

7. Repeat steps 4 through 6 to define other FTP sites.

8. When you're done, click OK.

Inserting Hyperlinks into Office Documents

Although it has been around for a while, one of the most interesting innovations in Office is still the capability to create hyperlinks in any kind of Office document: Word documents, Excel worksheets, Access databases, PowerPoint presentations, and even Outlook email messages. This section shows you the various techniques available for inserting hyperlinks in Office documents.

Hyperlinks and Word

Word accepts hyperlinks within the body of a document. This lets you create active documents that allow the reader to click special text sections and "surf" to another document, which may be on the Web, your corporate intranet, or your hard drive.

For example, consider the Word document shown in Figure 8.8. As you can see, the phrase "amortization schedule" is displayed underlined and in a different color (blue). This formatting indicates that this phrase is a hyperlink. Hovering the mouse pointer over the hyperlink displays a ScreenTip with the linked address and the message CTRL+click to follow link. Holding down Ctrl and clicking this link displays the linked Excel worksheet, as shown in Figure 8.9. (Yes, you Ctrl+click a Word hyperlink instead of just clicking as you would in a web browser. That's because you might need to position the cursor inside the link text, and to do that with a mouse you need to be able to click the text.)

Word gives you three methods for constructing a hyperlink:

- Using Word's AutoCorrect feature to create links automatically.
- Entering the appropriate information by hand.
- Pasting information from another document.

The next few sections discuss each method.

Using Drag and Drop to Create a Hyperlink

Word gives you a fourth method for creating a hyperlink: drag and drop. Right-click and drag a file from a folder window, a link from a web page, or an address displayed in the Internet Explorer Address bar (actually, you right-drag the page icon that appears on the left side of the Address bar). Drop the object inside a Word document and, in the shortcut menu that appears, click Create Hyperlink Here.

8

Figure 8.8
A Word document containing a hyperlink.

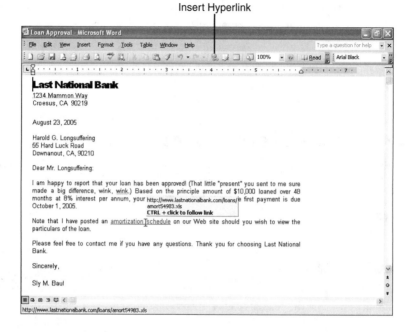

Figure 8.9
Holding down Ctrl and clicking the hyperlink displays this Excel worksheet.

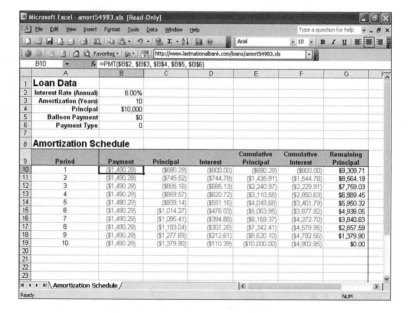

Creating a Hyperlink Using AutoCorrect

The easiest way to create a hyperlink in Word is to type the address into your document. As long as the address is a network path or an Internet URL, Word will convert the text into a hyperlink, no questions asked.

If this doesn't work for you, you'll need to turn on this feature by following these steps:

1. Select Tools, AutoCorrect Options to display the AutoCorrect dialog box.
2. Display the AutoFormat as You Type tab.
3. Activate the Internet and Network Paths with Hyperlinks check box.
4. Click OK.

Creating a Hyperlink from Scratch

For more control over your hyperlinks, you need to use Word's Insert Hyperlink feature, which lets you specify not only linked documents, but named locations within documents (such as a named range within an Excel worksheet). Here are the steps to follow:

1. Either select the text that you want to use for the hyperlink or select the position in the document where you want the link to appear. Note that if you don't select any text beforehand, the link text will be the hyperlink address.
2. Select Insert, Hyperlink, or click the Insert Hyperlink button in the Standard toolbar (refer to Figure 8.8; you can also press Ctrl+K). Word displays the Insert Hyperlink dialog box, shown in Figure 8.10.

Figure 8.10
Use the Insert Hyperlink dialog box to create your hyperlinks from scratch.

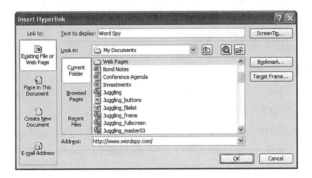

3. Use the Text to Display box to edit the link text, if necessary.
4. To set the ScreenTip text, click ScreenTip, type the ScreenTip text, and click OK. Note that this replaces the address that Word displays in the ScreenTip by default. Word still displays the CTRL+click to follow link message in the ScreenTip.
5. Use the Address text box to specify the name of the file or web page that the users jump to when they Ctrl+click the link. You can enter any of the following:
   - A path to another Word document
   - A path to a document from a different application on your hard drive
   - A path to a multimedia file (such as a sound or video file)
   - A network (UNC) path to a document on your company's intranet
   - A URL on the World Wide Web

6. If you want to link to a specific part of the file, you can do so in Word by linking to a bookmark. Click Bookmark, select the bookmark you want to link to, and click OK.

7. Click OK to insert the hyperlink.

Working with Hyperlinks

If you right-click a hyperlink, the shortcut menu that appears contains the following commands:

- Edit Hyperlink—Displays the Edit Hyperlink dialog box, which is identical to the Add Hyperlink dialog box.
- Select Hyperlink—Selects the hyperlink text.
- Open Hyperlink—Opens the linked document.
- Copy Hyperlink—Copies the hyperlink to the Clipboard.
- Remove Hyperlink—Deletes the hyperlink.

Pasting a Hyperlink in Word

The final method for creating a hyperlink is to paste an object from the Clipboard. That is, you copy an object to the Clipboard—it could be a section of text, an Excel range, some records from a table—position the cursor where you want the link to appear, and then select Edit, Paste Hyperlink. When you click this hyperlink, not only does Word load the application and document from which you copied the information, but it also moves to the spot in the document where the information resides.

Hyperlinks and Excel

Working with hyperlinks in Excel is similar to working with Word in that you have three main methods for inserting a hyperlink:

- Using AutoCorrect to create the link automatically. That is, you type a web address or network UNC path into a cell (don't type anything else) and AutoCorrect converts the text to a link.

- Entering the appropriate information by hand using the Insert, Hyperlink command. In Excel's version of the Insert Hyperlink dialog box, click Bookmark to specify either a range or range name as the target.

- Copying information from another document and then using the Edit, Paste as Hyperlink command.

The AutoCorrect option converts the address text to a HYPERLINK worksheet function. Here's the general format for this function:

HYPERLINK(*link_location* [,*friendly_name*])

link_location	The URL, local path, or network path of the document you want to link to.
friendly_name	(Optional) The text that will appear in the cell. If you omit this argument, Excel displays the *link_location* text, instead.

For example, the following formula sets up a link to the Budget.xls workbook in the \\Server\Public folder and displays Budget Workbook in the cell:

```
=HYPERLINK("\\Server\Public\Budget.xls", "Budget Workbook")
```

Hyperlinks and Access

Unlike with Word and Excel, you can't just insert hyperlinks into Access at random. Instead, to work with hyperlinks in Access tables, you have to create a special field. Specifically, you have to create a field that uses the Hyperlink data type. If you're experimenting with the Northwind sample database that ships with Access, check out the Suppliers table, shown in Design view in Figure 8.11, for an example of a Hyperlink field.

Figure 8.11
To add hyperlinks to an Access table, you need to create a field that uses the Hyperlink data type.

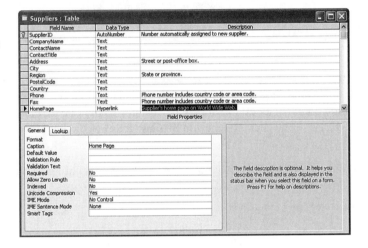

Inserting a Link Field in the Datasheet View
Rather than use Design view to add a Hyperlink column, you can do so quickly from Datasheet view by selecting Insert, Hyperlink Column.

After the Hyperlink field is in place, you have two options for inserting a hyperlink into a cell:

- Select the cell and then type the URL, path, or network path for the document to which you want to link.
- Select the cell and then select Insert, Hyperlink to use the Insert Hyperlink dialog box to specify the link.

After the link is in place, click the cell to jump to the specified document. Figure 8.12 shows the Northwind Suppliers table with a few hyperlinks added.

8

Figure 8.12
The Suppliers table with some sample hyperlinks.

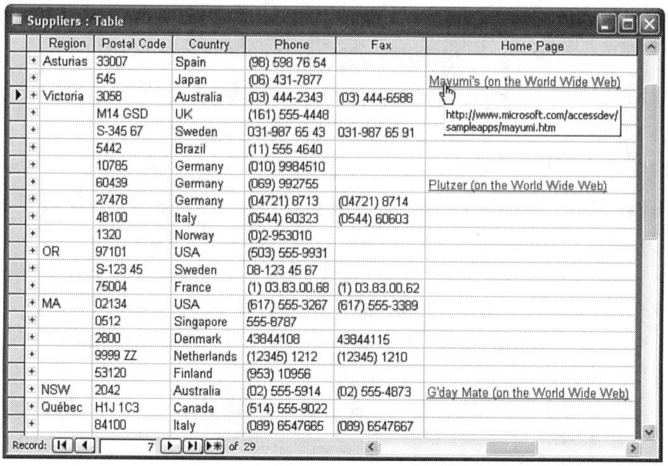

Suppliers : Table

Region	Postal Code	Country	Phone	Fax	Home Page
Asturias	33007	Spain	(98) 598 76 54		
	545	Japan	(06) 431-7877		Mayumi's (on the World Wide Web)
Victoria	3058	Australia	(03) 444-2343	(03) 444-6588	
	M14 GSD	UK	(161) 555-4448		http://www.microsoft.com/accessdev/sampleapps/mayumi.htm
	S-345 67	Sweden	031-987 65 43	031-987 65 91	
	5442	Brazil	(11) 555 4640		
	10785	Germany	(010) 9984510		
	60439	Germany	(069) 992755		Plutzer (on the World Wide Web)
	27478	Germany	(04721) 8713	(04721) 8714	
	48100	Italy	(0544) 60323	(0544) 60603	
	1320	Norway	(0)2-953010		
OR	97101	USA	(503) 555-9931		
	S-123 45	Sweden	08-123 45 67		
	75004	France	(1) 03.83.00.68	(1) 03.83.00.62	
MA	02134	USA	(617) 555-3267	(617) 555-3389	
	0512	Singapore	555-8787		
	2800	Denmark	43844108	43844115	
	9999 ZZ	Netherlands	(12345) 1212	(12345) 1210	
	53120	Finland	(953) 10956		
NSW	2042	Australia	(02) 555-5914	(02) 555-4873	G'day Mate (on the World Wide Web)
Québec	H1J 1C3	Canada	(514) 555-9022		
	84100	Italy	(089) 6547665	(089) 6547667	

Record: 7 of 29

When working with Access hyperlinks, bear in mind that some of the normal Access editing methods don't apply. For example, you might normally edit a cell by first clicking it to get the insertion point cursor and then making changes. With a Hyperlink field, however, you can't get the cursor by clicking (because that just activates the link). Instead, you need to select the cell and press F2.

Also, you need to be careful when you're editing a hyperlink. In general, Access hyperlinks take the following form:

```
friendly_name#link_location#
```

For example, suppose you enter the following into a cell:

```
Click here to load the memo#C:\My Documents\memo.doc#
```

Access will display only `Click here to load the memo` in the cell.

Access ignores anything you enter *after* the last pound sign. So if you're adding to the address, make sure you do it within the pound signs. Note, however, that anything *before* the first pound sign is used as link text. So instead of displaying, for instance, a URL, you can enter a description or name.

Hyperlinks and PowerPoint

You can also use two methods to add hyperlinks to your PowerPoint presentations:

- The Insert, Hyperlink command—Select some text or an image and then select this command (or click the Insert Hyperlink button on the toolbar). PowerPoint will display the usual Insert Hyperlink dialog box. Note that if the document you're linking to is a PowerPoint presentation, click Bookmark to select a slide.
- Pasting an object as a hyperlink—As with the other Office programs, you can copy data to the Clipboard and then select Edit, Paste as Hyperlink to insert the data as a hyperlink.

From Here

- Another way to put Office documents on the Web is to use a SharePoint site. In Chapter 7, see the section titled "Using SharePoint to Collaborate on Office Documents."

- Document hyperlinks can cause privacy breaches if they contain the addresses of sensitive or private locations. To learn how to remove hyperlinks before sharing a document, see the section in Chapter 14 titled "Removing Hyperlinks."

8

Collaborating with a Tablet PC and OneNote

9

In the old days, collaborating on a document often meant stuffing the hard copy into an interoffice envelope and routing it to another person. That person would remove the document, make notes on the page or edit the text with proofreader's marks, and then send the document back to the originator or on to the next person in the collaboration chain.

Although this red-pencil-and-paper method has largely been superseded by the electronic comments and annotations that we looked at in Chapter 7 "Working as a Team: Collaborating with Other Users," there are some businesses and even entire industries—notably trade publishing—where hard-copy collaboration is still the norm. Depending on your personality (and, likely, your age) the staying power of paper-based commenting and editing is either an inexplicable mystery or the most natural thing in the world. Those of us who incline toward the latter often see electronic documents as being decidedly less "real" than their hard-copy equivalents, so there's something that just feels "right" about reading and editing text on paper.

Unfortunately, for all but the most trivial applications, annotating on paper is inefficient because you either have to put the annotations in electronic form (by entering the annotation text itself or by performing the requested edits) or you have to scan the annotated document (to send the document as an email attachment, for example).

What the world has needed for a long time is a way to bridge the gap between purely digital and purely analog collaboration. We've needed a way to combine the convenience of the electronic format with the attraction of pen-based annotating and commenting. After several aborted attempts (think: the Apple Newton), that bridge was built in recent years: the Tablet PC and its unique operating system, Windows XP Tablet PC Edition. At first glance, the Tablet PC looks like a small notebook computer, and it certainly can be used like any notebook. However, a Tablet PC boasts three hardware innovations that make it unique:

- A pressure-sensitive touch screen that replaces the usual notebook LCD screen.

- A *digital pen* that acts as an all-purpose input device: You can use the pen to click, double-click, click and drag, as well as tap out individual characters using an onscreen keyboard. In certain applications, you can also use the pen to "write" directly on the screen—as though the screen is a piece of paper—thus enabling you to jot notes, sketch diagrams, add proofreader marks, or just doodle your way through a boring meeting. (And, as a bonus, many applications can also convert your handwriting into digital text.)

- The capability to physically reorient the screen so that it lies flat on top of the keyboard, thus making the machine appear like a tablet or pad of paper.

This chapter shows you how to take advantage of this unique hardware configuration by using it within Office 2003 to collaborate with other users in Word, Excel, and PowerPoint documents, as well as Outlook email messages. You'll also learn how to use OneNote, Microsoft's digital pen-based note-taking software.

Office and Windows XP Tablet PC Edition

Office 2003 was built with the Tablet PC in mind, so it not only recognizes that it's running under the Windows XP Tablet PC Edition, but it also adjusts the Office features and interface to take advantage of the Tablet PC. Some of these adjustments are relatively trivial—such as displaying the Task pane at the bottom of the screen instead of the right side—but others are more profound, as you'll see in this chapter.

Understanding Ink Integration

One of the biggest changes you get with Office 2003 running on the Windows XP Tablet PC Edition implements *ink integration*. This means that a new object type called *Digital Ink* or, simply, *Ink* becomes part of the Office system, like the AutoShape and Text Box object types, for instance. In fact, Ink objects are part of the Office drawing layer that holds AutoShapes, text boxes, WordArt, pictures, and so on, and you can format ink like other drawing layer objects by changing, for example, the text color and line weight.

From a collaboration point of view, ink enables you to mark up Office documents using the digital pen. You can do the following in Office 2003:

- Word—You can annotate a document directly, which means either writing notes in the margin using your own handwriting or adding highlighting, diagrams, proofreader marks, or other symbols. Also, you can create an ink area called a *canvas* that enables you to write text and symbols anywhere inside the area. Finally, Word also supports ink inside comments.

- Excel—You can annotate an Excel worksheet directly by adding highlights, arrows, or handwritten text.

- PowerPoint—You can annotate a PowerPoint slide to emphasize key points, record feedback, or jot down ideas that come up during a presentation run-through.

- Outlook—If you use Word as your email editor, you can send handwritten notes as messages, or you can spruce up a conventional message with your signature or other ink.

Using Office XP on a Tablet PC

If you're running Office XP, the programs don't automatically recognize when they're running on a Tablet PC. If you want to use your Tablet PC's capabilities in Office XP, you need to download the Microsoft Office XP Pack for Tablet PC, which is available here:

```
http://www.microsoft.com/downloads/details.aspx?
➥familyid=33790048-269B-4838-AB9E-74B64626A494
```

Entering Text with the Tablet PC Input Panel

Besides ink integration, Office (any version, not just 2003) also supports non-ink input with a digital pen. Windows XP Tablet Edition comes with a tool called the Tablet PC Input Panel that you use to enter text and other symbols with the digital pen instead of the keyboard. The Input Panel uses three views to enable you to enter your text; the view you use depends on the text you want to enter.

Using the Writing Pad

If you want to write a word or two or a short phrase, use the Writing Pad view. As you can see in Figure 9.1, this view displays a large box in which you handwrite words and phrases with the digital pen. When you're not writing, several keys appear to the right of the Writing Pad. Tap these keys to enter nonhandwritten characters such as a Tab or a Space, editing keys such as Bksp (Backspace) and Del (Delete), and navigation keys such as Enter and the left- and right-arrow keys.

Special Characters for Internet Addresses

The Writing Pad keyboard displays extra shortcut keys if you're entering an Internet address. If you tap inside Internet Explorer's Address bar, the Writing Pad keyboard displays shortcut keys for http://, www., .com, .org, . (dot), and / (slash).

To use the Writing Pad, first position the insertion point within the document at the spot where you want your text to appear. Then use the digital pen to write the word or phrase. As you complete each character, the Input Panel recognizes it and displays the recognized characters below, as shown in Figure 9.2. If the recognized text contains an error, click it to see a list of possible alternatives, as shown in Figure 9.3. To change an individual character, either write the correct character over top of the existing character or hover the pointer over the character and click the arrow that appears to see a list of alternative characters. Click OK when you're done. When the text is accurate, click Insert to add it to your document.

Writing Pad   Tools and Options

Figure 9.1
Use the Writing Pad to handwrite words or short phrases.

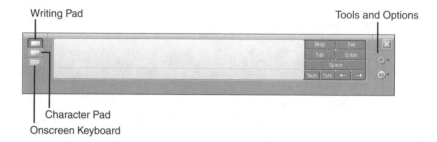

Character Pad
Onscreen Keyboard

Automatically Inserting Text

Rather than clicking Insert, you can get the Input Panel to recognize and insert your handwritten text automatically. Click the Tools and Options button (pointed out in Figure 9.1) and then click Options to display the Options dialog box. In the Writing Pad tab, activate the Automatically Insert Text After a Pause check box, and then use the slider to set the length of time (in seconds) after which Input Panel inserts your text.

Watch for Leading Spaces

If you elect to have the Input Panel insert text automatically, note that this method has an annoying habit of inserting a leading space along with your text. If you're using the Input Panel to enter a formula in a worksheet cell and Excel doesn't recognize the formula, a leading space in the cell may be the culprit.

Figure 9.2
When you handwrite your text in the Writing Pad, the Input Panel displays the recognized characters.

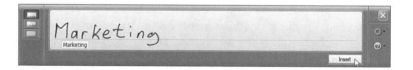

Figure 9.3
Click the recognized text to see a list of alternatives or to correct individual characters.

Using the Character Pad

If you want to insert just a few characters, use the Character Pad, which Microsoft added to the Input Panel in the Windows XP Tablet Edition 2005. This view displays a series of placeholders, each of which is designed to hold a single character. You write the character in the placeholder and after a second or two the Input Panel converts the written character to text, as shown in Figure 9.4. To correct a character, either write the correct character over top of the incorrect one, or hover the digital pen over the character and then click the arrow that appears. The Input Panel displays a list of alternatives (see Figure 9.4). When the text is accurate, click Insert to add the text to your document.

Figure 9.4
Use the Character Pad to handwrite text one character at a time.

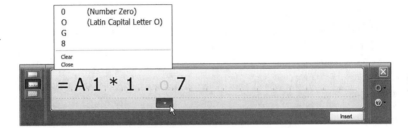

Using the Onscreen Keyboard

The Onscreen Keyboard view displays a graphical representation of a typical keyboard, as shown in Figure 9.5. After positioning the insertion point in your document at the spot where you want new text to appear, you input text by tapping the keys with your digital pen. The Input Panel inserts the characters directly into the document, just like a regular keyboard. Here are some techniques to bear in mind when using the onscreen keyboard:

- To access the function keys F1 through F12, tap the Func key. The onscreen keyboard reconfigures its layout to display the function keys along the top row. Tap the Func key again to return to the standard layout.

- To insert an uppercase letter or an "upper" symbol such as ? or :, tap the Shift key and then tap the symbol you want.

- To input shortcut keys, tap whatever combination of Ctrl, Alt, and Shift you require, and then tap the letter, number, or symbol that completes the shortcut. For example, to input Ctrl+O, tap Ctrl and then tap O; similarly, to input Alt+Shift+P, tap Alt, tap Shift, and then tap P.

Figure 9.5
Use the onscreen keyboard to insert text directly into a document one character at a time.

Using the Office Ink Tools

The Tablet PC Input Panel is designed to convert digital ink to text and insert it into just about any document, text box, or other input area. However, if you want to add digital ink to a Word document, Excel workbook, or PowerPoint presentation, you need to close the Input Panel and work instead with Office 2003's built-in ink tools.

To get started, in any Word, Excel, or PowerPoint document, select View, Toolbars, Ink Drawing and Writing (or right-click any toolbar and then click Ink Drawing and Writing).

Adding Ink to a Document

To add ink to your document, click the Drawing and Writing Pen button to use the default black felt tip pen, or drop down the arrow to display all the pens (see Figure 9.6) and then click the pen type and color you prefer.

Figure 9.6
Use the Drawing and Writing Pen button to select the pen you want to ink with.

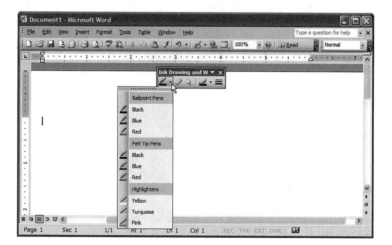

If you're working in Word, a drawing canvas appears on your document, and you use your digital pen to "ink" text or drawings within that canvas, as shown in Figure 9.7.

To gain some measure of control over Word's drawing canvas, right-click any canvas border and then click Show Drawing Canvas Toolbar to display a toolbar with the following four buttons:

 Click the Fit button to contract the canvas to the dimensions of the ink within it.

 Click the Expand button to increase the size of the drawing canvas.

Click the Scale Drawing button to add sizing handles to the canvas borders. When you click and drag a handle, Word increases or decreases the size of the canvas as well as the ink within it.

 Click the Text Wrapping button to display a list of options that determine how text wraps with respect to the drawing canvas.

Figure 9.7
In Word, you add digital ink within the displayed drawing canvas.

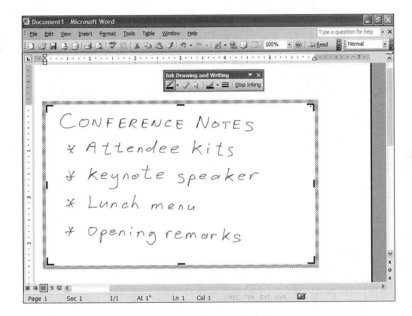

If you're working in Excel or PowerPoint, your ink appears in the document drawing layer and so sits on "top" of the worksheet or slide, as shown in Figure 9.8.

While you're inking, you can also change the ink color and weight by using the following buttons in the Ink Drawing and Writing toolbar:

 Drop down the Line Color button to display a color palette and then choose the ink color you want to use.

 Click the Line Style button to display a list of styles that determine the weight (thickness) of the ink.

When you're done, click Stop Inking in the Ink Drawing and Writing toolbar.

Figure 9.8
In Excel (and PowerPoint), the ink becomes part of the drawing layer.

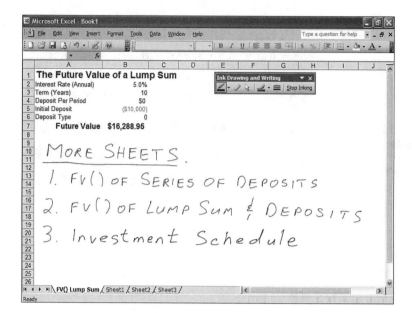

Editing Ink

If you need to make changes to your ink, note that the similarity between ink and objects such as AutoShapes and pictures extends to the ways you can manipulate Ink objects. That is, you can perform the following actions on an Ink object:

- To move an Ink object, click and drag it to the new location.

Watch the Space Between Characters

With text, Office divides the Ink objects into separate words. That is, if you click any inked character, Office selects the entire word. Office determines words based on the spacing between characters. Therefore, to ensure that you always select entire words, avoid putting too much space between the characters within your words.

Recombining Words

If you end up with a word that Office has interpreted as two separate Ink objects, you can recombine them. First, select both objects by clicking the first object, holding down Ctrl, and then clicking the second object. Right-click either object and then select Grouping, Group. Office combines the two objects into a single object.

- To change the size of an Ink object, select it and then click and drag one of the sizing handles.

- To format an Ink object, right-click it and then click Format Ink. Use the Format Ink dialog box to change the ink color, weight, or other formatting options. (You can also change the object's color and weight by clicking the object and then selecting options using the and buttons in the Ink Drawing and Writing toolbar.)
- To delete an Ink object, select it and press Delete.

Rather than deleting an entire Ink object, you may need to delete only a character or two, or you may need to delete stray lines that you accidentally inked. In either case, you can remove portions of an Ink object by using the Eraser tool. Here's how it works:

1. Click in the Ink Drawing and Writing toolbar.
2. Tap the ink you want to erase. If you have several characters to erase, drag the pointer over the characters.
3. Repeat step 2 until you have erased all the characters you no longer need.
4. Click Stop Erasing in the Ink Drawing and Writing toolbar.

Converting Ink to Text

After you add some ink, you may decide that you need some or all of the ink in text format. If so, Word, Excel, and PowerPoint enable you to convert the ink to regular text as follows:

1. Select the ink that you want to convert.
2. Right-click the selected ink and then click Copy Ink as Text. The program converts the ink to text and places the text on the Clipboard.
3. Paste the text into the document where you want it stored.

Inking an Email Message

If you use Word as your Outlook email editor, you can use Word's ink drawing canvas to ship out handwritten email messages. Just start a new email message in Outlook, fill in the recipients and subject, and then click inside the message body. Display the Ink Drawing and Writing toolbar and click a pen to bring up the drawing canvas. Dash off your note and tap Send to fire off the message.

Entering Recipient and Subject with a Pen

If you're using only the tablet when you write your email, entering the recipient's address and the message subject is problematic. For the address, either tap To and use the Address Book, or use the Tablet PC Input Panel. For the subject, you can use the Input Panel, but you can also handwrite the text in the drawing canvas, select it, copy it to text (as discussed in the previous section), and then paste it into the Subject line.

If your recipient's email program supports HTML messages, he or she will see the handwritten note in the body of the message as shown in Figure 9.9. Otherwise, the handwriting comes as a GIF attachment. (If you want to avoid the HTML format or the GIF attachment, you need to convert your ink to text, as I discussed in the previous section.)

Figure 9.9
If the recipient's email program supports HTML, your handwriting appears in the body of the message.

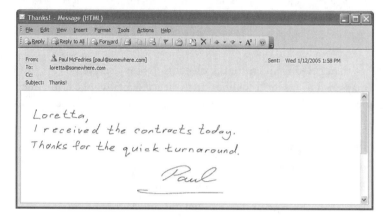

Collaborating with Ink

You can certainly use Ink created via the Ink Drawing and Writing toolbar in a collaborative way. You can jot notes or suggestions right on a worksheet or slide, or you can add them to Word's ink drawing canvas. But for truly collaborative work with Ink, you need to use the specific handwriting collaboration tools that come with Word, Excel, and PowerPoint. All three programs enable you to add Ink annotations, and Word goes one better by also enabling you to add Ink comments. The advantage to using these tools is that you (and any other reviewer) can then view and manipulate this Ink just like any other collaborative text. The next few sections provide you with the details.

Adding Ink Annotations

You can annotate any Word, Excel, or PowerPoint document with Ink. In Excel and PowerPoint, Ink is similar to the handwriting that results from using the Drawing and Writing pen in that it resides in the drawing layer and so appears to sit on top of the document. The only visual difference is that, by default, the Annotation Pen uses red ink. In Word, however, Ink annotations are different from Drawing and Writing annotations. Not only is the default color of the Annotation Pen red, but the Ink itself resides in the document's drawing layer, not in a separate drawing canvas. Therefore, your Ink markup appears directly on the document text.

 To get started, in any Word, Excel, or PowerPoint document, select View, Toolbars, Ink Annotations (or right-click any toolbar and click Ink Annotations). To add Ink annotations to your document, click the Annotations Pen button (which is also available on the Standard and Reviewing toolbars) to use the default red felt-tip pen, or drop down the arrow to display all the pens and then click the pen type and color you prefer. Then handwrite your markup. Figure 9.10 shows a PowerPoint slide with a few Ink annotations. Note that you can use the same Ink editing techniques that I outlined earlier for the Drawing and Writing pen (see "Editing Ink"). When you're done, click the Stop Inking button.

Figure 9.10
A PowerPoint slide with Ink annotations.

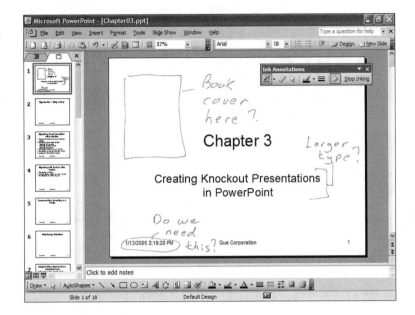

Adding Ink Comments in Word

Besides annotations, Word also enables you to add comments in Ink. To get started, you have two choices:

- Select Insert, Ink Comment.

- Click the Ink Comment button in the Reviewing toolbar.

Word then adds a comment box, which looks like a small sheet of lined writing paper. Write your Ink within the box, as shown in Figure 9.11. Use the Eraser to fix any mistakes you make, and then click the Pen button to continue inking. When you're done, click outside the comment box.

Working with Ink Annotations and Comments

As I mentioned earlier, Ink annotations (and Ink comments in Word) are different from Ink writing in that Ink annotations are grouped with other document markup, including typewritten changes and comments. Therefore, you can use the Reviewing toolbar to work with Ink annotations.

9

Figure 9.11
Word enables you to insert Ink comments in a document.

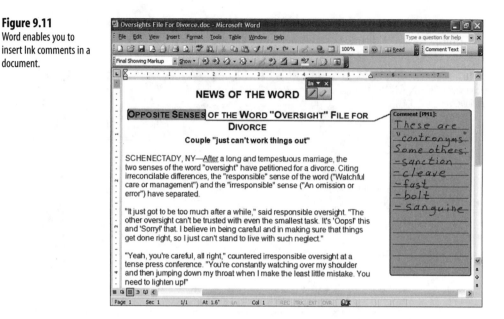

To toggle ink annotations and comments on and off, use the following techniques:

- In Word, select View, Markup or click Show/Hide Markup in the Ink Annotations toolbar. You can also click Show in the Reviewing toolbar and then click Ink Annotations. (Or you can click Comments to toggle both typed and inked comments on and off.)

- In Excel, click Show/Hide Ink Annotations in the Reviewing or Ink Annotations toolbars.

- In PowerPoint, select View, Markup or click Show/Hide Markup in the Reviewing or Ink Annotations toolbars.

To delete ink annotations or comments, use the following techniques:

- In Word, delete the current Ink comment by clicking the Reject Change/Delete Comment button in the Reviewing toolbar. To delete all the comments in the current document, drop down the Reject Change/Delete Comment list and select Delete All Comments in Document. To delete all Ink annotations in the document, drop down the Reject Change/Delete Comment list and select Delete All Ink Annotations in Document.

- In Excel, you can delete all the Ink annotations in the current workbook by clicking the Delete All Ink Annotations button in the Reviewing toolbar.

- In PowerPoint, drop down the Delete Comment list in the Reviewing toolbar and then click either Delete All Markup on the Current Slide or Delete All Markup in this Presentation.

Collaborating with OneNote 2003

Although not part of any Office 2003 suite, Microsoft's OneNote note-taking software is part of the Office "family" (its official name is Microsoft Office OneNote 2003). How does it fit in? It's all in the name: OneNote is designed to be the "one" place where you store all "notes." The metaphor is the pad of paper that many of us keep on our desks even in this digital age. We use the pad to save messages, jot down notes, brainstorm ideas, record inspirations, make quick to-do lists, and so on. With OneNote, you can do all of that (if you don't have a device for inputting Digital Ink, you can type your notes), but also much more:

- Paste pictures, text, even entire documents
- Import images from a digital camera or scanner
- Record audio or video
- Insert notes and recordings from a Pocket PC or Smartphone
- Share your notes with other people

It's the last of these features that I'll focus on in this chapter. You'll learn how to collaborate by combining OneNote and Outlook, sharing a note-taking session over the Internet, and sharing your notes with other people.

Collaborating with OneNote and Outlook

Of all the Office 2003 programs, OneNote gets along best with Outlook and boasts features that enable you to collaborate not only by sending email messages, but by creating Outlook appointments, contacts, and tasks directly from OneNote. This section shows you how to use these OneNote features.

Sending Email via OneNote

Perhaps the easiest way to collaborate with others using OneNote is to create a page and then email it to another person.

1. Create the page or pages you want to send.
2. If you want to send multiple pages from the same section, hold down Ctrl and click the tab of each page.

3. Select File, Send To, Mail Recipient. (You can also press Ctrl+Shift+E or click in the Standard toolbar.) OneNote opens a message window and displays the page (or pages) in the message body, as shown in Figure 9.12.
4. Fill in the email fields, such as To and Cc.
5. Click Send a Copy. OneNote sends the email.

OneNote sends the page as a .one file attachment. If the recipient's email program supports HTML, he or she sees the page in the body of the message; if not, the recipient can open the attachment to view the page in OneNote.

Figure 9.12
You can send one or more pages via Outlook email.

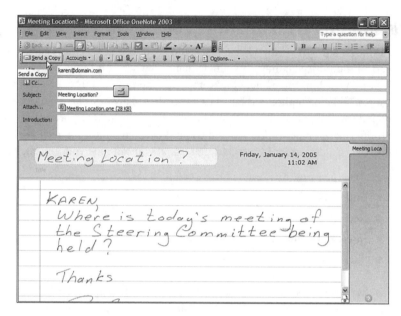

If the Recipient Doesn't Have OneNote

If the recipient doesn't have OneNote installed, he or she can still view the page Ink, but not conveniently. That's because OneNote sends the Ink as a series of GIF image attachments, one for each separate Ink object in the page.

Creating Outlook Items

Collaborating with Outlook often involves creating items for appointments, contacts, and tasks. You can create these items based on a note in a OneNote page, where the note is converted to text and stored in the item's Notes section. Here are the steps to follow:

1. Open the page that contains the note you want to work with.

2. Select the note or notes you want to include in the new Outlook item.

Selecting Notes

A quick way to select all the Ink in a note is to position the mouse pointer inside the note and then click the border that appears at the top of the note. To select multiple notes, hold down Ctrl and click the border of each note. Alternatively, click and drag the mouse over the notes you want to select.

3. Select Tools, Create Outlook Item, and then select one of the following commands:

Create Outlook Appointment—Select this command to create a new appointment item. You can also select this item by pressing Alt+Shift+A or by clicking in the Standard toolbar.

Create Outlook Contact—Select this command to create a new contact item. You can also select this item by pressing Ctrl+Shift+C or by clicking in the Standard toolbar.

 Create an Outlook Task—Select this command to create a new task item. You can also select this item by pressing Ctrl+Shift+K or by clicking in the Standard toolbar.

4. Switch to the new Outlook item and fill in the rest of the data, as required.

Inserting the Details of an Outlook Meeting

Typing notes during a meeting can be problematic because the noise of the typing is often distracting. A much better solution is to write the notes by hand, which is not only quieter, but gives you more freedom to construct the notes any way you want. OneNote's freeform structure is excellent for handwriting notes during a meeting. To get the page off to a great start, you can import the meeting details from Outlook, whether you've called the meeting yourself or have been invited by someone else. Here's how it's done:

1. Open or create the page where you want the meeting details to appear.

 2. Select Insert, Outlook Meeting Details, or click in the Standard toolbar. OneNote prompts you to select the meeting details.

3. Select the date on which the meeting occurs and then click the meeting.

4. Click Insert Details. OneNote inserts the meeting subject, data and location, attendees, and notes, as shown in Figure 9.13.

Figure 9.13
You can insert the details of an Outlook meeting in a OneNote page.

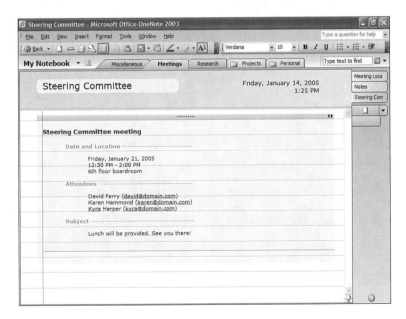

Sharing a Note-Taking Session

For true OneNote collaboration, you need to start or join a shared note-taking session. This is one of the most exciting features added to OneNote 2003 Service Pack 1, so be sure you download and install the service pack before continuing.

In a shared note-taking session, OneNote sets up a network or Internet address for the session, and invited participants use that address to access the session (entering a password, if necessary). The participants then take turns adding ink to a note in real-time.

The next few sections give you the details on starting, joining, and working in a shared note-taking session.

Starting a Shared Session

If you want to administer a shared note-taking session, you need to start the session and then invite others to join. Here are the steps to follow to get the session started:

1. Select File, Share with Others to display the Share with Others task pane.
2. Click Start a Session. The Start Shared Session task pane appears.
3. Type a password into the Session Password text box.
4. Select the pages you want to share. To share multiple pages, hold down Ctrl and click each page tab.
5. Click Start Shared Session.

After OneNote starts the session, it displays the Current Shared Session task pane. To invite one or more participants to join the session, follow these steps:

1. Click the Invite Participants button. OneNote creates a new email message, as shown in Figure 9.14.
2. Add the recipients and any other email data you require.
3. Click Send.

Note that the email message includes two IP addresses: one for participants joining via your local area network and one for participants joining via the Internet.

Getting Address Information

You can view the session addresses at any time by clicking the Shared Address Information button in the Current Shared Session task pane.

Figure 9.14
When you click Invite Participants, OneNote constructs an email message similar to the one shown here.

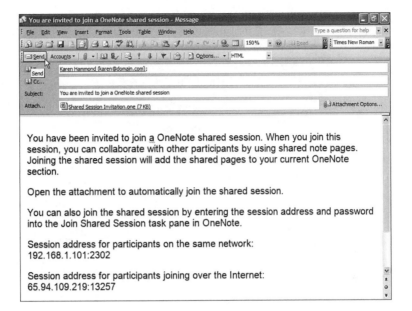

9

Joining a Shared Session

If you receive an invitation to join a shared note-taking session, you can use either of two methods to join the session:

- Open the Shared Session Invitation attachment that comes with the email.
- In OneNote, select File, Share with Others to display the Share with Others task pane, and then click Join a Session. Type the Shared Session Address and the Session Password, and then click Join Session. (If you don't know the password, contact the session administrator to get it.)

Unblocking OneNote

The first time you attempt to join a shared session, the Windows Firewall may appear to let you know that it's blocking OneNote. Click Unblock to let the session continue.

Working in a Shared Session

When the session is up and running, the Current Shared Session task pane shows you the names of the participants, as shown in Figure 9.15. In most sessions, each participant can add notes at will. If you're the session administrator and you want to be the only person who can make notes, scroll down to the bottom of the Current Shared Session task pane and deactivate the Allow Participants to Edit check box.

Figure 9.15
A shared note-taking session with a couple of participants.

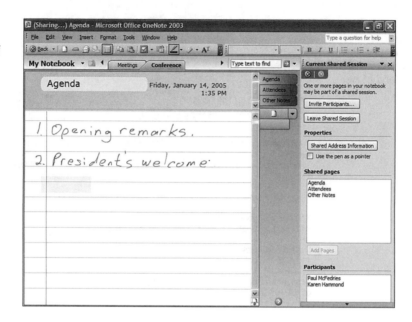

When you're done with a session, you can leave at any time by clicking the Leave Shared Session button.

Sharing Notes with Other People

Rather than working with other users in real-time using a shared note-taking session, you may prefer to allow other people to work with your notes at any time:

- If the other users have OneNote 2003 Service Pack 1, you can move the section to a shared network folder or a SharePoint site.
- If the other users don't have OneNote, you can publish the section to a web page or Word document on a shared network folder or SharePoint site.

The rest of this chapter takes you through these two scenarios.

Moving Notes to a Shared Network Folder

OneNote 2003 with Service Pack 1 gives you the capability to move a section to a shared network folder. Other users with OneNote 2003 SP1 can then open the section and use it as though it is part of their own notebook.

To move a section to a shared network folder, follow these steps:

1. Select File, Share with Others to display the Share with Others task pane.
2. Click the Browse and Move To button. The Save As dialog box appears.

3. Open a shared network folder or SharePoint document library and then click Save. OneNote asks if you want to create an email message with a link to the shared file.

4. Click Yes to create the email, or click No to bypass the email.

5. If you elected to send an email, fill in the message details and then click Send.

As you can see in Figure 9.16, the section tab now displays a shortcut icon. That's because you actually moved the section to the shared network folder, so the tab in your notebook is just a shortcut to the saved section.

Shortcut icon

Figure 9.16
When you save notes on your network, your version of the section becomes a shortcut to the saved file.

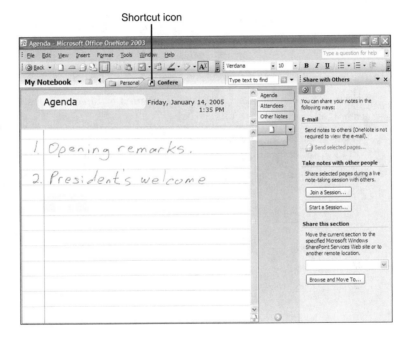

To access the shared notes, follow these steps:

1. Select File, Open, Section (or press Ctrl+O). The File Open dialog box appears.

2. Open the shared network folder or SharePoint document library that contains the OneNote file.

3. Click the OneNote file and then click Open.

Allowing Another User to Edit the Section

Shared notes are editable by only one person at a time. You can tell if you have permission to edit the notes by looking at the OneNote title bar: if you don't see (Read-Only), you can make changes to the section. To allow the other user to edit the notes, you can transfer permission by right-clicking the section tab and then clicking Allow Others to Edit.

Publishing to a Shared Network Folder

If you want to share your notes with another user who doesn't have OneNote 2003 Service Pack 1, you can publish the notes to a shared network folder or SharePoint library using a web page or Word document format. Here's how it's done:

1. Select the page or pages you want to publish.

2. Select File, Publish Pages. The Publish dialog box appears.

3. Open a shared network folder or SharePoint document library.

4. Use the Save as Type list to select the file format: Single File Web Page or Microsoft Word Document.

5. Click Publish.

From Here

- For the details on the other Office collaboration features, see Chapter 7, "Working as a Team: Collaborating with Other Users."

- You can also collaborate by publishing documents to the Web. See Chapter 8, "Office Without Borders: Using Office Documents on the Web."

- Security is an important collaboration issue. In Chapter 14, see the section "Using File Passwords and Encryption."

Office 2003 Customization Tricks

III

Customizing Office to Suit Your Style

10

The Microsoft programmers designed Office so that the commands and features commonly used by most people are within easy reach. This means that the setup of the menu system and toolbars reflects what the ordinary user might want. However, no one—particularly an Office guru—qualifies as an ordinary user; we all work with Office in our own way. What one person uses every day, another needs only once a year; one user's obscure technical feature is another's bread and butter.

To address these differences, Office provides what might be the most customizable interface on the market today. Office lets you create custom menus either by deleting some of an application's built-in commands or by adding new commands and attaching macros to them. You can also easily configure the toolbars by dragging buttons on or off them. You can even create your own button faces with the Button Editor. This chapter explores all of these customization features and more.

Displaying, Moving, and Sizing Toolbars

I'll lead off with a look at the simplest interface customization techniques, which involve displaying and hiding toolbars as well as moving and sizing them. First, though, you need to know the difference between docked and floating toolbars.

The Office programs designate the top and bottom of the application window, as well as the left and right sides of the window, as "docking" areas.

So a *docked toolbar* is one that is attached to one of these areas. Docked toolbars have the following characteristics:

- The buttons are arranged either in a single, horizontal row (in the case of a toolbar, docked at the top or bottom of the window; see Figure 10.1) or in a single, vertical column (in the case of a toolbar, docked at the left or right edge of the window).

- The toolbar becomes part of the application window interface, which leaves less room for document windows.

- A *move handle* appears on either the left side of the toolbar (if it's docked at the top or bottom; see Figure 10.1) or the top of the toolbar (if it's docked on the left or right).

Figure 10.1
You can display your toolbars either docked or floating.

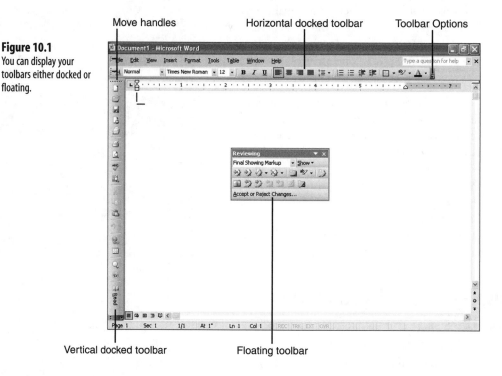

On the other hand, a *floating toolbar* is one that resides outside of these docking areas. Floating toolbars have the following characteristics:

- The toolbar forms a small window, and the buttons are arranged according to the shape of the window.

- The toolbar "floats" on top of the application (and can even be moved outside of the application window), so it leaves more room for document windows.

- The toolbar window includes a title bar, a Close button, and a border (refer to Figure 10.1).

Here's a summary of the various methods you can use to display, move, and size toolbars:

- To display a toolbar, first select View, Toolbars or right-click a visible toolbar. From the menu that appears, select the toolbar you want to display.

- If the toolbar you want doesn't appear in the list, select Tools, Customize to display the Customize toolbar. In the Toolbars tab, shown in Figure 10.2, activate the check box beside the toolbar you want and click Close.

Figure 10.2
The Toolbars tab lists all the application's available toolbars.

- To hide a docked toolbar, select View, Toolbars or right-click a visible toolbar; then deactivate the toolbar command in the menu that appears.

- To hide a floating toolbar, either use the procedure just discussed or click the toolbar's Close button.

- To move a docked toolbar, drag its move handle (pointed out in Figure 10.1). To turn it into a floating toolbar, drag the toolbar outside of the docking area.

- To move a floating toolbar, drag its title bar. To dock a floating toolbar, drag it to a docking area. When you see the toolbar outline snap into place either horizontally or vertically (depending on the docking area you're using), release the mouse button.

- To size a floating toolbar, drag the toolbar window borders.

Menu and Toolbar Customization Options

Let's now look at a few menu and toolbar customization options that are common to the Office applications. To view these options, first display the Customize dialog box using any of the following methods:

- Select Tools, Customize.

- Select View, Toolbars, Customize.

- Right-click the menu bar or any toolbar, and then select Customize.

When the Customize dialog box appears, activate the Options tab, shown in Figure 10.3. Here's a rundown of the controls in this tab:

Figure 10.3
The Options tab has a few settings for customizing menus and toolbars.

- **Show Standard and Formatting Toolbars on Two Rows**—By default, the Office applications display their Standard and Formatting toolbars in a single row. This means you don't see all the buttons, but Office tracks your usage and displays those buttons you've used most often. If you'd rather see all the buttons, you need to display these toolbars on separate rows by activating this check box.

A Quick Toolbar Move

A quicker way to display the Standard and Formatting buttons on separate rows is to click the Toolbar Options button (pointed out in Figure 10.1) and then click Show Buttons on Two Rows.

- **Always Show Full Menus**—By default, the Office application menus show only those commands that Microsoft has deemed to be the most popular among the majority of users. A downward-pointing double arrow appears at the bottom of each menu, and you can click it (or wait a few seconds) to see all the commands. Over time, the Office applications track your usage and begin displaying the commands you use most often, a feature called *Personalized Menus*. If you'd rather see all the commands by default, activate the Always Show Full Menus check box.

- **Show Full Menus After a Short Delay**—If you leave the Personalized Menus turned on, activating this check box tells the application to display all the commands automatically after about five seconds or so.

- Reset Menu and Toolbar Usage Data—Click this button to remove the usage data that the application has stored for your menu and toolbar choices and revert to the default menu and toolbar configuration.

- Large Icons—Many people have trouble seeing the toolbar icons, either because they're running their screen at a high resolution or because their eyesight isn't what it used to be. If this is the case for you, activate this check box to increase the size of the toolbar icons and make them easier to see.

- List Font Names in Their Font—When you activate this check box, the Formatting toolbar's Font list shows each font name in the actual typeface. This makes it much easier to choose the font you want, so I recommend leaving this option turned on.

- Show ScreenTips on Toolbars—When you activate this check box, Office displays the name of a toolbar button when you hover the mouse pointer over the button for a second or two.

- Show Shortcut Keys in ScreenTips—If you activate this check box, Office checks to see whether a toolbar button has a shortcut key equivalent. If it does, Office displays the key combination in the ScreenTip banner.

- Menu Animations—When you choose a menu from the menu bar, the associated menu usually appears instantly. You can use this drop-down list to make menus appear with an animated flourish. Your choices are System Default, Random, Unfold, Slide, and Fade.

10

The System Default Animation

The System Default choice in the Menu Animations list means that Office uses the same menu transition effect as Windows XP. To change the system default, right-click the desktop, click Properties, display the Appearance tab, click Effects, and then use the list under the Use the Following Transition Effect for Menus and Tooltips check box.

Creating Custom Menus

Office comes with a powerful set of tools called Command Bars that let you modify the Office application menus or create your own from scratch. Here's a list of some of the things you can do with the Command Bars feature:

- Move, rename, or delete existing menu commands.
- Add commands to or delete commands from an existing menu or shortcut menu.
- Create your own custom menus and attach them to any menu bar.
- Delete menus from any menu bar.
- Create your own menu bars.

The next few sections show you how to do all this and more.

Creating Custom Menu Bars

To create a custom menu bar, you use the same technique that you use to create a custom toolbar. See "Creating a New Toolbar" later in this chapter.

First, a Game Plan

Before you dive into the menu customization techniques outlined in the next few sections, you should take a step back to plan what you want to do and to consider the layout of your custom menus. You can use three levels of customization:

- Menu commands—This level involves adjusting existing commands or tacking new commands onto one or more of the application's built-in menus. Use this level when you have just a few changes to make.

- Submenus—This level involves adding one or more submenus to the application's built-in menu system. Use this level if you have several related procedures that you want to group together.

- Menus—This level involves creating an entirely new menu that appears in the application's menu bar. Use this level to create personalized menus or when you have many different procedures and you don't want to cram them all into the application's built-in menus.

Consider Other Users When You Customize

If other people use the Office programs on your computer, give some thought to what effect your menu customizations might have on them. People get used to the structure of menus, and you could seriously confuse other users if you make radical changes, especially to the built-in menus. Consider restricting your customizing to new menus that you create, or carefully document your changes and take the time to teach the new structure to the other users.

Customizing an Existing Menu

If all you need to do is customize one of the application's existing menus, follow the steps outlined earlier to display the Customize dialog box, and then use the following techniques:

- To move a menu item to a different location, drag it within the menu.

- To rename a menu item, right-click the item and then use the Name text box to edit the item name.

- To delete a menu item, either drag it off the menu or right-click it and then click Delete.

Resetting the Menu

If you no longer want to keep your changes, you can revert a built-in menu to its default configuration by right-clicking the menu name and then choosing Reset from the shortcut menu.

Creating a New Menu

If you'll be adding many new commands to the application's menu system, you might not want to bog down the existing menus with too many items. To keep things clean, you can create a custom menu just for your commands. Here are the steps to follow:

1. Select Tools, Customize to display the Customize dialog box.

2. Select the Commands tab.

3. In the Categories list, select New Menu, as shown in Figure 10.4.

Figure 10.4
Use the Commands tab in the Customize dialog box to create new menus in the application.

4. In the Commands list, click and drag the New Menu item up to the menu bar. You'll see a vertical bar that marks the spot where the new menu will appear. When the bar is positioned where you want your menu, drop the New Menu item.

5. Right-click the new menu and then use the Name box on the shortcut menu to name your new menu. Place an ampersand (&) before whichever letter you want to use as an accelerator key. (Make sure the key you choose doesn't conflict with an accelerator key used by any other menu.) For example, if your new menu is named Macros, entering the name as &Macros will set up the "M" as the accelerator key, which means you can select the menu by pressing Alt+M.

6. Press Enter.

Quickly Rearranging Menu Bar Items

If you want to change the order of the menu bar items, you can do so without displaying the Customize dialog box. Hold down the Alt key and drag the menu bar item left or right. You can also delete a menu bar item by holding down Alt and dragging the item off the menu bar.

Getting Easy Document Access with Word's Work Menu

If you have several documents that you use regularly, it's time consuming and inefficient to always use the Open command to locate and open these documents. You can save time by choosing documents from the File menu's list of most recently used files, but there's no guarantee all your regular documents will be available on that list.

To ensure easy access to your regular files, add Word's little-known Work menu to your menu bar by following these steps:

1. Select Tools, Customize to display the Customize dialog box.
2. Select the Commands tab.
3. In the Categories list, select Built-in Menus.
4. In the Commands list, click and drag the Work item and drop it on the menu bar.
5. Click Close.

To add a document to the Work menu, open the document and then select Work, Add to Work Menu.

Deleting an item from the Work menu takes a bit more work. You'd think you could just select Tools, Customize, drop down the Work menu, and then drag the item off the menu. That would be nice, but it doesn't work because when you drop down the Work menu while the Customize dialog box is displayed, you just see (List of Work Files) at the bottom of the menu. Instead, you have to add a special command to the Work menu, as detailed in the following steps:

1. Select Tools, Customize to display the Customize dialog box.
2. Select the Commands tab.
3. In the Categories list, select All Commands.
4. In the Commands list, click and drag the Tools Customize Remove Menu Shortcut item and drop it onto the Work menu.
5. Click Close.

To delete an item from the Work menu, select the Work, Tools Customize Remove Menu Shortcut command. The mouse pointer changes to a horizontal bar. Pull down the Work menu again and then click the item you want to delete. Word immediately removes the item from the Work menu.

Creating a New Submenu

To work with submenus, you have two choices:

- Add the submenu to the new menu you created in the preceding section.
- Add the submenu to one of the application's built-in menus.

Either way, you follow the steps outlined in the preceding section. However, instead of dragging the New Menu item to the menu bar, drag it to an existing menu. When the menu pulls down, drag the mouse pointer down into the menu to the position where you want the submenu to appear. (A black horizontal bar shows you where the menu will be positioned.) When you drop the item, a new submenu is created.

To rename the submenu item, right-click the item and then use the Name text box to enter the new name (including an accelerator key).

Adding Menu Commands

You're now ready to create custom menu commands. Remember that you can create these commands in any of the following locations:

- On a custom menu that you've created
- On a custom submenu that you've created
- On one of the application's built-in menus

Here are the steps you need to work through:

1. Select Tools, Customize to display the Customize dialog box.
2. In the Categories list, highlight the category that contains the command you want.
3. In the Commands list, click and drag the command you want to a custom menu, a custom submenu, or a built-in menu.
4. When the menu opens, drag the item down into the menu and then drop the item at the position where you want the command to appear.

Creating Custom Commands for Macros

In Chapter 11, "Maximizing Office with VBA Macros," I'll show you a number of methods for running your VBA macros. However, all these methods assume that you know which task each macro performs. If you're constructing procedures for others to wield, they might not be as familiar with what each macro name represents. Not only that, but you might not want novice users scrolling through a long list of procedures in the Macro dialog box or, even worse, having to use the Visual Basic Editor.

To help you avoid these problems, you can make your macros more accessible by assigning them to custom menu commands, as explained in the next two sections.

Custom Macro Commands in Word, PowerPoint, and Access

Follow these steps to add a custom command for a macro in Word, PowerPoint, and Access:

1. Select Tools, Customize to display the Customize dialog box and then select the Commands tab.

2. In the Categories list, select the Macros item. (In Access, select the All Macros item.)

3. In the Commands list, drag the macro you want to work with to a custom menu, a custom submenu, or a built-in menu.

4. When the menu opens, drag the item down into the menu and then drop the item at the position where you want the command to appear.

5. Right-click the item and then use the Name box on the shortcut menu to edit the macro name, if necessary. Place an ampersand (&) before whichever letter you want to use as an accelerator key.

6. Press Enter.

Creating Command Groups

You've probably noticed that Office applications group related menu commands by using separator bars. You can do the same for your custom menus. With the Customize dialog box displayed, pull down the menu, right-click the first command in the group you want to create, and then click Begin a Group. The application adds a separator bar above the selected command.

Custom Macro Commands in Excel

Excel uses a slightly different method for creating custom macro commands:

1. Select Tools, Customize to display the Customize dialog box and then select the Commands tab.

2. In the Categories list, select the Macros item.

3. In the Commands list, drag the Custom Menu Item command to a custom menu, a custom submenu, or a built-in menu.

4. When the menu opens, drag the item down into the menu, and then drop the item at the position where you want the command to appear.

5. Right-click the item and then use the Name box on the shortcut menu to name your new menu. As before, place an ampersand (&) in front of whichever letter you want to use as an accelerator key. (To ensure that the menu remains onscreen, don't press Enter when you're done.)

6. Click Assign Macro. The Assign Macro dialog box appears.

7. In the Macro Name list, select the macro you want to assign to the new menu command and then click OK.

Deleting Menus and Menu Commands

If you no longer need a custom menu, submenu, or command, you can use a couple of methods to delete these items. First, select Tools, Customize to display the Customize dialog box, and then try either of these techniques:

■ Use the mouse to drag the item off the menu or menu bar and drop it outside the application's menu system.

■ Right-click the item and then click Delete on the shortcut menu.

Creating Custom Toolbars

Menu commands are fine, but there's nothing like a toolbar's one-click access for making your macros easy to run. This section shows you how to create custom toolbars, populate them with buttons, and assign macros to these buttons.

Customizing an Existing Toolbar

If you want to make changes to one of the application's existing toolbars, display the toolbar, select Tools, Customize to load the Customize dialog box, and then use the following techniques:

■ To move a button to a different location, drag it within the toolbar.

■ To change the size of a toolbar drop-down list, click-and-drag either the left or right edge.

■ To change how the application displays a toolbar button, right-click the button and then choose one of the following commands from the shortcut menu:

  • Default Style—Uses the application's default style (only the button's image is shown).

  • Text Only (Always)—The button displays text (that is, the button name) whether it's displayed in a toolbar or on a menu.

  • Text Only (in Menus)—The button displays text only when it's displayed on a menu.

  • Image and Text—The button displays both its image and its name.

■ To delete a button, drag it off the toolbar.

Creating a New Toolbar

Theoretically, you *could* add new buttons to the application's built-in toolbars, but you run the risk of overcrowding them and possibly confusing your users. Instead, you can create a toolbar from scratch and add existing commands and custom buttons to it. Here are the steps to follow to create a new toolbar:

1. Select Tools, Customize to display the Customize dialog box.
2. Activate the Toolbars tab.
3. Click New. The New Toolbar dialog box appears.
4. Use the Toolbar Name text box to type the name you want to use for the toolbar.
5. In Word only, use the Make Toolbar Available To list to assign the new toolbar to a template.
6. Click OK. The application displays a new, empty toolbar.

Creating a New Menu Bar

There is no practical difference between a menu bar and a toolbar. (In fact, you can drag the menu bar from its top docking position and turn it into a floating toolbar.) Therefore, you can use the steps for creating a custom toolbar to create a custom menu bar as well.

Custom Toolbar Maintenance

After you've created a custom toolbar, activate the Toolbars tab in the Customize dialog box and then use the following techniques to work with it:

- To rename the toolbar, highlight it in the Toolbars list, click Rename, and then type the new name into the dialog box that appears.

- To delete the toolbar, highlight it in the Toolbars list and click Delete. When the application asks you to confirm the deletion, click OK.

Adding a Toolbar Submenu or Toolbar Button

After you have created your new toolbar, you can start adding submenus and buttons to it. This is the same as adding submenus and commands to a drop-down menu, so just follow the procedures described earlier. In this case, of course, you drag the menus, built-in commands, or macros and drop them on the toolbar of your choice.

Working with Button Images

If you add a button for a macro to a toolbar, you can leave the button as text, but you might prefer to assign a custom image. You can do this in three ways:

- Copy an image from another button.
- Use one of the application's predefined images.
- Use the Button Editor to edit an existing image or create an image from scratch.

Copying a Button Image

If another toolbar button has an image you want to use, follow these steps to copy the image and assign it to your custom button:

1. Select Tools, Customize to display the Customize dialog box and then select the Commands tab.
2. Display the toolbar that contains the button image you want, if it's not already displayed.
3. Right-click the button that contains the image you want.
4. Click Copy Button Image.
5. Right-click the button whose image you want to change.
6. Click Paste Button Image.

Assigning a Predefined Button Image

The Office applications come with more than 40 predefined button images that you can assign to your custom toolbar buttons. Follow these steps:

1. Select Tools, Customize to display the Customize dialog box and then select the Commands tab.
2. Right-click the button whose image you want to change.
3. Click Change Button Image.
4. In the submenu that appears, click the image you want.

Using the Button Editor

The Office Button Editor lets you modify an existing button image or create your own. The following procedure shows you how it's done:

1. Select Tools, Customize to display the Customize dialog box.
2. Right-click the button whose image you want to edit.

Starting with Another Button Image

If another toolbar button has an image that's close to the one you want, use the steps outlined earlier in the "Copying a Button Image" section to copy that image to your button. You can then edit this image as necessary using the Button Editor.

---

3. Click Edit Button Image. The application displays the Button Editor dialog box, shown in Figure 10.5.
4. If you want to create the button from scratch, click the Clear button.
5. Select a color by clicking one of the boxes in the Colors group.

Figure 10.5
The Button Editor lets you design your own toolbar buttons.

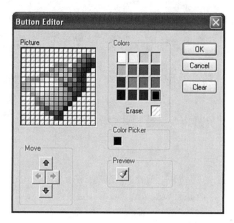

6. Add the color to the image by clicking one or more boxes in the Picture area. To clear a box, click it again. The Preview area shows you what the button looks like at regular size.

7. If necessary, use the buttons in the Move group to adjust the position of the image.

8. Repeat steps 5 through 7 to draw the complete image.

9. Click OK to assign the new image to the button.

Attaching a Toolbar to an Excel Workbook

If you're working in Excel and you need a custom toolbar only for a specific workbook, you can attach the toolbar to the workbook. This is also useful for developers who want to distribute custom toolbars with their projects. Here are the steps to follow:

1. Activate the workbook to which you want to attach the custom toolbar.

2. Select Tools, Customize to display the Customize dialog box and then select the Toolbars tab.

3. Click Attach. Excel displays the Attach Toolbars dialog box.

4. Select the custom toolbar and click Copy >>.

5. Click OK.

After you've attached a toolbar, it's automatically copied into the Excel workspace whenever you open the workbook.

Removing a Toolbar from a Workbook

If you accidentally copy a toolbar, you can remove it from the workbook. Display the Attach Toolbars dialog box and then select the toolbar in the Toolbars in Workbook list. The Copy >> button changes to a Delete button. Click Delete to remove the toolbar, and then click OK.

Creating Custom Keyboard Shortcuts in Word

Unlike the other Office applications, Word also lets you customize the third user-interaction element—the keyboard. Specifically, you can assign keyboard shortcuts to any of Word's commands (or change the existing keyboard shortcuts) or to your macros. Here are the steps to follow:

1. Select Tools, Customize.

2. Click the Keyboard button to display the Customize Keyboard dialog box.

3. Use the Save Changes In list to choose the document or template in which you want the new key combination stored.

4. Use the Categories list to select the category that contains the command you want to work with.

5. Use the Commands list to select the command. If the command already has a shortcut key assigned, it appears in the Current Keys list.

6. Click inside the Press New Shortcut Key text box.

7. Press the key combination you want to use. Word displays the keypress in the text box and tells you whether the key combination is already assigned, as shown in Figure 10.6.

Figure 10.6
Using the Customize Keyboard dialog box, you can assign key combinations to any Word command.

8. If this is the key combination you want to use, click Assign. Otherwise, repeat step 7 until you find a key combination you want.

9. Repeat steps 4 through 8 to assign other key combinations.

10. When you're done, click Close.

Customizing the Office Common Dialog Boxes

When you display the Open or Save As dialog boxes in any Office application, the left side of the dialog box holds a strip of icons called My Places. There are five icons in the default configuration: My Recent Documents, Desktop, My Documents, My Computer, and My Network Places. Clicking any of these icons places the corresponding folder in the Look In (or Save In) list and displays the folder contents in the dialog box.

This is handy behavior, and it gets even handier when you customize the My Places bar to include the folders that you use most often. You can also change the order of the icons and remove icons, as explained in the next few sections.

Adding a Folder to the My Places Bar

Follow these steps to add a folder to My Places:

1. In any Office application, select File, Open to display the Open dialog box. (You can also select File, Save As to display the Save As dialog box.)

2. Open the folder you want to add to My Places.

3. Drop down the Tools menu and select the Add to "My Places" command. Office adds the folder to My Places.

Figure 10.7 shows the Open dialog box with a folder named Conference Files added to My Places.

Figure 10.7
You can add your own folders to the My Places bar that is part of the Office Open and Save As dialog boxes.

Customizing the My Places Bar Icons

Here are a few useful techniques that enable you to customize the My Places bar:

- Keeping the icons in view—If you add more icons than can fit in the default height of the My Places bar, Office displays arrows at the bottom and/or top of the My Places bar to enable you to scroll down or up. One way to avoid this is to increase the height of the dialog box itself. Another method is to switch to smaller versions of the icons. To do that, right-click any icon in the My Places bar and then click Small Icons.

- Changing the icon order—If you have some icons that you use frequently, you might prefer to place them nearer the top of the list. You can change the position of an icon in the My Places bar by right-clicking the icon and then clicking either Move Up or Move Down.

- Renaming custom icons—You can rename the folder icons that you add to My Places. To do this, right-click the icon, click Rename, type the new name into the Rename Place dialog box, and then click OK.

Removing Icons from the My Places Bar

If you find that your My Places bar is getting overcrowded, you should delete any icons you no longer use. You can delete a custom icon by right-clicking it and then clicking Remove.

For the built-in icons, removing them involves editing the Windows Registry. (See Appendix A, "Working with the Windows Registry.") Open the Registry Editor and navigate to the following key:

```
HKEY_CURRENT_USER\Software\Microsoft\Office\11.0\Common\Open Find\Places\
➡StandardPlaces\
```

Here you see five subkeys: Desktop, MyComputer, MyDocuments, Publishing, and Recent. These correspond to the five built-in folder icons in the default My Places bar. (The Publishing key corresponds to the My Network Places icon.) Follow these steps to remove a built-in icon from My Places:

1. Click the key that corresponds to the icon you want to remove.
2. Select Edit, New, DWORD Value. The Registry Editor creates a new DWORD value in the key.
3. Type **Show** and press Enter.

Note that the default setting for a new DWORD value is 0, which is what we want. That is, when you add the Show value and set it to 0, Office doesn't display the corresponding icon in My Places. In Figure 10.8, for example, I've added the Show value to the Desktop key. As you can see in Figure 10.9, the Desktop icon no longer appears in the My Places bar.

If you change your mind, either change the Show value to 1 or delete the Show value.

10

10

Figure 10.8
To remove a built-in icon from My Places, add the Show value to the corresponding key and set the value to 0, as shown here for the Desktop key.

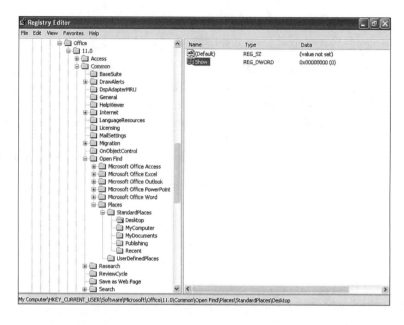

Figure 10.9
The Desktop icon no longer appears in the My Places bar.

From Here

- To learn how to create macros, see Chapter 11, "Maximizing Office with VBA Macros."

- For some examples of macros that you can assign to menu commands and toolbar buttons, see Chapter 12, "Putting VBA to Good Use: Practical Macros Everyone Can Use."

- To learn how to use the Registry Editor, see Appendix A, "Working with the Windows Registry."

Maximizing Office with VBA Macros

Office gurus know a secret that's crucial for mastering any or all of the Office applications: There are things you can make a program do that are *not* available via the program's interface (that is, its menu commands, toolbar buttons, and shortcut keys). To accomplish these extra tricks and techniques, you have to go under the program's hood and use Visual Basic for Applications (VBA), the programming language that comes with the Office suite. You use VBA to build small sets of instructions called *scripts*, or, more commonly, *macros*. With these instructions, you can make the program perform multiple tasks in a single operation or, as I mentioned earlier, perform tasks that aren't part of the interface. For example, in Chapter 1, "Building Dynamic Documents in Word," I showed you a simple macro that updates all the fields in a document (see Listing 1.1), a task that is otherwise cumbersome to accomplish using traditional methods.

This chapter introduces you to VBA programming. You learn how to run existing macros, record program actions as a macro, and the basics of creating your own macros. Chapter 12, "Putting VBA to Good Use: Practical Macros Everyone Can Use," offers a number of macros that you can use "as is" or modify to suit your needs.

11

Learning VBA

This chapter gives you only a minimal introduction to VBA programming. However, VBA is a relatively easy language to learn and is well worth the effort if you want to create truly custom functions that are designed to suit your needs and solve your worksheet problems. If you want to take the plunge into VBA programming, may I not-so-humbly suggest my book *The Absolute Beginner's Guide to VBA* (Que Publishing, 2004).

Using a VBA Macro

VBA macros come in two forms:

- Command macro—This is code that performs some action that usually has an effect on the program's environment. For example, the macro might insert text into a worksheet cell or change a Word option. In general, you can think of a command macro as being akin to a program menu command.

- Function macro—This is code that returns a result. A function often takes one or more values as inputs, manipulates those values in some way, and then sends back the result of those manipulations. In general, you can think of a function macro as being akin to an Excel worksheet function or a Word formula field.

You can run both command and function macros from within other macros and functions, but I'll ignore that here. Instead, the next two sections show you the techniques you need to use the macro examples provided in this chapter and in Chapter 12.

Running a Command Macro

To run a command macro in any Office program, follow these steps:

1. Choose Tools, Macro, Macros, or click Run Macro if you have the Visual Basic toolbar displayed (you can also press Alt+F8). The program displays the Macros dialog box.

2. (Optional) If you have a number of macros in different open documents, you can reduce the number of displayed macros by using the Macros In box to select the document that contains the macro you want to work with.

3. In the Macro Name list, select the macro you want to run.

4. Click Run.

Adding a Macro to a Custom Menu or Toolbar

If you have a macro that you use often, you should assign the macro to a menu command or toolbar button. In Chapter 10, see the section titled "Creating Custom Commands for Macros."

Using a Function Macro

You use functions as part of Excel worksheet formulas or as part of Access expressions that build calculated fields.

In Excel, as with the program's built-in functions, you can either type the function into the formula by hand, or you can use the Insert Function method. Assuming you're editing a cell formula, you enter a VBA function into the formula by hand by using the following general format:

`WorkbookName.xls!FunctionName(arguments)`

Here, `WorkbookName` is the filename of the workbook that contains the function, `FunctionName` is the name of the function, and `arguments` is the list of values for the arguments accepted by the function.

To use the Insert Function method, follow these steps:

1. Choose Insert, Function to display the Insert Function dialog box.
2. In the Or Select a Category list, click All to make sure that all the VBA functions are included in the Select a Function list.
3. The VBA functions appear in the list using the same *WorkbookName*.xls!*FunctionName* format that I described earlier. Therefore, first look for the workbook name in the list, and then select the function you want.
4. Click OK.
5. If the function accepts arguments, enter them and click OK.

In Access, you can enter the function into an expression either by hand or by using the Expression Builder. To insert a function by hand, place the cursor in the query Field cell or form text box and type the function using the following format:

`FunctionName(arguments)`

Here, `FunctionName` is the name of the function, and `arguments` is the list of values for the arguments accepted by the function.

To use the Expression Builder, follow these steps:

1. Place the cursor in the query Field cell or form text box.
 2. Click the Build toolbar button to display the Expression Builder dialog box.
3. In the left list, open the Functions branch.
4. Select the name of your database.
5. In the middle list, select the name of the module that contains your function.
6. In the right list, double-click the function you want to insert. Access inserts the function into the expression, as shown in Figure 11.1.

Figure 11.1
In Access, you can use the
Expression Builder to
insert a function into an
expression.

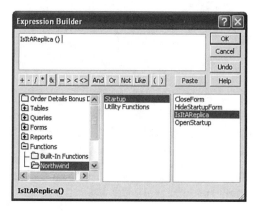

7. (Optional) Fill in the rest of your expression.
8. Click OK.

Using the Example Code

To use the macros presented in this chapter and in Chapter 12, you need to copy the code
into a VBA module on your computer. A *module* is an object that you insert into a document. The purpose of a module is to store VBA code, so to work with modules you need to
know how to get to the Visual Basic Editor, which I discuss a bit later (see "Working with
the Visual Basic Editor").

Recording a VBA Macro

By far the easiest way to create a command macro is to use the Macro Recorder. With this
method, you start the recorder and then run through the task you want to automate
(including selecting text, running menu commands, and choosing dialog box options). The
Recorder translates everything into the appropriate VBA statements and copies those statements to a command macro in a module. You can then use the recorded macro to replay
the entire procedure any time you like. This section shows you how to record a command
macro in Word, Excel, or PowerPoint. (The other programs in the Office suite don't have
macro recording capabilities.)

 To begin, set up the application so that it's ready to record. In Word, for example, if you
want to record a series of formatting options, select the text you want to work with. When
that's done, either select Tools, Macro, Record New Macro or click the Record Macro button in the Visual Basic toolbar. You'll see the Record Macro dialog box appear. Figure 11.2
shows the Excel version.

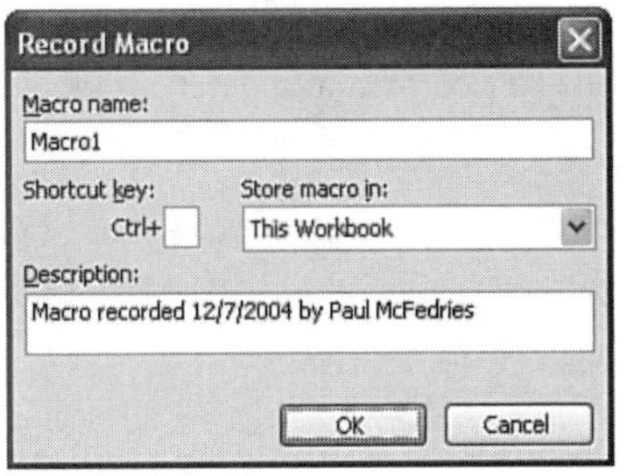

Figure 11.2
Use the Record Macro dia-
log box to name and
describe your macro.

The application proposes a name for the macro (such as Macro1), but you can use the
Macro Name text box to change the name to anything you like. However, you must follow
a few naming conventions: no more than 255 characters, the first character must be a letter
or an underscore (_), and no spaces or periods are allowed.

Word and Excel enable you to assign shortcuts to the macro:

- In Word, either click Toolbars to assign a toolbar button to the macro, or click
  Keyboard to assign a shortcut key to the macro.

- In Excel, enter a letter in the text box labeled Shortcut Key: Ctrl+.

Use the Store Macro In drop-down list to specify where the macro will reside:

- In Word, you can store the macro in any open template (which makes the macro available to any document that uses the template), or in any open document (which makes
  the macro available only to that document).

- In Excel, you can store the macro in the current workbook, a new workbook, or in the
  Personal Macro Workbook. If you use the latter, your macros will be available to all
  your workbooks.

The Personal Macro Workbook

The Personal Macro Workbook is a hidden workbook named Personal.xls that opens automatically when you start
Excel. This means that any macros contained in this file will be available to all your workbooks, which makes them easy
to reuse. If you want to see this workbook, you have to unhide it. To do this, select Window, Unhide, select PERSONAL.XLS
in the list of hidden files, and then click OK. Note, however, that this file is not created until you use it to store at least one
recorded macro.

- In PowerPoint, you can store the macro in any open presentation.

Finally, enter an optional description of the macro in the Description text box. When
you're ready to go, click OK. The application returns you to the document, displays
Recording or REC in the status bar, and displays the Stop Recording Macro toolbar. Now
perform the tasks you want to include in the macro. Because the macro recorder takes note

of nearly everything you do (except mouse movements and clicking the buttons in the Stop Recording Macro toolbar), be careful not to perform any extraneous actions or commands during the recording.

 When you finish the tasks, select Tools, Macro, Stop Recording, or click the Stop Macro button.

Viewing the Resulting Module

 To see your macro, select Tools, Macro, Macros, or click the Run Macro button (you can also press Alt+F8) to display the Macros dialog box. In the Macro Name list, select the macro you just recorded and then click the Edit button. The application opens the Visual Basic Editor window and then opens the module and displays the macro. As you can see in Figure 11.3, the application (Excel, in this case) translates your actions into VBA code and combines everything into a single macro.

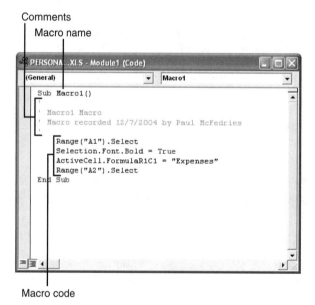

Figure 11.3
A sample recorded macro.

Macro code

A typical macro has the following features:

- Sub/End Sub—These keywords mark the beginning (Sub) and end (End Sub) of a command macro. The Sub keyword is the reason why command macros also are called *Subprocedures* (*sub* is short for *subroutine*).

- Macro name—After the Sub keyword, Excel enters the name of the macro followed by a left and right parenthesis (the parentheses are used for input values [arguments], as you'll see later).

- Comments—The first few lines begin with an apostrophe ('), which tells VBA that these lines are *comments*. As the name implies, comments are for show only; they aren't processed when you run the macro. In each recorded macro, the comments display the name of the macro and the description you entered in the Record New Macro dialog box. (In Excel, the comments also display the keyboard shortcut if you entered one.)

- Macro code—The main body of the macro (in other words, the lines between Sub and End Sub, not including the initial comments) consists of a series of statements. These are the application's interpretations of the actions you performed during the recording. In the example, four actions were performed in Excel:

  1. Cell A1 was selected.
  2. The cell was formatted as boldface.
  3. The string Expenses was typed into the cell.
  4. The Enter key was pressed (which moved the selection down to cell A2).

Editing a Recorded Macro

As you're learning VBA, you'll often end up with recorded macros that don't turn out quite right the first time. Whether the macro runs a command it shouldn't or is missing a command altogether, you'll often have to patch things up after the fact.

The lines within a VBA module are just text, so you make changes the same way you would in a word processor or text editor. If your macro contains statements that you want to remove, just delete the offending lines from the module.

If you want to add new recorded actions to the macro, VBA doesn't give you any way to record new statements into an existing macro. Instead, you should first record a new macro that includes the actions you want, and then display the macro. From here, you can use the standard Windows cut-and-paste techniques (including drag-and-drop) to move the statements from the new macro into the other macro.

Working with the Visual Basic Editor

 To add existing macro code to a module, edit a recorded macro, or build your own macros from scratch, you use the Visual Basic Editor. You saw earlier that one way to open the Visual Basic Editor is to display the Macros dialog box, select a macro, and then click Edit. However, if you just want access to the editor, the more normal route is to select Tools, Macro, Visual Basic Editor, or click the Visual Basic Editor button in the Visual Basic toolbar (you can also press Alt+F11).

The Visual Basic Editor is a so-called *integrated development environment*, which means it has tools and objects that enable programmers to write and edit VBA code. The Visual Basic Editor is divided into three areas (as shown in Figure 11.4):

11

- Project Explorer—This area shows the open VBA projects as well as a hierarchical view of the contents of each project. These contents include the open application objects (worksheets, documents, slides, and so on), any modules that have been created either by recording a macro or by creating one from scratch (explained later), and any user forms that you've built.

- Properties window—This area shows the various properties available for whatever object is highlighted in the Project Explorer. The Properties window is divided into two columns. The left column shows you the names of all the properties associated with the object, and the right side shows you the current value of each property. To change the value of a property, click the appropriate box in the right column and then either type in the new value or select it from a drop-down list (the method you use depends on the property).

- Work area—This is where the module windows you work with are displayed.

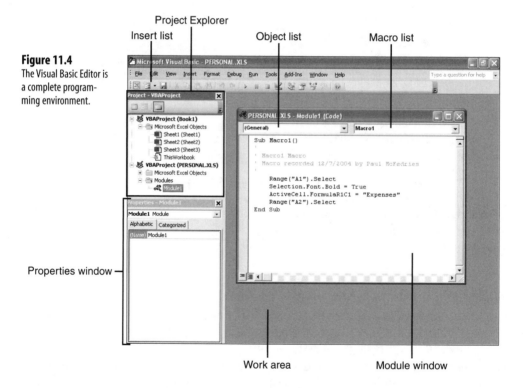

Figure 11.4
The Visual Basic Editor is a complete programming environment.

Creating a Module

To create a module, follow these steps:

1. In the Visual Basic Editor, use the Project pane to click the workbook project in which you want to insert the module. For example, if you want to use the Personal Macro Workbook in Excel, click the PERSONAL.XLS project.

2. Choose Insert, Module, or drop down the Insert list (pointed out in Figure 11.4) and select Module. The Visual Basic Editor adds a Modules branch (if one didn't already exist) to the workbook's project and opens the Module window.

Opening a Module

Later, when you've created modules in various workbooks, you'll need to know how to open the module that contains the code you want. You have two choices:

- Choose Tools, Macro, Macros (or press Alt+F8) to display the Macros dialog box, use the Macro Name list to click the macro you want to work with, and then choose Edit. The program launches the Visual Basic Editor and opens the module containing the macro.

- In the Visual Basic Editor, use the Project window to open the branch of the workbook that contains the module, open that project's Modules branch, and then double-click the name of the module you want to open.

I should also point out that each module window has two drop-down lists beneath the title bar (refer to Figure 11.4):

- Object list—This control contains a list of the available objects. Modules don't have objects, so this list contains only (General) for a module window.

- Macro list—This is a list of all the command macros and function macros in the module. Until you add a macro, this list shows only (Declarations).

11

Working with Macros

The basic unit of VBA programming is the *macro*, which is a block of code in a module that you reference as a unit. So far you've seen that there are two types of macros: command macros (also known as Subprocedures) and function macros (or Function procedures).

The Structure of Macro

To recap what you learned earlier, a command macro is allowed to modify its environment, but it can't return a value. Here is the basic structure of a command macro:

```
Sub MacroName (argument1, argument2, ...)
    [VBA statements]
End Sub
```

Here, *MacroName* is the name of the command macro, and *arguments* is the optional list of values for the arguments accepted by the macro. For example, Listing 11.1 presents a command macro that enters some values for a loan in various worksheet ranges and then adds a formula to calculate the loan payment.

This Chapter's Examples

You'll find the Word and Excel files used as examples in this chapter on my website at www.mcfedries.com/OfficeGurus.

Listing 11.1 A Sample Command Macro

```
Sub EnterLoanData()
    Range("A1").Value = .08
    Range("A2").Value = 10
    Range("A3").Value = 10000
    Range("A4").Formula = "=PMT(A1/12, A2*12, A3)"
End Sub
```

A Function macro, on the other hand, doesn't usually modify its environment, but it does return a value. Here is its structure:

```
Function MacroName (argument1, argument2, ...)
    [VBA statements]
    MacroName = returnValue
End Function
```

For example, Listing 11.2 is a function macro that sums two ranges, stores the results in variables named `totalSales` and `totalExpenses` (see "Understanding Program Variables," later in this chapter, to learn more about variables), and then uses these values and the `fixedCosts` argument to calculate the net margin:

Listing 11.2 A Sample Function Macro

```
Function CalcNetMargin(fixedCosts)
    totalSales = Application.Sum(Range("Sales"))
    totalExpenses = Application.Sum(Range("Expenses"))
    CalcNetMargin = (totalSales - totalExpenses - fixedCosts)/totalSales
End Function
```

Writing Your Own Macro

Although the Macro Recorder makes it easy to create your own homegrown command macros, you can't use it to create function macros, and there are plenty of macro features that you can't access with mouse or keyboard actions or by selecting menu options. In Excel, for example, VBA has a couple of dozen information macro functions that return data about cells, worksheets, workspaces, and more. Also, the VBA control functions enable you to add true programming constructs such as looping, branching, and decision making.

To access these macro elements, you need to write your own VBA routines from scratch. This is easier than it sounds because all you really need to do is enter a series of statements in a module. The problem here, of course, is that you likely don't know any VBA statements yet, so you're not in a position to write your own macros. That's fine, because I'll be introducing you to some VBA a bit later (see "VBA Programming Basics").

For now, let's work through a simple example to illustrate the process. With a module window open and active, follow these steps to write your own command macro:

1. Place the insertion point where you want to start the macro. (Make sure the insertion point isn't inside an existing macro.)

2. If you want to begin your macro with a few comments that describe what the macro does, type an apostrophe (') at the beginning of each comment line.

3. To start the macro, type **Sub**, followed by a space and the name of the macro. For the example, type **HelloWorld**. When you press Enter at the end of this line, VBA automatically adds a pair of parentheses at the end of the macro name. It also tacks on an End Sub line to mark the end of the procedure. Your code should now look like this:

```
Sub HelloWorld()

End Sub
```

4. Between the Sub and End Sub lines, type the VBA statements you want to include in the macro. For the example, type **MsgBox "Hello World!"**. Here's the final macro:

```
Sub HelloWorld()
    MsgBox "Hello World!"
End Sub
```

Indent Statements for Clarity

To make your code easier to read, you should indent each line by pressing the Tab key at the beginning of the line. Note that VBA preserves the indentation on subsequent lines, so you have to indent only the first line.

11

When you press Enter to start a new line, VBA analyzes the line you just entered and performs three chores:

- It formats the color of each word in the line: by default, VBA keywords are blue, comments are green, errors are red, and all other text is black.

- VBA keywords are converted to their proper case. For example, if you type end sub, VBA converts this to End Sub when you press Enter.

- It checks for syntax errors. VBA signifies a syntax error either by displaying a dialog box to let you know what the problem is, or by not converting a word to its proper case or color.

Always Enter Keywords in Lowercase

By always entering VBA keywords in lowercase letters, you'll be able to catch typing errors by looking for those keywords that VBA doesn't recognize (in other words, the ones that remain in lowercase).

Running a Command Macro from the Visual Basic Editor

After you create a command macro, you can run it directly from the Visual Basic Editor:

1. Open the module containing the command macro.

2. Place the insertion point anywhere inside the macro.

3. Select Run, Run Sub/User Form or press F5.

VBA Programming Basics

The rest of this chapter gives you a very basic introduction to programming VBA code. What you learn won't make you an expert VBA programmer by any means, but you'll learn enough to write your own simple macros and understand the examples I take you through in Chapter 12.

Understanding Program Variables

Your VBA procedures often will need to store temporary values for use in later statements and calculations. For example, you might want to store values for total sales and total expenses to use later in a gross margin calculation. Although you probably could get away with using the underlying application to store these values (for example, in a cell in an Excel worksheet), this almost always isn't practical. Instead, VBA (like all programming languages) lets you store temporary values in *variables*.

Declaring Variables

Declaring a variable tells VBA the name of the variable you're going to use. (It also serves to specify the *data type* of the variable, which I'll explain later in this section; see "Variable Data Types.") You declare variables by including Dim statements (Dim is short for *dimension*) at the beginning of each Sub or Function procedure.

The Placement of Variable Declarations

Technically, you can put variable declarations anywhere you like within a procedure and VBA won't complain. The only real restriction is that the Dim statement must precede the first use of the variable in a procedure. However, it's not only traditional to list all your Dim statements together at the top of a procedure, it's also clearer.

In its simplest form, a Dim statement has the following syntax:

```
Dim variableName
```

Here, *variableName* is the name of the variable. The name must begin with a letter, it can't be longer than 255 characters, it can't be a VBA keyword, and it can't contain a space or any of the following characters:

```
. ! # $ % & @
```

For example, the following statement declares a variable named `totalSales`:

```
Dim totalSales
```

Variable Case Considerations

To avoid confusing variables with the names of objects, properties, or methods, many programmers begin their variable names with a lowercase letter. This is the style I use in this book.

Also, note that VBA preserves the case of your variable names throughout a procedure. For example, if you declare a variable named `totalSales` and you later enter this variable name as, for instance, `totalsales`, VBA will convert the name to `totalSales` automatically as part of its syntax checking. This means two things:

- If you want to change the case used in a variable, change the *first* instance of the variable (usually the `Dim` statement).

- After you've declared a variable, you should enter all subsequent references to the variable entirely in lowercase. Not only is this easier to type, but you'll immediately know if you've misspelled the variable name if you see that VBA doesn't change the case of the variable name after you enter the line.

Most programmers set up a declaration section at the beginning of each procedure and use it to hold all their `Dim` statements. Then, after the variables have been declared, they can use them throughout the procedure. Listing 11.3 shows a `function` macro that declares two variables—`totalSales` and `totalExpenses`—and then uses Excel's `Sum` function to store a range sum in each variable. Finally, the `GrossMargin` calculation uses each variable to return the function result.

11

Listing 11.3   A Function That Uses Variables to Store the Intermediate Values of a Calculation

```
Function GrossMargin()
    '
    ' Declarations
    '
    Dim totalSales
    Dim totalExpenses
    '
    ' Code
    '
    totalSales = Application.Sum(Range("Sales"))
    totalExpenses = Application.Sum(Range("Expenses"))
    GrossMargin = (totalSales - totalExpenses) / totalSales
End Function
```

In the `GrossMargin` function, notice that you store a value in a variable with a simple assignment statement of the following form:

```
variableName = value
```

Variable Data Types

The *data type* of a variable determines the kind of data the variable can hold. Table 11.1 lists all the VBA data types.

Table 11.1 The VBA Data Types

Data Type	Description
Boolean	Takes one of two logical values: True or False.
Byte	Used for small, positive integer values (from 0 to 255).
Currency	Used for monetary or fixed-decimal calculations where accuracy is important. The value range is from –922,337,203,685,477.5808 to 922,337,203,685,477.5807.
Date	Used for holding date data. The range is from January 1, 0100 to December 31, 9999. When setting a value to a Date variable, enclose the date in pound signs (for example, newDate = #8/23/2005#).
Double	Double-precision floating point. Negative numbers range from –1.79769313486232E308 to –4.94065645841247E–324. Positive numbers range from 4.94065645841247E–324 to 1.79769313486232E308.
Integer	Used for integer values in the range –32,768 to 32,767.
Long	Large integer values. The range is from –2,147,483,648 to 2,147,483,647.
Object	Used for objects (see "Working with Objects," later in this chapter).
Single	Single-precision floating point. Negative numbers range from –3.402823E38 to –1.401298E–45. Positive numbers range from 1.401298E–45 to 3.402823E38.
String	Holds text values.
Variant	Can take any kind of data.

You specify a data type by including the As keyword in a Dim statement. Here's the general syntax:

```
Dim variableName As DataType
```

variableName is the name of the variable and *DataType* is one of the data types from Table 11.1. For example, the following statement declares a variable named textString to be of type String:

```
Dim textString As String
```

Building VBA Expressions

VBA variables aren't much use unless you do something with them. In other words, a procedure is merely a lifeless collection of Dim statements until you define some kind of relationship among the variables and your program objects. To establish these relationships, you need to create *expressions* that perform calculations and produce results. This section introduces you to the basics of building VBA expressions.

Understanding Expression Structure

You can think of an expression as being like a compact version of a function macro. In other words, in the same way that a function takes one or more arguments, combines them in various ways, and returns a value, so too does an expression take one or more inputs (called *operands*), combine them with special symbols (called *operators*), and produce a result. The main difference, though, is that an expression must do everything in a single VBA statement.

For example, consider the following statement:

```
might = "right"
```

Here, the left side of the equation is a variable named `might`. The right side of the equation is the simplest of all expressions: a text string. In other words, a string value is being stored in a variable.

Here's a slightly more complex example:

```
energy = mass * (speedOfLight ^ 2)
```

Again, the left side of the equation is a variable (named `energy`) and the right side of the equation is an expression. For the latter, a variable named `speedOfLight` is squared and then this result is multiplied by another variable named `mass`. In this example, you see the two main components of any expression:

- Operands—These are the "input values" used by the expression. They can be variables, object properties, function results, or literals. (A *literal* is a specific value, such as a number or text string. In the first expression example, `"right"` is a string literal.)

- Operators—These are symbols that combine the operands to produce a result. In the example just shown, the `*` symbol represents multiplication and the `^` symbol represents exponentiation.

This combination of operands and operators produces a result that conforms to one of the variable data types outlined earlier: `Date`, `String`, `Boolean`, `Object`, `Variant`, or one of the numeric data types—`Byte`, `Integer`, `Long`, `Single`, `Double`, or `Currency`. When building your expressions, the main point to keep in mind is that you must maintain *data type consistency* throughout the expression. This means you must watch for three things:

- The operands must use compatible data types. Although it's okay to combine, for example, an `Integer` operand with a `Long` operand (because they're both numeric data types), it wouldn't make sense to use a `Double` operand and a `String` operand, for instance.

- The operators you use must match the data types of the operands. For example, you wouldn't want to multiply two strings together.

11

- If you're storing the expression result in a variable, make sure the variable's data type is consistent with the type of result produced by the expression. For example, don't use a Currency variable to store the result of a string expression.

VBA Operators

You've already seen the first of VBA's operators: the *assignment operator*, which is just the humble equal sign (=). You use the assignment operator to assign the result of an expression to a variable or to an object property.

Note that the assignment operator is not the same as the equal sign from mathematics. To understand why, you need to bear in mind that VBA always derives the result of the right side of the equation (that is, the expression) before it modifies the value of the left side of the equation. This seems like obvious behavior, but it's the source of a handy trick that you'll use quite often. In other words, you can use the current value of whatever is on the left side of the equation *as part of the expression* on the right side. For example, consider the following code fragment:

```
currYear = 2005
currYear = currYear + 1
```

The first statement assigns the literal value 2005 to the currYear variable. The second statement also changes the value stored in the currYear, but it uses the expression currYear + 1 to do it. This looks weird until you remember that VBA always evaluates the expression first. In other words, it takes the current value of currYear, which is 2005, and adds 1 to it. The result is 2006 and *that* is what's stored in currYear when all is said and done.

VBA has a number of different operators that you can use to combine functions, variables, and values in a VBA expression. These operators work much like the operators—such as addition (+) and multiplication (*)—that you use to build formulas in Excel worksheets and Word tables. VBA operators fall into four general categories: arithmetic, concatenation, comparison, and logical.

VBA's arithmetic operators are similar to those you use to build Excel formulas, Word fields, and Access expressions. Table 11.2 lists each of the arithmetic operators you can use in your VBA statements.

Table 11.2   The VBA Arithmetic Operators

Operator	Name	Example	Result
+	Addition	10+5	15
-	Subtraction	10-5	5
-	Negation	-10	-10
*	Multiplication	10*5	50
/	Division	10/5	2

Operator	Name	Example	Result
\	Integer division	11\5	2
^	Exponentiation	10^5	100000
Mod	Modulus	10 Mod 5	0

You use the concatenation operator (&) to combine text strings within an expression. One way to use the concatenation operator is to combine string literals. For example, the expression "soft" & "ware" returns the string software. Note that the quotation marks and ampersand aren't shown in the result. You can also use & to combine any kind of operand, as long as the operands use the String data type.

You use the comparison operators in an expression that compares two or more numbers, text strings, variables, or function results. If the statement is true, the result of the formula is given the logical value True (which is equivalent to any nonzero value). If the statement is false, the formula returns the logical value False (which is equivalent to 0). Table 11.3 summarizes VBA's comparison operators.

Table 11.3   The VBA Comparison Operators

Operator	Name	Example	Result
=	Equal to	10=5	False
>	Greater than	10>5	True
<	Less than	10<5	False
>=	Greater than or equal to	"a">="b"	False
<=	Less than or equal to	"a"<="b"	True
<>	Not equal to	"a"<>"b"	True
Like	Like	"Smith" Like "Sm?th"	True

You use the logical operators to combine or modify True/False expressions. Table 11.4 summarizes VBA's logical operators.

Table 11.4   The VBA Logical Operators

Operator	General Form	What It Returns
And	*Expr1* And *Expr2*	True if both *Expr1* and *Expr2* are True; False otherwise.
Eqv	*Expr1* Eqv *Expr2*	True if both *Expr1* and *Expr2* are True or if both *Expr1* and *Expr2* are False; False otherwise.
Imp	*Expr1* Imp *Expr2*	False if *Expr1* is True and *Expr2* is False; True otherwise.

continues

Table 11.4 **Continued**

Operator	General Form	What It Returns
Or	*Expr1* Or *Expr2*	True if at least one of *Expr1* and *Expr2* are True; False otherwise.
Xor	*Expr1* Xor *Expr2*	False if both *Expr1* and *Expr2* are True or if both *Expr1* and *Expr2* are False; True otherwise.
Not	Not *Expr*	True if *Expr* is False; False if *Expr* is True.

Working with Objects

Many of your VBA procedures will perform calculations using simple combinations of numbers, operators, and the host application's built-in functions. You'll probably find, however, that most of your code manipulates the application environment in some way, whether it's formatting document text, entering data in a worksheet range, or setting application options. Each of these items—the document, the range, the application—is called an *object* in VBA.

You can manipulate objects in VBA in various ways, but we'll concentrate on the following two:

- You can make changes to the object's *properties*.
- You can make the object perform a task by activating a *method* associated with the object.

Each Office application's objects are arranged in a hierarchy. The most general object—the Application object—refers to the program itself. In Word, for example, the Application object contains more than 30 objects, including the Documents object (the collection of all open documents, each one a Document object), the Options object (the settings available in the Options dialog box), and the RecentFiles object (the names of the files that have been used most recently).

Many of these objects have objects beneath them in the hierarchy. A Document object, for example, contains objects that represent the document's characters, words, sentences, paragraphs, bookmarks, and much more. Similarly, a Paragraph object contains objects for the paragraph format and the tab stops.

To specify an object in the hierarchy, you usually start with the uppermost object and add the lower objects, separated by periods. For example, following is one way you could specify the first word in the second paragraph in a document named Memo.doc:

```
Application.Documents("Memo.doc").Paragraphs(2).Range.Words(1)
```

As you'll see, there are ways to shorten such long-winded "hierarchical paths."

Working with Object Properties

Every object has a defining set of characteristics. These characteristics are called the object's *properties*, and they control the appearance and position of the object. For example, each Window object has a `WindowState` property you can use to display a window as maximized, minimized, or normal. Similarly, a Word `Document` object has a `Name` property to hold the filename, a `Saved` property that tells you whether the document has changed since the last save, a `Type` property to hold the document type (regular or template), and many more.

When you refer to a property, you use the following syntax:

`Object.Property`

For example, the following expression refers to the `ActiveWindow` property of the `Application` object:

`Application.ActiveWindow`

Setting the Value of a Property   To set a property to a certain value, you use the following syntax:

`Object.Property = value`

Here, `value` is an expression that returns the value to which you want to set the property. As such, it can be any of VBA's recognized data types, including the following:

- A numeric value—For example, the following statement sets the size of the font in the active cell to 14:

  `ActiveCell.Font.Size = 14`

- A string value—The following example sets the font name in the active cell to Times New Roman:

  `ActiveCell.Font.Name = "Times New Roman"`

- A logical value (in other words, `True` or `False`)—The following statement turns on the `Italic` property in the active cell:

  `ActiveCell.Font.Italic = True`

Returning the Value of a Property   Sometimes you need to know the current setting of a property before changing the property or performing some other action. You can store the current value of a property in a variable by using the following syntax:

`variable = Object.Property`

Here, `variable` is a variable or another property. For example, the following statement stores the contents of the active cell in a variable named `cellContents`:

`cellContents = ActiveCell.Value`

Working with Object Methods

An object's properties describe what the object is, whereas its *methods* describe what you can do with the object. For example, in Word you can spellcheck a `Document` object using the `CheckSpelling` method. Similarly, you can sort a `Table` object by using the `Sort` method.

How you refer to a method depends on whether the method uses any arguments. If it doesn't, the syntax is similar to that of properties:

```
Object.Method
```

For example, the following statement saves the active document:

```
ActiveDocument.Save
```

If the method requires arguments, you use the following syntax:

```
Object.Method (argument1, argument2, ...)
```

When to Use Method Parentheses

Technically, the parentheses around the argument list are necessary only if you'll be storing the result of the method in a variable or object property.

For example, Word's Document object has a Close method that you can use to close a document programmatically. Here's the syntax:

```
Object.Close(SaveChanges[, OriginalFormat, RouteDocument])
```

Object	The Document object.
SaveChanges	A constant that specifies whether the file is saved before closing.
OriginalFormat	A constant that specifies whether the file is saved in its original format.
RouteDocument	A True or False value that specifies whether the document is routed to the next recipient.

Formatting Required Arguments

For many VBA methods, not all the arguments are required. For the Close method, for example, only the SaveChanges argument is required. In this chapter and in Chapter 12, I differentiate between required and optional arguments by displaying the optional arguments in square brackets ([]).

For example, the following statement prompts the user to save changes, saves the changes (if applicable) in the original file format, and routes the document to the next recipient:

```
ActiveDocument.Close wdPromptToSaveChanges, wdOriginalFormat, True
```

To make your methods clearer to read, you can use VBA's predefined *named arguments*. For example, the syntax of the Close method has three named arguments: SaveChanges, OriginalFormat, and RouteDocument. Here's how you would use them in the preceding example:

```
ActiveDocument.Close _
    SaveChanges:=wdPromptToSaveChanges, _
    OrignalFormat:=wdOriginalFormat, _
    RouteDocument:=True
```

Notice how the named arguments are assigned values by using the := operator.

Working with Object Collections

A *collection* is a set of similar objects. For example, Word's `Documents` collection is the set of all the open `Document` objects. Similarly, the `Paragraphs` collection is the set of all `Paragraph` objects in a document. Collections are objects, too, so they have their own properties and methods, and you can use the properties and methods to manipulate one or more objects in the collection.

The members of a collection are called the *elements* of the collection. You can refer to individual elements using either the object's name or by using an *index*. For example, the following statement closes a document named `Budget.doc`:

```
Documents("Budget.doc").Close
```

On the other hand, the following statement uses an index to select the first `Bookmark` object in the active document:

```
ActiveDocument.Bookmarks(1).Select
```

If you don't specify an element, VBA assumes you want to work with the entire collection.

Assigning an Object to a Variable

As you learned earlier in this chapter (see "Understanding Program Variables") you can declare a variable as an `Object` data type by using the following form of the `Dim` statement:

```
Dim variableName As Object
```

After you've set up your object variable, you can assign an object to it by using the `Set` statement. `Set` has the following syntax:

```
Set variableName = ObjectName
```

variableName	The name of the variable.
ObjectName	The object you want to assign to the variable.

For example, the following statements declare a variable named `budgetSheet` to be an `Object` and then assign it to the `2005 Budget` worksheet in the `Budget.xls` workbook:

```
Dim budgetSheet As Object
Set budgetSheet = Workbooks("Budget.xls").Worksheets("2005 Budget")
```

11

Declare Specific Object Types

For faster performance, use specific object types instead of the generic Object type in your Dim statements. For example, the following statement declares the budgetSheet variable to be of type Worksheet:

```
Dim budgetSheet As Worksheet
```

Working with Multiple Properties or Methods

Because most objects have many properties and methods, you'll often need to perform multiple actions on a single object. This is accomplished easily with multiple statements that set the appropriate properties or run the necessary methods. However, this can be a pain if you have a long object name.

For example, take a look at the FormatParagraph procedure shown in Listing 11.4. This procedure formats a paragraph with six statements. Note that the Paragraph object name—ThisDocument.Paragraphs(1)—is quite long and is repeated in all six statements.

Listing 11.4   A Procedure That Formats a Range

```
Sub FormatParagraph()
    ThisDocument.Paragraphs(1).Style = "Heading 1"
    ThisDocument.Paragraphs(1).Alignment = wdAlignParagraphCenter
    ThisDocument.Paragraphs(1).Range.Font.Size = 16
    ThisDocument.Paragraphs(1).Range.Font.Bold = True
    ThisDocument.Paragraphs(1).Range.Font.Color = RGB(255, 0, 0) ' Red
    ThisDocument.Paragraphs(1).Range.Font.Name = "Times New Roman"
End Sub
```

To shorten this procedure, VBA provides the With statement. Here's the syntax:

```
With object
    [statements]
End With
```

object	The name of the object.
statements	The statements you want to execute on object.

The idea is that you strip out the common object and place it on the With line. Then all the statements between With and End With need only reference a specific method or property of that object. In the FormatParagraph procedure, the common object in all six statements is ThisDocument.Paragraphs(1). Listing 11.5 shows the FormatParagraph2 procedure, which uses the With statement to strip out this common object and make the previous macro more efficient.

Listing 11.5   A More Efficient Version of FormatParagraph()

```
Sub FormatParagraph2()
    With ThisDocument.Paragraphs(1)
        .Style = "Heading 1"
```

```
        .Alignment = wdAlignParagraphCenter
        .Range.Font.Size = 16
        .Range.Font.Bold = True
        .Range.Font.Color = RGB(255, 0, 0) ' Red
        .Range.Font.Name = "Times New Roman"
    End With
End Sub
```

Code That Makes Decisions

A smart macro performs tests on its environment and then decides what to do next based on the results of each test. For example, suppose you've written a function macro that uses one of its arguments as a divisor in a formula. You should test the argument before using it in the formula to make sure that it isn't 0 (to avoid producing a Division by zero error). If it is, you could then display a message that alerts the user of the illegal argument.

Using If...Then to Make True/False Decisions

The most basic form of decision is the simple true/false decision (which could also be seen as a yes/no or an on/off decision). In this case, your program looks at a certain condition, determines whether it is currently true or false, and acts accordingly. In VBA, simple true/false decisions are handled by the If...Then statement. You can use either the *single-line* syntax:

```
If condition Then statement
```

or the *block* syntax:

```
If condition Then
    [statements]
End If
```

condition   You can use either a logical expression that returns True or False, or you can use any expression that returns a numeric value. In the latter case, a return value of zero is functionally equivalent to False, and any nonzero value is equivalent to True.

statements   The VBA statement or statements to run if *condition* returns True. If *condition* returns False, VBA skips over the statements.

Whether you use the single-line or block syntax depends on the statements you want to run if the *condition* returns a True result. If you have only one statement, you can use either syntax. If you have multiple statements, you must use the block syntax.

Listing 11.6 shows a revised version of the GrossMargin procedure from Listing 11.3, earlier in this chapter. This version—called GrossMargin2—uses If...Then to check the totalSales variable. The procedure calculates the gross margin only if totalSales isn't zero.

11

Listing 11.6 An If...Then **Example**

```
Function GrossMargin2()
    Dim totalSales
    Dim totalExpenses
    totalSales = Application.Sum(Range("Sales"))
    totalExpenses = Application.Sum(Range("Expenses"))
    If totalSales <> 0 Then
        GrossMargin2 = (totalSales - totalExpenses) / totalSales
    End If
End Function
```

You Don't Need to Test for Zero

You can make the If...Then statement in the GrossMargin2 procedure slightly more efficient by taking advantage of the fact that in the condition, zero is equivalent to False and any other number is equivalent to True. This means you don't have to explicitly test the totalSales variable to see whether it's zero. Instead, you can use the following statements:

```
If totalSales Then
    GrossMargin2 = (totalSales - totalExpenses) / totalSales
End If
```

Using If...Then...Else **to Handle a** False **Result**

Using the If...Then statement to make decisions suffers from an important drawback: A False result only bypasses one or more statements; it doesn't execute any of its own. This is fine in many cases, but there will be times when you need to run one group of statements if the condition returns True and a different group if the result is False. To handle this, you need to use an If...Then...Else statement:

```
If condition Then
    [TrueStatements]
Else
    [FalseStatements]
End If
```

condition	The logical expression that returns True or False.
TrueStatements	The statements to run if condition returns True.
FalseStatements	The statements to run if condition returns False.

If the condition returns True, VBA runs the group of statements between If...Then and Else. If it returns False, VBA runs the group of statements between Else and End If.

Let's look at an example. Suppose you want to calculate the future value of a series of regular deposits, but you want to differentiate between monthly deposits and quarterly deposits. Listing 11.7 shows a function macro called FutureValue that does the job.

Listing 11.7   A Procedure That Uses `If...Then...Else`

```
Function FutureValue(Rate, Nper, Pmt, Frequency)
    If Frequency = "Monthly" Then
        FutureValue = FV(Rate / 12, Nper * 12, Pmt / 12)
    Else
        FutureValue = FV(Rate / 4, Nper * 4, Pmt / 4)
    End If
End Function
```

The first three arguments—`Rate`, `Nper`, and `Pmt`—are, respectively, the annual interest rate, the number of years in the term of the investment, and the total deposit available annually. The fourth argument—`Frequency`—is either `Monthly` or `Quarterly`. The idea is to adjust the first three arguments based on the `Frequency`. To do that, the `If...Then...Else` statement runs a test on the `Frequency` argument:

```
If Frequency = "Monthly" Then
```

If the logical expression `Frequency = "Monthly"` returns `True`, the procedure divides the interest rate by 12, multiplies the term by 12, and divides the annual deposit by 12. Otherwise, a quarterly calculation is assumed, and the procedure divides the interest rate by 4, multiplies the term by 4, and divides the annual deposit by 4. In both cases, VBA's `FV` (future value) function is used to return the future value. (In Chapter11.xls on my website, the Tests worksheet shows an example of this function at work.)

Indent Statements for Easier Readability

`If...Then...Else` statements are much easier to read when you indent the expressions between `If...Then`, `Else`, and `End If`, as I've done in Listing 11.7. This lets you easily identify which group of statements will be run if there is a `True` result and which group will be run if the result is `False`. Pressing the Tab key once at the beginning of the first line in the block does the job.

Using the `Select Case` **Statement**

If you need to perform multiple tests on some data, VBA's `Select Case` statement is a good choice. The idea is that you provide a logical expression at the beginning and then list a series of possible results. For each possible result—called a *case*—you provide one or more VBA statements to execute should the case prove to be true. Here's the syntax:

```
Select Case TestExpression
    Case FirstCaseList
        [FirstStatements]
    Case SecondCaseList
        [SecondStatements]
    <etc.>
    Case Else
        [ElseStatements]
End Select
```

TestExpression	This expression is evaluated at the beginning of the structure. It must return a value (logical, numeric, string, and so on).
CaseList	A list of one or more possible results for *TestExpression*. These results are values or expressions separated by commas. VBA examines each element in the list to see whether one matches the *TestExpression*. The expressions can take any one of the following forms:

Expression

Expression To *Expression*

Is *LogicalOperator Expression*

The To keyword defines a range of values (for example, 1 To 10). The Is keyword defines an open-ended range of values (for example, Is >= 100).

Statements	These are the statements VBA runs if any part of the associated *CaseList* matches the *TestExpression*. VBA runs the optional *ElseStatements* if no *CaseList* contains a match for the *TestExpression*.

Handling Multiple Matches

If more than one *CaseList* contains an element that matches the *TestExpression*, VBA runs only the statements associated with the *CaseList* that appears *first* in the Select Case structure.

Listing 11.8 shows how you would use Select Case to handle the Frequency argument problem.

Listing 11.8   A Procedure That Uses Select Case **to Test Multiple Values**

```
Function FutureValue4(Rate, Nper, Pmt, Frequency)
    Select Case Frequency
        Case "Monthly"
            FutureValue4 = FV(Rate / 12, Nper * 12, Pmt / 12)
        Case "Quarterly"
            FutureValue4 = FV(Rate / 4, Nper * 4, Pmt / 4)
        Case Else
            MsgBox "The Frequency argument must be either " & _
                   """Monthly"" or ""Quarterly""!"
    End Select
End Function
```

Code That Loops

It makes sense to divide up your VBA chores and place them in separate command or function macros. That way, you need to write the code only once and then call it any time you need it. This is known in the trade as *modular programming*; it saves time and effort by helping you avoid reinventing too many wheels.

There are also wheels to avoid reinventing *within* your procedures and functions. For example, consider the following code fragment:

```
MsgBox "The time is now " & Time
Application.Wait Now + TimeValue("00:00:05")
MsgBox "The time is now " & Time
Application.Wait Now + TimeValue("00:00:05")
MsgBox "The time is now " & Time
Application.Wait Now + TimeValue("00:00:05")
```

The Wait Method

This code fragment uses the Excel `Application` object's `Wait` method to produce a delay. The argument `Now +` `TimeValue("00:00:05")` pauses the procedure for about five seconds before continuing.

This code does nothing more than display the time, delay for five seconds, and repeat this two more times. Besides being decidedly useless, this code just reeks of inefficiency. It's clear that a far better approach would be to take the first two statements and somehow get VBA to repeat them as many times as necessary.

The good news is that not only is it possible to do this, but VBA also gives you a number of methods to perform this so-called *looping*. I spend the rest of this chapter investigating each of these methods.

11

Using Do...Loop **Structures**

What do you do when you need to loop but you don't know in advance how many times to repeat the loop? This could happen if, for example, you want to loop only until a certain condition is met, such as encountering a blank cell in an Excel worksheet. The solution is to use a Do...Loop.

The Do...Loop has four syntaxes:

`Do While condition`
    `[statements]`
`Loop`
	Checks *condition* before entering the loop. Executes the *statements* only while *condition* is True.

`Do`
    `[statements]`
`Loop While condition`
	Checks *condition* after running through the loop once. Executes the *statements* only while *condition* is True. Use this form when you want the loop to be processed at least once.

`Do Until condition`
    `[statements]`
`Loop`
	Checks *condition* before entering the loop. Executes the *statements* only while *condition* is False.

`Do`
  `[statements]`
`Loop Until condition`
	Checks *condition* after running through the loop once. Executes the *statements* only while *condition* is False. Again, use this form when you want the loop to be processed at least once.

Listing 11.9 shows a procedure called `BigNumbers` that runs down a worksheet column and changes the font color to magenta whenever a cell contains a number greater than or equal to 1,000.

Listing 11.9   A Procedure That Uses a Do...Loop **to Process Cells Until It Encounters a Blank Cell**

```
Sub BigNumbers()
    Dim rowNum As Integer, colNum As Integer, currCell As Range
    '
    ' Initialize the row and column numbers
    '
    rowNum = ActiveCell.Row
    colNum = ActiveCell.Column
    '
    ' Get the first cell
    '
    Set currCell = ActiveSheet.Cells(rowNum, colNum)
    '
    ' Loop while the current cell isn't empty
    '
    Do While currCell.Value <> ""
        '
        ' Is it a number?
        '
        If IsNumeric(currCell.Value) Then
            '
            ' Is it a big number?
            '
            If currCell.Value >= 1000 Then
                '
                ' If so, color it magenta
                '
                currCell.Font.Color = VBAColor("magenta")
            End If
        End If
        '
        ' Increment the row number and get the next cell
        '
        rowNum = rowNum + 1
        Set currCell = ActiveSheet.Cells(rowNum, colNum)
    Loop
End Sub
```

The idea is to loop until the procedure encounters a blank cell. This is controlled by the following `Do While` statement:

```
Do While currCell.Value <> ""
```

`currCell` is an object variable that is `Set` using the `Cells` method. Next, the first `If...Then` uses the `IsNumeric` function to check if the cell contains a number, and the second `If...Then` checks if the number is greater than or equal to 1,000. If both conditions are `True`, the font color is set to magenta using the `VBAColor` function described earlier in this chapter.

Using `For...Next` **Loops**

The most common type of loop is the `For...Next` loop. Use this loop when you know exactly how many times you want to repeat a group of statements. The structure of a `For...Next` loop looks like this:

```
For counter = start To end [Step increment]
    [statements]
Next [counter]
```

`counter`	A numeric variable used as a *loop counter*. The loop counter is a number that counts how many times the procedure has gone through the loop.
`start`	The initial value of `counter`. This is usually 1, but you can enter any value.
`end`	The final value of `counter`.
`increment`	This optional value defines an increment for the loop counter. If you leave this out, the default value is 1. Use a negative value to decrement `counter`.
`statements`	The statements to execute each time through the loop.

The basic idea is simple. When VBA encounters the `For...Next` statement, it follows this five-step process:

1. Set `counter` equal to `start`.
2. Test `counter`. If it's greater than `end`, exit the loop (that is, process the first statement after the `Next` statement). Otherwise, continue. If `increment` is negative, VBA checks to see whether `counter` is less than `end`.
3. Execute each statement between the `For` and `Next` statements.
4. Add `increment` to `counter`. Add 1 to `counter` if `increment` isn't specified.
5. Repeat steps 2 through 4 until done.

Listing 11.10 shows a simple Subprocedure—`LoopTest`—that uses a `For...Next` statement. Each time through the loop, the procedure uses the `Application` object's `StatusBar` property to display the value of `counter` (the loop counter) in the status bar. When you run this

11

procedure, `counter` gets incremented by 1 each time through the loop, and the new value gets displayed in the status bar.

Listing 11.10   A Simple `For...Next` **Loop**

```
Sub LoopTest()
    Dim counter
    For counter = 1 To 10
        '
        'Display the message
        '
        Application.StatusBar = "Counter value: " & counter
        '
        ' Wait for 1 second
        '
        Application.Wait Now + TimeValue("00:00:01")
    Next counter
    Application.StatusBar = False
End Sub
```

Mimicking the `Wait` Method

The `LoopTest` procedure works fine in Excel, but it will fail in the other Office applications because they don't implement the `Wait` method. If you need to get your code to delay for a short while, here's a simple procedure that does the trick:

```
Sub VBAWait(delay As Integer)
    Dim startTime As Long
    startTime = Timer
    Do While Timer - startTime < delay
        DoEvents
    Loop
End Sub
```

Note the use of the `DoEvents` function inside the `Do While...Loop` structure. This function yields execution to the operating system so that events such as keystrokes and application messages are processed while the procedure delays.

Following are some notes on `For...Next` loops:

- If you use a positive number for *increment* (or if you omit *increment*), *end* must be greater than or equal to *start*. If you use a negative number for *increment*, *end* must be less than or equal to *start*.

- If *start* equals *end*, the loop will execute once.

- As with `If...Then...Else` structures, indent the statements inside a `For...Next` loop for increased readability.

- To keep the number of variables defined in a procedure to a minimum, always try to use the same name for all your `For...Next` loop counters. The letters *i* through *n* traditionally are used for counters in programming. For greater clarity, you might want to use names such as `counter`.

■ For the fastest loops, don't use the counter name after the `Next` statement. If you'd like to keep the counter name for clarity (which I recommend), precede the name with an apostrophe (`'`) to comment out the name, like this:

```
For counter = 1 To 10
    [statements]
Next 'counter
```

■ If you need to break out of a `For...Next` loop before the defined number of repetitions is completed, use the `Exit For` statement, described in the later section "Using `Exit For` or `Exit Do` to Exit a Loop."

Using `For Each...Next` Loops

A useful variation of the `For...Next` loop is the `For Each...Next` loop, which operates on a collection of objects. You don't need a loop counter because VBA just loops through the individual elements in the collection and performs on each element whatever operations are inside the loop. Here's the structure of the basic `For Each...Next` loop:

```
For Each element In group
    [statements]
Next [element]
```

element	A variable used to hold the name of each element in the collection.
group	The name of the collection.
statements	The statements to be executed for each element in the collection.

As an example, let's create a command procedure that converts a range of text into proper case (that is, the first letter of each word is capitalized). This function can come in handy if you import mainframe text into your worksheets, because mainframe reports usually appear entirely in uppercase. This process involves three steps:

1. Loop through the selected range with `For Each...Next`.
2. Convert each cell's text to proper case. Use Excel's `PROPER()` function to handle this:

   ```
   PROPER(text)
   ```

text	The text to convert to proper case.

3. Enter the converted text into the selected cell. This is the job of the `Range` object's `Formula` method:

   ```
   object.Formula = Expression
   ```

object	The `Range` object in which you want to enter *Expression*.
Expression	The data you want to enter into object.

Listing 11.11 shows the resulting procedure, `ConvertToProper`. Note that this procedure uses the `Selection` object to represent the currently selected range.

Listing 11.11   A Subprocedure That Uses For Each...Next **to Loop Through a Selection and Convert Each Cell to Proper Text**

```
Sub ConvertToProper()
    Dim cellObject As Object
    For Each cellObject In Selection
        cellObject.Formula = Application.Proper(cellObject)
    Next
End Sub
```

Using Exit For or Exit Do to Exit a Loop

Most loops run their natural course and then the procedure moves on. There might be times, however, when you want to exit a loop prematurely. For example, you might come across a certain type of cell, or an error might occur, or the user might enter an unexpected value. To exit a For...Next loop or a For Each...Next loop, use the Exit For statement. To exit a Do...Loop, use the Exit Do statement.

Listing 11.12 shows a revised version of the BigNumbers procedure, which exits the Do...Loop if it comes across a cell that isn't a number.

Listing 11.12   In This Version of the BigNumbers **Procedure, the** Do...Loop **Is Terminated with the** Exit Do **Statement If the Current Cell Isn't a Number**

```
Sub BigNumbers2()
    Dim rowNum As Integer, colNum As Integer, currCell As Range
    '
    ' Initialize the row and column numbers
    '
    rowNum = ActiveCell.Row
    colNum = ActiveCell.Column
    '
    ' Get the first cell
    '
    Set currCell = ActiveSheet.Cells(rowNum, colNum)
    '
    ' Loop while the current cell isn't empty
    '
    Do While currCell.Value <> ""
        '
        ' Is it a number?
        '
        If IsNumeric(currCell.Value) Then
            '
            ' Is it a big number?
            '
            If currCell.Value >= 1000 Then
                '
                ' If so, color it magenta
                '
                currCell.Font.Color = VBAColor("magenta")
            End If
            '
```

```
        ' Otherwise, exit the loop
        '
        Else
            Exit Do
        End If
        '
        ' Increment the row number and get the next cell
        '
        rowNum = rowNum + 1
        Set currCell = ActiveSheet.Cells(rowNum, colNum)
    Loop
End Sub
```

From Here

- For lots of examples of command and function macros, see Chapter 12, "Putting VBA to Good Use: Practical Macros Everyone Can Use."

- You can combine repetitive or complex Access tasks into another kind of macro. To learn how, see Chapter 13, "Taking Advantage of Access Macros."

- For the details on using macros securely, in Chapter 14, see the section titled "Controlling VBA Security."

Putting VBA to Good Use: Practical Macros Everyone Can Use

12

Learning VBA, or any programming language for that matter, is always easiest when the concepts are buttressed by examples that are both numerous *and* useful. Having lots of good examples to study enables you to immerse yourself in the language and see how things work first-hand. It's a lot like learning a human language: Classroom theory and practice will get you only so far; to really learn the tongue, you have to converse with native speakers all day long.

This book isn't designed to teach you VBA, but it *is* designed to offer you techniques both numerous and useful that will help you get the most out of Office and get your work done faster and more efficiently. VBA can be a big help here because you can use it to perform tasks that by hand would be inordinately time-consuming or even downright impossible. As proof, this chapter presents a bunch of VBA macros for Word, Excel, and Outlook. These procedures show you many techniques for programming these applications, but, more importantly, I chose the macros because they're all truly useful and time-saving. So even if you have no desire to learn VBA, you can still implement these macros on your own system to work faster and more efficiently.

Word Macros

This section takes you through a few useful macros that you can use when working with Word documents.

Saving Frequently

Word enables you to save AutoRecovery info at specified intervals (select Tools, Options, Save and set the number of minutes using the Save AutoRecovery Info Every spin box). However, the shortest interval is one minute, and fast writers could still lose work. If you want a way to automatically save your work at a faster interval, use Word's handy OnTime method, which enables you to run a procedure at a specified time. Here's the syntax:

```
Application.OnTime(When, Name [, Tolerance])
```

When | The time (and date, if necessary) you want the procedure to run. Enter a date/time serial number.

Name | The name (entered as text) of the procedure to run when the time given by When arrives.

Tolerance | If Word isn't ready to run the procedure at When, it will keep trying for the number of seconds specified by Tolerance. If you omit Tolerance, VBA waits until Word is ready.

The easiest way to enter a time serial number for When is to use the TimeValue function:

```
TimeValue(Time)
```

Time | A string representing the time you want to use (such as "5:00PM" or "17:00").

For example, the following code runs a procedure called MakeBackup at 5:00 p.m.:

```
Application.OnTime _
    When:=TimeValue("5:00PM"), _
    Name:="MakeBackup"
```

If you want the OnTime method to run after a specified time interval (for example, an hour from now), use Now + TimeValue(Time) for When (where Time is the interval you want to use). For example, if you want to save your work every 10 seconds, use the OnTime method as shown in Listing 12.1.

This Chapter's Examples

You'll find the Word and Excel files used as examples in this chapter on my website at www.mcfedries.com/OfficeGurus.

Listing 12.1   A Macro That Saves the Active Document Every 10 Seconds

```
Public Sub FileSave()
    ActiveDocument.Save
    DoEvents
    Application.OnTime _
        When:=Now + TimeValue("00:00:10"), _
        name:="FileSave"
    Application.StatusBar = "Saved: " & ActiveDocument.name
End Sub
```

The `FileSave` procedure saves the current document by running the `Save` method on the `ActiveDocument` object. The `DoEvents` method processes any keystrokes that occurred during the save, and then the `OnTime` method sets up the `FileSave` procedure to run again in 10 seconds. To remind you that the procedure is on the job, the procedure closes by displaying a message in the status bar.

Giving a Macro the Same Name as a Word Command

`FileSave` is also the internal name of Word's File, Save command. By giving your procedure the same name (and procedure the `Sub` keyword with `Public` to make it available to all documents), you intercept any calls to the Save command and replace Word's internal procedure with your own. This isn't strictly necessary, but it's handy because it means that your procedure will run as soon as the File, Save command is chosen.

To find out the internal names of Word's commands, select View, Toolbars, Customize, and then click Keyboard to display the Customize Keyboard dialog box. Select an item in the Categories list and then look up the internal command name in the Commands list. Alternatively, hold down Ctrl and Alt, press the + key on your numeric keypad, and then either click the toolbar button or select the menu command associated with the command you want to use. Word displays the Customize Keyboard dialog box with only the selected command displayed.

Making Backups as You Work

We've all learned from hard experience not only to save our work regularly, but also to make periodic backup copies. The macro I use most often in Word is one that does both in a single procedure! That is, the macro not only saves your work, but it also makes a backup copy on another drive, such as a removable disk, a second hard drive, or a network folder. Listing 12.2 shows the code.

Listing 12.2 A Procedure That Creates a Backup Copy of the Active Document on Another Drive

```
Sub MakeBackup()
    Dim currFile As String
    Dim backupFile As String
    Const BACKUP_FOLDER = "A:\"
    With ActiveDocument
        '
        ' Don't bother if the document is unchanged or new
        '
        If .Saved Or .Path = "" Then Exit Sub
        '
        ' Mark current position in document
        '
        .Bookmarks.Add Name:="LastPosition"
        '
        ' Turn off screen updating
        '
        Application.ScreenUpdating = False
        '
```

continues

Listing 12.2   Continued

```
            ' Save the file
            '
            .Save
            '
            ' Store the current file path, construct the path for the
            ' backup file, and then save it to the backup drive
            '
            currFile = .FullName
            backupFile = BACKUP_FOLDER + .Name
            .SaveAs FileName:=backupFile
    End With
    '
    ' Close the backup copy (which is now active)
    '
    ActiveDocument.Close
    '
    ' Reopen the current file
    '
    Documents.Open FileName:=currFile
    '
    ' Return to pre-backup position
    '
    Selection.GoTo What:=wdGoToBookmark, Name:="LastPosition"
End Sub
```

The backupFile and currFile variables are strings that store the full pathnames for the active document and the backup version of the document. Use the BACKUP_FOLDER constant to specify the folder in which you want the backup stored.

The procedures first check to see if the backup operation is necessary. In other words, if the document has no unsaved changes (the Saved property returns True) or if it's a new, unsaved document (the Path property returns ""), bail out of the procedure (by running Exit Sub).

Otherwise, a new Bookmark object is created to save the current position in the document, screen updating is turned off, and the file is saved.

We're now ready to perform the backup. First, the currFile variable is used to stored the full pathname of the document, and the pathname of the backup file is built with the following statement:

```
backupFile = BACKUP_FOLDER + .Name
```

This will be used to save the file to the specified folder. The actual backup takes place via the SaveAs method, which saves the document to the path given by backupFile. From there, the procedure closes the backup file, reopens the original file, and uses the GoTo method to return to the original position within the document.

Returning to the Last Edited Position

Using a `Bookmark` object to reset the insertion point is useful because it takes you back to the exact point in the document where you were before the backup started. However, you may be interested only in returning to the last position within the document where an edit occurred. If that's the case, use the following statement in place of the `Selection.GoTo` statement:

```
Application.GoBack
```

Note, however, that there's a bug in the `GoBack` method whereby Word doesn't save the last edit position (technically, it's a hidden bookmark named `\PrevSel1`) in some cases. Specifically, when you exit Word, if you elect to save changes in the last document that gets closed, Word doesn't save the last edit position in that document.

Opening the Most Recently Used Document at Startup

Word's `RecentFiles` object represents the collection of most-recently used files displayed near the bottom of Word's File menu. Each item on this list is a `RecentFile` object. You specify a `RecentFile` object by using `RecentFiles(Index)`, where `Index` is an integer that specifies the file you want to work with. The most-recently used file is 1, the second most-recently used file is 2, and so on.

It would be handy to have Word open the most-recently used file each time you start the program. If you want Word to run some code each time it's started, open the Normal project in the VBA Editor's Project Explorer and then create a new module name `AutoExec`. In this module, create a `Sub` procedure named `Main` and enter your code in that procedure. Listing 12.3 shows such a procedure:

Listing 12.3   A Procedure That Opens the Most-Recently Used Document

```
Sub Main()
    With RecentFiles(1)
        Documents.Open .Path & "\" & .Name
    End With
End Sub
```

12

Creating and Opening a Word Workspace

In Excel, you can define a *workspace* of files. When you then open that workspace, Excel opens all the files at once. If you often work with two or more files as a group, you can use VBA to create your own workspace functionality. Listing 12.4 shows two procedures that act as a workspace function for Word:

- `CreateWorkspace`—This procedure uses the Windows Registry to store a list of open documents. Before running this procedure, make sure that only those files you want to include in the workspace are currently open.

- `OpenWorkspace`—This procedure accesses the Registry and runs through the list of saved files. For each setting, the procedure checks to see if the file is already open. If it's not, the procedure runs the `Documents.Open` method to open the file.

Listing 12.4   Procedures That Create and Open a Workspace of Files

```
' CreateWorkspace()
' Saves the path and filename data of all the
' open files to the Windows Registry. Before
' running this procedure, make sure only the
' files you want in the workspace are open.
'
Sub CreateWorkspace()
    Dim total As Integer
    Dim doc As Document
    Dim i As Integer
    '
    ' Delete the old workspace Registry settings
    ' First, get the total number of files
    '
    total = GetSetting("Word", "Workspace", "TotalFiles", 0)
    For i = 1 To total
        '
        ' Delete each Registry setting
        '
        DeleteSetting "Word", "Workspace", "Document" & i
    Next 'i
    '
    ' Create the new workspace
    '
    i = 0
    For Each doc In Documents
        '
        ' Make sure it's not a new, unsaved file
        '
        If doc.Path <> "" then
            '
            ' Use i to create unique Registry setting names
            '
            i = i + 1
            '
            ' Save the FullName (path and filename) to the Registry
            '
            SaveSetting "Word", "Workspace", "Document" & i, doc.FullName
        End If
    Next 'doc
    '
    ' Save the total number of files to the Registry
    '
    SaveSetting "Word", "Workspace", "TotalFiles", i
End Sub
'
' OpenWorkspace()
' Accesses the Registry's workspace settings
' and then opens each workspace file.
'
Sub OpenWorkspace()
    Dim total As Integer
    Dim i As Integer
```

```
    Dim filePath As String
    Dim doc As Document
    Dim fileAlreadyOpen As Boolean
    '
    ' Get the total number of files from the Registry
    '
    total = GetSetting("Word", "Workspace", "TotalFiles", 0)
    For i = 1 To total
        '
        ' Get the path and filename
        '
        filePath = GetSetting("Word", "Workspace", "Document" & i)
        '
        ' Make sure the file isn't already open
        '
        fileAlreadyOpen = False
        For Each doc In Documents
            If filePath = doc.FullName Then
                fileAlreadyOpen = True
                Exit For
            End If
        Next 'doc
        '
        ' Open it
        '
        If Not fileAlreadyOpen Then
            Documents.Open filePath
        End If
    Next 'i
End Sub
```

Add the Workspace Macros to the Menus

For easy access to the workspace macros, add them to one of your Word menus. I use the Work menu, which I discussed in the Chapter 10 section "Getting Easy Document Access with Word's Work Menu."

Displaying Sentence Word Counts

When you grammar check a document, you can elect to display the document's readability statistics. (Select Tools, Options, Spelling & Grammar, and activate the Show Readability Statistics check box.) Among other values, the Readability Statistics dialog box offers the average number of words per sentence. This is useful because you don't want your average sentence to be too long or too short. However, writing gurus also stress that you should have a variety of sentence lengths in your prose, with some shorter and longer sentences thrown in for reading variety. Unfortunately, the Readability Statistics dialog box doesn't tell you the lengths of your sentences, but it's easy enough to get a VBA macro to do it for you, as shown in Listing 12.5.

12

Listing 12.5   A Macro That Displays the Lengths of Sentences in the Active Document

```
Sub DisplaySentenceLengths()
    Dim s As Range
    Dim maxWords As Integer
    Dim i As Integer
    Dim sentenceLengths() As Integer
    Dim str As String

    With ActiveDocument
        '
        ' Run through all the sentences to find the longest
        '
        maxWords = 0
        For Each s In .Sentences
            If s.Words.Count > maxWords Then
                maxWords = s.Words.Count
            End If
        Next 's
        '
        ' Redimension the array of sentence lengths
        '
        ReDim sentenceLengths(maxWords)
        '
        ' Run through the sentences again to count
        ' the number of sentences for each length
        '
        For Each s In .Sentences
            sentenceLengths(s.Words.Count - 1) = sentenceLengths(s.Words
➥.Count - 1) + 1
        Next 's
        '
        ' Construct the string that displays the sentence lengths
        ' and their frequencies
        '
        str = "Sentence Length:" & vbTab & "Frequency:" & vbCrLf & vbCrLf
        '
        ' The UBound() function tells you the upper bound of an array.
        ' In this case, it tells us the largest value in sentenceLengths.
        '
        For i = 0 To UBound(sentenceLengths) - 1
            '
            ' The code below uses the IIf() function, which is similar to
            ' the If...End If structure from Chapter 12.
            ' Also, vbTab represents a Tab character and
            ' vbCrLf represents a Control/Line Feed character.
            '
            str = str & IIf(i + 1 < 10, "  ", "") & i + 1 & _
                IIf(i = 0, " word:  ", " words: ") & _
                vbTab & sentenceLengths(i) & vbCrLf
        Next 'i
        '
        ' Display the string
        '
        MsgBox str
    End With
End Sub
```

Using the `ActiveDocument` object, the macro makes a first pass through all the sentences to find the one with the most words. The macro then uses this maximum word count to redimension the `sentenceLengths` array, which is used to hold the number of occurrences of each sentence length within the document. To calculate these frequencies, the macro then runs through all the sentences again and increments the array values for each length. The macro finishes by constructing and then displaying a string that holds the sentence lengths and frequencies. Figure 12.1 shows an example.

Figure 12.1

The `DisplaySentence Lengths` macro displays a message box such as this to show you the document's sentence lengths and the frequency with which each length occurs.

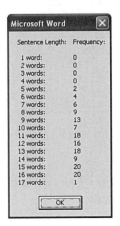

Sentence Length:	Frequency:
1 word:	0
2 words:	0
3 words:	0
4 words:	0
5 words:	2
6 words:	4
7 words:	6
8 words:	9
9 words:	13
10 words:	7
11 words:	18
12 words:	16
13 words:	18
14 words:	9
15 words:	20
16 words:	20
17 words:	1

Displaying Paragraph Word Counts

If you're also interested in displaying data for each paragraph, replace `.Sentences` in Listing 12.5 with `.Paragraphs`. Because the variable `s` is a `Range` object, you can work with either the words in each paragraph—`s.Words.Count`—or the sentences in each paragraph—`s.Sentences.Count`.

Finding the Longest Sentence

One of the hallmarks of good business writing is that it's succinct and to the point: no digressions, minimal adjectives and adverbs, and no run-on sentences. If you use the code in Listing 12.5 to study the sentence lengths of your document, you may find one sentence that's quite a bit longer than the others. For example, all your sentences might be fewer than 25 words, but there may be one that's 50 words. That one sentence is obviously far too long, and the problem may be mistaken punctuation (such as a comma instead of a period) or a too-long sentence that needs to be broken up into two or three smaller sentences. Either way, you need to find the problem sentence, and the code in Listing 12.6 does just that.

12

Listing 12.6   Finding the Longest Sentence in a Document

```vba
Sub FindLongestSentence()
    Dim s As Range
    Dim maxWords As Integer
    Dim longestSentence As String

    With ActiveDocument
        '
        ' Run through all the sentences to find the longest
        '
        maxWords = 0
        For Each s In .Sentences
            If s.Words.Count > maxWords Then
                maxWords = s.Words.Count
                longestSentence = s.Text
            End If
        Next 's
        '
        ' Move to the top of the document
        '
        Selection.HomeKey Unit:=wdStory
        '
        ' Set up the Find object
        '
        With Selection.Find
            '
            ' Clear Find object formatting
            '
            .ClearFormatting
            '
            ' Check the length of the sentence
            '
            If Len(longestSentence) <= 256 Then
                '
                ' The length of the sentence is okay,
                ' so go ahead and find the text.
                '
                .Text = longestSentence
                .Execute
            Else
                ' The sentence is too long for the Text
                ' property, so find just the first 256 characters
                '
                .Text = Left(longestSentence, 256)
                .Execute
                '
                ' Extend the selection to the entire sentence
                '
                Selection.MoveEnd Unit:=wdSentence
            End If
        End With
        '
        ' Display a message
        '
```

```
        MsgBox "The selected sentence is the longest in the document " & _
                "at " & maxWords & " words."
    End With
End Sub
```

As in Listing 12.5, the `FindLongestSentence` macro runs through the active document's sentences to find the longest one. In this case, however, the macro stores not only the length of the longest sentence, but its text, as well. The macro then uses this text to locate the sentence using the `Find` object. Note, however, that the `Find` object's `Text` property can accept only up to 256 characters. Because a long sentence can easily have more characters than that, the macro checks the length of the sentence: if it's too long, the `Find` object is set up to look for only the first 256 characters in the sentence.

Toggling Hidden Codes and Text

 When you click the Show/Hide button, Word displays symbols that represent hidden "characters" such as tabs, spaces, paragraph marks, and optional hyphens, as well as any text formatted as hidden. This is handy for looking "under the hood" of the document. However, a thorough check of a document's inner workings should also include other normally hidden items: bookmarks, comments, revisions, and field codes. You can toggle all of these by hand individually, but if you need to do this often, the procedure in Listing 12.7 is much easier.

Listing 12.7 Toggling Hidden Codes and Text

```
Public Sub ShowAll()
    Dim currentState As Boolean
    With ActiveWindow.View
        currentState = .ShowBookmarks
        .ShowBookmarks = Not currentState
        .ShowComments = Not currentState
        .ShowFieldCodes = Not currentState
        .ShowHiddenText = Not currentState
        .ShowHyphens = Not currentState
        .ShowOptionalBreaks = Not currentState
        .ShowParagraphs = Not currentState
        .ShowRevisionsAndComments = Not currentState
        .ShowSpaces = Not currentState
        .ShowTabs = Not currentState
        .Type = wdNormalView
    End With
End Sub
```

The procedure is named `ShowAll`, which is the internal name of the command that Word runs when you click the Show/Hide button. Therefore, clicking Show/Hide will then run the `ShowAll` procedure. Using the active window's `View` object, the program first checks the current state of the `ShowBookmarks` property and stores the state in the `currentState` variable. Then each of the `View` properties is set to the opposite value. Figure 12.2 and 12.3 show the two states produced by the procedure.

12

Figure 12.2
The document view with the hidden codes and text turned off.

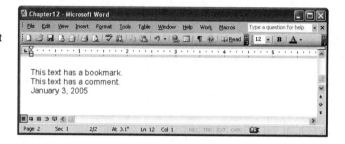

Figure 12.3
The document view with the hidden codes and text turned on.

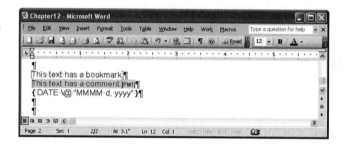

Excel Macros

This section takes you through a few useful macros that you can use when working with Excel worksheets.

Assigning Shortcut Keys to Excel Macros

Before getting to some specific procedures, let's take a brief side trip to discuss assigning shortcut keys to Excel macros. The easiest way to assign a shortcut key to an existing macro (or change a macro's current shortcut key) is to follow these steps:

1. Select Tools, Macro, Macros (or press Alt+F8) to display the Macro dialog box.

2. Select the macro you want to work with.

3. Click Options to display the Macro Options dialog box shown in Figure 12.4.

Figure 12.4
Use the Macro Options dialog box to assign a shortcut key to a macro.

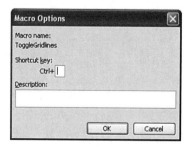

4. In the Shortcut Key Ctrl+ text box, type the letter you want to use with Ctrl for the key combination. For example, if you type **e**, you can run the macro by pressing Ctrl+E.

Excel Shortcuts Are Case Sensitive

Excel shortcut keys are case sensitive, meaning you can create separate shortcuts with uppercase and lowercase letters. For example, if you type **e** into the Ctrl+ text box, you would have to press Ctrl+E to run the macro. However, if you type **E** into the Ctrl+ text box, you would have to press Ctrl+Shift+E to run the macro.

---

5. Click OK to return to the Macro dialog box.

6. Click Cancel.

Avoid Shortcut Key Conflicts

Make sure you don't specify a shortcut key that conflicts with Excel's built-in shortcuts (such as Ctrl+B for Bold or Ctrl+C for Copy). If you use a key that clashes with an Excel shortcut, Excel will override its own shortcut and run your macro instead (provided that the workbook containing the macro is open).

There are only five letters not assigned to Excel commands that you can use with your macros: e, j, m, q, and t. You can get extra shortcut keys by using uppercase letters. For example, Excel differentiates between Ctrl+b and Ctrl+B (or, more explicitly, Ctrl+Shift+b). Note, however, that Excel uses four built-in Ctrl+Shift shortcuts: A, F, O, P.

There are two major drawbacks to assigning Ctrl+*key* combinations to your Excel macros:

- Excel uses some Ctrl+*key* combinations for its own use (such as Ctrl+O for Open and Ctrl+G for Go To), which limits the key combinations that you can use.

- It doesn't help if you would like your procedures to respond to "meaningful" keys such as Delete and Esc.

To remedy these problems, use the `Application` object's `OnKey` method to run a procedure when the user presses a specific key or key combination:

```
Application.OnKey(Key, Procedure)
```

Key	The key or key combination that runs the procedure. For letters, numbers, or punctuation marks, enclose the character in quotes (for example, `"a"`). For other keys, see Table 12.1.
Procedure	The name (entered as text) of the procedure to run when the user presses a key. If you enter the null string (`""`) for *Procedure*, a key is disabled. If you omit *Procedure*, Excel resets the key to its normal state.

12

Table 12.1 Key Strings to Use with the OnKey **Method**

Key	What to Use
Backspace	"{BACKSPACE}" or "{BS}"
Break	"{BREAK}"
Caps Lock	"{CAPSLOCK}"
Delete	"{DELETE}" or "{DEL}"
Down arrow	"{DOWN}"
End	"{END}"
Enter (keypad)	"{ENTER}"
Enter	"~" (tilde)
Esc	"{ESCAPE}" or "{ESC}"
F1 through F12	"{F1}" through "{F15}"
Help	"{HELP}"
Home	"{HOME}"
Insert	"{INSERT}"
Left arrow	"{LEFT}"
Num Lock	"{NUMLOCK}"
Page Down	"{PGDN}"
Page Up	"{PGUP}"
Right arrow	"{RIGHT}"
Scroll Lock	"{SCROLLLOCK}"
Tab	"{TAB}"
Up arrow	"{UP}"

You also can combine these keys with the Shift, Ctrl, and Alt keys. You just precede these codes with one or more of the codes listed in Table 12.2.

Table 12.2 Symbols That Represent Alt, Ctrl, and Shift in OnKey

Key	What to Use
Alt	% (percent)
Ctrl	^ (caret)
Shift	+ (plus)

For example, pressing Delete normally wipes out a cell's contents only. If you would like a quick way of deleting everything in a cell (contents, formats, comments, and so on), you could set up (for example) Ctrl+Delete to do the job. Listing 12.8 shows three procedures that accomplish this:

- `SetKey`—This procedure sets up the Ctrl+Delete key combination to run the `DeleteAll` procedure. Notice how the *Procedure* argument includes the name of the workbook; therefore, this key combination will operate in any workbook.

- `DeleteAll`—This procedure runs the `Clear` method on the current selection.

- `ResetKey`—This procedure resets Ctrl+Delete to its default behavior.

Listing 12.8   Procedures That Set and Reset a Key Combination Using the `OnKey` Method

```
Sub SetKey()
    Application.OnKey _
        Key:="^{Del}", _
        Procedure:="Chapter12.xls!DeleteAll"
End Sub

Sub DeleteAll()
    Selection.Clear
End Sub

Sub ResetKey()
    Application.OnKey _
        Key:="^{Del}"
End Sub
```

Toggling Gridlines On and Off

If you find yourself regularly turning gridlines off and then back on for a particular window, it's a hassle to be constantly opening the Options dialog box to do this. For faster service, use the macro in Listing 12.9 and assign it to a toolbar button or keyboard shortcut.

Listing 12.9   A Macro That Toggles Gridlines On and Off

```
Sub ToggleGridlines()
    With ActiveWindow
        .DisplayGridlines = Not .DisplayGridlines
    End With
End Sub
```

Creating a Workbook with a Specified Number of Sheets

By default, Excel provides you with three worksheets in each new workbook. You can change the default number of sheets by selecting Tools, Options, displaying the General tab, and then adjusting the Sheets in New Workbook value. However, what if you want more control over the number of sheets in each new workbook? For example, a simple loan amortization model might require just a single worksheet, whereas a company budget workbook might require a dozen worksheets.

The macro in Listing 12.10 solves this problem by enabling you to specify the number of sheets you want in each new workbook.

Listing 12.10   A Macro That Creates a New Workbook with a Specified Number of Worksheets

```
Sub NewWorkbookWithCustomSheets()
    Dim currentSheets As Integer
    With Application
        currentSheets = .SheetsInNewWorkbook
        .SheetsInNewWorkbook = InputBox("How many sheets do you want
➥in the new workbook?", , 3)
        Workbooks.Add
        .SheetsInNewWorkbook = currentSheets
    End With
End Sub
```

The value of the Sheets in New Workbook setting is given by the `Application` object's `SheetsInNewWorkbook` property. The macro first stores the current `SheetsInNewWorkbook` value in the `currentSheets` variable. Then the macro runs the `InputBox` function to get the number of required sheets (with a default value of 3), and this value is assigned to the `SheetsInNewWorkbook` property. Then the `Workbooks.Add` statement creates a new workbook (which will have the specified number of sheets) and the `SheetsInNewWorkbook` property is returned to its original value.

Automatically Sorting a Range After Data Entry

If you have a sorted range, you might find that the range requires resorting after data entry because the values on which the sort is based have changed. Rather than constantly invoking the Sort command, you can set up a macro that sorts the range automatically every time the relevant data changes.

As an example, consider the simple parts database shown in Figure 12.5. The range is sorted on the Gross Margin column (H), the values of which are determined using a formula that requires input from cells in columns E and G. In other words, each time a value in column E or G changes, the corresponding Gross Margin value changes. We want to keep the list sorted based on these changes.

Listing 12.11 shows a couple of macros that serve to keep the range sorted automatically.

Listing 12.11   Two Macros That Keep the Parts Database Sorted Automatically

```
Sub Auto_Open()
    ThisWorkbook.Worksheets("Parts").OnEntry = "SortParts"
End Sub

Sub SortParts()
    Dim currCell As Range
    Set currCell = Application.Caller
    If currCell.Column = 5 Or currCell.Column = 7 Then
        Selection.Sort Key1:=Range("H1"), _
```

```
                    Order1:=xlDescending, _
                    Header:=xlYes, _
                    OrderCustom:=1, _
                    MatchCase:=False, _
                    Orientation:=xlTopToBottom

        End If
End Sub
```

Figure 12.5
The parts database range is sorted on the Gross Margin column (H).

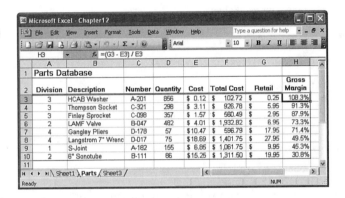

Auto_Open is a macro that runs automatically when the workbook containing the code is opened. In this case, the statement sets the OnEntry event of the Parts worksheet to run the SortParts macro. The OnEntry event fires whenever data entry occurs in the specified object (in this case, the Parts worksheet).

The SortParts macro begins by examining the value of the Application object's Caller property, which returns a Range object that indicates which cell invoked the SortParts macro. In this context, Caller tells us in which cell the data entry occurred, and that cell address is stored in the currCell variable. Next, the macro checks currCell to see if the data entry occurred in either column E or column G. If so, the new value changes the calculated value in the Gross Margin column, so the range needs to be resorted. This is accomplished by running the Sort method, which sorts the range based on the values in column H.

Selecting A1 on All Worksheets

When you open an Excel file that you've worked on before, the cells or ranges that were selected in each worksheet when the file was last saved remain selected upon opening. This is handy behavior because it often enables you to resume work where you left off previously. However, when you've completed work on an Excel file, you may prefer to remove all the selections. For example, you might run through each worksheet and select cell A1 so that you or anyone else opening the file can start "fresh."

Selecting all the A1 cells manually is fine if the workbook has only a few sheets, but it can be a pain in a workbook that contains many sheets. Listing 12.12 presents a macro that selects cell A1 in all of a workbook's sheets.

Listing 12.12   A Macro That Selects Cell A1 on All the Sheets in the Active Workbook

```
Sub SelectA1OnAllSheets()
    Dim ws As Worksheet
    '
    ' Run through all the worksheets in the active workbook
    '
    For Each ws In ActiveWorkbook.Worksheets
        '
        ' Activate the worksheet
        '
        ws.Activate
        '
        ' Select cell A1
        '
        ws.[A1].Select
    Next 'ws
    '
    ' Activate the first worksheet
    '
    ActiveWorkbook.Worksheets(1).Activate
End Sub
```

The macro runs through all the worksheets in the active workbook. In each case, the work-sheet is first activated (you must activate a sheet before you can select anything on it), and then the Select method is called to select cell A1. The macro finishes by activating the first worksheet.

Selecting the "Home Cell" on All Worksheets

Many worksheets have a "natural" starting point, which could be a model's first data entry cell or a cell that displays a key result. In such a case, rather than selecting cell A1 on all the worksheets, you might prefer to select each of these "home cells."

One way to do this is to add a uniform comment to each home cell. For example, you could add the comment Home Cell. Having done that, you can then use the macro in Listing 12.13 to select all these home cells.

Listing 12.13   A Macro That Selects the "Home Cell" on All the Sheets in the Active Workbook

```
Sub SelectHomeCells()
    Dim ws As Worksheet
    Dim c As Comment
    Dim r As Range
    '
    ' Run through all the worksheets in the active workbook
    '
    For Each ws In ActiveWorkbook.Worksheets
        '
        ' Activate the worksheet
        '
        ws.Activate
        '
```

```
        ' Run through the comments
        '
        For Each c In ws.Comments
            '
            ' Look for the "Home Cell" comment
            '
            If InStr(c.Text, "Home Cell") <> 0 Then
                '
                ' Store the cell as a Range
                '
                Set r = c.Parent
                '
                ' Select the cell
                '
                r.Select
            End If
        Next 'c
    Next 'ws
    '
    ' Activate the first worksheet
    '
    ActiveWorkbook.Worksheets(1).Activate
End Sub
```

The `SelectHomeCells` procedure is similar to the `SelectA1OnAllSheets` procedure from
Listing 12.12. That is, the main loop runs through all the sheets in the active workbook and
activates each worksheet in turn. In this case, however, another loop runs through each
worksheet's `Comments` collection. The `Text` property of each `Comment` object is checked to see
if it includes the phrase `Home Cell`. If so, the cell containing the comment is stored in the `r`
variable (using the `Comment` object's `Parent` property) and then the cell is selected.

Selecting the Named Range That Contains the Active Cell

It's often handy to be able to select the name range that contains the current cell (for example, to change the range formatting). If you know the name of the range, you need only
select it from the Name box. However, in a large model or a workbook that you're not
familiar with, it may not be obvious which name to choose. Listing 12.14 shows a function
and procedure that will handle this chore for you.

**Listing 12.14   A Function and Procedure That Determine and Select the Named Range
Containing the Active Cell**

```
Function GetRangeName(r As Range) As String
    Dim n As Name
    Dim rtr As Range
    Dim ir As Range
    '
    ' Run through all the range names in the active workbook
    '
    For Each n In ActiveWorkbook.Names
        '
```

continues

Listing 12.14   Continued

```
            ' Get the name's range
            '
            Set rtr = n.RefersToRange
            '
            ' See if the named range and the active cell's range intersect
            '
            Set ir = Application.Intersect(r, rtr)
            If Not ir Is Nothing Then
                '
                ' If they intersect, then the active cell is part of a
                ' named range, so get the name and exit the function
                GetRangeName = n.Name
                Exit Function
            End If
        Next 'n
        '
        ' If we get this far, the active cell is not part of a named range,
        ' so return the null string
        '
        GetRangeName = ""
End Function

Sub SelectCurrentNamedRange()
    Dim r As Range
    Dim strName As String
        '
        ' Store the active cell
        '
        Set r = ActiveCell
        '
        ' Get the name of the range that contains the cell, if any
        '
        strName = GetRangeName(r)
        If strName <> "" Then
            '
            ' If the cell is part of a named range, select the range
            '
            Range(strName).Select
        End If
End Sub
```

The heart of Listing 12.14 is the GetRangeName function, which takes a range as an argument. The purpose of this function is to see whether the passed range—r—is part of a named range and if so, to return the name of that range. The function's main loop runs through each item in the active workbook's Names collection. For each name, the RefersToRange property returns the associated range, which the function stores in the rtr variable. The function then uses the Intersect method to see if the ranges r and rtr intersect. If they do, it means that r is part of the named range (because, in this case, r is just a single cell), so GetRangeName returns the range name. If no intersection is found for any name, the function returns the null string (""), instead.

The `SelectCurrentNamedRange` procedure makes use of the `GetRangeName` function. The procedure stores the active cell in the `r` variable and then passes that variable to the `GetRangeName` function. If the return value is not the null string, the procedure selects the returned range name.

Saving All Open Workbooks

In Word, if you hold down Shift and then drop down the File menu, the Save command changes to Save All; selecting this command saves all the open documents. Unfortunately, this very useful feature isn't available in Excel. Listing 12.15 presents a macro named `SaveAll` that duplicates Word's Save All command.

Listing 12.15   A Macro That Saves All Open Workbooks

```
Sub SaveAll()
    Dim wb As Workbook
    Dim newFilename As Variant
    '
    ' Run through all the open workbooks
    '
    For Each wb In Workbooks
        '
        ' Has the workbook been saved before?
        '
        If wb.Path <> "" Then
            '
            ' If so, save it
            '
            wb.Save
        Else
            '
            ' If not, display the Save As dialog box
            ' to get a path and filename for the workbook
            '
            newFilename = Application.GetSaveAsFilename(FileFilter:= _
                        "Microsoft Office Excel Workbook (*.xls), *.xls")
            '
            ' Did the user click Cancel?
            '
            If newFilename <> False Then
                '
                ' If not, save the workbook using the
                ' specified path and filename
                '
                wb.SaveAs fileName:=newFilename
            End If
        End If
    Next 'wb
End Sub
```

The main loop in the `SaveAll` macro runs through all the open workbooks. For each workbook, the loop first checks the `Path` property to see if it returns the null string (""). If not, it means the workbook has been saved previously, so the macro runs the Save method to save the file. If Path does return the null string, it means we're saving the workbook for the first time. In this case, the macro runs the GetSaveAsFilename method. It displays the Save As dialog box so that the user can select a save location and filename, which are stored in the newFilename variable. If this variable's value is False, it means the user clicked Cancel in the Save As dialog box, so the macro skips the file; otherwise, the macro saves the workbook using the specified path and filename.

Outlook Macros

The rest of this chapter presents a selection of macros for automating tasks in Outlook.

Creating Advanced Rules for Handling Incoming Messages

Outlook's Rules Wizard is a powerful tool for processing incoming messages, but it has some unfortunate limitations. Here are two examples:

→ To learn how to use the Rules Wizard, see "Using Rules to Process Messages Automatically," p. 190

- Suppose you create a rule where you specify both an address in the "from people or distribution list" condition and a word in the "with specific words in the body" condition. Outlook applies this rule only to a message that satisfies *both* conditions. However, what if you want to apply the rule to messages that satisfy *either* condition?

- Suppose you create a rule where you enter two words in the "with specific words in the subject" condition. Outlook applies this rule to any message that contains *either* word. However, what if you want to apply the rule only to messages that contain *both* words in the subject?

To work around these limitations, you need to turn to VBA. Specifically, you need to set up the Inbox folder as a programmable object, which enables you to write code that examines every incoming message and applies your own rules.

Open Outlook's VBA Editor, open the default project (VbaProject.OTM), and then open the Microsoft Office Outlook Objects branch. Double-click ThisOutlookSession to open the module window you'll use to enter the code. At the top of the module, add the following statements to declare two global variables:

```
Dim ns As NameSpace
Private WithEvents inboxItems As Items
```

Listing 12.16 shows two event handlers that you also need to add to the module. (An *event handler* is a Sub procedure that runs when a particular event fires. For example, Outlook's Application object has a Startup event that fires each time you launch Outlook.)

Listing 12.16   Event Handlers for Outlook's Startup and Quit Events

```
Private Sub Application_Startup()
    '
    ' Use the MAPI namespace object
    '
    Set ns = Application.GetNamespace("MAPI")
    '
    ' Get the Inbox Items object
    '
    Set inboxItems = ns.GetDefaultFolder(olFolderInbox).Items
End Sub

Private Sub Application_Quit()
    '
    ' Clear the objects to save memory
    '
    Set inboxItems = Nothing
    Set ns = Nothing
End Sub
```

The `Application_Startup` event handler runs automatically each time you start Outlook. The procedure initializes two variables: ns, which stores the MAPI `NameSpace` object that enables you to work with Outlook folders and items, and inboxItems, which stores the `Item` objects (messages) in the Inbox folder. The `Application_Quit` event handler runs when you shut down Outlook, and it sets the inboxItems and ns objects to `Nothing` to save memory.

Listing 12.17 shows a procedure that implements a couple of custom rules for handling incoming messages.

Listing 12.17   Event Handler for the Inbox Folder's ItemAdd Event—Use the Event Handler to Specify Your Custom Rule

```
Private Sub inboxItems_ItemAdd(ByVal Item As Object)
    Dim topFolder As Outlook.MAPIFolder
    Dim rule1Folder As Outlook.MAPIFolder
    '
    ' Store the Personal Folders folder
    '
    Set topFolder = ns.Folders("Personal Folders")
    '
    ' Custom Rule #1
    ' Move messages from "president@whitehouse.gov"
    ' OR with "politics" in the body
    '
    If Item.SenderEmailAddress = "president@whitehouse.gov" _
        Or InStr(Item.Body, "politics") <> 0 Then
            Set rule1Folder = topFolder.Folders("Politics")
            Item.Move rule1Folder
    End If
    '
    ' Custom Rule #2
```

continues

Listing 12.17   Continued

```
    ' Flag messages with "Conference" AND "2005" in the subject
    '
    If InStr(Item.Subject, "Conference") <> 0 _
       And InStr(Item.Subject, "2005") <> 0 Then
         Item.FlagStatus = olFlagMarked
         Item.FlagRequest = "Review"
         Item.FlagIcon = olBlueFlagIcon
         Item.FlagDueBy = Now() + 7
         Item.Save
    End If
End Sub
```

This code is the event handler for the Inbox folder's ItemAdd event, which runs automatically each time a new message is added to the Inbox. The procedure is passed the Item object, which represents the message added to the Inbox. The procedure begins by storing the Folder object for Personal Folders in the topFolder variable. Now the code implements two custom rules:

- Custom Rule #1—This is an example of a rule that looks for messages that satisfy one condition *or* another. In this case, the If test checks to see if the Item object's SenderEmailAddress property equals "president@whitehouse.gov" or the Item object's Body property (the message body) contains the word "politics." If either condition is true, the message is moved to the "Politics" folder.

- Custom Rule #2—This is an example of a rule that uses two criteria in a single condition and looks for messages that satisfy *both* criteria. In this case, the If test checks to see if the Item object's Subject property includes the word "Conference" and the word "2005." If both criteria are true, the code applies a blue "Review" flag to the message and sets the flag to expire seven days from today.

Supplementing a Reminder with an Email Message

If you set up an appointment or task with a reminder, or if you set up a message or contact with a flag that has a due date, Outlook displays a Reminder window that tells you the item is due. That's a useful visual cue, unless you're out of the office or away from your desk, in which case the reminder becomes far less helpful.

If you have email access when you're away, one way to work around this problem is to have Outlook send you an email message when it processes the reminder. The procedure in Listing 12.18 shows you how to set this up.

Listing 12.18   A Procedure to Send an Email Message When Outlook Processes a Reminder

```
Private Sub Application_Reminder(ByVal Item As Object)
    Dim msg As MailItem
    '
    ' Create a new message
    '
```

```
    Set msg = Application.CreateItem(olMailItem)
    '
    ' Set up the message with your address and the reminder subject
    '
    msg.To = "youraddress@wherever.com"
    msg.Subject = Item.Subject
    msg.Body = "Reminder!" & vbCrLf & vbCrLf
    '
    ' Set up the message body using properties
    ' appropriate to the different reminder types
    '
    Select Case Item.Class
        Case olAppointment
            msg.Body = "Appointment Reminder!" & vbCrLf & vbCrLf & _
            "Start: " & Item.Start & vbCrLf & _
            "End: " & Item.End & vbCrLf & _
            "Location: " & Item.Location & vbCrLf & _
            "Appointment Details: " & vbCrLf & Item.Body
        Case olContact
            msg.Body = "Contact Reminder!" & vbCrLf & vbCrLf & _
            "Contact: " & Item.FullName & vbCrLf & _
            "Company: " & Item.CompanyName & vbCrLf & _
            "Phone: " & Item.BusinessTelephoneNumber & vbCrLf & _
            "E-mail: " & Item.Email1Address & vbCrLf & _
            "Contact Details: " & vbCrLf & Item.Body
        Case olMail
            msg.Body = "Message Reminder!" & vbCrLf & vbCrLf & _
            "Sender: " & Item.SenderName & vbCrLf & _
            "E-mail: " & Item.SenderEmailAddress & vbCrLf & _
            "Due: " & Item.FlagDueBy & vbCrLf & _
            "Flag: " & Item.FlagRequest & vbCrLf & _
            "Message Body: " & vbCrLf & Item.Body
        Case olTask
            msg.Body = "Task Reminder!" & vbCrLf & vbCrLf & _
            "Due: " & Item.DueDate & vbCrLf & _
            "Status: " & Item.Status & vbCrLf & _
            "Task Details: " & vbCrLf & Item.Body
    End Select
    '
    ' Send the message
    '
    msg.Send
    '
    ' Release the msg object
    '
    Set msg = Nothing
End Sub
```

The Application_Reminder procedure is an event handler that runs whenever Outlook processes a reminder, and the Item variable that's passed to the procedure represents the underlying Outlook item: an appointment, contact, message, or task. The procedure declares a MailItem (message) variable named msg, uses it to store a new message, and then sets up the message's To, Subject, and initial Body properties. Then a Select Case statement processes the four possible Item classes: olAppointment, olContact, olMail, and olTask.

In each case, the message body is extended to include data from the item. Finally, the message is sent using the Send method and the msg variable is released.

Adding More Recipients

If you want to send the email to multiple recipients, one option is to use the MailItem object's Cc or Bcc properties. If you prefer to place multiple addresses in the message's To field, use the Recipients.Add method as often as needed, like so:

```
msg.Recipients.Add "another@domain.com"
```

Prompting to Save Messages in the Sent Items Folder

By default, Outlook saves a copy of all of your outgoing messages in the Sent Items folder. That's a good idea for important messages that you may need to refer to later on. However, we all send out plenty of unimportant messages, too, and there's no sense in saving those messages to Sent Items because doing so not only increases the size of the message store but also makes it harder to find messages in Sent Items. Listing 12.19 shows a procedure that enables you to decide whether Outlook should save an outgoing message to Sent Items.

Listing 12.19 An Event Handler That Asks Whether Outlook Should Save a Copy of an Outgoing Message in the Sent Items Folder

```vba
Private Sub Application_ItemSend(ByVal Item As Object, Cancel As Boolean)
    Dim result As Integer
    '
    ' Display the prompt
    '
    result = MsgBox("Save this message in Sent Items?", vbSystemModal+vbYesNo)
    '
    ' Check the result
    '
    If result = vbNo Then
        '
        ' If the user clicked No, don't save the message in Sent Items
        '
        Item.DeleteAfterSubmit = True
    End If
End Sub
```

This procedure is an event handler for the ItemSend event, which fires each time you send a message. The message is passed to the handler as the Item object. The procedure uses MsgBox to display a message asking the user whether the message should be saved in Sent Items. If the user clicks No, the result is vbNo and the procedure sets the Item object's DeleteAfterSubmit property to True to bypass saving the message in Sent Items.

Setting Up a Password-Protected Folder

If you use Outlook to exchange messages containing confidential data such as trade secrets, budget plans, payroll details, or proprietary information, the data may be vulnerable to snooping if you leave your desk. You could prevent this by storing the confidential messages in a folder protected by a password, but, unfortunately, Outlook doesn't give you any way to do this. Fortunately, it's fairly easy to set up a password-protected folder using some VBA code.

You begin by adding a global variable to the top of the `ThisOutlookSession` module:

```
Private WithEvents myExplorer As Explorer
```

This enables you to trap events for the `Explorer` object, which represents the Outlook interface. In particular, you want to trap the `BeforeFolderSwitch` event. This event fires when the user tries to display a different folder. The idea is that because this event fires before the other folder is displayed, you can use the event handler to ask the user for a password. If the correct password isn't given, you cancel the folder switch.

To use the `myExplorer` object, set `myExplorer` to Outlook's active `Explorer` object:

```
Set myExplorer = Application.ActiveExplorer
```

Place this statement within the `Application_Startup` event handler (refer to Listing 12.16).

With that done, you can now set up the handler for the `BeforeFolderSwitch` event, as shown in Listing 12.20.

Listing 12.20   An Event Handler That Asks the User for a Password Before Switching to the "Confidential" Folder

```
Private Sub myExplorer_BeforeFolderSwitch(ByVal NewFolder As Object,
➥Cancel As Boolean)
    Dim pwd as String
    '
    ' Are we switching to the "Confidential" folder?
    '
    If NewFolder.Name = "Confidential" Then
        '
        ' If so, ask the user for the password
        '
        pwd = InputBox("Please enter the password for this folder:")
        '
        ' Check the password
        '
        If pwd <> "password" Then
            '
            ' If the password doesn't match, cancel the switch
            '
            Cancel = True
        End If
    End If
End Sub
```

12

This procedure accepts an argument named `NewFolder`, which represents the folder to which the user is trying to switch. If this folder's name is "Confidential," the procedure asks the user to enter the password. If the password doesn't match, the `Cancel` argument is set to `True`, which means the folder isn't displayed.

Change the Password

The code in Listing 12.20 uses the word "password" as the folder password. If you use this code on your system, be sure to change the password to a less obvious word or phrase.

You're probably wondering just how secure this method is if the password appears right in the code. As things stand, it's not very secure at all because a savvy user would know to examine the VBA code. Therefore, you need to prevent others from viewing the project. Here are the steps to follow:

1. In the VBA Editor, select Tools, *Project* Properties, where *Project* is the name of your VbaProject.OTM project (the default name is Project1).

2. Display the Protection tab, as shown in Figure 12.6.

Figure 12.6
Use the Protection tab to prevent unauthorized users from viewing your Outlook VBA code.

3. Activate the Lock Project for Viewing check box.

4. Type a password into the Password and Confirm Password text boxes.

5. Click OK.

Shut down and then restart Outlook to put the password into effect.

From Here

- To learn how to set up a menu command to run a macro, see the section titled "Creating Custom Commands for Macros" in Chapter 10.

- You can also set up toolbar buttons to run macros. In Chapter 10, see the section titled "Creating Custom Toolbars."

- For some VBA basics, see Chapter 11, "Maximizing Office with VBA Macros."

- For other ways to secure Outlook, see Chapter 15, "Enhancing Outlook Email Security and Privacy."

Taking Advantage of Access Macros

13

As you learned in Chapter 11, "Maximizing Office with VBA Macros," a macro is a series of statements packaged as a procedure or function. In an Access database, you can also create a second type of macro that's a series of actions—such as opening a form, applying a filter, and displaying a message— packaged as a single database object. In this case, when the user runs the macro, Access executes each of the defined actions in the order specified within the macro.

You can use macros to automate tasks by building lists of actions that occur in response to events, such as a command button being clicked. You build the list in the order you want these actions to occur. The list can cover all the features available through the program's menus, as well as some that aren't. By using macros, you can automate the process of importing and exporting data, create buttons that perform complex queries, and create other useful functions.

Why not use VBA, instead? Actually, if you're comfortable with VBA, you should skip this chapter and just do all your coding in the VBA language. That's because there's nothing an Access macro can do that VBA can't do at least as well, and usually with more power and flexibility. However, if you're not familiar with VBA, you'll love Access macros because they require no programming skill, and building them isn't much harder than building a table or query.

In this chapter, you learn how to create simple and complex macros, work with existing macros, associate macros with various events, and troubleshoot your macros.

Writing Access Macros

Unlike writing a VBA program, where you can be as structured or unstructured as you want, writing a macro tends to be a very regimented process. That sounds like a bad thing, but it isn't—because this regimentation means that Access macros are easy to learn and you're far less likely to make programming errors. To get started, use any of the following methods:

- Select the Macros tab in the Database window and click the New button.
- Select Insert, Macro.
- Click Macro in the toolbar's New Object drop-down list.

Figure 13.1 shows the initial screen for creating a new macro.

Figure 13.1
The initial screen for a new macro.

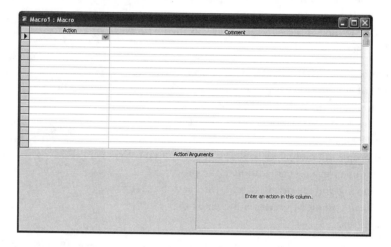

Notice that each line has two columns:

- Action—You use the cells in this column to choose the specific actions you want to include in your macro. Access runs the actions in order from top to bottom. For a complete list of the available actions, see "Summary of Macro Actions," later in this chapter.
- Comment—You use the cells in this column to describe or store notes about each action. Comments are an important part of Access macros because they help you decipher what each action is doing, and that helps you figure out the overall purpose of the macro. That may not seem like a big deal now, but it will in a few months when you don't remember why you created the macro in the first place. A quick glance at the comments is usually enough to get your bearings.

When you choose a cell in the Action column, a drop-down list appears, and this list contains all the possible actions that you can include in your macro. When you choose an action, the arguments for that action appear in the Action Arguments panel, as shown in Figure 13.2.

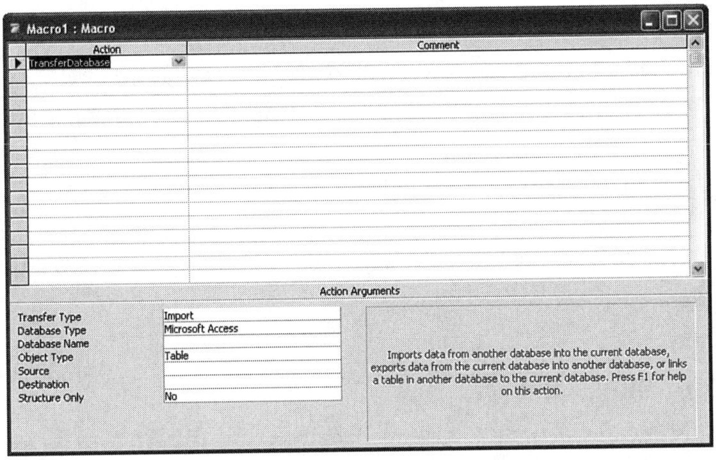

Figure 13.2
When you choose an action, its arguments appear in the bottom panel.

Notice that in some cases, the default arguments for the action are already filled in. For the TransferDatabase action (which you use to import data from or export data to a database), the Transfer Type, Database Type, Object Type, and Structure Only arguments are filled in automatically. You complete the current action by filling in the arguments as required:

- Some arguments accept text (such as the TransferDatabase action's Database Name argument). In this case, type the argument value you want to use.

- Other arguments provide you with a list of choices. For example, the TransferDatabase action's Transfer Type argument uses a list with three values, as shown in Figure 13.3: Import, Export, and Link.

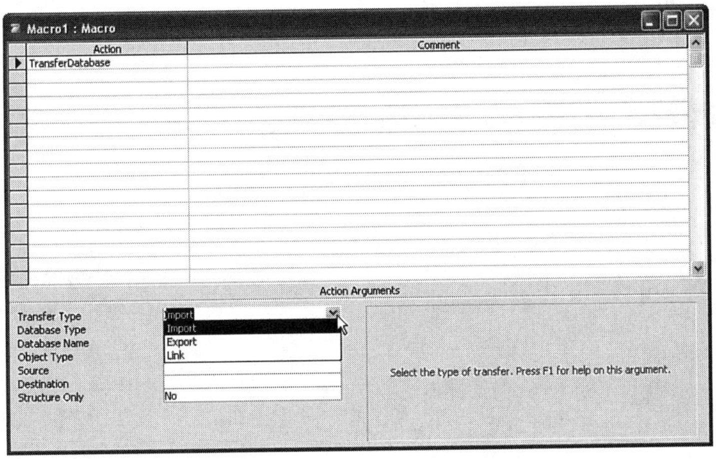

Figure 13.3
Some action arguments offer a drop-down list of possible values.

13

Creating an Access macro involves the following steps:

1. In the first unused Action cell, choose the next action you want your macro to perform.
2. Use the corresponding Comment column to write a brief description of what the action does in your macro.
3. Use the cells in the Action Arguments panel to specify the argument values to use with the action.
4. Repeat steps 1–3 until you've added all the actions your macro requires.
5. Save the macro.

Example: Opening a Report

To illustrate this a little more clearly, let's look at a sample macro for opening a report. I want this macro to perform three actions:

1. Open the Northwind database's Catalog report showing just the Beverages category in Print Preview view.
2. Maximize the report window.
3. Skip the report's opening two pages so that the Beverages data appears immediately.

Figure 13.4 shows the completed macro, and Table 13.1 lists the actions as well as their arguments and values.

This Chapter's Examples

You'll find the Access database that contains the macro examples in this chapter on my website at www.mcfedries.com/OfficeGurus.

Table 13.1   An Access Macro That Opens a Report

Action	Action Arguments	Values
OpenReport	Report Name	Catalog
	View	Print Preview
	Where Condition	[CategoryName]='Beverages'
	Window Mode	Normal
Maximize	None	
SendKeys	Keystrokes	{PGDN 2}
	Wait	No

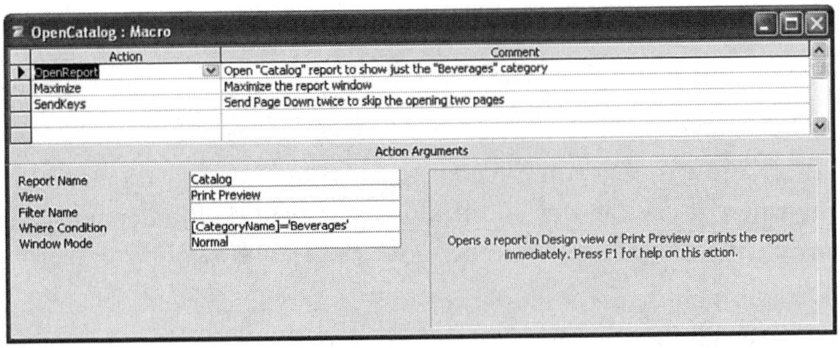

Figure 13.4
An Access macro that
opens a report.

You open a report by using the OpenReport action. In this example, I set the Report Name argument to Catalog, the View argument to Print Preview, set the Where Condition argument so that only the Beverages category will display, and set the Window Mode argument to Normal. I then used the Maximize action (which takes no arguments) to maximize the report window. Finally, I used the SendKeys action to send the Page Down key—{PGDN}—twice to bypass the report's two introductory pages.

→ The string values used in the SendKeys action's Keystroke argument are nearly identical to those used with the OnKey method in Excel VBA. (The exception is that you can't use the Alt key with SendKeys.) See "Assigning Shortcut Keys to Excel Macros," p. 406

Running Your Macro

There are several ways to run a macro after it's written and saved (you must save your macro before you can run it):

- Click the Run toolbar button that appears both in the macro design window and in the database window.
- Select Run, Run.
- Select Tools, Macro, Run Macro to display the Run Macro dialog box. Select the macro you want to run, and then click OK.
- Associate the macro with a specific event, such as clicking a button on a form or moving from one record to another. See "Associating Macros with Events," later in this chapter.
- Use the RunMacro action in another macro. In this case, specify the macro you want to run as the value of the Macro Name argument.

Modifying Existing Macros

After you have a macro, you might decide to make changes to it. Or you might need to modify someone else's macro to perform a specific task for you. To modify an existing macro, activate the Macros tab, highlight the macro you want to edit, and click the Design button. This brings the macro sheet back up.

13

To modify a macro, you usually have several choices:

- Change the existing actions or comments, or edit the arguments of an existing action.
- Add new actions to the bottom of the macro.

- Insert a row so that you can add an action between existing actions. Begin by clicking anywhere inside the row above which you want the new action to appear. Then either select Insert, Rows, or click the toolbar's Insert Rows button.

- Delete a row that contains an action you no longer need. Select the row you want to remove and then either select Edit, Delete Rows, or click the toolbar's Delete Rows button.

Using Names to Create Macro Groups

If you use Access macros a lot, you may find that you have a number of related macros. For example, you could have several macros that perform similar tasks, such as opening reports. Similarly, you may have several macros associated with the events of a specific form or report (see "Associating Macros with Events," later in this chapter). Rather than cluttering the Macros tab with all these different macros, Access enables you to group related macros within a single macro object. You do this by assigning a name to each macro within the object. This requires the Macro Name column, which you display as follows:

- Select View, Macro Names.

- Click the Macro Names toolbar button.

Access adds the Macro Name column to the macro sheet. Type the name of the macro in the Macro Name column beside the first action, as shown in Figure 13.5.

Figure 13.5
Use the Macro Name column to name multiple macros within a single macro object.

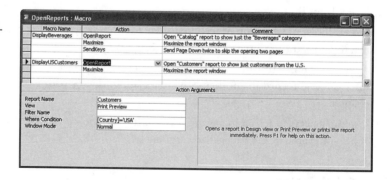

After you add two or more macro names to a macro object, selecting the Run command or clicking the Run button only launches the first macro. To run the macro, you need to select Tools, Macro, Run Macro to open the Run Macro dialog box, and then use the Macro

Name list to select the specific macro you want to run. When you use macro names, the individual macros now appear in the list with the following syntax:

`MacroObjectName.MacroName`

For example, if the macro object is named OpenReports and the macro is named DisplayBeverages, the full macro name is OpenReports.DisplayBeverages, as shown in Figure 13.6.

Figure 13.6
When you use macro names, you run a macro by specifying both the macro object and the macro name.

Example: Creating Access Shortcut Keys

Macro names are useful for keeping related macros together in a single object and for reducing the number of objects that appear in the database window's Macros tab. However, macro names also have another, rather unexpected, benefit: you can use them to create shortcut keys that launch Access macros.

To do this, you first need to create a new macro object and give it the name AutoKeys. Within that macro object, type the shortcut key combination as the macro name and then set up one or more macro actions to run when the user presses the shortcut key. Specify the shortcut keys using the same strings as in the SendKeys action.

For example, the string ^+b corresponds to the shortcut key combination Ctrl+Shift+B. In Figure 13.7, you can see that I've set up this shortcut to run the DisplayBeverages macro. However, you can select any action, so you could use the shortcut to open a form, show a toolbar, or run a VBA procedure. Note that the shortcut keys are ready to go as soon as you save the AutoKeys macro object.

Figure 13.7
In a macro object named AutoKeys, use the Macro Name column to enter shortcut key strings and associate them with one or more macro actions.

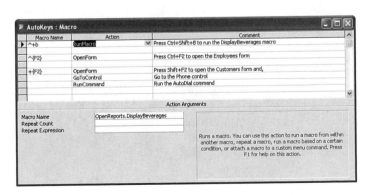

13

Adding Macro Conditions

In Figure 13.7, the third macro—the one that sets up the Shift+F2 shortcut key—opens the Customers form, selects the Phone field, and then runs the Access AutoDialer feature. Table 13.2 summarizes the macro actions and argument values.

Table 13.2 An Access Macro That Runs the Access AutoDialer		
Action	**Action Arguments**	**Values**
OpenForm	Report Name	Customers
	View	Form
	Window Mode	Normal
GoToControl	Control Name	Phone
RunCommand	Command	AutoDial

This works well as long as there is a value in the Phone field. It would be nice if the macro could somehow check the value of the Phone field in advance and then bail if no phone number is present.

This is possible by using a macro condition, which requires the Condition column. To display the Condition column, follow these steps:

1. Select View, Conditions.

2. Click the Conditions toolbar button.

Access adds the Condition column to the macro sheet. The idea here is that you add a logical expression to the Condition column: If the expression returns True, Access runs the macro action in the same row as the condition; if the expression returns False, Access skips the macro action in the same row as the condition. Either way, Access then continues with the rest of the macro's actions.

For the AutoDialer example, we can use the following condition to test whether the Phone field is blank:

```
Forms!Customers!Phone Is Null
```

If this expression returns True, no phone number is present. Figure 13.8 shows a revised version of the macro that uses this expression. (Notice that Access adds square brackets around each term; I've left these off here in the chapter to make the expression easier to read.) Table 13.3 shows the complete macro.

Table 13.3   An Access Macro That Bypasses the AutoDialer If No Phone Number Is Present

Condition	Action	Arguments	Values
	OpenForm	Report Name	Customers
		View	Form
		Window Mode	Normal
	GoToControl	Control Name	Phone
Forms!Customers!Phone Is Null	MsgBox	Message	No phone number for this customer!
		Beep	Yes
		Type	Critical
		Title	AutoDialer
...	StopMacro	None	
	RunCommand	Command	AutoDial

Figure 13.8
Use the Condition column to use logical expressions that determine whether a macro action runs.

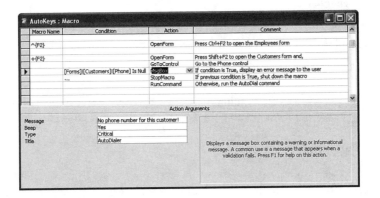

If the condition returns True, no phone number is present, so the macro runs the MsgBox action to display the message No phone number for this customer!, as shown in Figure 13.9. On the next line, the Condition column shows an ellipsis (...); this tells Access to apply the previous condition to the current line. Because the condition is True, the next action runs as well—in this case, StopMacro—which shuts down the macro so that the AutoDial command doesn't run.

13

Figure 13.9
If the Phone field is blank, the `MsgBox` action displays this message to the user.

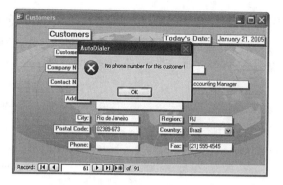

Associating Macros with Events

Although it's certainly possible to run an Access macro on its own, most macros run as a result of a specific event occurring. Following is a partial list of events that you can use to initiate a macro:

- Clicking a button
- Moving between fields
- Making changes in a record
- Opening or closing tables and forms
- Selecting a custom command from a custom menu

Depending on what you're trying to do, you might want a macro in a form, in a section of a form, in a report, or in a section of a report. All of these options are covered in this section.

Adding a Macro to a Form

To add a macro to a form, you can either create a control (such as a command button) that you associate the macro with, or you can edit the Event properties of the form itself, one of its sections, or one of its fields to call the macro. In each case, you must first open the form in Design view to make the necessary changes.

In Design view, display the properties sheet for the object either by clicking the object and then selecting View, Properties, or by right-clicking the object and then clicking Properties in the shortcut menu. (If you want to associate a macro with a form-level event, select the Edit, Select Form command—or press Ctrl+R—and then select View, Properties.)

In the properties sheet, display the Event tab to see a list of the events you can use to trigger the macro. For example, a macro associated with the On Click event will run whenever the user clicks the control. For each event, a drop-down list contains all the available macros, as shown in Figure 13.10.

Figure 13.10
The Event tab lists all the events available for the selected object. You can associate a macro with any of those events.

If you need to create a macro from scratch, click the ellipsis (...) button to display the Choose Builder dialog box. Select the Macro Builder option and then click OK to begin building your macro directly.

To determine which event to use, think about when you want your actions to occur and then match the macro accordingly. If you're unsure of how a specific event works, click in the field for the event and then press F1 to bring up the online help for the event.

Creating a Macro Command Button

One of the most common macro scenarios is to add a command button to the form and then associate a macro with that button so that it runs when the user clicks the button. The easiest way to set this up is to use the Command Button Wizard, as shown in the following steps:

1. In the Toolbox, make sure the Control Wizards button is activated.
2. Click the Command Button control and then click and drag within the form to create the button. When you release the mouse button, the Command Button Wizard appears.
3. In the Categories list, select Miscellaneous.
4. In the Actions list, select Run Macro.
5. Click Next.
6. Select the macro you want to associate with the command button and click Next.
7. Select a button label and click Next.
8. Type a name for the command button and click Finish.

Example: Confirming Changes to a Record

If you have a form where you don't expect users to make changes to the records, you can prevent accidental edits by asking the user to confirm any changes he or she has made. This way, the user can cancel the changes before committing them to disk.

First, create the macro as shown in Table 13.4, and save the macro with the name ConfirmChanges.

Table 13.4   An Access Macro That Asks the User to Confirm Changes

Condition	Action	Arguments	Values
MsgBox("Save changes to this record?",289)=2	Cancel Event	None	
...	SendKeys	Keystroke	{ESC}

The ConfirmChanges macro's first action uses a MsgBox function in the Condition column. This function displays a message using the following syntax:

MsgBox(*Prompt*[, *Buttons*] [, *Title*])

Prompt	The message you want to display in the dialog box. (You can enter a string up to 1,024 characters long.)
Buttons	A number that specifies, among other things, the command buttons that appear in the dialog box (explained next). The default value is 0.
Title	The text that appears in the dialog box title bar. If you omit the title, the name of the underlying application appears (for example, Microsoft Office Access).

Table 13.5 lists the values you can use for the *Buttons* parameter.

Table 13.5   The MsgBox Buttons Parameter Options

Value	Description
Buttons	
0	Displays only an OK button. (This is the default.)
1	Displays the OK and Cancel buttons.
2	Displays the Abort, Retry, and Ignore buttons.
3	Displays the Yes, No, and Cancel buttons.
4	Displays the Yes and No buttons.
5	Displays the Retry and Cancel buttons.
Icons	
16	Displays the Critical Message icon.
32	Displays the Warning Query icon.
48	Displays the Warning Message icon.
64	Displays the Information Message icon.

Value	Description
Default Buttons	
0	The first button is the default (that is, the button selected when the user presses Enter).
256	The second button is the default.
512	The third button is the default.

You derive the *Buttons* argument by adding up the values for each option. For this example, we want to use a dialog box with the OK and Cancel buttons (value 1), the Warning Query icon (32), and with the Cancel button as the default (256). So the *Buttons* argument is 1+32+256, which equals the 289 value shown in the condition in Table 13.4.

The MsgBox function returns a value depending on which button the user clicked, as detailed in Table 13.6.

Table 13.6   The MsgBox Function's Return Values

Value	User Clicked...
1	OK
2	Cancel
3	Abort
4	Retry
5	Ignore
6	Yes
7	No

In the macro, the condition checks to see if the user pressed the Cancel button (value 2). If that's true, the macro runs the CancelEvent procedure, which prevents the event the macro is associated with from firing. The second macro action (which also runs if the MsgBox function returns 2) uses SendKeys to send an Escape keystroke to the form, which cancels any changes the user made.

With the macro set up, you now add it to your form's BeforeUpdate event (see Figure 13.11), which fires if the user has made changes to the current record and is trying to save those changes (for example, by navigating to a different record). In this case, the dialog box shown in Figure 13.12 appears so that the user can confirm or cancel the changes.

13

Figure 13.11
Associate the
ConfirmChanges macro
with the form's
BeforeUpdate event.

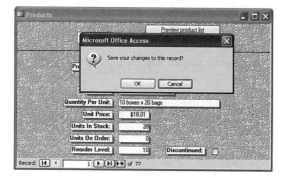

Figure 13.12
When the user attempts
to save changes to a
record, the confirmation
dialog box appears.

Example: Transferring Data from One Form to Another

One powerful application of macros within forms is the capability to transfer data between forms. For example, suppose you're viewing the Northwind sample database's Suppliers form, and you decide to add a new product for the current supplier. Normally you'd start this process by opening the Products form and selecting the supplier. However, with a macro you can perform these steps with the click of a button.

Table 13.7 presents a macro named AddProducts that comes with the default Northwind database (see the Suppliers macro object).

Table 13.7 A Macro That Transfers Data from One Form to Another

Action	Action Arguments	Values
Echo	Echo On	Off
Close	Object Type	Form
	Object Name	Product List
	Save	No
OpenForm	Form Name	Products
	View	Form
	Data Mode	Add
	Window Mode	Normal

Action	Action Arguments	Values
SetValue	Item	Forms!Products!SupplierID
	Expression	SupplierID
GoToControl	Control Name	ProductName

Following is a summary of the five actions performed by this macro:

1. Run the `Echo` action and set the `Echo On` argument to `Off`. This freezes the screen display until the macro finishes, which is useful for preventing the user from seeing unnecessary information as the macro goes about its business.

2. Run the `Close` action to close the Product List form, just in case (another macro in the Suppliers object opens the Product List form).

3. Run the `OpenForm` action to open the Products form in Add mode.

4. The `SetValue` action takes the `SupplierID` value from the current record in the Suppliers form (this is the `Expression` argument's value) and stores it in the `SupplierID` field of the Products form (this is the `Item` argument's value).

5. The `GoToControl` action sets the focus on the Products form's Product Name field.

Go to Product Name, Instead

In the original version of AddProducts that ships with the Northwind sample database, the `GoToControl` action is used to set the focus on the Category field instead of the Product Name field. This is inefficient because the first field you need to fill in when using the Products form is the Product Name field. Therefore, I edited the macro to use the more efficient method.

In Northwind, the Suppliers form includes an Add Products button (see Figure 13.13) with which the AddProducts macro is associated (via the `On Click` event). In Figure 13.13, notice that the current supplier name is Exotic Liquids. When you click Add Products, the Products form that appears already has Exotic Liquids in the Supplier field, as shown in Figure 13.14.

Adding a Macro to a Report

Reports are another area where macros are often very useful. Just like forms, reports have two levels of events. Figure 13.15 shows the events associated with the report object. You display this dialog box by selecting View, Select Report (or by pressing Ctrl+R) and then selecting View, Properties.

13

Figure 13.13
In the Northwind sample database, the Supplier form has an Add Products button with which the AddProducts macro is associated via the On Click event.

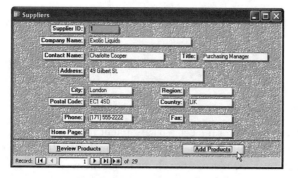

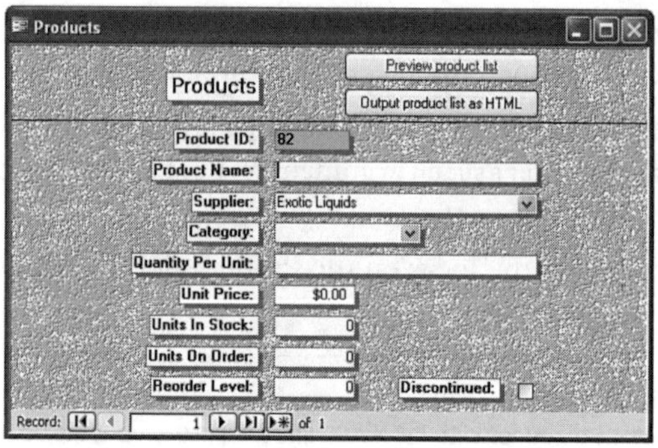

Figure 13.14
When you click Add Products, the Products form appears with the current supplier name already filled in.

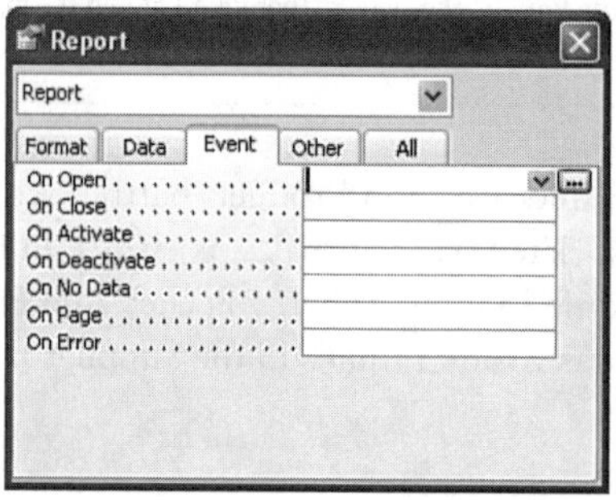

Figure 13.15
Access reports generate seven different events.

For more details on these events, you can again rely on the online help system to assist you in choosing the proper event for your macro.

Report Section Events

Within a report there are also the Report Header, the Page Header, the Detail, the Report Footer, and the Page Footer sections, each of which can have its events associated with a macro. These events are listed in Table 13.8.

Table 13.8 Report Section Events

Event	Description
On Format	Fires after Access has accumulated or calculated the data for the section but before it has printed the section.
On Print	Fires after the data in a section is laid out but before printing.
On Retreat	Fires when Access returns to a previous report section during report formatting. (This event doesn't fire with the Page Header and Page Footer sections.)

Example: Calculating Page Totals

One of the most frustrating quirks of the Access reporting engine is that is doesn't allow you to sum a field over a page. That is, if you place an unbound text box in the Page Footer section and include a Sum function that totals one of the report fields, Access always displays #Error as the result. Dumb! Fortunately, you can work around this limitation by using a macro that does the summing for you.

The first thing you need to do is insert an unbound text box in the Page Footer section of your report. Right-click the text box, click Properties, display the Other tab, and then change the Name property to PageTotal, as shown in Figure 13.16.

→ For more information on using calculated text boxes in reports, see "Adding Calculations to a Report," p. 174

Figure 13.16
Create an unbound text box named PageTotal in your report's Page Footer section.

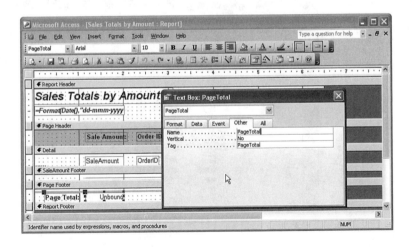

Next, you need to create two macros that you'll later associate with events in the report. Because both macros are related, you should place them both into a single macro object and use the Macro Name column to separate them. Table 13.9 shows the macros. (You can find these macros in the Northwind sample database in the Sales Totals by Amount macro object.)

Table 13.9   Access Macros Control the Summing of a Field Over a Page

Macro Name	Action	Arguments	Values
Page Total	SetValue	Item	[PageTotal]
		Expression	[PageTotal]+[SaleAmount]
New Page	SetValue	Item	[PageTotal]
		Expression	0

The `Page Total` macro uses the `SetValue` action to set the value of the unbound `PageTotal` text box to the following:

```
[PageTotal]+[SaleAmount]
```

This expression takes the current value of the `PageTotal` field and then adds the value of the `SaleAmount` field. For this to work properly, you must associate this macro with the `On Print` event in the report's Detail section. By using the Detail section, the macro runs after each record, so you get a running sum of the records on the page.

After each page is done, you need to reset the `PageTotal` field to `0`, and that's the job of the `New Page` macro. To make this work, you must associate this macro with the `On Print` event of the report's Page Header section.

Figure 13.17 shows a print preview of the report with the sum at the bottom of the page.

Figure 13.17
Using two simple macros, you can work around the Access reporting engine's inability to calculate totals over a page.

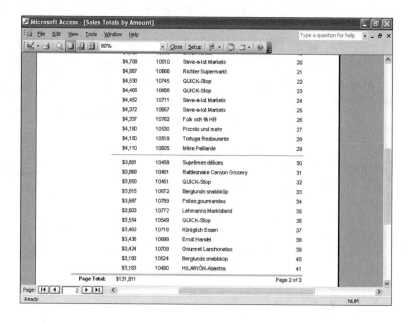

Troubleshooting Macros

Although it's nice to think that every macro you write will run correctly the first time you code it, the reality is that sometimes it won't. Usually you'll build a simple macro, test it, get it working, and then add more complex statements and so on until you get the final version. One way you'll know that your macro isn't working is when you see the Action Failed dialog box, shown in Figure 13.18. It shows you which macro has failed, what step it was on when it failed, and the arguments that were being used for that step.

Figure 13.18
The Action Failed dialog box appears when Access encounters a problem running your macro.

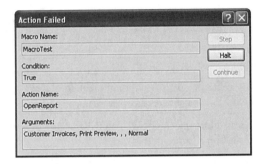

If you get the Action Failed dialog box, you'll want to jot down the macro name and the step as well as any open forms, reports, or queries. Then click the Halt button to close the dialog box. If you don't already have the macro sheet open for the offending macro, open it and see if you can figure out why that step caused the particular failure. Things to look at are whether what you thought should happen matched what appeared to be happening (particularly a problem with reports), whether the logic in the conditions matches what you thought you coded, and whether there was a condition in the data being analyzed that you didn't expect.

 After you've looked at these items, if there still is no apparent problem, it's time to try "stepping" through the macro one action at a time. To do this, begin by opening the macro and any forms or reports that would normally be open when it runs. Select Run, Single Step, or click the Single Step toolbar button to activate the Single Step feature. Then run the macro. As the macro goes through each step, you get a dialog box (similar to the one shown in Figure 13.19) that shows the step being executed. The information about that step is displayed in the dialog box.

13

Figure 13.19
Use the Macro Single Step dialog box to step through your macro one action at a time.

Macro Single Step

Macro Name:	Step
MacroTest	Halt
Condition:	Continue
True	
Action Name:	
OpenReport	
Arguments:	
Customer Invoices, Print Preview, , , Normal	

You have three choices at each step: You can click Step (which is the default) to go to the next action, click Halt to stop execution of the macro, or click Continue to run the macro from that point on without stopping until the end of the macro or until an error is encountered.

Summary of Macro Actions

To close this chapter, Table 13.10 presents a complete list of the macro actions you can use.

Table 13.10   Macro Actions and Their Descriptions

Action	Description
AddMenu	Replaces a built-in menu bar for a form or report with a custom menu bar; replaces a built-in shortcut menu for a form, report, or form control with a custom shortcut menu.
ApplyFilter	Uses a filter, query, or SQL WHERE clause to restrict and/or sort the records in a form or report.
Beep	Beeps the computer's speakers.
CancelEvent	Cancels the event that caused the macro to run.
Close	Closes the active window or a specified window.
CopyDatabaseFile	Makes a copy of the current Access database file.
CopyObject	Copies a database object to another database or to the current database with a different name.
DeleteObject	Deletes a specified database object or the selected object in the database window.
Echo	Hides or shows the macro's actions while it runs.
FindNext	Finds the next record that meets the criteria used in the most recent FindRecord action or Find dialog box usage.
FindRecord	Finds the first record in a table or form that meets the specified criteria.
GoToControl	Moves the focus to the specified field or control on the current datasheet or form.
GoToPage	Moves the focus to the first field or control on the specified page in the active form.
GoToRecord	Makes the specified record the current record in a table, query result, or form.
Hourglass	Changes the mouse pointer from the normal icon to an hourglass icon; the pointer is restored when the macro stops.
Maximize	Enlarges the active window to fill the Access window.

Action	Description
Minimize	Reduces the active window to a title bar at the bottom of the Access window.
MoveSize	Moves or resizes the active window.
MsgBox	Displays a message to the user.
OpenDataAccessPage	Opens a specified data access page.
OpenDiagram	Opens a specified database diagram.
OpenForm	Opens a specified form.
OpenFunction	Opens a specified function.
OpenModule	Opens a specified Visual Basic module at a specified procedure or function.
OpenQuery	Opens a specified query.
OpenReport	Opens a specified report.
OpenStoredProcedure	Opens a specified stored procedure.
OpenTable	Opens a specified table.
OpenView	Opens a specified view.
OutputTo	Exports data from a database object to a file in another format, such as HTML, Excel, or text.
PrintOut	Prints the active datasheet, form, report, data access page, or module.
Quit	Shuts down Access.
Rename	Renames the specified database object.
RepaintObject	Completes any pending screen updates or control recalculations for the specified database object.
Requery	Updates data in the specified control in the active database object.
Restore	Restores a maximized or minimized window to its original location and size.
RunApp	Runs the specified application.
RunCode	Runs the specified VBA function. (To run a procedure, create a function that calls the procedure and then use RunCode to run the function.)
RunCommand	Runs the specified command in a built-in menu or toolbar.
RunMacro	Runs the specified Access macro.
RunSQL	Runs the specified SQL statement for an action or data definition query.
Save	Saves the specified database object.

13

continues

Table 13.10 Continued

Action	Description
SelectObject	Selects the specified database object.
SendKeys	Sends one or more keystrokes to Access or the active application.
SendObject	Includes the specified database object in an email message.
SetMenuItem	Sets the state of menu items (such as checked or unchecked) on the custom or global menu bar for the active window.
SetValue	Sets the value of a field, control, or property on a form or report.
SetWarnings	Turns system messages on or off.
ShowAllRecords	Removes any applied filter from the active table, query, or form.
ShowToolbar	Displays or hides a built-in or custom toolbar.
StopAllMacros	Stops all currently running macros.
StopMacro	Stops the currently running macro.
TransferDatabase	Imports, exports, or links data between the current Access database and another database.
TransferSpreadsheet	Imports, exports, or links data between the current Access database and a spreadsheet file.
TransferSQLDatabase	Transfers an SQL database from one server to a SQL database on another server.
TransferText	Imports, exports, or links data between the current Access database and a text file.

From Here

- For more information on using calculated text boxes in reports, see the section titled "Adding Calculations to a Report" in Chapter 4.

- VBA can do everything Access macros can do, and much more. To learn VBA basics, see Chapter 11, "Maximizing Office with VBA Macros."

- The strings used in the SendKeys action's Keystroke argument are identical to those used with the OnKey method in Excel VBA. In Chapter 12, see the section titled "Assigning Shortcut Keys to Excel Macros."

13

Office 2003 Security Tricks

IV

Securing Office 2003

14

Microsoft has estimated that there are more than 400 million Office users around the world. That's a large number, to be sure, but it shouldn't come as a big surprise. After all, you only have to ask around a bit to realize that, for all intents and purposes, *everyone* uses at least a subset of the Office suite. (More evidence: Microsoft's share of the productivity suite market is more than 90%.)

What this means in the real world is that we all use Office for a variety of documents, from simple letters to full-blown corporate budgets. Inevitably, some of those documents will be vitally important, either to you personally or to your business, or they'll be of a sensitive or private nature. Whatever the reason, you might be looking for increased security, either because you want to protect important data or because you want to restrict access to sensitive data. Whether it's preservation or privacy you seek, Outlook 2003 offers a number of tools that can help you secure your documents, and you learn about many of them in this chapter.

Setting Document Security Options

Your first step toward a secure Office environment involves securing your documents. Office 2003 offers a number of security levels, which range from merely suggesting that users don't edit a file to requiring strong passwords to open otherwise-encrypted documents. The next few sections take you through some of these document security options.

Preventing Changes by Opening a Document as Read-Only

One way to prevent unauthorized changes to a document is to open it as read-only. You can still make changes to the document, but you can't save those changes (except to a different file).

If you're opening the file yourself, you can open it as read-only by following these steps:

1. Select File, Open (or press Ctrl+O) to display the Open dialog box.

2. Open the folder containing the document and then select the document.

3. Pull down the Open list and click Open Read-Only, as shown in Figure 14.1.

Figure 14.1
To open a document as read-only, pull down the Open list and click Open Read-Only.

As an extra measure of safety, you can also tell Word and Excel to recommend that a document be opened as read-only. Select File, Save As to open the Save As dialog box, and then use the following techniques:

- In Word, select Tools, Security Options, activate the Read-Only Recommended check box, and then click OK.

- In Excel, select Tools, General Options, activate the Read-Only Recommended check box, and then click OK.

Click Save to finish saving the document.

A More Direct Route

Rather than using the Save As dialog box, you can set the read-only recommendation directly. In Word and Excel, select Tools, Options, display the Security tab, and then activate the Read-Only Recommended check box.

When you attempt to open the document now, Word or Excel displays a dialog box similar to the one shown in Figure 14.2. Click Yes to open the document as read-only; click No if you want to make changes to the document.

Figure 14.2
With the Read-Only Recommended check box activated, Word or Excel displays this dialog box before opening the document.

Using File Passwords and Encryption

The Read-Only Recommended option places a hurdle in front of a user bent on modifying a document, but only a very small one. To defeat this protection, he or she need only click No at the Open as Read-Only? prompt shown in Figure 14.2.

If you are serious about protecting the contents of a document, you need to take the security to a higher level by assigning a password to the document. You can assign passwords to Word documents, Excel workbooks, and PowerPoint presentations. In each case, the program uses the password as a key to encrypt the document contents. The only way to view or modify the document is to supply the password.

Here are the steps to follow to assign a password to encrypt a Word document, an Excel workbook, or a PowerPoint presentation:

1. Select Tools, Options to display the Options dialog box.
2. Display the Security tab.
3. Type a password into one or both of the following text boxes:

Creating Strong Passwords
To get the most out of any password-based security, select a strong password, which is one that's meaningful to you (and so easier to remember), but is not easy for someone else to guess (such as your name or your spouse's name). The password should be a minimum of eight characters (longer is better) and should be a mix of letters and numbers. Note, too, that the Office applications differentiate between uppercase and lowercase letters, so remember the capitalization you use.

Password to Open—This password is required to view the document (see Figure 14.3). If you don't include the password to modify, the user can edit the document.

Password to Modify—This password is required to edit the document's contents. If you don't include the password to open, the user has the option of opening the document as read-only (see Figure 14.4).

14

Figure 14.3
You see this dialog box when you assign a password to open a document.

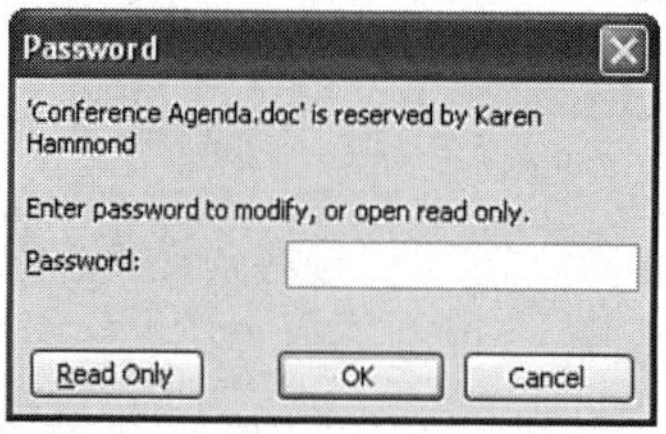

Figure 14.4
You see this dialog box when you assign a password to modify a document.

4. Click OK. The program prompts you to enter the password to open and/or to modify the password. In each case, re-enter the password and click OK.

5. Save the document to put the password into effect.

Don't Forget Your Password

If you forget your password, there's no way to retrieve it, and you'll never be able to access your document. As a precaution, you might want to write down your password and store it in a safe place.

Enhancing Security with Windows Permissions and Encryption

If you're running Windows XP Professional and using NTFS as your hard disk file system, you can add another layer of security by applying advanced permissions to the appropriate folders or files. Right-click the folder or file, click Properties, and then display the Security tab. You can also encrypt a folder or file to make it impossible for other people to read the contents. Again, right-click the folder or file, click Properties, and then display the General tab. Click Advanced and then activate the Encrypt Contents to Secure Data check box.

More Options for Protecting Word Documents

Applying a password that allows the user to open or modify a Word document is an all-or-nothing strategy. That is, the user can either edit all of the document—the text and the formatting—or none of it. However, there may be scenarios where you want to give someone access to one or the other. For example, you might need someone to modify just the document text, but you want to prevent him or her from messing with the formatting. The next two sections show you how to protect the document formatting and text separately.

Locking Document Formatting

Like most modern word processors, Word fits into the category of *fritterware*—programs with so many formatting bells and whistles that you can end up frittering away hours and hours by tweaking fonts, colors, alignments, and so on. Whether you think of such activity as frittering depends on your point of view, but we all agree that a well-formatted document makes a better impression than a plain or sloppy-looking one. So no matter how much time you've devoted to getting your document just so, the last thing you want is another person running roughshod over your careful look and layout.

Fortunately, Word 2003 offers the capability to lock your document's formatting, which prevents others from changing the formatting unless they know the password. Here are the steps to follow:

1. Display the Protect Document task pane by using either of the following techniques:
   - Select Tools, Protect Document.
   - Select Tools, Options, select the Security tab, and then click Protect Document.
2. Activate the Limit Formatting to a Selection of Styles check box.
3. Click Settings to display the Formatting Restrictions dialog box, shown in Figure 14.5.

Figure 14.5
Use the Formatting Restrictions dialog box to restrict the formatting another user can apply to a document.

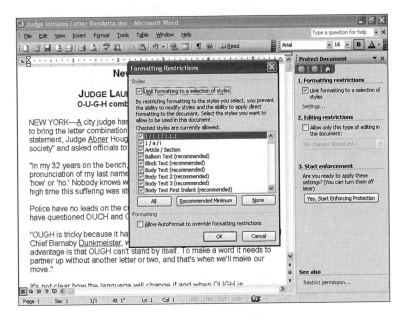

4. In the Checked Styles Are Currently Allowed list, deactivate the check box beside each style that you want to disallow. Alternatively, use the following buttons to set the check boxes:

14

- All—Click this button to activate all the check boxes and thus enable unauthorized users to apply formatting using only the existing styles; these users can't modify the existing styles or create new styles.

- Recommended Minimum—Click this button to activate the check boxes for only those styles that Word determines are necessary for the document.

- None—Click this button to deactivate all the check boxes and thus prevent unauthorized users from changing any document formatting.

5. If the user applies an AutoFormat and you want the AutoFormat to apply restricted styles, activate the Allow AutoFormat to Override Formatting Restrictions check box.

6. Click OK.

7. If Word warns you that the document contains disallowed styles, click Yes to remove them or click No to keep them.

8. In the Protect Document task pane, click Yes, Start Enforcing Protection. The Start Enforcing Protection dialog box appears.

9. Type the password twice and then click OK.

If you or another authorized user need to change the document formatting, select Tools, Unprotect Document, type the password, and then deactivate the Limit Formatting to a Selection of Styles check box.

Preventing Untracked Changes

When you share a Word document, it's common to turn on the Track Changes feature so that you can see all the edits made by the other person. Unfortunately, it's easy to turn off Track Changes (either accidentally or on purpose), so you can never be sure whether your document contains any untracked changes.

→ For the details on tracking changes in a Word document, see "Tracking Word Document Changes," p. 264

If it's important that you track all edits, it's possible to set up Word to prevent untracked changes, and even to enforce this option with a password. Here are the steps to follow:

1. Display the Protect Document task pane by using either of the following techniques:
   - Select Tools, Protect Document.
   - Select Tools, Options, select the Security tab, and then click Protect Document.

2. Activate the Allow Only This Type of Editing in the Document check box.

3. In the Editing Restrictions list, select Tracked Changes.

4. Click Yes, Start Enforcing Protection. The Start Enforcing Protection dialog box appears.

5. Type the password twice and then click OK.

User-Based Read-Only

If you're using Word 2003 in a Windows domain or an Exchange shop, you can set up portions of a document as read-only and you can make exceptions for certain users. In the Protect Document task pane, use the Editing Restrictions list to select No Changes (Read-only). If you want users to edit only a portion of the document, select that portion. In the Exceptions group, click More Users and then type the usernames or email addresses of the users you want to be able to freely edit in the document of the selected portion.

If you or another authorized user need to freely edit the document text, select Tools, Unprotect Document, type the password, and then deactivate the Allow Only This Type of Editing in the Document check box.

More Options for Protecting Excel Workbooks

When you've labored long and hard to get your worksheet formulas or formatting just right, the last thing you need is to have a cell or range accidentally deleted or copied over. You can prevent this by using Excel's worksheet protection features, which enable you to prevent changes to anything from a single cell to an entire workbook.

Protecting Individual Cells, Objects, and Scenarios

Protecting cells, objects, and scenarios in Excel is a two-step process:

1. Set up the item's protection formatting. You have four options:
   - Cells, objects, and scenarios can be either *locked* or *unlocked*. As soon as protection is turned on (see step 2), a locked item can't be changed, deleted, moved, or copied over.
   - You can protect ranges with a password so that only users who know the password can edit the cells within the range.
   - Cell formulas and scenarios can be either *hidden* or *visible*. With protection on, a hidden formula doesn't appear in the formula bar when the cell is selected; a hidden scenario doesn't appear in the Scenario Manager dialog box.
   - Text boxes, macro buttons, and some worksheet dialog box controls also can have *locked text*, which prevents the text they contain from being altered.
2. Turn on the worksheet protection.

These steps are covered in more detail in the following sections.

Setting Up Protection Formatting for Cells

By default, all worksheet cells are formatted as locked and visible. This means that you have three options when setting up your protection formatting:

- If you want to protect every cell, leave the formatting as it is and turn on the worksheet protection.

14

- If you want certain cells unlocked (for data entry, for example), select the appropriate cells and unlock them before turning on worksheet protection. Similarly, if you want certain cells hidden, select the cells and hide them.

- If you want only selected cells locked, select all the cells and unlock them. Then select the cells you want protected and lock them. To keep only selected formulas visible, hide every formula and then make the appropriate range visible.

Here are the steps to follow to set up protection formatting for worksheet cells:

1. Select the cells for which you want to adjust the protection formatting.

2. Select the Format, Cells command, and in the Format Cells dialog box, select the Protection tab.

3. To lock the cells' contents, activate the Locked check box. To unlock cells, deactivate this check box.

4. To hide the cells' formulas, activate the Hidden check box. To make the cells' formulas visible, deactivate the check box.

Hiding Cell Contents

Hiding a formula prevents only the formula from being displayed in the formula bar; the results appear inside the cell itself. If you also want to hide the cell's contents, create an empty custom numeric format (;;;), and assign this format to the cell. To create a custom numeric format, select the Number tab, click Custom in the Category list, and then type the format into the Type list.

---

5. Click OK.

Protecting a Range with a Password

If you want to prevent unauthorized users from editing within a range, you can set up that range with a password. After you protect the sheet, only authorized users who know the password can edit the range. Here are the steps to follow:

1. Select Tools, Protection, Allow Users to Edit Ranges. Excel displays the Allow Users to Edit Ranges dialog box.

2. Click New. Excel displays the New Range dialog box.

3. Type a Title for the range.

4. Use the Refers to Cells range box to select the range you want to protect.

5. Type a password into the Range Password box.

6. Click OK. Excel prompts you to re-enter the password.

7. Type the password and click OK. Excel adds the range to the Allow Users to Edit Ranges dialog box, as shown in Figure 4.6.

Figure 14.6
Use the Allow Users to Edit Ranges dialog box to specify ranges you want to protect with a password.

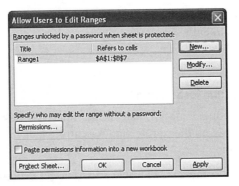

8. Repeat steps 2–7 to protect other ranges.

9. Click OK. (Alternatively, click Protect Sheet to go directly to the sheet protection stage. See "Protecting a Worksheet," later in this chapter.)

Setting Up Protection Formatting for Objects

Excel locks all worksheet objects by default (and it locks the text in text boxes, macro buttons, and some worksheet dialog box controls). As with cells, you have three options for protecting objects:

- If you want to protect every object, leave the formatting as it is and turn on the worksheet protection.

- If you want certain objects unlocked, select the appropriate objects and unlock them before turning on worksheet protection.

- If you want only selected objects locked, select all the objects and unlock them. Then select the objects you want to protect and lock them.

Selecting All Objects
To select all the objects in a sheet, select Edit, Go To, click the Special button in the Go To dialog box, activate the Objects option, and then click OK.

Follow these steps to set up protection formatting for worksheet objects:

1. Select the objects for which you want to adjust the protection formatting.

2. Pull down the Format menu and select the command for the selected object or objects (such as Object, Text Box, or Picture), and in the Format Object dialog box, activate the Protection tab.

3. To lock the objects, activate the Locked check box. To unlock them, deactivate this check box.

14

4. For text boxes or macro buttons, activate the Lock Text check box to protect the text. Deactivate this check box to unlock the text.

5. Click OK.

Setting Up Protection Formatting for Scenarios

Similar to cells, scenarios are normally locked and visible. You can't work with scenarios in groups, however, so you must set up their protection formatting individually. The following procedure shows you the steps:

1. Select the Tools, Scenarios command. The Scenario Manager dialog box appears.

2. Select the scenario in the Scenarios list and then click the Edit button. Excel displays the Edit Scenario dialog box.

3. To lock the scenario, activate the Prevent Changes check box. To unlock it, deactivate this check box.

4. To hide the scenario, activate the Hide check box; deactivate it to unhide the scenario.

5. Click OK. Excel displays the Scenario Values dialog box.

6. Enter new values, if necessary, and then click OK.

7. Repeat steps 2–6 to set the protection formatting for other scenarios.

8. When you're done, click Close to return to the worksheet.

Protecting a Worksheet

At this point, you've formatted the cells, ranges, objects, or scenarios for protection. To activate the protection, follow these steps:

1. Select Tools, Protection, Protect Sheet. (If you're in the Allow Users to Edit Ranges dialog box, click Protect Sheet.) Excel displays the Protect Sheet dialog box, shown in Figure 14.7.

Figure 14.7
Use the Protect Sheet dialog box to activate your protection formatting.

2. For added security, enter a password in the Password to Unprotect Sheet text box. This means that no one can turn off the worksheet's protection without first entering the password.

Protection Without a Password

You might wonder why Excel makes the password for unprotecting the sheet optional. That's because the concern here is worksheet integrity: you don't want a user accidentally modifying or deleting formulas or data. When faced with a protected sheet, most users don't automatically look to unprotect it, so protection without a password is almost always a safe option.

---

3. Use the check boxes to select the actions unauthorized users are allowed to perform.

4. Click OK.

5. If you entered a password, Excel asks you to confirm it. Re-enter the password and then click OK.

To turn off the protection, select the Tools, Protection, Unprotect Sheet command. If you entered a password, Excel displays the Unprotect Sheet dialog box. Type the password into the Password text box and then select OK.

Protecting Windows and Workbook Structures

You also can protect your windows and workbook structures. When you protect a window, Excel takes the following actions:

- Hides the window's Maximize and Minimize buttons, Control-menu box, and borders. This means the window can't be moved, sized, or closed.
- Disables the window menu's New Window, Split, and Freeze Panes commands when the window is active. The Arrange command remains active, but it has no effect on the protected window. The Hide and Unhide commands remain active.

When you protect a workbook's structure, Excel takes the following actions:

- Disables the Edit menu's Delete Sheet and Move or Copy Sheet commands.
- Prevents the Insert menu's Worksheet and Chart commands from having any effect on the workbook.
- Keeps the Scenario Manager from creating a summary report.

Follow these steps to protect windows and workbook structures:

1. Activate the window or workbook you want to protect.

2. Select the Tools, Protection, Protect Workbook command. Excel displays the Protect Workbook dialog box, shown in Figure 14.8.

14

Figure 14.8
Use the Protect Workbook dialog box to protect your workbook structure and windows.

3. Activate the check boxes for the workbook items you want to protect: Structure and/or Windows.

4. Enter a password into the Password text box, if required.

5. Click OK.

6. If you entered a password, Excel asks you to confirm it. Re-enter the password and click OK.

Assigning a Password to Your Outlook Personal Folders

If your Outlook data file (the one that stores your Personal Folders) resides on a shared network folder, other people can add that file to their own list of Outlook data files. This means they can view your email and other Outlook data as easily as you can. Also, anyone who has physical access to your computer can start Outlook and view your Outlook data.

Locking Your Computer

If you're concerned that an unauthorized user may sit down at your computer while you're at a meeting or at lunch, you should lock your computer before leaving. In Windows XP, you do this by pressing the Windows Logo+L keys. Alternatively, press Ctrl+Alt+Delete and then click Lock Computer. Note, however, that to truly lock your computer, you must assign a password to your Windows XP user account. This means that another user can't get to Windows unless they enter your password.

To prevent both scenarios, you should set up your Outlook data file with a password by following these steps:

1. In Outlook, select Tools, Options to display the Options dialog box.

2. Select the Mail Setup tab.

3. Click Data Files to display the Outlook Data Files dialog box.

4. Select the data file you want to protect and then click Settings.

5. Click Change Password to display the Change Password dialog box.

6. Type your Old Password (this will likely be blank if you haven't done this before), type your New Password and Verify Password, and then click OK.

7. Close the remaining dialog boxes.

Protecting Access Data with Passwords and Permissions

Access database security usually falls into one or both of the following categories:

- The database contains sensitive or private data that should be viewed or edited only by authorized users.
- The database contains production versions of tables, queries, forms, reports, and other objects that should be modified only by authorized users.

To handle both categories, Access offers two types of security: a database password and user-level permissions. The next two sections show you how to implement both types of security.

Setting a Database Password

If you want to restrict the opening of a database to authorized users only, you need to set up the database with a password. This is useful only for controlling access to sensitive or private data because after authorized users open the database, they're free to modify the data and objects.

Following are the steps to set up an Access database (.mdb file) with a password:

1. Close the database if it's currently open.
2. Select File, Open to display the Open dialog box.
3. Open the folder containing the database and select the database file.
4. Pull down the Open button's list and click Open Exclusive. The database opens with exclusive access.
5. Select Tools, Security, Set Database Password. The Set Database Password dialog box appears.
6. Type the password into the Password and Verify boxes, and then click OK.
7. Close and reopen the database and enter the password when prompted.

Removing the Password

To remove the password from the database, select Tools, Security, Unset Database Password. Type the Password and click OK.

Setting User-Level Database Permissions

Even Access experts who wouldn't blink an eye when asked, for instance, to replicate a database or program ActiveX Data Objects can get the shakes when asked to implement user-level security for a database. The problem isn't that user-level database security is so hard, it's more that it's notoriously arcane. Matters are made worse by the fact that although Access database permissions bear a distinct resemblance to NTFS file permissions in Windows, the two are not in any way related, and the Access version is just different enough to cause confusion.

14

Normally I'm a big believer in bypassing wizards and getting one's hands dirty with the actual program features that the wizard acts as a front-end for. However, I'm happy to make an exception with Access security because the User-Level Security Wizard is a powerful and easy-to-use alternative to the normal security interface.

Here's how the Security Wizard works:

1. Select Tools, Security, User-Level Security Wizard to open the first Security Wizard dialog box.

2. Activate the Create a New Workgroup Information File option (it may be the only option available to you) and click Next.

3. In the next wizard dialog box, Access generates a unique workgroup ID (WID) and prompts you to enter your name and company name (although these are optional). You also get two choices (click Next when you've made your selection):

   - I Want to Make This My Default Workgroup Information File—Activate this option to use the new workgroup information file for all your databases.

   - I Want to Create a Shortcut to Open My Security-Enhanced Database—Activate this option to use the new workgroup information file for the current database only (as well as for other selected files you secure down the road). In this case, the wizard creates a shortcut file to load the database using the /wrkgrp parameter, which specifies your new workgroup information file.

4. The Security Wizard displays the dialog box shown in Figure 14.9 to enable you to specify which database objects you want to secure. Leave the check boxes activated beside each object you want to secure, and then click Next.

Figure 14.9
Activate the check boxes beside the database objects you want to secure.

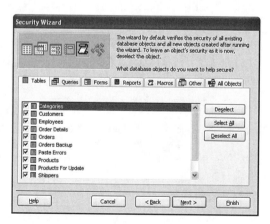

5. The Security Wizard displays a list of security group accounts that you can add to your workgroup information file, as shown in Figure 14.10. Each group has a specific set of permissions. (Click a group's name to see a description of the group's permissions.) For example, the Read-Only Users group can view data, but they can't edit data or modify

object designs. Activate the check box beside each group you want to include in your workgroup information file, and then click Next.

Figure 14.10
Activate the check boxes beside the security groups you want to include in your workgroup information file.

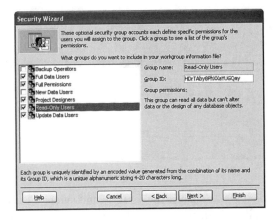

6. The wizard asks if you want to assign specific permissions to the Users group (which, by definition, includes all users). The safest way to secure an Access database is to assign permissions to the groups you chose in step 5 and to specific users. Therefore, you should leave the No, the Users Group Should Not Have Any Permissions option activated. Click Next.

7. Use the next Security Wizard to add users to your workgroup information file. For each user, type a User Name and Password and then click Add This User to the List. (If you add a user by mistake, select the user in the list and then click Delete User from the List.) When you're done, click Next.

Add Test Users for Each Group

In step 8 the wizard will ask you to assign users to one or more of the groups you chose in step 5. It's a good idea to test the security for each group, and the easiest way to do that is to add dummy users for testing purposes. For example, to test the Full Data Users group, add a user named FullDataUser. For each of these dummy users, assign a common password to make it easier to remember when you're doing the group testing.

---

8. The Security Wizard prompts you to assign the users from step 7 to the security groups from step 5. You have two ways to proceed (click Next when you're done):

   • Select a User and Assign the User to Groups—If you activate this option, use the Group or User Name list to select a user, and then use the check boxes to assign groups to that user, as shown in Figure 14.11.

   • Select a Group and Assign Users to That Group—If you activate this option, use the Group or User Name list to select a group, and then use the check boxes to assign users to that group.

14

Figure 14.11
You can assign groups to the selected user (as shown) or users to the selected group.

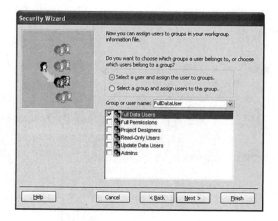

9. In the final wizard dialog box, change the location and name of the unsecured backup copy of the database, if desired, and then click Finish. The wizard displays a security report.

10. Close the report window. The Security Wizard asks if you want to create a Snapshot file of the report. (A Snapshot file is viewable with the Access Snapshot Viewer.) Click Yes. Access creates the Snapshot file and displays it in the Snapshot Viewer.

Save Your Snapshot File

If you need to re-create your workgroup information file later, you can do so only if you know the exact WID, name, and company name, all of which are included in the Snapshot file. Therefore, be sure to save a copy of the Snapshot file in a secure location.

---

11. Select File, Exit to close the Snapshot view. The Security Wizard tells you that your database is now secured.

12. Click OK.

13. Shut down Access.

14. If you chose to create a shortcut to the secured database in step 3, display the Windows desktop and double-click the shortcut file; otherwise, reopen the secured database. The Logon dialog box appears, as shown in Figure 14.12.

Figure 14.12
When you open a secured database, you must log on with a user-name and password.

15. Enter the Name and Password of the user and then click OK.

To make changes to the user-level security, you have two choices:

- Select Tools, Security, User-Level Security Wizard to run the wizard again. In the initial dialog box, leave the Modify My Current Workgroup Information File option activated and then follow steps 4–14.

- Select Tools, Security. In the submenu that appears, select User and Group Permissions to set specific database object permissions for users or groups. Select User and Group Accounts to add and remove users and groups and change passwords.

Protecting Your Privacy

Office documents may not look like privacy nightmares, but many of them are actually riddled with data that can unwittingly disclose information about you, other people who have used the document, file locations, email addresses, and much more. This type of information is known as *metadata*, and if you're even slightly concerned about maintaining your privacy, you should take steps to minimize or remove metadata.

That's not to say that metadata is always evil. Much metadata is generated by the collaboration techniques you learned about in Chapter 7, "Working as a Team: Collaborating with Other Users" and Chapter 9, "Collaborating with a Tablet PC and OneNote." Tracked changes, comments, and annotations all generate metadata about the reviewers, which is truly useful in a collaborative environment. However, after the document is finished, all that metadata is no longer required; and if you'll be publishing the document, the metadata is a serious privacy concern, as well.

The next three sections show you how to eliminate metadata as much as possible in your Office documents.

Setting Document Privacy Options

Word, Excel, PowerPoint, and Publisher all contain an option that automatically eliminates much metadata—including the document author, track changes authors, and comment authors—each time you save a document. Follow these steps to activate this option:

1. Select Tools, Options to display the Options dialog box.
2. Select the Security tab.
3. Activate the Remove Personal Information from File Properties on Save check box.
4. Click OK.

Note that Word's Security tab also contains the following privacy options:

- Warn Before Printing, Saving or Sending a File that Contains Tracked Changes or Comments—When you activate this option, any attempt to print, save, or email a document that has tracked changes or comments results in a query dialog box similar to the one shown in Figure 14.13. Click OK to continue with the operation; click Cancel to end the operation.

Figure 14.13
You can set up Word to warn you when you attempt to print, save, or email a document that contains tracked changes or comments.

■ Store Random Number to Improve Merge Accuracy—When this option is activated, Word stamps a document with a unique random number. When you attempt to merge two versions of a document, Word uses this random number to enhance the merge process. However, a savvy user could theoretically use the random number to prove that two documents are related (that is, one is an earlier version of the other). If you removed sensitive data from one version, but the other version still contains this data, the random number tells the snoop that's he's found the scrubbed data. Although this isn't a serious privacy threat, it's probably still a good idea to deactivate this option.

Preventing Outlook from Adding Properties
Even if you scrub your Word document clean, you could still be foiled by Outlook if you send the document as an attachment, because Outlook automatically adds properties that identify the sender, among other privacy-busting items. To prevent this, select Tools, Options, select the Preferences tab, click E-mail Options, click Advanced E-mail Options, and then deactivate the Add Properties to Attachments to Enable Reply with Changes check box.

■ Make Hidden Markup Visible When Opening or Saving—When this option is activated, Word displays markup (such as tracked changes, comments, and ink annotations) when you open a document. To leave markup hidden after opening a document, deactivate this option.

Using the Remove Hidden Data Tool

Word, Excel, and PowerPoint documents actually have a lot more privacy problems than simply the personal information of the document authors and editors. Document versions, routing slips, Excel scenario comments, and even recorded VBA macro descriptions (which include your name) are all potential privacy problems.

All these items can be scrubbed from a document by hand, but Microsoft has given us an easier method: an Office add-in called the Remove Hidden Data tool, which you can download here:

```
http://www.microsoft.com/downloads/details.aspx?
➥FamilyID=144e54ed-d43e-42ca-bc7b-5446d34e5360
```

This add-in enhances privacy by automating the removal of the following document data:

- Your username
- Your personal summary information
- The names of previous authors and editors
- Revision marks (all revisions are accepted)
- Reviewer comments
- Deleted text
- Document versions
- Routing slips
- Email headers
- Descriptions added as comments to recorded VBA macros
- In Excel, comments attached to scenarios
- In Office 97 documents only, unique identifiers (which included information about the computer and the person who registered the software)

Remove Hidden Data Tool Issues

Before running the Remove Hidden Data add-in, you might want to take a look at the known issues (none of which are terribly serious) for this program, as described here:

    http://support.microsoft.com/default.aspx?scid=kb;en-us;834636

After you install the Remove Hidden Data tool, follow these steps to use it on a document:

1. Open the document you want to work with.
2. Select File, Remove Hidden Data. The Remove Hidden Data dialog box appears, as shown in Figure 14.14.

Figure 14.14
Use the Remove Hidden Data add-in to remove private data from a document.

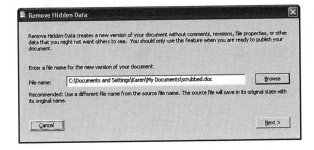

3. Enter the path and filename of the new version of the document that will have the private data removed, and then click Next. The add-in removes the private data.
4. Click Finish. The add-in displays a report of the data it removed.

Removing Other Private Data

The Remove Hidden Data add-in does a good job of removing the major sources of private data, but it doesn't get them all. The next few sections take you through a few other potential sources of privacy breaches.

Removing Hidden Text

If you use hidden text in a Word document to store sensitive information, you need to be sure to delete that text before publishing the document. One way to do this is to display hidden text (select Tools, Options, select the View tab, and activate the Hidden Text check box) and then use the Find feature to locate text where the font is formatted as hidden. You could also use a VBA macro like the one shown in Listing 14.1.

This Chapter's Examples

You'll find the Word, Excel, and PowerPoint files used as examples in this chapter on my website at www.mcfedries.com/OfficeGurus.

Listing 14.1   A Procedure That Finds the Hidden Text in the Active Document and Prompts to Delete It

```
Sub RemoveHiddenText()
    Dim nResult As Integer
    Dim nDeletes As Integer
    Dim nRemaining As Integer
    '
    ' Start from the top of the document
    '
    Selection.HomeKey Unit:=wdStory
    '
    ' Display hidden text
    '
    ActiveDocument.ActiveWindow.View.ShowHiddenText = True
    '
    ' Find and display all instances of hidden text
    '
    nDeletes = 0
    nRemaining = 0
    Do While True
        '
        ' Find the next instance
        '
        With Selection.Find
            .ClearFormatting
            .Text = ""
            .Replacement.Text = ""
            .Forward = True
            .Wrap = wdFindStop
            .Format = True
            .Font.Hidden = True
```

```
        .Execute
        '
        ' Was it found?
        '
        If .Found Then
            '
            ' If so, ask the user if they want to delete it
            '
            nResult = MsgBox("The following hidden text was found " & _
                            "in the document:" & vbCrLf & vbCrLf & _
                            Selection.Text & vbCrLf & vbCrLf & _
                            "Do you want to delete it?", _
                            vbYesNo, "Found Hidden Text")
            '
            ' If Yes, delete it
            '
            If nResult = vbYes Then
                Selection.Range.Delete
                nDeletes = nDeletes + 1
            Else
                nRemaining = nRemaining + 1
            End If
        Else
            '
            ' If no more hidden text was found,
            ' we're done, so exit the loop
            '
            Exit Do
        End If
    End With
Loop
MsgBox "Instances of hidden text deleted: " & nDeletes & vbCrLf & _
       "Instances of hidden text remaining: " & nRemaining,,"Done!"
End Sub
```

This procedure sets the ShowHiddenText property to True to display the active document's hidden text. A Do loop then calls the Find method to look for the next instance of hidden text (where the Font.Hidden property is True). If an instance is found (the Find object's Found property is True), a message is displayed, like the example shown in Figure 14.15. Click Yes to delete the hidden text (and increment the nDeletes counter) or click No to leave it (and increment the nRemaining counter). When all the instances of hidden text have been found, the code exits the Do loop and another message box shows the number of instances of hidden text deleted and still remaining in the document.

Figure 14.15
When the RemoveHiddenText macro finds an instance of hidden text in the active document, it displays a message box like the one shown here.

14

Removing Hyperlinks

Hyperlinks in a document can cause privacy problems because they may point to local files, network shares, or web pages that contain sensitive data. Just in case, use the VBA procedure in Listing 14.2 to examine the hyperlinks and handle them accordingly (delete the entire hyperlink, including the display text; delete just the link; or do nothing).

This Chapter's Examples

Listing 14.2 applies to a Word document, but you can also remove hyperlinks from Excel and PowerPoint documents using a similar technique. See my website for the Excel and PowerPoint versions of Listing 14.2.

Listing 14.2   A Procedure That Finds the Hyperlinks in the Active Document and Prompts to Delete the Entire Hyperlink or Just the Link

```
Sub RemoveHyperlinks()
    Dim nResult As Integer
    Dim nHDeletes As Integer
    Dim nLDeletes As Integer
    Dim nRemaining As Integer
    Dim r As Range
    Dim hl As Hyperlink
    '
    ' Initialize counters
    '
    nHDeletes = 0
    nLDeletes = 0
    nRemaining = 0
    '
    ' Run through all the hyperlinks in the document
    '
    For Each r In ActiveDocument.StoryRanges
        For Each hl In r.Hyperlinks
            nResult = MsgBox("The following hyperlink was found in " & _
                        "the document:" & vbCrLf & vbCrLf & _
                        "Text: " & hl.TextToDisplay & vbCrLf & _
                        "Link: " & hl.Address & vbCrLf & vbCrLf & _
                        "Click Yes to delete entire hyperlink" & vbCrLf & _
                        "Click No to delete just the link" & vbCrLf & _
                        "Click Cancel to leave the hyperlink", _
                        vbYesNoCancel, "Found Hyperlink")
            '
            ' Handle the result
            '
            Select Case nResult
                Case vbYes
                    '
                    ' Delete the entire hyperlink
                    '
                    hl.Range.Delete
                    nHDeletes = nHDeletes + 1
                Case vbNo
                    '
```

```
                          ' Delete just the link
                          '
                          hl.Delete
                          nLDeletes = nLDeletes + 1
                    Case vbCancel
                          '
                          ' Leave the hyperlink as is
                          '
                          nRemaining = nRemaining + 1
                End Select
          Next
    Next
    MsgBox "Hyperlinks deleted: " & nHDeletes & vbCrLf & _
            "Links deleted: " & nLDeletes & vbCrLf & _
            "Hyperlinks remaining: " & nRemaining, , "Done!"

End Sub
```

The `RemoveHyperlinks` procedure runs through all the hyperlinks in the active document. For each one, it displays a message that lists the hyperlink text and address and asks the user what to do with the hyperlink: delete it, delete just the link, or ignore it (refer to Figure 14.15). A `Select Case` structure handles the three possibilities and increments the corresponding counters. When all the hyperlinks have been handled, a message box displays the final counter totals, as shown in Figure 14.16.

Figure 14.16
When the `RemoveHyperlinks` procedure finds a hyperlink, it displays a message box similar to the one shown here.

Remove Document Variables

As you learned in Chapter 11, "Maximizing Office with VBA Macros," you can use program variables to store data for later use in a procedure. One common problem that VBA programmers face is how to store data between macro sessions. That is, if I run a macro today, how can I preserve the results for when I run the macro again tomorrow?

→ See "Understanding Program Variables," p. 372

You can use a number of methods to overcome this program—for example, by storing the data in the Windows Registry—but one solution that Word VBA programmers often turn to is the *document variable*. This is a storage location similar to a program variable, except that instead of being stored in memory, the variable is stored in a Word document. The variable isn't visible to the user, but any VBA programmer can easily write a short procedure to enumerate a document's variables and their values.

14

If you or someone else has used document variables to store private or sensitive data, you should clear the document variables before making the document available for public consumption. Listing 14.3 shows a procedure that removes the document variables from a Word document. Click Yes to delete the document variable (and increment the nDeletes counter) or No to leave it (and increment the nRemaining counter). When all the instances of document variables have been handled, the code displays another message box showing the number of variables deleted and still remaining in the document.

Listing 14.3   A Procedure That Finds the Variables in a Document and Prompts to Delete Them

```
Sub RemoveDocumentVariables()
    Dim nresult As Integer
    Dim nDeletes As Integer
    Dim nRemaining As Integer
    Dim v As Variable
    '
    ' Find and display all instances of document variables
    '
    nDeletes = 0
    nRemaining = 0
    For Each v In ActiveDocument.Variables
        '
        ' In each case, ask the user if they want to delete it
        '
        nresult = MsgBox("The following variable was found " & _
                         "in the document:" & vbCrLf & vbCrLf & _
                         "Name: " & v.Name & vbCrLf & _
                         "Value: " & v.Value & vbCrLf & vbCrLf & _
                         "Do you want to delete it?", _
                         vbYesNo, "Found Document Variable")
        '
        ' If Yes, delete it
        '
        If nresult = vbYes Then
            v.Delete
            nDeletes = nDeletes + 1
        Else
            nRemaining = nRemaining + 1
        End If
    Next 'v
    MsgBox "Document variables deleted: " & nDeletes & vbCrLf & _
           "Document variables remaining: " & nRemaining, , "Done!"
End Sub
```

The RemoveDocumentVariables procedure runs through the collection of Variable objects in the active document. In each case, the procedure displays a message box showing the variable name and value, as shown in Figure 14.17.

Figure 14.17
When the
RemoveDocument
Variables procedure
finds a document vari-
able, it displays a mes-
sage box similar to the
one shown here.

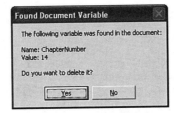

Removing Field Codes with Links

Another potential Word privacy breach is a field in which the code contains a link. For
example, the IncludePicture field inserts a picture into a document by linking to an image
file on a local hard disk, network share, or remote server. Similarly, the Link field inserts an
object based on a pathname or URL. You should examine your document for linked field
codes before publishing it.

→ For the details on using fields in Word, see "Using Fields to Insert Dynamic Data," p. 21

If you have only a few fields, one way to prevent privacy problems is to display all the field
codes (select Tools, Options, display the View tab, activate the Field Codes check box, and
select Always in the list box). For each field that contains a link, click the field and then
press Ctrl+Shift+F9 to unlink the field.

If you have a number of fields, however, use the procedure in Listing 14.4 to run through
all the fields automatically.

Listing 14.4   A Procedure That Finds the Fields in a Document and Prompts to Delete Them

```
Sub RemoveLinkedFields()
    Dim nresult As Integer
    Dim nDeletes As Integer
    Dim nUnlinks As Integer
    Dim nRemaining As Integer
    Dim f As Field
    '
    ' Find and display all instances of document variables
    '
    nDeletes = 0
    nUnlinks = 0
    nRemaining = 0
    For Each f In ActiveDocument.Fields
        '
        ' Check for a linked field
        '
        If f.Type = wdFieldIncludePicture Or _
            f.Type = wdFieldIncludeText Or _
            f.Type = wdFieldLink Then
            '
            ' In each case, ask the user if they want to delete it
            '
```

continues

14

Listing 14.4 **Continued**

```
            nresult = MsgBox("The following linked field was found " & _
                       "in the document:" & vbCrLf & vbCrLf & _
                       "Code: " & f.Code & vbCrLf & vbCrLf & _
                       "Click Yes to delete the field" & vbCrLf & _
                       "Click No to unlink the field" & vbCrLf & _
                       "Click Cancel to leave the field", _
                       vbYesNoCancel, "Found Linked Field")
            '
            ' Handle the result
            '
            Select Case nresult
                Case vbYes
                    '
                    ' Delete the field
                    '
                    f.Delete
                    nDeletes = nDeletes + 1
                Case vbNo
                    '
                    ' Unlink the field
                    '
                    f.Unlink
                    nUnlinks = nUnlinks + 1
                Case vbCancel
                    '
                    ' Leave the field as is
                    '
                    nRemaining = nRemaining + 1
            End Select
        End If
    Next 'f
    MsgBox "Fields deleted: " & nDeletes & vbCrLf & _
           "Fields unlinked: " & nUnlinks & vbCrLf & _
           "Fields remaining: " & nRemaining, , "Done!"
End Sub
```

The RemoveLinkedFields procedure runs through all the fields in the active document. For each one, it tests for a linked field type; if it finds one, it displays a message that lists the field code and asks the user what to do with the field: delete it, unlink it, or ignore it (see Figure 14.18). A Select Case structure handles the three possibilities and increments the corresponding counters. When all the fields have been handled, a message box displays the final counter totals.

Figure 14.18
When the RemoveLinked Fields procedure finds a field, it displays a message box similar to the one shown here.

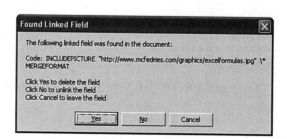

Controlling VBA Security

With a full-blown programming language—Visual Basic for Applications—built in to the very fabric of the major Office applications, the security of that language becomes a major issue. With VBA and Office, you need to think of security from two perspectives:

- The user—From the user's perspective, VBA is a security threat because scripts attached to other people's documents can be malicious (for example, deleting the user's files or folders).

- The developer—From the developer's perspective, VBA is a security threat because other people can easily open the VBA Editor and accidentally or purposely alter or delete code.

The next few sections show you how to set up VBA security to handle both scenarios.

Setting the Macro Security Level

Go to any antivirus site and run a search on the words "VBA" and "virus" and you'll probably come up with thousands—yes, *thousands*—of hits. Malicious programs coded in VBA and attached to innocent-looking Word, Excel, and PowerPoint files are legion and are one of the most common sources of virus infection. In Chapter 15, "Enhancing Outlook Email Security and Privacy," you'll learn that Outlook 2003 blocks most potentially dangerous attachments, including executable files, batch files, and Windows Scripting Host files. However, Outlook 2003 doesn't block Word, Excel, and PowerPoint documents, so you need an extra layer or two of defense.

→ For more information on Outlook and email attachments, see "Handling Attachments," p. 486

Your first line of defense should always be a top-of-the-line virus scanner, particularly one that scans Office documents for viruses before allowing you to open them. Install the scanner and, most importantly, keep its virus definitions up-to-date.

Even with a high-end antivirus program on the job, it's still possible (although highly unlikely) for a virus that the scanner doesn't recognize to sneak through. Because of this, you should add a second line of defense: setting the macro security level in each Office application that can run macros. Here are the steps to follow:

1. In any VBA-enabled Office application, select Tools, Macro Security to display the Security dialog box shown in Figure 14.19.

2. In the Security Level tab, activate one of the following security levels (not all levels are available in some Office applications):
   - Very High—If you select this option, the Office application enables macros only if they're installed in a trusted folder on your hard disk. This gives you near-total macro safety, but for most applications, the need to set up a trusted location is overkill.

14

Figure 14.19
Use the Security dialog box to set the macro security level in each VBA-enabled Office application.

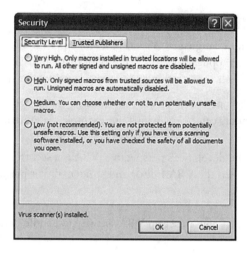

- High—If you select this option, the Office application enables macros only if they come from a trusted source—that is, a source that has digitally signed the VBA project using a trusted code-signing certificate. Macros from any other source are automatically disabled. This is the default security level for all Office applications and it gives you almost total macro safety. (If you develop macros for your own use, this level can cause problems. See "Self-Certifying Your VBA Projects," later in this chapter, for more information.) To use macros with this security level, look for the Security Warning dialog box when you open a document with a digitally signed VBA project. Activate the Always Trust Macros from This Publisher check box and then click Enable Macros.

- Medium—If you select this option, the Office application warns you when a document you're about to open contains macros and gives you the option of enabling or disabling the macros. This is a useful option if you often open third-party documents. If you're expecting the document to contain macros, you can go ahead and enable them; if you're not expecting macros, disable them and then check out the code to see if it's malicious.

- Low—If you select this option, the Office application runs all macros without prompting. If you don't have a virus scanner installed, use this level if you run only your own macros and you never open documents created by a third-party. If you do have a virus scanner, this level is probably safe if you open third-party documents only from people or sources you know. (However, you run the risk of opening documents containing malicious code that the scanner doesn't recognize.)

3. Click OK.

Self-Certifying Your VBA Projects

If you're a VBA developer and you set the macro security level to High, you'll immediately run into a problem: Office won't allow you to run your own macros! The problem is an obvious one, if you think about it: Office doesn't know that you created the macros yourself. Fortunately, it's possible to "prove" that you're the author of your own macros. You do that by *self-certifying*, which creates a trust certificate that applies only to your own work and to using that work on your own computer. The certificate is not valid on any other computer and so isn't a substitute for getting a proper code-signing digital certificate. However, if you all you want to do is run your own macros, self-certifying enables you to do that while still using the High macro security level.

Getting a Code-Signing Certificate

If you distribute your VBA projects to people running High macro security, the only way they'll be able to run your macros is if you get a proper code-signing digital certificate from a trusted certification authority. If you work for a large corporation or a software company, your network administrator may be able to generate a certificate for you. Otherwise, you'll need to purchase a certificate from a third-party certification authority. To see a list of trusted authorities, check out the following page on Microsoft's MSDN site:

```
msdn.microsoft.com/library/en-us/dnsecure/html/rootcertprog.asp
```

You self-certify by using a program that ships with Office 2003. Here's how it works:

1. Select Start, Run to open the Run dialog box.
2. Type the following and click OK (change *d* to the letter of the drive in which you installed Office 2003):
   ```
   d:\Program Files\Microsoft Office\OFFICE11\SELFCERT.EXE
   ```
3. In the Create Digital Certificate dialog box, type your name into the text box and then click OK.
4. When SelfCert reports that the certificate has been created, click OK.

Now that you are self-certified, you need to digitally sign your VBA project to enable its macros. Here are the steps to follow:

1. In the VBA Editor, select the VBA project you want to digitally sign.
2. Select Tools, Digital Signature to display the Digital Signature dialog box.
3. Click Choose to display the Select Certificate dialog box, shown in Figure 14.20.
4. Select your certificate and click OK to return to the Digital Signature dialog box.
5. Click OK.
6. Save the document, close it, and then reopen it. The Office application displays a Security Warning dialog box similar to the one shown in Figure 14.21.
7. Activate the Always Trust Macros from This Publisher check box.
8. Click Enable Macros.

14

Figure 14.20
Use the Select Certificate dialog box to select the digital certificate you created via self-certification.

Figure 14.21
When you reopen the document that contains your digitally signed VBA project, the Security Warning dialog box appears.

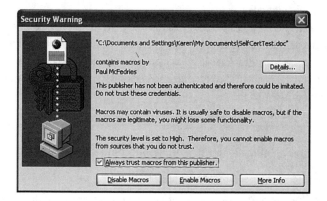

Using Your Certificate on Another Computer

In theory, a certificate generated by self-certifying will be authenticated only on the some computer that generated the certificate. However, in practice it's possible to also use the certificate on other computers by telling Windows in advance that the certificate is to be fully trusted. First you need to export your certificate to a file. In the VBA Editor, select Tools, Digital Signature, click Detail, display the Details tab, and then click Copy to File. This launches the Certificate Export Wizard, which takes you step-by-step through the process of exporting your certificate. (Be sure to export the file to a network share or other location that's accessible by the other computer.) After that's done, switch to the other computer, select Start, Run, type `certmgr.msc`, and click OK. In the Certificates window, select Trusted Root Certification Authority and then select Action, All Tasks, Import. This launches the Certificate Import Wizard. Use the wizard to locate the exported certificate and place it into the Trusted Root Certification Authorities store.

Locking a VBA Project

If you're a VBA developer and you distribute your projects to other users, it's unlikely that you want those users to tamper with your code, either accidentally or purposely. You can prevent that by locking your VBA project, as shown in the following steps:

1. In the VBA Editor, select the VBA project you want to lock.

2. Select Tools, *Project* Properties, where *Project* is the name of the VBA project.

3. Select the Protection tab.

4. Activate the Lock Project for Viewing check box.

5. Type a password required for viewing the project into both the Password and Confirm Password boxes.

6. Click OK.

From Here

- For information on using fields in Word, see the section titled "Using Fields to Insert Dynamic Data" in Chapter 1.

- For the details on tracking changes in a Word document, see the section titled "Tracking Word Document Changes" in Chapter 7.

- To learn about variables in VBA programming, see the section titled, "Understanding Program Variables" in Chapter 11.

- For an in-depth look at Outlook email security, see Chapter 15, "Enhancing Outlook Email Security and Privacy."

14

Enhancing Outlook Email Security and Privacy

15

As more people, businesses, and organizations establish a presence online, the world becomes an increasingly connected place. And the more connected the world becomes, the more opportunities arise for communicating with others, doing research, sharing information, and collaborating on projects. The flip side to this new connectedness is the increased risk of connecting with a remote user whose intentions are less than honorable. It could be a *packet sniffer*—a person who monitors network traffic to steal sensitive data—who steals your password or credit card number, a cracker who breaks into your Internet account, a virus programmer who sends a Trojan-horse virus attached to an email, or a spammer looking to dupe you out of your hard-earned money.

Admittedly, online security threats are relatively rare and are no reason to swear off the online world. However, these threats *do* exist, and people fall victim to them every day. Luckily, protecting yourself from these and other e-menaces doesn't take much effort or time, as you'll see in this chapter, in which I discuss the security tools built into Microsoft Outlook.

Guarding Against Email Viruses

Until just a few years ago, the primary method that computer viruses used to propagate themselves was the floppy disk. A user with an infected machine would copy some files to a floppy, and the virus would surreptitiously add itself to the disk. When the recipient inserted the disk, the virus copy would come to life and infect yet another computer.

When the Internet became a big deal, viruses adapted and began propagating either via malicious websites or via infected program files downloaded to users' machines.

Over the past few years, however, by far the most productive method for viruses to replicate has been the humble email message. Melissa, I Love You, BadTrans, Sircam, Klez. The list of email viruses and Trojan horses is a long one, but they all operate more or less the same way: they arrive as a message attachment, often from someone you know. When you open the attachment, the virus infects your computer and then, without your knowledge, uses Outlook and your address book to ship out messages with more copies of itself attached. The nastier versions will also mess with your computer, including deleting data and corrupting files.

You can avoid getting infected by one of these viruses by implementing a few common-sense procedures:

- Never open an attachment that comes from someone you don't know.

- Even if you know the sender, if the attachment isn't something you're expecting, assume the sender's system is infected. Write back and confirm that he or she sent the message.

- Some viruses come packaged as scripts that are hidden within messages that use the Rich Text or HTML formats. This means that the virus can run just by your viewing the message! If a message looks suspicious, don't open it, just delete it. (Note that you'll need to turn off the Outlook Reading pane before deleting the message. Otherwise, when you highlight the message, it will appear in the Reading pane and set off the virus. Select View, Reading Pane, Off.)

- Install a top-of-the-line antivirus program, particularly one that checks incoming email. Also, be sure to keep your antivirus program's virus list up-to-date. As you read this, there are probably dozens, maybe even hundreds, of morally challenged scumnerds designing even nastier viruses. Regular updates will help you keep up.

Checking Antivirus Compatibility

Most major antivirus programs integrate well with Office 2003, meaning that the programs automatically run a virus scan on all Word, Excel, and PowerPoint documents that you open. To check whether your antivirus software integrates with Office, select Tools, Macro, Security in Word, Excel, or PowerPoint to open the Security dialog box. You'll know that your antivirus program is compatible with Office if you see the following message near the bottom of the Security Level tab:

```
Virus scanner(s) installed
```

Besides these general procedures, Outlook also comes with its own set of virus-protection features. The next few sections show you how to use them.

Working with Security Zones

When implementing security for Internet Explorer, Microsoft realized that different sites have different security needs. For example, it makes sense to have fairly stringent security for Internet sites, but you can probably scale the security back a bit when browsing pages on your corporate intranet.

The way Internet Explorer handles security is to classify web pages according to different security *zones*. Each zone is a collection of web pages that implements a common security level. From the perspective of Outlook, you use the security zones to determine whether active content inside a HTML-format message is allowed to run.

Checking the Outlook Security Zone

To check your Outlook security zone setting, follow these steps:

1. Select Tools, Options to display the Options dialog box.
2. Select the Security tab.
3. In the Zone list, you have two choices:
    - Internet Zone—If you choose this zone, active content is allowed to run.
    - Restricted Sites Zone—If you choose this option, active content is disabled. This is the default setting and it's the one I recommend.
4. Click OK.

Changing a Zone's Security Level

To change the security level for a zone, display the Security tab and then click the Zone Settings button. When Outlook warns you that you're about to change security settings, click OK to display the Security dialog box. In the Select a Web Content Zone to Specify Its Security Settings list, select the zone you want to work with, then use the Security Level for This Zone slider to set the level. (If you don't see this slider, click Default Level.) To set up your own security settings, click Custom Level to display the Security Settings dialog box, which provides you with a long list of possible security issues. Your job is to specify how you want to handle each issue. You usually have three choices: Disable (security is turned on), Enable (security is turned off), or Prompt (you're asked how you want to handle the issue).

Viewing a Restricted Message Using the Internet Zone

The Restricted Sites zone blocks ActiveX controls, scripts, and other potentially unsafe content in HTML messages. Considering that such content is rarely required in an email message, you shouldn't feel like you're missing much when you use the Restricted Sites zone with Outlook. However, that doesn't mean that ActiveX controls and scripts are *never* useful in an email. Some data require active content, so you may occasionally get an email that doesn't display properly because of the Restricted Sites zone's proscriptions. Fortunately, you don't have to abandon the security of the Restricted Sites zone to view the active content of the occasional message. Instead, you can ask Outlook to view the message using the Internet Zone, which does allow active content. Here's how you do this:

1. Double-click the message to open it in its own window.
2. Select View, View in Internet Zone. Outlook displays the warning shown in Figure 15.1.

Figure 15.1
When you select the View in Internet Zone command, Outlook displays this warning message.

3. If you are absolutely certain that the message is safe, click Yes to allow the active content to run; if you have even the smallest doubt about the message's active content, click No.

Disabling HTML and Rich Text

Using the Restricted Sites zone gives you a high level of email security, but does it make email completely safe? I'd really like to be able to tell you that it does, but if the Internet's relatively short history tells us anything, it's that virus writers and other online miscreants *always* find a way around even the toughest restrictions. So even though I can't even imagine *how* someone would break through the Restricted Sites zone's barriers, I'm paranoid enough to believe that someday someone *will* do it.

If you're as paranoid as I am, you need to augment the Restricted Sites settings with the highest level of protection possible: plain text. That is, you need to tell Outlook to eschew HTML and Rich Text formatting and, instead, display all your messages using plain text: no fancy fonts, no colors, no HTML tags, no images, no sounds: just simple, unadorned text where no virus or other malicious content can hide. Here are the steps to follow:

1. Select Tools, Options to display the Options dialog box.
2. In the Preference tab, click E-mail Options.
3. Activate the Read All Standard Mail in Plain Text check box.
4. If you also want to view digitally signed messages as text-only, activate the Read All Digitally Signed Mail in Plain Text check box.
5. Click OK.

When you receive an HTML or Rich Text message, Outlook converts the message to plain text when you view it either in the Reading pane or in its own window, as shown in Figure 15.2. Notice that the Information pane includes the following message:

```
This message was converted to plain text.
```

Changing the Plain Text Font
The default plain text font is 10-point Courier New, which isn't particularly attractive as fonts go. To change the plain text font, select Tools, Options, display the Mail Format tab, and then click Fonts. Beside the When Composing and Reading Plain Text box, click Choose Font and then use the Font dialog box to select the font you prefer.

Figure 15.2
When you view an HTML or Rich Text message, Outlook converts it to plain text.

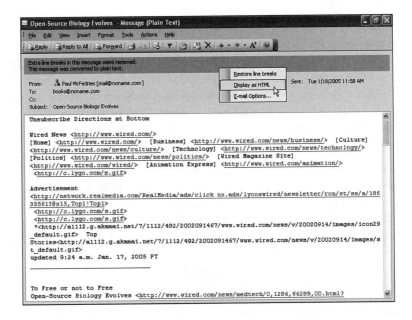

Note that this conversion is for display purposes only. The original message remains in its original format in your Inbox. To prove this for yourself, you can easily view the original formatting by clicking the Information pane and then clicking Display as HTML (refer to Figure 15.2). Outlook converts the message to its original format, as shown in Figure 15.3.

Figure 15.3
Click the Information pane and then click Display as HTML to view the message using its original formatting.

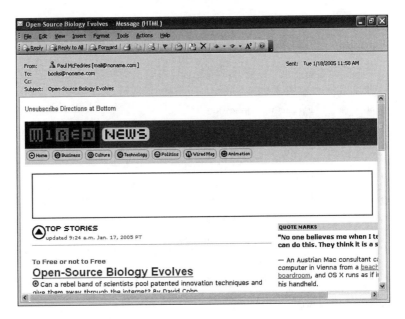

15

Handling Attachments

It is sobering to contemplate the billions of dollars and hundreds of thousands of man-hours lost because of major virus outbreaks over the past few years. It is saddening to realize that almost all of those outbreaks were started and escalated by a simple action repeated thousands of times: opening an email attachment. For Microsoft, it was no doubt frightening to realize that most of the damage was caused by Outlook users because, in most cases, these viruses took advantage of security holes to not only infect each user's PC, but also to pass along copies of the virus to other users.

Chastened by all of this, Microsoft designed Outlook 2003 with a grim determination to avoid similar problems. Most drastically, Microsoft identified around 70 file types that could potentially cause problems as attachments, and then simply disallowed the opening of those file types. Note that Microsoft didn't merely make it inconvenient to open these file types; no, they made it *impossible* without high-level tweaks (that I'll show you a bit later). If someone sends you, for instance, a file with the .exe extension (an executable file), Outlook displays the following message in the Information pane:

```
Outlook blocked access to the following potentially unsafe attachments: filename
```

Here, *filename* is the name of the blocked file. If you select the File, Save Attachments command, the blocked file does *not* appear in the submenu. There is, in short, no way to view, open, or save the attachment.

Table 15.1 runs through all the file types and their associated extensions that Outlook 2003 blocks.

Table 15.1	File Extensions Blocked by Outlook on Incoming Attachments
Extension	**File Type**
.ade	Access Project Extension
.adp	Access Project
.app	Executable Application
.asp	Active Server Page
.bas	BASIC Source Code
.bat	Batch File
.cer	Internet Security Certificate
.chm	Compiled HTML Help
.cmd	Command File for Windows NT
.com	Command File
.cpl	Windows Control Panel Extension
.crt	Security Certificate
.csh	Unix C Shell Script

Extension	File Type
.exe	Executable File
.fxp	FoxPro Compiled Source
.hlp	Windows Help File
.hta	Hypertext Application
.inf	Information or Setup File
.ins	IIS Internet Communications Settings
.isp	IIS Internet Service Provider Settings
.its	Internet Document Set
.js	JavaScript Source Code
.jse	JScript Encoded Script File
.ksh	Unix korn Shell Script
.lnk	Windows Shortcut File
.mad	Access Module Shortcut
.maf	Access Form Shortcut
.mag	Access Diagram Shortcut
.mam	Access Macro Shortcut
.maq	Access Query Shortcut
.mar	Access Report Shortcut
.mas	Access Stored Procedures
.mat	Access Table Shortcut
.mau	Media Attachment Unit
.mav	Access View Shortcut
.maw	Access Data Access Page
.mda	Access Add-in
.mdb	Access Application, Access Database
.mde	Access MDE Database File
.mdt	Access Add-in Data
.mdw	Access Workgroup Information
.mdz	Access Wizard Template
.msc	Microsoft Management Console Snap-in Control File
.msi	Windows Installer File

15

continues

15

Table 15.1 Continued	
Extension	**File Type**
.msp	Windows Installer Patch
.mst	Windows SDK Setup Transform Script
.ops	Office Profile Settings File
.pcd	Visual Test Script
.pif	Windows Program Information File
.prf	Windows System File
.prg	Program File
.pst	Outlook Personal Folder File
.reg	Registry Data File
.scf	Windows Explorer Command
.scr	Windows Screen Saver
.sct	Windows Script Component, Foxpro Screen
.shb	Windows Shortcut into a Document
.shs	Shell Scrap Object File
.tmp	Temporary File/Folder
.url	Internet Uniform Resource Locator
.vb	VBScript File, Visual Basic Source
.vbe	VBScript Encoded Script File
.vbs	VBScript Script, VBA Script
.vsmacros	Visual Studio .NET Binary-based Macro Project
.vss	Visio Stencil
.vst	Visio Template
.vsw	Visio Workspace File
.ws	Windows Script File
.wsc	Windows Script Component
.wsf	Windows Script File
.wsh	Windows Script Host Settings File

There is, to be sure, much that is potentially dangerous in Table 15.1, but also much that is potentially useful: Registry files, screen savers, Access databases, and batch files, to name just a few. How do you sneak such files past Outlook in cases where you know the files are safe? Here are some ideas:

- Compress the file into a ZIP archive. The .zip extension isn't blocked by Outlook, so your recipient can easily open or save the archive and then extract the original file.

- Rename the file's extension to one that isn't listed in Table 15.1. For example, rename script.wsh to script.wsh.delete. When your recipient saves the attachment, he or she can remove the extra extension to restore the original filename.

- If you have a website, put a copy of the file on the site and then send the file's URL in the message instead of the file itself.

- If you're working on a network, put a copy of the file in a shared network folder and then put the folder's network address in your message instead of attaching the file.

Virus-Check the Files!

No matter how you fool or bypass Outlook's attachment security, you still need to be smart about the attachments themselves. That is, always scan the files for viruses before opening them.

If you regularly get attachments of a certain file type, the preceding solutions may be more of a hassle than they're worth. Fortunately, there is a Registry tweak you can perform that enables you to specify one or more extensions that Outlook should open with less paranoia. Notice that I didn't say with *no* paranoia; even with the tweak, you still have a hurdle or two to jump through. To see why, first understand that the file types in Table 15.1 are what Microsoft calls *Level 1* file types. With Level 1, you don't get access to the files, period. However, Microsoft also defines *Level 2* file types. With these file types, you can access them as attachments, but *only* by first saving the files to your hard disk. That is, you can't open the files directly from the message. The assumption here is that saving the files to your hard disk gives you the opportunity to virus-check the files before opening them.

To specify a file type as Level 2 (there are no default Level 2 file types in Outlook 2003), follow these steps:

1. Open the Registry Editor.

→ For detailed information on using the Registry and the Registry Editor, see Appendix A, "Working with the Windows Registry," p. 507

2. Navigate to the following key:
   `HKEY_CURRENT_USER\Software\Microsoft\Office\11.0\Outlook\Security`

3. Select Edit, New, String Value.

4. Type **Level1Remove** and press Enter.

5. Press Enter to open the Level1Remove setting.

6. Type the extension of each file type you want to move to Level 2, separated by semicolons. For example, the following string moves the Registry Data File, Screen Saver, and Access Database file types to Level 2:
   `.reg;.scr;.mdb`

7. Shut down and restart Outlook to put the new setting into effect.

When you attempt to open a Level 2 file type attachment from a message, Outlook displays the warning dialog box shown in Figure 15.4. You need to click the Save to Disk button to save the attachment to your hard disk before you can open it.

Figure 15.4
You can work with Level 2 file types, but you must save them to your hard disk before you can open them.

Controlling Third-Party Access to Your Contacts

One of the biggest reasons that some recent email viruses have done such damage is that they've found a powerful new way to propagate themselves: they access the user's Contacts list and use it to send out dozens of new messages, each with its own infected file attached. In fact, it's not at all hard to access the Contacts list programmatically. Listing 15.1 shows a short bit of VBA code that does just that.

This Chapter's Examples
You'll find Outlook code used as examples in this chapter on my website at www.mcfedries.com/OfficeGurus.

Listing 15.1   A Procedure That Accesses the Outlook Contacts List from Another Application

```
Sub AccessOutlookAddressBook()
    Dim ol As Outlook.Application ' Outlook Automation object
    Dim ns As Namespace          ' Outlook NameSpace object
    Dim addr As AddressEntry      ' Outlook AddressEntry object
    '
    ' Establish a connection and log on to Outlook
    '
    Set ol = CreateObject("Outlook.Application")
    Set ns = ol.GetNamespace("MAPI")
    ns.Logon
    '
    ' Grab the first Contacts address
    ' This is where the Address Book security kicks in
    '
    Set addr = ns.AddressLists("Contacts").AddressEntries(1)
    '
    ' Display the name and address
    '
    MsgBox "The first Contacts entry is " & _
            addr.name & " <" & addr.Address & ">"
    '
```

```
    ' Log off the session and clear the objects
    '
    ns.Logoff
    Set addr = Nothing
    Set ns = Nothing
    Set ol = Nothing
End Sub
```

Referencing the Outlook Object Library

For the code in Listing 15.1 to work, your VBA project must include a reference to Outlook's object library. To set up that reference, select Tools, References to display the References dialog box. In the Available References list, activate the check box beside Microsoft Outlook 11.0 Object Library, and then click OK.

In Outlook 2003 (as well as older versions of Outlook with the E-mail Security Update installed), programmatic access to Contacts isn't forbidden (many legitimate applications require it), but it is monitored. When Outlook detects a script accessing any `AddressList` object, it immediately displays the dialog box shown in Figure 15.5. You now have two choices:

- If you're not running any applications that require access to your Contacts list, some funny business is almost certainly going on, so you should click No to prevent access.

- If you know the access is legitimate, activate the Allow Access For check box, select a time value in the list, and then click Yes.

Other Ways to Trigger the Warning

If you're writing VBA code or running third-party applications, you should know that a few other VBA techniques also trigger the warning dialog box shown in Figure 15.5. For example, if your code uses the `Body` or `HTMLBody` properties of a message, the warning appears because some malicious code uses these properties to extract addresses from the body text of stored messages. Similarly, the warning appears if the `WordEditor` and `HTMLEditor` properties are used, because these return the Word document object model and the HTML document object model, respectively, both of which can be used to compromise security.

Figure 15.5
Outlook enables you to control whether a script can access your Contacts list.

Controlling Third-Party Access to Sending Messages

It's still possible for a virus or script to propagate itself without accessing your Contacts list. For example, it might have its own database of addresses. For that reason, Outlook also guards against third-party scripts that send messages. Listing 15.2 shows such a procedure, which you can run from Word, Excel, or PowerPoint.

Listing 15.2   A Procedure That Sends an Email Message from Another Application

```
Sub SendMessage()
    Dim ol As Outlook.Application ' Outlook Automation object
    Dim ns As Namespace          ' Outlook NameSpace object
    Dim mi As MailItem           ' Outlook Mailitem object
    '
    ' Establish a connection and log on to Outlook
    '
    Set ol = CreateObject("Outlook.Application")
    Set ns = ol.GetNamespace("MAPI")
    ns.Logon
    '
    ' Create a new message
    '
    Set mi = ol.CreateItem(olMailItem)
    '
    ' Add a recipient without using Contacts
    '
    mi.To = "blah@yadda.com"
    mi.Subject = "Just Testing"
    '
    ' Send it
    ' This is where the Send security kicks in
    '
    mi.Send
    '
    ' Log off the session
    '
    ns.Logoff
    Set mi = Nothing
    Set ns = Nothing
    Set ol = Nothing
End Sub
```

As with access to the Contacts list, third-party sending requires your permission, so Outlook displays the dialog box shown in Figure 15.6. Again, click Yes to allow the send or click No to block it.

Figure 15.6
Outlook enables you to control whether a third-party script can send a message.

Blocking Spam Messages

Spam—unsolicited commercial messages—has become a plague upon the earth. Unless you've done a masterful job at keeping your address secret, you probably receive at least a few spam emails every day, and it's more likely that you receive a few dozen. The bad news is that most experts agree that it's only going to get worse. And why not? Spam is one of the few advertising mediums where the costs are substantially borne by the users, not the advertisers.

The best way to avoid spam is to not get on a spammer's list of addresses in the first place. That's hard to do these days, but there are some steps you can take:

- Never use your actual email address in a newsgroup account. The most common method that spammers use to gather addresses is to harvest them from newsgroup posts. One common tactic you can use is to alter your email address by adding text that invalidates the address but is still obvious for other people to figure out:

  `user@myisp.remove_this_to_email_me.com`

- When you sign up for something online, use a fake address if possible. If you need or want to receive email from the company and so must use your real address, make sure you deactivate any options that ask if you want to receive promotional offers. Alternatively, enter the address from a free web-based account (such as a Hotmail account), so that any spam you receive will go there instead of to your main address.

- Never open suspected spam messages, because doing so can sometimes notify the spammer that you've opened the message, thus confirming that your address is legit. For the same reason, you should never display a spam message in the Outlook Reading pane. As I described earlier, shut off the Reading pane before selecting any spam messages that you want to delete.

- Never, I repeat, *never*, respond to spam, even to an address within the spam that claims to be a "removal" address. By responding to the spam, all you're doing is proving that your address is legitimate, so you'll just end up getting *more* spam.

If you do get spam despite these precautions, the good news is that Outlook 2003 comes with a Junk E-mail feature that can help you cope. Junk E-mail is a *spam filter*, which means that it examines each incoming message and applies sophisticated tests to determine whether the message is spam. If the tests determine that the message is probably spam, the email is exiled to a separate Junk E-mail folder. It's not perfect (no spam filter is), but with a bit of fine-tuning, as described in the next few sections, it can be a very useful anti-spam weapon.

Setting the Junk E-mail Protection Level

Filtering spam is always a tradeoff between protection and convenience. That is, the stronger the protection you use, the less convenient the filter becomes, and vice versa. This inverse relationship is caused by a filter phenomenon called the *false positive*. This is a legitimate message that the filter has pegged as spam and so (in Outlook's case) moves the message to the Junk E-mail folder. The stronger the protection level, the more likely it is that false positives will occur, and the more time you must spend checking the Junk E-mail folder for legitimate messages that need to be rescued. Fortunately, Outlook gives you several Junk E-mail levels to choose from, so you can choose a level that gives the blend of protection and convenience that suits you.

Here are the steps to follow to set the Junk E-mail level:

1. Select Actions, Junk E-mail, Junk E-mail Options. Outlook displays the Junk E-mail Options dialog box.

2. The Options tab, shown in Figure 15.7, gives you four options for the Junk E-mail protection level:

   - No Automatic Filtering—This option turns off the Junk E-mail filter. However, Outlook still moves messages from blocked senders to the Junk E-mail folder (see "Blocking Senders," later in this chapter). Choose this option only if you use a third-party spam filter or if you handle spam using your own message rules.

   - Low—This is the default protection level and it's designed to move only messages with obvious spam content to the Junk E-mail folder. This is a good level to start with—particularly if you get only a few spams a day—because it catches most spam and has only a minimal risk of false positives.

   - High—This level handles spam aggressively and only rarely misses a junk message. On the downside, the High level also catches the occasional legitimate message in its nets, so you need to check the Junk E-mail folder regularly to look for false positives. Use this level if you get a lot of spam—a few dozen messages or more each day.

Turn Off the Reading Pane

To make checking the Junk E-mail folder more palatable, display it and then turn off the Reading pane (View, Reading Pane, Off). That way, you need to deal only with the Subject lines, which in the vast majority of cases are enough to let you know whether a message is spam or legitimate.

Marking False Positives as Not Junk

If you get a false positive in your Junk E-mail folder, click the message and then select Actions, Junk E-mail, Mark as Not Junk. (You can also click the Not Junk toolbar button or press Ctrl+Alt+J.) To prevent messages from the sender from being classified as spam in the future, leave the Always Trust E-mail From check box activated. Outlook adds the address to your Safe Senders list. If the message came from a mailing list, activate the check box (or boxes) in the Always Trust E-mail Sent to the Following Addresses list to place the addresses in your Safe Recipients list.

   - Safe Lists Only—This level treats all incoming messages as spam, except for those messages that come from people or domains in your Safe Senders list (see "Specifying Safe Senders," later in this chapter) or that are sent to addresses in your Safe Recipients list (see "Specifying Safe Recipients," later in this chapter).

Use this level if your spam problem is out of control (a hundred or more spams each day) and if most of your nonspam email comes from people you know or from mailing lists you subscribe to.

Figure 15.7
Use the Options tab to set the Junk E-mail protection to the level you prefer.

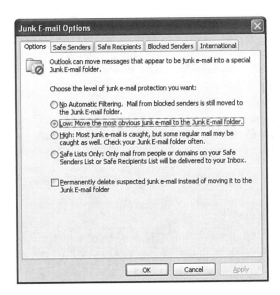

3. If you hate spam so much that you never want to even *see* it, much less deal with it, activate the Permanently Delete Suspected Junk E-mail check box.

Don't Permanently Delete Spam

Spam is so hair-pullingly frustrating that you may be tempted to activate the Permanently Delete Suspected Junk E-mail check box out of sheer spite. I don't recommend this, however. The danger of false positives is just too great, even with the Low level, and it's not worth missing a crucial message.

---

4. Click OK (or click Apply if you want to keep the Junk E-mail Options dialog box open).

Specifying Safe Senders

If you use the Low or High Junk E-mail protection level, you can reduce the number of false positives by letting Outlook know about the people or institutions that regularly send you mail. By designating these addresses as Safe Senders, you tell Outlook to automatically leave their incoming messages in your Inbox and to never redirect them to the Junk E-mail folder. And certainly if you use the Safe Lists Only protection level, you must specify some Safe Senders because Outlook treats everyone else as a spammer (unless they send mail to an address in your Safe Recipients list; see the next section).

Your Safe Senders list can consist of three types of addresses:

- Individual email addresses of the form *someone@somewhere.com*. All messages from these individual addresses will not be treated as spam.

- Domain names of the form *@somewhere.com*. All messages from any address within that domain will not be treated as spam.

- Your Contacts list. You can tell Outlook to treat everyone in your Contacts list as a Safe Sender, which makes sense because you're unlikely to be spammed by someone you know.

You can specify a Safe Sender either by entering the address by hand or by using an existing message from the sender. Let's start with the steps to follow to specify a Safe Sender by hand:

1. Select Actions, Junk E-mail, Junk E-mail Options to display the Junk E-mail Options dialog box.

2. Display the Safe Senders tab.

3. Click Add to display the Add Address or Domain dialog box.

4. Type the individual address or domain name and then click OK.

5. Repeat steps 3 and 4 to add more addresses to your Safe Senders list.

Adding Safe Senders in Bulk

If you have a lot of addresses to designate as Safe Senders, it can quickly grow tedious to use the Add Address or Domain dialog box. A much quicker method is to create a text file in which each address and domain appears on its own line. In the Safe Senders tab, click Import from File, select the text file in the Import Safe Senders dialog box, and then click Open.

---

6. To ensure that your Contacts are treated as Safe Senders, leave the Also Trust E-mail from My Contacts check box activated.

7. If you initiate an email to someone, it makes sense that you could treat that person as a Safe Sender because it's unlikely you'd ever send email to a spammer. To treat your recipients as Safe Senders, activate the Automatically Add People I E-mail to the Safe Senders List check box. (To see this feature, you need to have Office 2003 Service Pack 1 or later.)

8. Click OK (or click Apply if you want to keep the Junk E-mail Options dialog box open).

You can also populate your Safe Senders list using individual messages sent to you. Select the message you want to work with, select Actions, Junk E-mail, and then select one of the following commands:

- Add Sender to Safe Senders List—This command places the address of the message sender on your Safe Senders list.

- Add Sender's Domain (@example.com) to Safe Sender's List—This command places the domain name of the message sender's address on your Safe Senders list.

Backing Up Your Safe Senders

If you spend a lot of time populating and maintaining your Safe Senders list, it's a good idea to create a backup from time to time. In the Safe Senders tab, click Export to File, select a location and filename, and then click Save.

Specifying Safe Recipients

The Safe Recipients list is almost identical to the Safe Senders list. The difference is that Outlook examines the address to which each message was sent instead of the address from which it was sent. This is useful when you receive mail as part of a distribution list or mailing list, the posts to which are often sent to a list address instead of to individual subscriber addresses. By specifying this list address as a Safe Recipient, Outlook won't treat list messages as spam.

Again, you can specify a Safe Recipient either by entering the address by hand or by using an existing message from the sender. Here are the steps to follow to specify a Safe Recipient by hand:

1. Select Actions, Junk E-mail, Junk E-mail Options to display the Junk E-mail Options dialog box.
2. Display the Safe Recipients tab.
3. Click Add to display the Add Address or Domain dialog box.
4. Type the individual address or domain name and then click OK.
5. Repeat steps 3 and 4 to add more addresses to your Safe Recipients list.
6. Click OK (or click Apply if you want to keep the Junk E-mail Options dialog box open).

You can also populate your Safe Recipients list using individual messages sent to you. Select the message you want to work with and then select Actions, Junk E-mail, Add Recipient to Safe Recipients List.

Blocking Senders

If you notice that a particular address is the source of much spam or other annoying email, the easiest way to block the spam is to block all incoming messages from that address. You can do this using the Blocked Senders list, which watches for messages from a specific address and relegates them to the Junk E-mail folder.

As with Safe Senders and Safe Recipients, you can specify a Blocked Sender either by entering the address by hand or by using an existing message from the sender. Here are the steps to follow to specify a Blocked Sender by hand:

1. Select Actions, Junk E-mail, Junk E-mail Options to display the Junk E-mail Options dialog box.

2. Display the Blocked Senders tab.

3. Click Add to display the Add Address or Domain dialog box.

4. Type the individual address or domain name and then click OK.

5. Repeat steps 3 and 4 to add more addresses to your Blocked Senders list.

6. Click OK (or click Apply if you want to keep the Junk E-mail Options dialog box open).

You can also populate your Blocked Senders list using individual messages sent to you. Select the message you want to work with and then select Actions, Junk E-mail, Add Sender to Blocked Senders List.

Blocking Countries and Languages

Office 2003 Service Pack 1 gives you new Junk E-mail features that enable you to handle spam that has an international flavor:

- Spam that comes from a particular country or region—If you receive no legitimate messages from that country or region, you can treat all messages from that location as spam. Outlook does this by using the *top-level domain* (TLD), which is the final suffix that appears in a domain name. There are two types: a *generic top-level domain* (gTLD), such as "com," "edu," and "net"; and a *country code top-level domain* (ccTLD), such as "ca" (Canada) and "fr" (France). Outlook uses the latter to filter spam that comes from certain countries.

- Spam that comes in a foreign language—If you don't understand the language, you can safely treat all messages that appear in that language as spam. The character set of a foreign language always appears using a special *encoding* unique to that language. (An encoding is a set of rules that establishes a relationship between the characters and their representations.) Outlook uses this encoding to filter spam that appears in a specified language.

Follow these steps to filter spam based on countries and languages:

1. Select Actions, Junk E-mail, Junk E-mail Options to display the Junk E-mail Options dialog box.

2. Display the International tab.

3. To filter spam based on one or more countries, click Blocked Top-Level Domain List, activate the check box beside each of the countries you want to filter, and then click OK.

4. To filter spam based on one or more languages, click Blocked Encodings List, activate the check box beside each of the languages you want to filter, and then click OK.

5. Click OK (or click Apply if you want to keep the Junk E-mail Options dialog box open).

Maintaining Your Privacy While Reading Email

You wouldn't think that the simple act of reading an email message would have privacy implications, but you'd be surprised. There are actually three scenarios that compromise your privacy: read receipts, web bugs, and unauthorized forwarding. The next three sections explain each issue and show you how to maintain your privacy in each case.

Controlling Read Receipts

A *read receipt* is an email notification that tells the sender that you've opened the message that he or she sent you. If the sender requests a read receipt, Outlook displays a dialog box similar to the one shown in Figure 15.8, if you do the following:

- Double-click the message to open it.
- Move the selection off the message. (This works only if you have the Mark Item as Read When Selection Changes check box activated; select Tools, Options, display the Other tab, and then click Reading Pane.)
- Select the message so that the message text appears in the Reading pane. (This works only if you have the Mark Items as Read When Viewed in the Reading Pane check box activated; select Tools, Options, display the Other tab, and then click Reading Pane.)

Click Yes to send the receipt, or click No to skip it.

Figure 15.8
You see this dialog box when you open a message for which the sender has requested a read receipt.

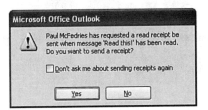

Many people like asking for read receipts because they offer "proof" not just that the message has been delivered, but also that the recipient has at least looked at the message. It has been my experience, however, that getting a read receipt back starts a kind of internal clock that the sender uses to "measure" how long it takes you to respond after reading the message. Because of this annoyance, and because you may feel, as I do, that it's nobody's business to know when you read a message, you should always click No when asked to send a read receipt.

15

In fact, you can go one better and tell Outlook to never send a read receipt. To do this, you have two choices:

- In the dialog box shown in Figure 15.8, activate the Don't Ask Me About Sending Receipts Again check box.
- Select Tools, Options, display the Preferences tab, click E-mail Options, click Tracking Options, and then activate the Never Send A Response option.

Squashing Web Bugs

A *web bug* is an image that resides on a remote server and that is added to an HTML-formatted email message by referencing a URL on the remote server. (Images and other objects that reside on a remote server rather than being embedded in the message are called *external content*.) When you open the message, Outlook uses the URL to download the image for display within the message. That sounds harmless enough, but if the message is junk email, it's likely that the URL will also contain either your email address or a code that points to your email address. When the remote server gets a request for this URL, it knows not only that you've opened their message, but also that your email address is legitimate.

Fortunately, Outlook 2003 is hip to the web bug menace, and it's set up to automatically block *any* external content (including sound files). When you receive an HTML message with links to remote images, Outlook blocks the images and, for each one, displays instead a placeholder containing a red X and a message telling you that the image has been blocked. The Information pane also tells you that the message's pictures have been blocked, as shown in Figure 15.9.

Figure 15.9
Outlook 2003 automatically blocks external images in HTML messages.

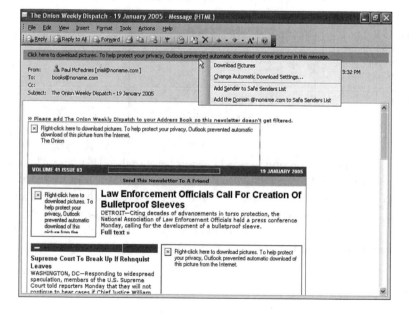

If you know the message isn't spam, you can view the images using either of the following techniques:

■ Click the Information pane and then click Download Pictures (refer to Figure 15.9).

■ Right-click an image placeholder and then click Download Pictures.

Note that the menus displayed using these techniques also give you commands for adding the sender's address or domain to the Safe Senders list. Placing the sender on your Safe Senders list means that in the future, Outlook will display the external content automatically.

To control the way Outlook handles external content, follow these steps:

1. Select Tools, Options to display the Options dialog box.

2. Display the Security tab.

3. Click Change Automatic Download Settings. Outlook displays the Automatic Picture Download Settings dialog box, shown in Figure 15.10.

Faster Access to Automatic Download Settings
A quicker way to get to the Automatic Picture Download Settings dialog box is to display a message with blocked external content, click the Information pane, and then click Change Automatic Download Settings.

Figure 15.10
Use this dialog box to control how Outlook downloads external content referenced in HTML messages.

4. Use the following four check boxes to control the external content:

• Don't Download Pictures or Other Content Automatically in HTML E-mail—This check box toggles Outlook's automatic blocking of external content on and off.

• Permit Downloads in E-mail Messages—When activated, this option tells Outlook to automatically download external content for addresses and domains in your Safe Senders and Safe Recipients lists.

- Permit Downloads from Web Sites in this Security Zone: Trusted Sites—When activated, this option tells Outlook to automatically download external content that comes from sites specified in your Trusted Sites security zone.

Adding Trusted Sites

To add a website to your Trusted Sites security zone, select Tools, Options, display the Security tab, click Zone Settings, and then click OK. In the Security dialog box, click the Trusted Sites zone and then click Sites. In the Trusted Sites dialog box, type the site address and click Add.

- Warn Me Before Downloading Content when Editing, Forwarding, or Replying to E-mail—When activated, this option tells Outlook to warn you that external content will be downloaded when you attempt to edit, reply to, or forward a message that contains external references, as shown in Figure 15.11.

Figure 15.11
Be default, Outlook displays this warning message when you attempt to edit, reply to, or forward a message that references external content.

5. Click OK.

Sending and Receiving Secure Email

When you connect to a website, your browser sets up a direct connection—called a *channel*—between your machine and the web server. Because the channel is a direct link, it's relatively easy to implement security because all you have to do is secure the channel, which is what security protocols such as Private Communication Technology (PCT) and Secure Sockets Layer (SSL) do.

However, email security is entirely different and much more difficult to set up. The problem is that email messages don't have a direct link to a Simple Mail Transfer Protocol (SMTP) server. Instead, they must usually "hop" from server to server until the final destination is reached. Combine this with the open and well-documented email standards used on the Internet, and you end up with three email security issues:

- Privacy—Because messages often pass through other systems and can even end up on a remote system's hard disk, it isn't that difficult for someone with the requisite know-how and access to the remote system to read a message.

- Tampering—Because a user can read a message passing through a remote server, it comes as no surprise that he or she can also change the message text.
- Authenticity—With the Internet email standards an open book, it isn't difficult for a savvy user to forge or *spoof* an email address.

To solve these issues, the Internet's gurus came up with the idea of *encryption*. When you encrypt a message, a complex mathematical formula scrambles the message content to make it unreadable. In particular, a *key value* is incorporated into the encryption formula. To unscramble the message, the recipient feeds the key into the decryption formula.

This *single-key encryption* works, but its major drawback is that the sender and the recipient must both have the same key. *Public-key encryption* overcomes that limitation by using two related keys: a *public key* and a *private key*. The public key is available to everyone, either by sending it to them directly or by offering it in an online key database. The private key is secret and is stored on the user's computer.

Here's how public-key cryptography solves the issues discussed earlier:

- Solving the privacy issue—When you send a message, you obtain the recipient's public key and use it to encrypt the message. The encrypted message can now only be decrypted using the recipient's private key, thus assuring privacy.
- Solving the tampering issue—An encrypted message can still be tampered with, but only randomly because the content of the message can't be seen. This thwarts the most important skill used by tamperers: making the tampered message look legitimate.
- Solving the authenticity issue—When you send a message, you use your private key to digitally sign the message. The recipient can then use your public key to examine the digital signature to ensure the message came from you.

If there's a problem with public-key encryption, it is that the recipient of a message must obtain the sender's public key from an online database. (The sender can't just send the public key because the recipient would have no way to prove that the key came from the sender.) Therefore, to make all this more convenient, a *digital ID* is used. This is a digital certificate that states the sender's public key has been authenticated by a trusted certifying authority. The sender can then include his or her public key in any outgoing messages.

Setting Up an Email Account with a Digital ID

To send secure messages using Outlook, you first have to obtain a digital ID. Here are the steps to follow:

1. In Outlook, select Tools, Options to display the Options dialog box.
2. Select the Security tab.
3. Click Get a Digital ID. Internet Explorer loads and takes you to the Office Digital ID page on the Web.
4. Click a link to the certifying authority (such as VeriSign) that you want to use.

5. Follow the authority's instructions for obtaining a digital ID. (Note that digital IDs are not free; they typically cost about $20 (U.S.) per year. However, some authorities enable you to set up a trial digital ID.)

Backing Up Your Digital ID

You should make a backup copy of your digital ID for safekeeping. Open Internet Explorer and select Tools, Internet Options. Display the Content tab and click Certificates to see a list of your installed certificates (be sure to use the Personal tab). Click your digital ID and then click Export.

Obtaining Another Person's Public Key

Before you can send an encrypted message to another person, you must obtain his or her public key. How you do this depends on whether you have a digitally signed message from that person.

If you do have a digitally signed message, follow these steps to store the sender's public key:

1. Open the digitally signed message.
2. Right-click the sender's name or address in the From line.
3. Click Add to Outlook Contacts. Outlook adds the sender to your Contacts list and includes the sender's digital ID in the Certificates tab, as shown in Figure 15.12.

Figure 15.12
When you receive a digitally signed message, add the sender to your Contacts to store his or her digital ID (and public key).

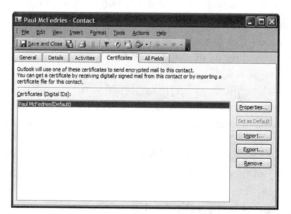

4. Click Save and Close. If you already have the sender in your Contacts folder, the Duplicate Contact Detected dialog box appears.
5. Activate the Update New Information from This Contact to the Existing One option and click OK.

If you don't have a digitally signed message for the person you want to work with, you have to visit a certifying authority's website and find the person's digital ID. For example, you can go to the VeriSign site (directory.verisign.com) to search for a digital ID and then download it to your computer. After that, follow these steps:

1. Open the Contacts folder.
2. Open the person's contact info or create a new contact.
3. Enter one or more email addresses and fill in the other data as necessary.
4. Display the Certificates tab.
5. Click the Import button to display the Locate Certificate dialog box.
6. Find and select the downloaded digital ID file and then click Open.
7. Click Save and Close.

Sending a Secure Message

After your digital ID is installed, you can start sending out secure email messages. You have two options:

- Digitally sign a message to prove that you're the sender.
- Encrypt a message to avoid snooping and tampering.

Follow these steps to secure your message using one or both options:

1. Start a new email message.
2. Click the Options toolbar button to display the Message Options dialog box.
3. Click Security Settings to display the Security Properties dialog box, shown in Figure 15.13.

Figure 15.13
Use the Security Properties dialog box to set the message security options.

4. To digitally sign the message with the sender's public key, activate the Add Digital Signature to This Message check box. Outlook enables the following check boxes:

   - Send This Message as Clear Text Signed—Activate this check box if your recipient doesn't have Secure Multipurpose Internet Mail Extensions (S/MIME), which is a specification for secure email messages.

   - Request S/MIME Receipt for This Message—Activate this check box to request an S/MIME receipt, which tells you when (and if) your message was "cryptographically verified."

5. To encrypt the message with your private key, activate the Encrypt Message Contents and Attachments check box.

6. Click OK to return to the Message Options dialog box.

7. Click Close.

Faster Message Security

 If you use Word as your email editor, you can apply default message security quicker by using a couple of toolbar buttons. Click the Digitally Sign button to add your digital signature to the message; click the Encrypt Message button to encrypt the message.

Automating Message Security

You can tell Outlook to digitally sign and/or encrypt all your outgoing messages. Select Tools, Options, and display the Security tab. To encrypt all your messages, activate the Encrypt Contents and Attachments for All Outgoing Messages check box. To sign all your messages, activate the Add Digital Signature to Outgoing Messages check box.

From Here

- For other Outlook tricks, see Chapter 5, "Getting the Most Out of Outlook."

- To learn the basics of VBA, see Chapter 11, "Maximizing Office with VBA Macros."

- To see other Outlook VBA code, see the section titled "Outlook Macros" in Chapter 12.

- For more on Office security, see Chapter 14, "Securing Office 2003."

- To learn how to apply a password to your Outlook data files, see the section titled "Assigning a Password to Your Outlook Personal Folders" in Chapter 14.

- To learn how to work with the Registry Editor and the Windows Registry, see Appendix A, "Working with the Windows Registry."

Working with the Windows Registry

In some parts of this book, you learn tricks that involve changing a setting or two in the Windows Registry. To use these examples—and, indeed, to get the most out of this book and Windows XP itself—you need to know what the Registry is and how to use it efficiently and safely. This appendix helps you do that by telling you everything you need to know to become comfortable working with this most important of Windows configuration tools.

Understanding the Registry

When you change the desktop wallpaper using Control Panel's Display icon, the next time you start your computer, how does Windows know which wallpaper you selected? If you change your video display driver, how does Windows know to use that driver at startup and not the original driver loaded during Setup? In other words, how does Windows "remember" the various settings and options either that you've selected yourself or that are appropriate for your system?

The secret to prodigious memory of Windows is the Registry. The Registry is a central database that Windows uses to store anything and everything that applies to the configuration of your system. This includes all of the following:

- Information about all the hardware installed on your computer.
- The resources used by those devices.
- A list of the device drivers that get loaded at startup.
- Settings used internally by Windows XP.
- File type data that associates a particular type of file with a specific application.

- Wallpaper, color schemes, and other interface customization settings.
- Other customization settings for things such as the Start menu and the taskbar.
- Settings for accessories such as Windows Explorer and Internet Explorer.
- Internet and network connections.
- Settings and customization options for many applications.

Even better, thanks to a handy tool called the Registry Editor (discussed later in this chapter), it's yours to play with (carefully!) as you see fit.

Taking a Tour of the Registry

As you'll see a bit later, the Registry's files are binary files, so you can't edit them directly. Instead, you use a program called the Registry Editor, which enables you to view, modify, add, and delete any Registry setting. It has a search feature to help you find settings, and export and import features enable you to save settings to and from a text file.

Playing It Safe with the Registry

The Registry is so important that you don't want to ever mess anything up or you could trash your system. Before making any changes to the Registry, consider reviewing the techniques outlined later in this chapter in the "Keeping the Registry Safe" section.

To launch the Registry Editor, select Start, Run to open the Run dialog box, type **regedit**, and click OK. Figure A.1 shows the Registry Editor window that appears.

Figure A.1
Running the REGEDIT command launches the Registry Editor, a front-end that enables you to work with the Registry's data.

The Registry Editor is reminiscent of Windows Explorer, and it works in basically the same way. The left side of the Registry Editor window is similar to Explorer's Folders pane, except that rather than folders, you see *keys*. For lack of a better phrase, I'll call the left pane the *Keys pane*.

Navigating the Keys Pane

The Keys pane, like Explorer's Folders pane, is organized in a treelike hierarchy. The five keys that are visible when you first open the Registry Editor are special keys called *handles* (which is why their names all begin with HKEY). These keys are referred to collectively as the Registry's *root keys*. I'll tell you what to expect from each of these keys later (see the section called "Getting to Know the Registry's Root Keys," later in this chapter).

These keys all contain subkeys, which you can display by clicking the plus sign (+) to the left of each key or by highlighting a key and pressing the plus-sign key on your keyboard's numeric keypad. When you open a key, the plus sign changes to a minus sign (–). To close a key, click the minus sign or highlight the key and press the minus-sign key on the numeric keypad. (Again, this is just like navigating folders in Explorer.)

You often have to drill down several levels to get to the key you want. For example, Figure A.2 shows the Registry Editor after I've opened the HKEY_CURRENT_USER key, then the Control Panel subkey, and then clicked the Keyboard subkey. Notice how the status bar tells you the exact path to the current key, and that this path is structured just like a folder path.

A

Resizing the Keys Pane

To see all the keys properly, you likely have to increase the size of the Keys pane. To do this, use your mouse to drag the split bar to the right. Alternatively, select View, Split, use the right-arrow key to adjust the split bar position, and then press Enter.

Figure A.2
Open the Registry's keys and subkeys to find the settings you want to work with.

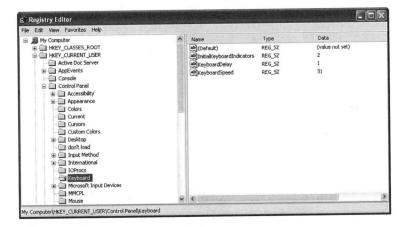

Understanding Registry Settings

If the left side of the Registry Editor window is analogous to Explorer's Folder pane, the right side is analogous to Explorer's Contents pane. In this case, the right side of the Registry Editor window displays the settings contained in each key (so I'll call it the *Settings pane*). The Settings pane is divided into three columns:

■ Name—This column tells you the name of each setting in the currently selected key (analogous to a filename in Explorer).

- Type—This column tells you the data type of the setting. There are five possible data types:
  - REG_SZ—This is a string value.
  - REG_MULTI_SZ—This is a series of strings.
  - REG_EXPAND_SZ—This is a string value that contains an environment variable name that gets "expanded" into the value of that variable. For example, the %SystemRoot% environment variable holds the folder in which Windows XP is installed. So if you see a Registry setting with the value %SystemRoot%\System32\, and Windows XP is installed in C:\Windows, then the setting's expanded value is C:\Windows\System32\.
  - REG_DWORD—This is a double word value: a 32-bit hexadecimal value arranged as eight digits. For example, 11 hex is 17 decimal, so this number would be represented in DWORD form as 0x00000011 (17). (Why "double word"? A 32-bit value represents four bytes of data, and because a *word* in programming circles is defined as two bytes, a four-byte value is a *double word*.)
  - REG_BINARY—This value is a series of hexadecimal digits.
- Data—This column displays the value of each setting.

Getting to Know the Registry's Root Keys

The root keys are your Registry starting points, so you need to become familiar with what kinds of data each key holds. The next few sections summarize the contents of each key.

HKEY_CLASSES_ROOT (HKCR)

HKEY_CLASSES_ROOT—usually abbreviated as HKCR—contains data related to file extensions and their associated programs, the objects that exist in the Windows XP system, as well as applications and their OLE Automation information. There are also keys related to shortcuts and other interface features.

The top part of this key contains subkeys for various file extensions. You see .bmp for Bitmap (Paint) files, .doc for Word.Document.8 (Word) files, and so on. In each of these subkeys, the Default setting tells you the name of the registered file type associated with the extension. For example, the .txt extension is associated with the txtfile file type.

These registered file types appear as subkeys later in the HKEY_CLASSES_ROOT branch, and the Registry keeps track of various settings for each registered file type. In particular, the shell subkey tells you the actions associated with this file type. For example, in the shell\open\command subkey, the Default setting shows the path for the executable file that opens. Figure A.3 shows this subkey for the Word.Document.8 file type.

HKEY_CLASSES_ROOT is actually a copy (or an *alias*, as these copied keys are called) of the following HKEY_LOCAL_MACHINE key:

```
HKEY_LOCAL_MACHINE\Software\Classes
```

Figure A.3
The registered file type subkeys specify various settings associated with each file type, including its defined actions.

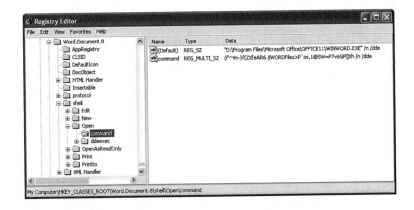

The Registry creates an alias for HKEY_CLASSES_ROOT to make these keys easier for applications to access and to improve compatibility with legacy programs.

HKEY_CURRENT_USER (HKCU)

HKEY_CURRENT_USER (usually abbreviated as HKCU) contains data that applies to the user who is currently logged on. It contains user-specific settings for Control Panel options, network connections, applications, and more. Following is a summary of the most important HKEY_CURRENT_USER subkeys:

- AppEvents—Contains sound files that play when particular system events occur (such as the maximizing of a window).

- Control Panel—Contains settings related to certain Control Panel icons.

- Identities—Contains settings related to Outlook Express, including mail and news options and message rules.

- InstallLocationsMRU—Contains a list of the drives and folders that were most recently used (MRU) to install software or drivers.

- Keyboard Layout—Contains the keyboard layout as selected via Control Panel's Keyboard icon.

- Network—Contains settings related to mapped network drives.

- RemoteAccess—Contains settings related to remote network access.

- Software—Contains user-specific settings related to installed applications and Windows. For example, Window stores the user-specific settings for Office 2003 in the following subkey:

  `HKEY_CURRENT_USER\Software\Microsoft\Office\11.0`

HKEY_LOCAL_MACHINE (HKLM)

HKEY_LOCAL_MACHINE (HKLM) contains non-user–specific configuration data for your system's hardware and applications. There are three subkeys that you'll use most often:

- Hardware—Contains subkeys related to serial ports and modems, as well as the floating-point processor.

- Software—Contains computer-specific settings related to installed applications. The Classes subkey is aliased by HKEY_CLASSES_ROOT. The Microsoft subkey contains settings related to Windows and Office (as well as any other Microsoft products you have installed on your computer).

- System—Contains subkeys and settings related to Windows startup.

HKEY_USERS (HKU)

HKEY_USERS (HKU) contains settings that are similar to those in HKEY_CURRENT_USER. HKEY_USERS is used to store the settings for users with group policies defined, as well as the default settings (in the .DEFAULT subkey) that get mapped to a new user's profile.

HKEY_CURRENT_CONFIG (HKCC)

HKEY_CURRENT_CONFIG (HKCC) contains settings for the current hardware profile. If your machine uses only one hardware profile, HKEY_CURRENT_CONFIG is an alias for HKEY_LOCAL_MACHINE\SYSTEM\ControlSet001. If your machine uses multiple hardware profiles, HKEY_CURRENT_CONFIG is an alias for HKEY_LOCAL_MACHINE\SYSTEM\ControlSet$n$, where n is the numeric identifier of the current hardware profile. This identifier is given by the Current setting in the following key:

```
HKEY_LOCAL_MACHINE\SSYSTEM\CurrentControlSet\Control\IDConfigDB
```

Understanding Hives and Registry Files

The Registry database consists of a number of files that contain a subset of the Registry called a *hive*. A hive consists of one or more Registry keys, subkeys, and settings. Each hive is supported by several files that use the extensions listed in Table A.1.

Table A.1   Extensions Used by Hive Supporting Files

Extension	File Contains
None	A complete copy of the hive data.
.alt	A backup copy of the hive data.
.log	A log of the changes made to the hive data.
.sav	A copy of the hive data from the text mode portion of the Windows XP setup.

Table A.2 shows the supporting files for each hive (note that not all of these files may appear on your system).

Table A.2   Supporting Files Used by Each Hive

Hive	Files
HKLM\SAM	%SystemRoot%\System32\config\SAM
	%SystemRoot%\System32\config\SAM.LOG
	%SystemRoot%\System32\config\SAM.SAV
HKLM\Security	%SystemRoot%\System32\config\SECURITY
	%SystemRoot%\System32\config\SECURITY.LOG
	%SystemRoot%\System32\config\SECURITY.SAV
HKLM\Software	%SystemRoot%\System32\config\SOFTWARE
	%SystemRoot%\System32\config\SOFTWARE.LOG
	%SystemRoot%\System32\config\SOFTWARE.SAV
HKLM\System	%SystemRoot%\System32\config\SYSTEM
	%SystemRoot%\System32\config\SYSTEM.ALT
	%SystemRoot%\System32\config\SYSTEM.LOG
	%SystemRoot%\System32\config\SYSTEM.SAV
HKU\.DEFAULT	%SystemRoot%\System32\config\DEFAULT
	%SystemRoot%\System32\config\DEFAULT.LOG
	%SystemRoot%\System32\config\DEFAULT.SAV

Also, each user has his or her own hive, which gets mapped to HKEY_CURRENT_USER during logon. The supporting files for each user hive are stored in \Documents and Settings*User*, where *User* is the username. In each case, the NTUSER.DAT file contains the hive data, and the NTUSER.LOG file tracks the hive changes.

Keeping the Registry Safe

The sheer wealth of data stored in one place makes the Registry convenient, but it also makes it very precious. If your Registry went missing somehow, or if it got corrupted, Windows XP simply would not work. With that scary thought in mind, let's take a moment to run through several protective measures. The techniques in this section should ensure that Windows XP never goes down for the count because you made a mistake while editing the Registry.

Backing Up the Registry

Windows XP maintains what is known as the *system state*: the crucial system files that Windows XP requires to operate properly. Included in the system state are the files used during system startup, the Windows XP protected system files, and, naturally, the Registry files. The Backup utility has a feature that enables you to easily back up the current system state, so it's probably the most straightforward way to create a backup copy of the Registry should anything go wrong. Here are the steps to follow to back up the system state:

1. Select Start, All Programs, Accessories, System Tools, Backup. (Note that if you're using Windows XP Home, you might need to install Backup from the Windows XP CD.)

2. If the Backup or Restore Wizard appears, click the Advanced Mode link.

3. Display the Backup tab.

4. In the folder tree, open the Desktop branch and then the My Computer branch, if they're not open already.

5. Activate the System State check box.

6. Choose your other backup options, click Start Backup, and then follow the usual backup procedure.

Leave Room for the System State

Depending on the configuration of your computer, the system state can be quite large—up to 350MB. Therefore, make sure the destination you choose for the backup has enough free space to handle such a large file.

Saving the Current Registry State with System Restore

Another easy way to save the current Registry configuration is to use Windows XP's System Restore utility. This program takes a snapshot of your system's current state, including the Registry. Then, if anything should go wrong with your system, the program enables you to restore a previous configuration. It's a good idea to set a system restore point before doing any work on the Registry:

1. Select Start, All Programs, Accessories, System Tools, System Restore. The System Restore window appears.

2. Activate the Create a Restore Point option and click Next.

3. Use the Restore Point Description text box to enter a description for the new checkpoint, and then click Create. System Restore creates the restore point and displays the Restore Point Created window.

4. Click Close.

Protecting Keys by Exporting Them to Disk

If you're just making a small change to the Registry, backing up all of its files may seem like overkill. Another approach is to back up only the part of the Registry that you're working on. For example, if you're about to make changes within the HKEY_CURRENT_USER key, you could back up just that key, or even a subkey within HKCU. You do that by exporting the key's data to a hive file, which is a binary file (meaning you can't edit it). That way, if the change causes a problem, you can import the hive file back into the Registry to restore things the way they were.

Exporting a Key to a Hive File

Here are the steps to follow to export a key to a hive file:

1. Open the Registry Editor and highlight the key you want to export.
2. Select File, Export to display the Export Registry File dialog box.
3. Select a location for the file.
4. Use the File Name text box to enter a name for the file.
5. In the Save as Type list, select Registry Hive Files.
6. If you want to export only the currently highlighted key, make sure the Selected Branch option is activated. If you'd prefer to export the entire Registry, activate the All option.
7. Click Save.

Importing a Hive File

If you need to restore the key that you backed up to a hive file, follow these steps:

1. Open the Registry Editor.
2. Select File, Import to display the Import Registry File dialog box.
3. In the Files of Type list, select Registry Hive Files.
4. Find and highlight the file you want to import.
5. Click Open. The Registry Editor asks you to confirm.
6. Click Yes.
7. When Windows XP tells you that the information has been entered into the Registry, click OK.

Working with Registry Keys and Settings

Now that you've had a look around, you're ready to start working with the Registry's keys and settings. In this section, I'll give you the general procedures for basic tasks, such as modifying, adding, renaming, deleting, and searching for entries, and more.

Changing the Value of a Registry Entry

Changing the value of a Registry entry is a matter of finding the appropriate key, displaying the setting you want to change, and editing the setting's value. Unfortunately, finding the key you need isn't always a simple matter. Knowing the root keys and their main subkeys, as

A

described earlier, will certainly help, and the Registry Editor also has a Find feature that's invaluable (I'll show you how to use it later).

To illustrate how this process works, let's work through an example: changing your Windows XP registered owner name and company name. During the Windows XP installation process, Setup may have asked you to enter your name and, optionally, your company name. (If you upgraded to Windows XP, this data was brought over from your previous version of Windows.) These "registered names" appear in several places as you work with Windows XP:

- If you open the Control Panel's System icon, your registered names appear in the General tab of the System Properties dialog box.

- If you select Help, About in most Windows XP programs, your registered names appear in the About dialog box.

- If you install a 32-bit application (including Office), the installation program uses your registered names for its own records (although you usually get a chance to make changes).

With these names appearing in so many places, it's good to know that you can change either or both names (for example, if you give the computer to another person). The secret lies in the following key:

```
HKLM\SOFTWARE\Microsoft\WindowsNT\CurrentVersion
```

To get to this key, open the branches in the Registry Editor's tree pane: HKEY_LOCAL_MACHINE, SOFTWARE, Microsoft, and then WindowsNT. Finally, click the CurrentVersion subkey to highlight it. Here you'll see a number of settings, but two are of interest to us:

Saving Favorite Keys

If you have keys that you visit often, you can save them as "favorites" to avoid trudging through endless branches in the Keys pane. To do this, navigate to the key and then select Favorites, Add to Favorites. In the Add to Favorites dialog box, edit the Favorite Name text box, if necessary, and then click OK. To navigate to a favorite key, pull down the Favorites menu and select the key name from the list that appears at the bottom of the menu.

- RegisteredOrganization—This setting contains the registered company name.
- RegisteredOwner—This setting contains your registered name.

Now you open the setting for editing by using any of the following techniques:

- Highlight the setting name and either select Edit, Modify or press Enter.
- Double-click the setting name.
- Right-click the setting name and click Modify from the shortcut menu.

The dialog box that appears depends on the value type you're dealing with, as discussed in the next few sections. Note that edited settings are written to the Registry right away, but the changes might not go into effect immediately. In many cases, you need to exit the Registry Editor and then either log off or restart Windows XP.

Editing a String Value

If the setting is a REG_SZ value (as it is in our example), a REG_MULTI_SZ value, or a REG_EXPAND_SZ value, you see the Edit String dialog box, shown in Figure A.4. Use the Value Data text box to enter a new string or modify the existing string, and then click OK. (For a REG_MULTI_SZ multi-string value, Value Data is a multiline text box. Type each string value on its own line. That is, after each string, press Enter to start a new line.)

Figure A.4
You use the Edit String dialog box to modify a string value.

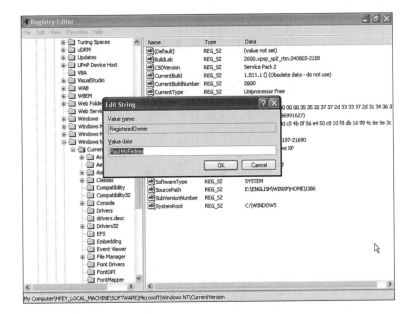

Editing a DWORD Value

If the setting is a REG_DWORD value, you see the Edit DWORD Value dialog box shown in Figure A.5. In the Base group, select either Hexadecimal or Decimal, and then use the Value Data text box to enter the new value of the setting. (If you chose the Hexadecimal option, enter a hexadecimal value; if you chose Decimal, enter a decimal value.)

Figure A.5
You use the Edit DWORD
Value dialog box to mod-
ify a DWORD value.

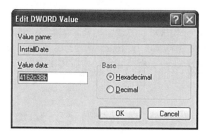

Editing a Binary Value

If the setting is a REG_BINARY value, you see an Edit Binary Value dialog box like the
one shown in Figure A.6.

Figure A.6
You use the Edit Binary
Value dialog box if you're
modifying a binary
value.

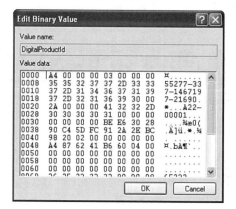

For binary values, the Value Data box is divided into three vertical sections:

- Starting byte number—The four-digit values on the left of the Value Data box tell you
  the sequence number of the first byte in each row of hexadecimal numbers. This
  sequence always begins at 0, so the sequence number of the first byte in the first row is
  0000. There are 8 bytes in each row, so the sequence number of the first byte in the
  second row is 0008, and so on. These values can't be edited.

- Hexadecimal numbers (bytes)—The eight columns of two-digit numbers in the middle
  section display the setting's value, expressed in hexadecimal numbers, where each two-
  digit number represents a single byte of information. These values are editable, but
  because of the obvious complexities involved with hexadecimal numbers, few computer
  users take advantage of this "feature."

- ASCII equivalents—The third section on the right side of the Value Data box shows
  the ASCII equivalents of the hexadecimal numbers in the middle section. In Figure
  A.6, for example, the first byte of the second row is the hexadecimal value 35, which
  represents the number 5. The values in this column are also editable.

Renaming a Key or Setting

You won't often need to rename existing keys or settings. Just in case, though, here are the steps to follow:

1. In the Registry Editor, find the key or setting you want to work with, and then highlight it.

2. Select Edit, Rename, or press F2.

3. Edit the name and then press Enter.

A

Rename with Care

Rename only those keys or settings that you created yourself. If you rename any other key or setting, Windows XP might not work properly.

Creating a New Key or Setting

Many Registry-based customizations don't involve editing an existing setting or key. Instead, you have to create a new setting or key. Here's how you do it:

1. In the Registry Editor, highlight the key in which you want to create the new subkey or setting.

2. Select Edit, New. (Alternatively, right-click an empty section of the Settings pane and then click New.) A submenu appears.

3. If you're creating a new key, select the Key command. Otherwise, select the command that corresponds to the type of setting you want: String Value, Binary Value, DWORD Value, Multi-String Value, or Expandable String Value.

4. Type a name for the new key or setting.

5. Press Enter.

For example, Office versions prior to 2003 have a feature called AutoSelect that automatically selects the first available document when you display the Open dialog box. If that was the document you wanted, you only had to press Enter to open it. This was an occasionally handy feature that Microsoft disabled in Office 2003 because AutoSelect would sometimes cause long delays when displaying a network folder. Fortunately, you can tweak the Registry to enable AutoSelect again. First, head for the following key:

```
HKEY_CURRENT_USER\Software\Microsoft\Office\11.0\Common\Open Find
```

Add a new DWORD value named DisableAutoSelect and set its value to 0.

Deleting a Key or Setting

Follow these steps to delete a key or setting:

1. In the Registry Editor, highlight the key or setting that you want to delete.

2. Select Edit, Delete, or press Delete. The Registry Editor asks if you're sure.

3. Click Yes.

A

Delete with Care, Too

Again, to avoid problems you should delete only those keys or settings that you created yourself. If you're not sure about deleting a setting, try renaming, instead. If a problem arises, you can also return the setting back to its original name.

Finding Registry Entries

The Registry contains only five root keys, but these root keys contain hundreds of subkeys. And the fact that some root keys are aliases for subkeys in a different branch only adds to the confusion. If you know exactly where you're going, the Registry Editor's treelike hierarchy is a reasonable way to get there. If you're not sure where a particular subkey or setting resides, however, you could spend all day poking around in the Registry's labyrinthine nooks and crannies.

To help you get where you want to go, the Registry Editor has a Find feature that lets you search for keys, settings, or values. Here's how it works:

1. In the Keys pane, select My Computer at the top of the pane (unless you're certain which root key contains the value you want to find; in this case, you can select the appropriate root key instead).

2. Select Edit, Find or press Ctrl+F. The Registry Editor displays the Find dialog box.

3. Use the Find What text box to enter your search string. You can enter partial words or phrases to increase your chances of finding a match.

4. In the Look At group, activate the check boxes for the elements you want to search. For most searches, you want to leave all three check boxes activated.

5. If you want to find only those entries that exactly match your search text, activate the Match Whole String Only check box.

6. Click the Find Next button. The Registry Editor highlights the first match.

7. If this isn't the item you want, select Edit, Find Next (or press F3) until you find the setting or key you want.

When the Registry Editor finds a match, it displays the appropriate key or setting. Note that if the matched value is a setting name or data value, Find doesn't highlight the current key. This is a bit confusing, but remember that the current key always appears at the bottom of the Keys pane.

INDEX